Embedded Linux Essentials Handbook

Build embedded Linux systems and real-world apps with Yocto, Buildroot, and RPi

Mohammed Billoo

<packt>

Embedded Linux Essentials Handbook

Portfolio Director: Rohit Rajkumar
Relationship Lead: Kaustubh Manglurkar
Project Manager: Sandip Tadge
Content Engineer: Shazeen Iqbal
Technical Editor: Tejas Mhasvekar
Copy Editor: Safis Editing
Indexer: Hemangini Bari
Proofreader: Safis Editing
Production Designer: Jyoti Kadam
Growth Lead: Namita Velgekar

First published: January 2026

Production reference: 1230126

Published by Packt Publishing Ltd.
Grosvenor House
11 St Paul's Square
Birmingham
B3 1RB, UK.

ISBN 978-1-83546-930-9
www.packtpub.com

To my mother, Rukshana, and the memory of my father, Abdur Rashid, for their tremendous sacrifices and for making me the person I am today. To my wife, Nida, for her titanic patience and support in this tough journey when writing my first book. To my daughters, Haneefa and Husna, who taught me that life shouldn't be taken too seriously.

– Mohammed Billoo

Contributors

About the author

Mohammed Billoo is an Embedded Software Consultant with over 14 years of experience across a multitude of domains, including Defense, Space, and Commercial. He is an avid blogger and contributor to the open-source community. He specializes in Embedded Linux systems, including driver development to interface with custom hardware (including FPGAs), BSP customizations (specifically The Yocto Project), and user-space applications across different verticals. Mohammed also carries expertise in developing microcontroller-based solutions using The Zephyr Project.

About the reviewer

Matt St. Onge is an Associate Principal Solutions Architect at Red Hat, focused on providing enablement through their Embedded Systems partner program. Since 2015, his activities at Red Hat have ranged from best practices sessions to design reviews and even leading rapid prototyping workshops. Matt has assisted hundreds of product teams over the past decade in building quality, secure Linux appliances. Matt has been active in the open source and Linux communities for over 30 years by contributing to solutions via GitHub, creating new projects for the benefit of the embedded systems community, and hosting webinars and user group meetings. When not building solutions in the lab, Matt can be found hiking with his dog in the mountains, golfing, or cooking elaborate meals on the grill for his extended family.

Table of Contents

Chapter 3: Navigating the Linux Kernel 49

Chapter 4: Describing Hardware Using the Devicetree 75

Chapter 6: Building an Image Using the Yocto Project 123

Chapter 7: Building an Image Using Buildroot 155

Part 3: Developing Applications 191

Chapter 8: Building, Debugging, and Launching Applications on Startup 193

Chapter 10: Project 2: Using Qt to Build a Scientific Instrument 251

Chapter 11: Project 3: Using Qt to Build a Medical Device 299

Part 4: Advanced Topics, Implementing CI/CD, Best Practices, and Looking Ahead 317

Preface

Hi there! **Embedded software** is aimed at specialized devices rather than typical computers we use every day. Unlike *general-purpose software* which runs on standard computers, embedded software runs on systems with limited hardware resources, called **embedded systems**. However, with the recent explosion of the computational capabilities of embedded systems, **Embedded Linux** is becoming an increasingly popular paradigm for embedded software.

As Embedded Linux becomes available on more platforms, it's important for embedded software engineers to be comfortable customizing, installing, using, and developing on it.

Embedded Linux systems can be broken into three distinct categories:

- Portions responsible for interfacing with hardware, such as the bootloader, kernel, and **Devicetree**.
- Frameworks that can be used to build entire Embedded Linux software systems.
- Applications running on Embedded Linux systems that are meant to serve specific purposes.

While some books and resources cover each of the three bullet points above, no single resource covers all three. This book aims to address all three in detail.

I will provide relevant information and guide you through key topics needed to gain a sound understanding of Embedded Linux systems. The best way to learn a topic is through examples, so this book includes timely hands-on examples for many of the topics covered.

Who this book is for

Embedded software engineers should be familiar with existing paradigms, including Embedded Linux, to ensure their designs are well suited to the target product, application, and hardware.

The three main personas this book is written for are:

- *Technical leads and architects*: Embedded Linux differs significantly from other embedded software paradigms. A solid understanding of Embedded Linux will help technical leads and architects decide when it's the right solution for their application. It will also help them understand the tasks involved in building an Embedded Linux system and the timelines associated with them.

- *Embedded software engineers*: This book is for engineers who want to gain practical experience with Embedded Linux. They will learn the essential concepts and tools needed to perform key tasks involved in developing an Embedded Linux system.
- *Hardware engineers*: Hardware engineers can benefit from a cursory understanding of Embedded Linux, since they're often responsible for board bring-up and design verification.

What this book covers

Chapter 1, Exploring Embedded Linux's Architecture and Its Use Cases, shows the reader when to choose Embedded Linux over other software paradigms. It covers the use cases of Embedded Linux, its architecture, and its hardware requirements. This chapter also teaches the reader about the different components of an Embedded Linux system.

Chapter 2, Learning About U-Boot, describes the structure of U-Boot's codebase and how to build it. It dives into key **U-Boot** subsystems and demonstrates how to run U-Boot on QEMU and a Raspberry Pi5.

Chapter 3, Navigating the Linux Kernel, provides details about the **Linux kernel**. It describes the codebase's structure and how to build it. This chapter dives into key subsystems of the Linux kernel, the ARM architecture, and the device driver model.

Chapter 4, Describing Hardware Using the Devicetree, describes the Devicetree in detail. This chapter demonstrates how the Linux kernel uses the Devicetree to configure itself to interact with the hardware on an embedded system. It walks through examples showing how to add specific peripherals, including an ADC and DAC, over the I2C bus, and a device of the SPI bus.

Chapter 5, Exploring Frameworks to Build an Image, teaches the reader how the different components of Embedded Linux can be combined to form a singular image. This chapter briefly describes the two most popular frameworks for this purpose: **Buildroot** and **The Yocto Project**. It compares these two frameworks and provides guidance on when to select the appropriate framework.

Chapter 6, Building an Image Using the Yocto Project, provides an in-depth review of The Yocto Project. It covers how to add an application to an Embedded Linux image using this framework and how to customize an existing image.

Chapter 7, Building an Image Using Buildroot, describes how to use Buildroot to create an Embedded Linux image. It also demonstrates how to add an application and customize an existing image.

Chapter 8, Building, Debugging, and Launching Applications on Startup, describes the basics of application development on an Embedded Linux system. It teaches the steps necessary to compile an application. This chapter also provides recommendations on testing and debugging an application and identifying functional and performance issues. It describes the `Systemd` framework, which is used to automatically launch applications on boot.

Chapter 9, Project 1: Using Python to Build a Web Server to Display Sensor Data, walks through the development of a **Python** application executed on a **Raspberry Pi**. The application is a web server that retrieves data from a sensor over the I2C bus and stores it in a database. It also retrieves data from the database and presents it to a user when queried.

Chapter 10, Project 2: Using Qt to Build a Scientific Instrument, demonstrates the development of an application using the **Qt** framework. It describes the features and components used in a scientific instrument. This chapter provides a detailed description of QML and how it is used to develop sophisticated UI. It also demonstrates how to use C++ to implement the business logic backend.

Chapter 11, Project 3: Using Qt to Build a Medical Device, walks through another application developed using the Qt framework. It demonstrates how to use **Qt Widgets** to develop a sample medical device application.

Chapter 12, Debugging the Linux Kernel, teaches the reader how to debug the Linux kernel. It demonstrates functional and performance issues that can be encountered when working with the Linux kernel, how these issues can manifest, and the different mechanisms available to help debug these issues. This chapter provides specific examples of the topics covered.

Chapter 13, Securing Code Execution with eBF, demonstrates how to execute applications inside the Linux kernel using the extended **Berkeley Packet Filter** (**eBPF**) securely and safely. It teaches the reader some of the capabilities that this feature enables, the syntax of an eBPF application, and how to execute an eBPF application on an Embedded Linux system. This chapter provides specific examples to demonstrate the topics covered.

Chapter 14, Rust in Embedded Linux: The Kernel and Applications, briefly teaches the reader about **Rust**, a new programming language gaining significant popularity. This chapter describes Rust's syntax, basic data types, and Rust mechanisms to guarantee memory safety.

Chapter 15, Implementing Continuous Integration/Continuous Delivery (CI/CD), teaches readers the importance of **Continuous Integration** and **Continuous Delivery**, also known as **CI/CD**. It provides specific use cases in the context of Embedded Linux systems. This chapter demonstrates examples of processes using GitHub Actions.

Chapter 16, Looking to the Future, concludes the book with a review of the topics covered in the previous chapters. It covers some future trends that Embedded Linux software engineers should be aware of.

To get the most out of this book

You should be familiar with general embedded software concepts, comfortable reading C and Python code, and able to use a Linux terminal confidently.

In this book, we will use the following hardware and software packages. If you would like, you can obtain them or become familiar with them ahead of time:

Software/Hardware	Version
Raspberry Pi	4
Raspberry Pi	5
Ubuntu	22.04
Qt Framework	5.15.2
Qt Creator	13.0.2

> **Important note**
>
> **If you are using the digital version of this book, we advise you to type the code yourself or access the code from the book's GitHub repository (a link is available in the next section). Doing so will help you avoid any potential errors related to the copying and pasting of code.**

You will gain a thorough understanding of Embedded Linux internals, learn how to create a custom image from scratch, flash it onto a Raspberry Pi, develop simple device drivers that can be tested on simulated or real hardware, and build and run applications using a sophisticated framework.

Download the example code files

You can download the example code files for this book from GitHub at `https://github.com/PacktPublishing/Embedded-Linux-Essentials-Handbook`. If there's an update to the code, it will be updated in the GitHub repository.

We also have other code bundles from our rich catalog of books and videos available at `https://github.com/PacktPublishing/`. Check them out!

Download the color images

We also provide a PDF file that has color images of the screenshots/diagrams used in this book. You can download it here: `https://packt.link/gbp/9781835469309`.

Conventions used

There are a number of text conventions used throughout this book.

`Code in text`: Indicates code words in text, database table names, folder names, filenames, file extensions, pathnames, dummy URLs, user input, and Twitter handles. Here is an example: "The `ENTRY` directive in the preceding linker script specifies that execution starts at the function dictated by the `CONFIG_PLATFORM_ELFENTRY` configuration option."

A block of code is set as follows:

```
config PLATFORM_ELFENTRY
        string
        default "__start" if MIPS
        default "_start"
```

When we wish to draw your attention to a particular part of a code block, the relevant lines or items are set in bold:

```
static init_fnc_t init_sequence_r[] = {
        initr_trace,
        initr_reloc,
        event_init,
.
.
.
        INIT_FUNC_WATCHDOG_RESET
.
.
.
        run_main_loop,
};
```

Any command-line input or output is written as follows:

```
$ git clone git://git.denx.de/u-boot.git
```

Bold: Indicates a new term, an important word, or words that you see onscreen. For instance, words in menus or dialog boxes appear in **bold**. Here is an example: "We can examine U-Boot's **linker script** to discover which function is executed first when U-Boot is launched."

Warnings or important notes appear like this.

Tips and tricks appear like this.

Get in touch

Feedback from our readers is always welcome.

General feedback: If you have questions about any aspect of this book, email us at `customercare@packtpub.com` and mention the book title in the subject of your message.

Errata: Although we have taken every care to ensure the accuracy of our content, mistakes do happen. If you have found a mistake in this book, we would be grateful if you would report this to us. Please visit `www.packtpub.com/support/errata` and fill in the form.

Piracy: If you come across any illegal copies of our works in any form on the internet, we would be grateful if you would provide us with the location address or website name. Please contact us at `copyright@packt.com` with a link to the material.

If you are interested in becoming an author: If there is a topic that you have expertise in and you are interested in either writing or contributing to a book, please visit `authors.packtpub.com`.

Share your thoughts

Once you've read *Embedded Linux Essentials Handbook*, we'd love to hear your thoughts! Scan the QR code below to go straight to the Amazon review page for this book and share your feedback.

`https://packt.link/r/1835469302`

Your review is important to us and the tech community and will help us make sure we're delivering excellent quality content.

Free benefits with your book

This book comes with free benefits to support your learning. Activate them now for instant access (see the "*How to Unlock*" section for instructions).

Here's a quick overview of what you can instantly unlock with your purchase:

DRM-Free PDF Version

Download DRM-free PDF and ePub copies of this book.

7-Day Packt Library Access

Get 7-day unlimited access to 8,000+ books and videos. No credit card required.

Available for first-time Packt+ trial users only.

Next-Gen Reader Access

Read this book on Packt Reader with progress sync, dark mode and note-taking.

How to Unlock

Scan the QR code (or go to `packtpub.com/unlock`). Search for this book by name, confirm the edition, and then follow the steps on the page.

UNLOCK NOW

Note: Keep your invoice handy. Purchases made directly from Packt don't require one

Part 1

Getting Started with Embedded Linux

In this part, you will gain an understanding of the fundamentals of Embedded Linux. Upon the completion of this part, you will be comfortable retrieving, navigating, and customizing specific components of an Embedded Linux system.

This part has the following chapters:

1

Exploring Embedded Linux's Architecture and Its Use Cases

With the recent massive increase in processor density, **embedded Linux** is becoming an increasingly popular **operating system** (**OS**) for embedded systems. Silicon vendors have recognized this increased popularity and provide reference implementations of embedded Linux to run on their hardware.

Embedded Linux offers a paradigm different from those that traditional embedded software engineers are accustomed to, such as **bare-metal** development or using a **real-time operating system** (**RTOS**). Traditional embedded software development usually involves 2–3 steps to allow an embedded software engineer to get up and going. Typically, they connect a debugger to their board, write embedded software in an IDE provided by the silicon vendor, and use a debugger to flash and debug their application. However, the development workflow when working with an embedded Linux system is usually more complicated.

In this chapter, we will understand the architecture of embedded Linux and how it differs from other embedded software paradigms. We will also learn when embedded Linux is the ideal choice for our applications. Due to its nature, embedded Linux has unique hardware requirements that ease deployment, which we will also cover in this chapter. Finally, we will understand the different components of embedded Linux and how they fit together in the boot process.

I believe that embedded software development is best learned using actual hardware. To make it easier for you, I have chosen the Raspberry Pi 5, which is an easily accessible platform.

However, I recognize that it may be difficult for certain readers to procure the Raspberry Pi 5, due to cost and availability based on region. This difficulty may preclude them from learning the concepts covered in this book since they may be unable to try the examples.

Fortunately, we can simulate hardware using a tool called QEMU. At the end of the chapter, we will learn how to set up and use QEMU. This understanding will allow you to use QEMU to follow along with the examples in later chapters in case you don't have access to the Raspberry Pi 5.

In this chapter, we are going to cover the following topics:

- Understanding embedded Linux use cases
- Understanding the hardware requirements
- Reviewing embedded Linux's architecture
- Booting embedded Linux
- Learning about U-Boot
- Reviewing the Linux kernel
- Understanding the Devicetree
- QEMU: stimulating an embedded Linux system

Technical requirements

This chapter assumes that you are familiar with and have hands-on experience with embedded software. You should also be familiar with relevant terminology, such as *bare-metal* and *RTOS*. You should also know about common peripherals used in embedded systems, such as GPIO, I2C, SPI, and UART.

Understanding embedded Linux use cases

In this section, we will learn when embedded Linux is applicable to embedded systems. As mentioned earlier, embedded Linux usually involves a different development strategy and workflow from other embedded software patterns. Thus, it's important to understand the types of systems and applications that are ideal to use and when not to use them.

When to use embedded Linux

To best understand when to use embedded Linux, I'd like to present the following figure, which represents a block diagram of a scientific instrument that I worked on:

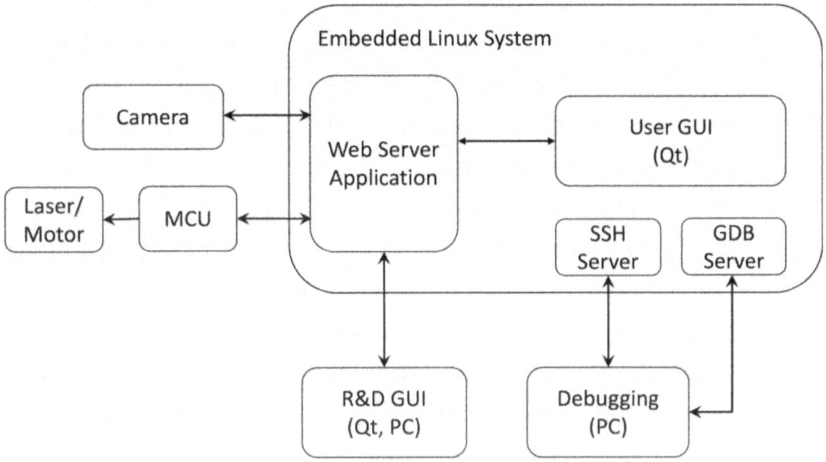

Figure 1.1 – Typical embedded Linux system

The system consists of the following relevant hardware elements:

- A **system-on-module (SoM)**, which contains a **system-on-chip (SoC)** along with other components to facilitate the operation of the SoC. For example, the SoM usually contains flash storage and RAM external to the SoC. The SoC, containing the CPU and other peripheral controllers, runs the embedded Linux OS. For example, while the flash storage and RAM may be external to the SoC, the controllers used to access flash and RAM are on the SoC.
- A camera, which interfaces with the embedded Linux system over the MIPI bus. The web server application retrieves the images captured from the camera.
- An external **microcontroller unit (MCU)** running bare-metal embedded software is responsible for actuating the motor and controlling the laser based on instructions from the web server application running on the embedded Linux system.

The preceding system has the following software components:

- **Web server application**: This application, which was inherited from another team, performs the crux of the operations on the system and has the following responsibilities:
    - It interacts with a microcontroller over a UART interface to actuate a motor and control a laser
    - It captures images from a camera, runs an algorithm on the captured images, and generates results
    - It also exposes an HTTP interface, allowing other applications and systems to interact with it
- **User GUI**: This application, implemented using the Qt framework, is how the user interacts with the system. The user interacts with the GUI application through a touchscreen display. In turn, the GUI commands the web server application through the HTTP interface to take measurements and collect results.
- **R&D GUI**: This application, also implemented using the Qt framework, runs on an external PC. This application has more capabilities than the user GUI application running on the system. It allows the user to view the images from the camera as they are being captured in near-real time. This application allows the user to view intermediate results as the web server application runs its algorithm. This application also uses the HTTP interface to interact with the web server application. However, unlike the user GUI, the communication occurs over a network interface.
- **SSH server**: This utility allows users, including developers, to log in to the system remotely for diagnostic purposes. For example, they can view logs on the system, see what data has been stored, and even load new versions of the applications. For security purposes, typically, this utility is removed from this application to avoid unauthorized access to the system.
- **gdbserver**: This application is meant for developers. As we know, embedded software development mostly always involves debugging. However, due to the nature of embedded Linux, it is difficult to follow the same debugging workflow. We can't connect a debugger to our system and expect to begin debugging our application easily. Instead, debugging applications on embedded Linux systems involves an intermediary application called "**gdbserver**". This application translates commands sent by **GDB**, a debugger running on our PC, over the network to commands to step through the application. We will learn more about debugging embedded Linux applications in *Chapter 10*.

Why was embedded Linux chosen for this system? In this instance, the hardware was already selected and designed before I got involved with the project. Because the chosen SoC already had embedded Linux support from the vendor, it made sense to use it.

However, in retrospect, choosing embedded Linux was the correct decision because it offers the following advantages:

- A Linux driver to interface with the camera was already available. Writing a driver from scratch in bare metal or using an RTOS would have required significant effort.
- The web server application was originally designed for a Linux desktop PC, and my responsibility was to migrate it to the embedded system. The following features of the web server application made embedded Linux an ideal platform:
    - The image processing algorithm uses the OpenCV framework. OpenCV has resource requirements that would make it unsuitable for a bare-metal implementation on a microcontroller.
    - The implementation uses features of the C++ Standard Library relevant to an embedded Linux system. For example, the application performs many file operations, which are ideally suited for embedded Linux. While it is still possible, migrating the implementation to a microcontroller would have been a substantial undertaking.
- The support for remote login using the SSH server and remote debugging via the GDB server was invaluable during development and testing. Although it is possible to include these capabilities on a microcontroller-based system running a bare-metal application, it is not a trivial effort. Including these features on an embedded Linux system is practically trivial.

When not to use embedded Linux

Previously, we saw an example of a system where embedded Linux was beneficial. Now, we will see an example of a system that I worked on where a portion of it was purposely implemented on a microcontroller running a bare-metal application. This will provide some insight into where embedded Linux is *not* appropriate.

The following figure shows the block diagram of a medical device I worked on, where blood from a patient is run through the system:

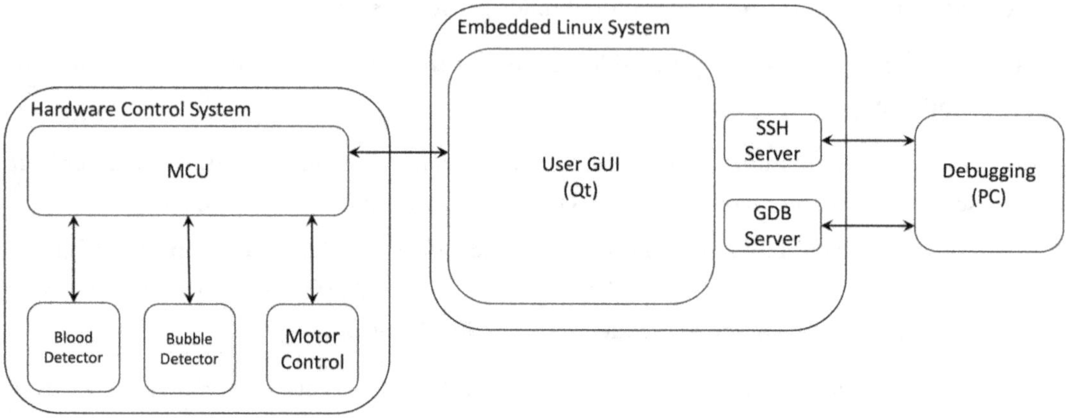

Figure 1.2 – Example medical device

The embedded Linux system has the elements we discussed previously, including an SSH server and a GDB server. A single application running in embedded Linux serves as the main application that the user interacts with. This application interfaces with the microcontroller over UART.

Unlike the previous example, the hardware control system has stringent requirements due to the nature of the product. There are strict requirements associated with controlling the motor in response to the blood and bubble detectors.

For example, if blood is pumping through the system and it is not being detected, then clearly something is wrong, and the microcontroller must stop the motor and inform the user GUI on the embedded Linux system of the condition. The time between when the absence of blood is detected and when the motor is stopped *must* be deterministic and clearly defined.

Similarly, the presence of a bubble in the bloodstream can be fatal. Thus, if the microcontroller detects a bubble, it must stop the motor within a deterministic amount of time.

These two conditions are examples of *hard* real-time requirements. Real-time requirements in an embedded system mean that the system must respond to inputs and generate outputs within a specified time frame or *deadline*. There are two categories of real-time requirements, *hard* and *soft*:

- An embedded system with hard real-time requirements has absolute deadlines. If a deadline is missed, the system fails and stops operating.
- An embedded system with soft real-time requirements doesn't have absolute deadlines. The system continues functioning but may not perform optimally.

Embedded systems such as the medical device just described may have hard real-time requirements. In these instances, embedded Linux may not be suitable. Although there are ways to configure an embedded Linux system to support real-time requirements, it is generally better to implement such a system using another embedded software pattern on a microcontroller. Nonetheless, as we have seen, running embedded Linux on other system components can be valuable. For example, the user interface may be implemented using embedded Linux.

While the *standard* Linux kernel does not guarantee precise timing or predictability, there are ways to adapt it.

The Linux kernel contains patches to enable real-time operation, called `PREEMPT_RT` patches (`https://wiki.linuxfoundation.org/realtime/start`). While these patches enable real-time operation, they don't necessarily support hard real-time requirements. Instead, `PREEMPT_RT` patches should only be used for embedded systems with soft real-time requirements. An RTOS with documented support for hard real-time requirements should be used if such requirements must be met.

Xenomai (`https://xenomai.org/`) is a real-time development framework that coexists with the Linux kernel, providing a real-time kernel alongside the standard kernel.

Besides hard real-time requirements, the target hardware may preclude us from using embedded Linux. Generally, if the **size, weight, power, and cost** (**SwaP-C**) requirements are extremely stringent, such that only a small microcontroller would meet these requirements, then embedded Linux will not be applicable.

In the next section, we will learn about embedded Linux's hardware requirements.

Understanding the hardware requirements

As embedded software engineers, we usually work in tandem with hardware engineers when designing and bringing up the custom hardware for our system. Typically, the hardware engineering team selects the components based on the system's overall SWaP-C requirements. Once they have completed their initial selection, they work with us to confirm the selection and plan out design details, such as pin selection.

We must know whether the SoM/SoC selected by the hardware will support embedded Linux. The processor must be 32- or 64-bit. Extremely low-cost and low-power microcontrollers that use an 8- or 16-bit instruction set architecture generally won't be able to run embedded Linux.

RAM and storage are also important requirements of an embedded Linux system. The minimum RAM requirement for embedded Linux is usually around 4 MB to 8 MB. However, for typical embedded applications requiring more robust networking, filesystem support, and a lightweight graphical interface, 64 MB to 128 MB of RAM may be required. Also, 4 MB to 8 MB of flash storage is usually the minimum necessary to run a minimal embedded Linux system. However, the flash requirement will increase as more applications, features, and frameworks are added.

Usually, the RAM and flash requirements are where microcontrollers fall short. Low-end microcontrollers, which are selected for their cost and power consumption, have up to 2 KB of RAM and 16 KB of flash. Mid-range microcontrollers, such as the popular STMicroelectronics STM32F0 series or the Microchip ATMega328, have up to 64 KB of RAM and 512 KB of flash. High-end microcontrollers, such as the STMicroelectronics STM32F4 series or NXP Kinetis K series, have up to 512 KB of RAM and 2 MB of flash. Finally, specialized or high-performance microcontrollers have up to 1 MB of RAM and 4 MB of flash. As we can see, high-end or high-performance microcontrollers don't meet the minimum requirements to run embedded Linux.

The other key hardware requirement to run embedded Linux is a **memory management unit (MMU)**. One of the most significant differences between embedded Linux and other embedded software patterns is that applications in embedded Linux have a distinct region of memory in which they can operate. Suppose an application accesses memory outside of this region. In that case, the MMU raises an exception to the Linux kernel, which raises a **segmentation fault** on the system and terminates the application. This capability is possible via the MMU.

The following diagram, retrieved from ARM's documentation, briefly describes the MMU's operation:

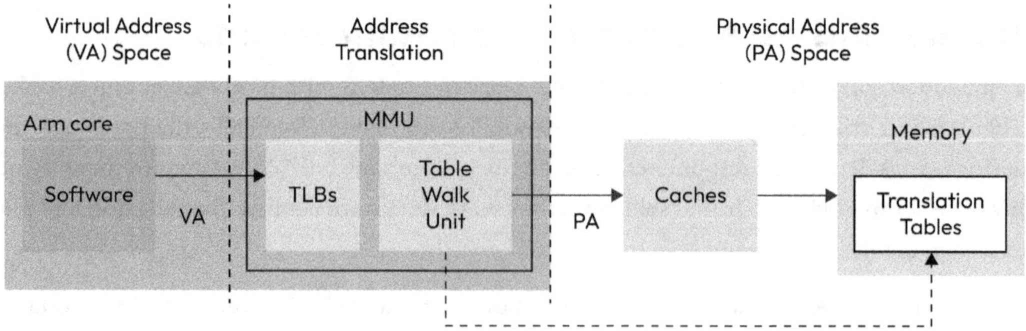

Figure 1.3 – MMU operation

As seen in the preceding figure, there are two types of addresses to access the underlying memory. A **virtual address**, as its name implies, is a software-generated address used to access the underlying memory. The MMU converts a virtual memory address into a physical one and accesses the underlying memory, using the **Translation Lookaside Buffer (TLB)**. This mechanism allows the Linux kernel to manage memory regions within applications.

While non-MMU support does exist in the Linux kernel, it is not often tested, and support is limited. Thus, if we wish to run embedded Linux on a particular system, we must ensure that the underlying hardware platform contains an MMU. Instead, if we opt for a system that doesn't have an MMU, we may spend a considerable amount of time getting embedded Linux to run successfully on our system.

Now that we know whether embedded Linux will run on the hardware selected, we can understand the different software components that comprise an embedded Linux system. In the next section, we will learn about these components and how they fit together.

Reviewing embedded Linux's architecture

In this section, we will review the architecture of embedded Linux. Specifically, we will briefly learn about the different software components that are typically part of an embedded Linux system. In future chapters, we will discuss each element in more detail.

Architecture

There are four distinct software elements in most embedded Linux systems, as shown in the following figure.

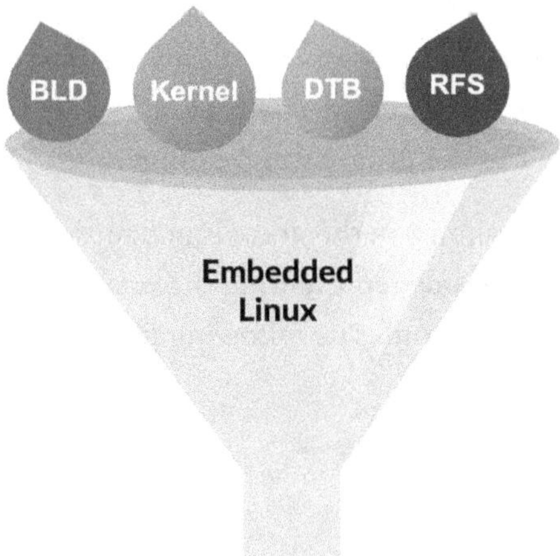

Figure 1.4 – embedded Linux components

Let us understand each of the components in detail:

- The first software component of embedded Linux is the **bootloader**, shown as **BLD** in the preceding figure. The bootloader is responsible for initializing the CPU and the necessary peripherals before launching the kernel. This can include clock configurations and RAM, which the Linux kernel may need to run correctly. The bootloader is also responsible for configuring the kernel itself, such as passing arguments to the kernel during boot and informing the kernel about the Devicetree. The most popular bootloader used in embedded Linux is **U-Boot. BareBox** is another popular bootloader. While it has a smaller user base than U-Boot, BareBox focuses on clean and modular code and has a robust scripting infrastructure. We will go into more detail about U-Boot in a later section.
- The second software component of embedded Linux is the **Linux kernel**. The kernel is perhaps the most essential software component. It constitutes the crux of embedded Linux and has several responsibilities. It is responsible for launching applications on the system and ensuring that the application can safely access the needed hardware. For example, the kernel allocates the RAM needed by the application. If the application requires peripheral access, the kernel provides a software interface for the application to access the hardware safely. The kernel is also responsible for ensuring that all applications are granted sufficient execution time on the processor.
- The third software component of embedded Linux is the **Devicetree**, noted by **DTB** in the preceding figure. The Devicetree describes the hardware of the system. For example, it describes the CPU, RAM, and any buses connected to the processor. The Devicetree also describes the different peripherals on the system, including controllers that exercise specific protocols.
- The final software component of embedded Linux is the **root filesystem**, shown as **RFS** in the preceding figure. The root filesystem contains all of the files present on the system. This includes the applications, libraries, and configuration files needed by the applications.

One important component not shown in the preceding figure is the **toolchain**. The toolchain is a utility that converts the source code representing the previous components into binaries and applications that the processor can run. The following figure presents a high-level view of the toolchain's function:

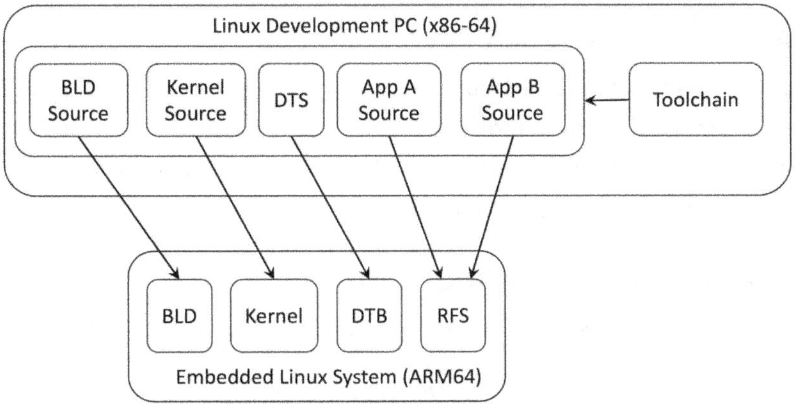

Figure 1.5 – Toolchain operation

The toolchain runs on our Linux development PC and converts the source code for each component of an embedded Linux system into its binary format. These outputs are then placed on the embedded Linux system for the processor to execute. The toolchain is an application designed to run on the x86 or x86-64 **instruction set architecture** (**ISA**) of our Linux development PC. It produces applications or binaries that are compatible with the **ARM64 ISA**. The operation in the preceding figure and just described involves running an application on one ISA (x86-64, in this case) to generate outputs that can be executed on another ISA (ARM64, in this case). This process is known as **cross-compilation**.

In fact, as embedded software engineers, we always perform cross-compilation for bare-metal development. We write source code, use a build system to compile the final binary, and load the final binary generated by the compiler onto the target microcontroller.

> Important note
>
> Novice embedded software engineers may use the IDE to compile their source code into the final binary. They may not realize that the build system is usually a separate set of applications that the IDE invokes during compilation. Certain advanced embedded software engineers recognize this and directly use the underlying build system without the IDE.

Now that we understand the different software components of a typical embedded Linux system, we can see how they fit together in the boot process.

Booting embedded Linux

In this section, we will learn about the embedded Linux boot process. Due to the different software components of an embedded Linux system and their complex structure, the boot process requires a detailed review. By the end of this section, we will have a comprehensive understanding of the Linux boot process, from power-up to a console terminal.

From power-up to kernel loading

The following diagram shows one variant of the first stage of the embedded Linux boot process:

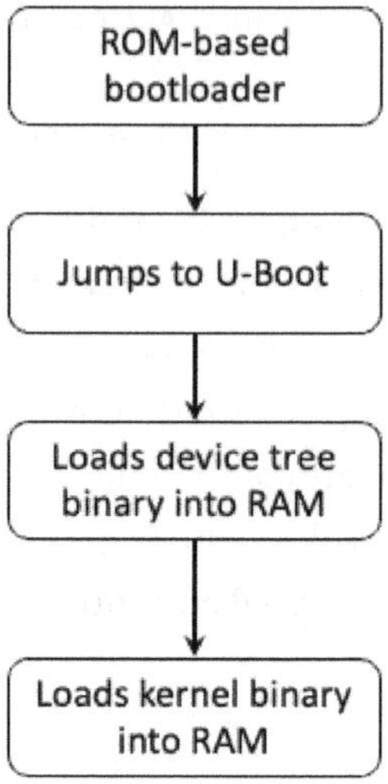

Figure 1.6 – Bootloader operations during boot

When power is applied to the processor, it usually launches an initial bootloader in the read-only portion of its memory. Depending on the SoC, the ROM-based bootloader jumps to a fixed location in flash. This location contains another bootloader, usually U-Boot.

Another variant of this process involves another bootloader, the **secondary program loader (SPL)**, which runs after the ROM-based bootloader and before U-Boot. The ROM-based bootloader loads the SPL into RAM from a predefined memory location, such as on-chip flash. The SPL then performs the necessary setup and configuration operations to load and execute U-Boot from external flash.

Why would an SPL be necessary? Depending on the hardware architecture and constraints of the onboard ROM, the necessary drivers to communicate with the external flash may result in a bootloader that may not fit in the ROM. On-chip flash storage is usually larger than ROM and can contain another bootloader to interface with external flash.

The bootloader configures and initializes essential peripherals to facilitate kernel booting.

After the bootloader configures these peripherals, it loads the Devicetree binary from flash and stores it in a fixed location in RAM. Then, the bootloader loads the kernel binary from flash and stores it in a fixed location in RAM.

Loading and launching the kernel

After the bootloader loads the kernel into RAM, the next step is to launch it. The following diagram illustrates that process:

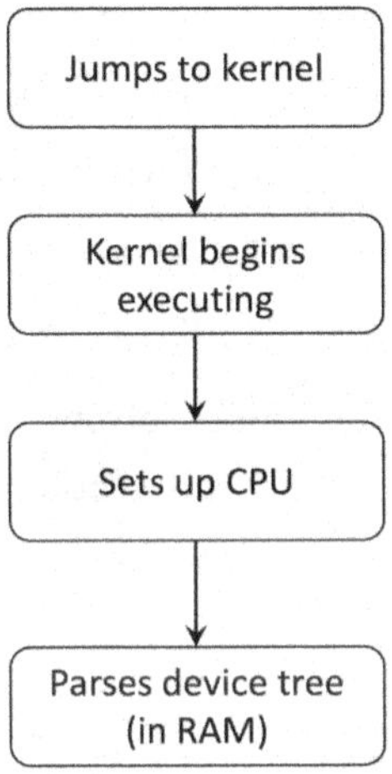

Figure 1.7 – Kernel operations during boot

The bootloader jumps to that location after loading the Linux kernel into RAM. First, the kernel configures the processor to allow essential components and subsystems to run successfully. Then, the kernel parses the Devicetree from RAM to gain more insight into the system's hardware and loads the appropriate drivers to configure the detected hardware. This process is shown briefly in the first box of the following figure:

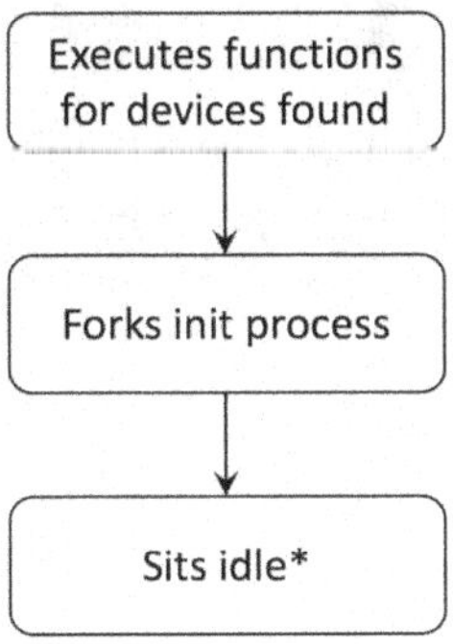

Figure 1.8 – Kernel operations during and after boot

We will learn more about the details of this process in *Chapter 3* and see examples in *Chapter 4*.

Then, the kernel starts the `init` process. A **process** in embedded Linux is an application running on the system. A process has an area of RAM that it can operate in without interference from other applications. The `init` process is a special application in embedded Linux. Since it is the first process to start, it is the parent of all other processes in Linux. Then, `init` launches other applications using one of two popular frameworks, which we will discuss in *Chapter 8*.

After the `init` process is launched, the kernel sits idle and has three primary responsibilities:

- It facilitates launching other applications, including allocating an initial amount of RAM for each application and providing any other hardware access
- It ensures that each application has sufficient time for execution on the processor
- It handles any interrupts triggered by the CPU

Now that we understand the overall boot process of an embedded Linux system, we can explore each component in more detail. In the next few sections, we will learn about the individual components of embedded Linux in more detail. Subsequent chapters will be devoted to each component and describe it extensively.

Learning about U-Boot

U-Boot is the most popular bootloader used on embedded Linux systems. It borrows a good deal of source code from the Linux kernel. U-Boot and the Linux kernel have header files in common, and U-Boot supports loading different variants of the Linux kernel.

Let's briefly dive into U-Boot's source code since I firmly believe we can truly understand how any application works by understanding the source code behind the implementation. We can retrieve U-Boot's source code by executing the following command:

```
$ git clone git://git.denx.de/u-boot.git
```

We can retrieve version 2024.07 by executing the following command:

```
$ git checkout tags/v2024.07
```

Finally, we can use the `ls` command to view the directory structure of U-Boot's source code, which is shown here:

```
[u-boot]$ ls
api    boot    config.mk  doc      env       include  lib          Makefile  README   tools
arch   cmd     configs    drivers  examples  Kbuild   Licenses     net       scripts
board  common  disk       dts      fs        Kconfig  MAINTAINERS  post      test
```

Figure 1.9 – U-Boot source tree (version 2024.07)

Let's review some of the more interesting directories:

- The `api` directory contains hardware-independent source code. It serves as an interface to standalone U-Boot applications, giving them access to some of the underlying functionality of U-Boot itself.
- The `arch` directory contains CPU-specific and SoC-specific implementations.
- The `board` directory contains source code used to initialize and interface with boards provided by vendors.
- The `boot` directory contains source code to parse and boot different variants of the Linux kernel.
- The `cmd` directory contains the implementation of all the commands available in U-Boot.
- The `configs` directory contains the different configuration options enabled and specified for the boards that U-Boot supports.
- Like the Linux kernel, U-Boot uses the `kconfig` infrastructure to configure U-Boot before compilation. We will discuss the `kconfig` infrastructure in more detail in *Chapter 3*.
- The `env` directory contains the source code to manage U-Boot's environment variables. Environment variables are one of the most powerful features of U-Boot. In addition to dictating U-Boot's behaviour and boot process, U-Boot environment variables are also used by Linux applications.
- The `examples` directory contains samples of different standalone U-Boot applications.
- The `script` directory contains numerous utilities implemented as scripts and as source code.

We will go into more detail about U-Boot in *Chapter 2*. In the next section, we will review the basics of the Linux kernel, arguably the most essential component used in embedded Linux systems.

Reviewing the Linux kernal

The Linux kernel has over 30 million lines of code, and its development has spanned nearly 35 years.

We can retrieve version 6.9 of the Linux kernel by executing the following commands:

```
$ git clone https://git.kernel.org/pub/scm/linux/kernel/git/torvalds/
linux.git/
$ cd linux
$ git checkout tags/v6.9
```

The following figure shows the structure of the Linux kernel source code:

```
[linux]$ ls
arch     CREDITS        fs        ipc      lib          mm      samples   tools
block    crypto         include   Kbuild   LICENSES     net     scripts   usr
certs    Documentation  init      Kconfig  MAINTAINERS  README  security  virt
COPYING  drivers        io_uring  kernel   Makefile     rust    sound
```

Figure 1.10 – Linux kernel code base

Similar to the previous section, we will review some of the more exciting directories:

- The `arch` directory contains source code specific to a particular CPU and SoC. For example, `arch/arm/boot` contains source files relevant to the boot process of ARM CPUs, and `arch/arm/boot/dts` contains Devicetree files for platforms with ARM-based processors. `arch/arm/crypto` contains hardware-accelerated cryptographic implementations, and `arch/arm/kernel` contains hardware-specific implementations of certain kernel functions. We will learn more about these directories in *Chapter 3*.
- The `drivers` directory forms the majority of the Linux kernel code base. It is the largest directory in the Linux kernel. We can confirm this by executing the following commands:

```
$ du sh . -exclude ".git"
1.6G
$ du -sh drivers/
1.1G
```

The preceding output shows that the size of the entire Linux kernel is 1.6 GB, and the size of the `drivers` directory is roughly 1.1 GB. The `drivers` directory constitutes roughly 69% of the entire Linux kernel!

Besides drivers, the Linux kernel also consists of numerous subsystems.

For example, the following figure shows the contents of the sound directory:

```
[sound]$ ls
ac97        arm    drivers   i2c      last.c    oss     pcmcia  soc           spi    virtio
ac97_bus.c  atmel  firewire  isa      Makefile  parisc  ppc     sound_core.c  synth  x86
aoa         core   hda       Kconfig  mips      pci     sh      sparc         usb    xen
```

Figure 1.11 – Linux kernel sound directory

The preceding image shows the relevant directories that comprise the entire sound subsystem of the Linux kernel. Specifically:

- The `soc` directory contains source code to interface with the sound controller hardware inside the processor
- The `i2c` directory contains the interface logic between the Linux sound subsystem and the `i2c` subsystem

This section briefly introduced the Linux kernel. We will thoroughly review it and learn how to build it in *Chapter 3*. We will learn how to debug it in *Chapter 12*.

In the next section, we will briefly review the Devicetree, a unique concept that may be difficult for engineers from a typical embedded software background to grasp.

Understanding the Devicetree

The **Devicetree** allows the Linux kernel to learn about the hardware present on the system. The Linux kernel uses the information in the Devicetree to make the necessary function calls to initialize the underlying hardware.

The Devicetree is not specific to the Linux kernel. The Devicetree, abbreviated as **DTS** and more formally known as the **Open Firmware Device Tree**, is a construct initially conceived to describe hardware. It is both a data structure and a language, and is meant to be read by any OS, not just Linux, so that it can identify hardware during runtime and configure itself appropriately.

The Linux kernel uses the Devicetree for three main reasons:

- The first is to identify the system. Ideally, the devicetree could consistently describe all system details. However, there are some nuanced differences across systems. Thus, the kernel must be able to identify the machine early in the boot process to execute code specific to the machine.
- The second reason is to configure certain parameters during runtime. For example, certain memory regions may be defined in the Devicetree that the Linux kernel uses for initial configuration.

- The third primary purpose of the devicetree is for the Linux kernel to identify the buses and peripherals present on the system and to load the appropriate drivers.

Again, this chapter is meant to introduce the core elements of an embedded Linux system. We will cover the devicetree in more detail, including hands-on examples, in *Chapter 4*. In the next section, we will learn about **QEMU**, a tool we can use to simulate embedded Linux systems on our PC!

QEMU: simulating an embedded Linux system

While I firmly believe that embedded software engineers function best when they are running their software on real hardware, that may not always be the case. The examples in this book are intended to be executed on a Raspberry Pi 5. However, not everyone may have access to the Raspberry Pi 5 and may not be able to take advantage of the examples.

As an alternative, we can use the **Quick Emulator (QEMU)**. QEMU is an open source virtualization application that allows us to run an embedded Linux system targeting an architecture or platform different from our development PC. We can use QEMU to simulate a good deal of the Raspberry Pi hardware to run our embedded Linux system. This will allow us to learn about the different components, even U-Boot, without having hardware. We will learn how to use QEMU to learn about the relevant component in future chapters.

> Important note
>
> Unfortunately, Ubuntu 24.04, the version of Ubuntu that was used at the time of writing, contains QEMU 8.2.2, which doesn't support the Raspberry Pi 4B. That is why we needed to install QEMU from source.

In preparation, let's see how we can build QEMU by following the steps outlined here:

1. Retrieve the archive containing the source code for QEMU 9.0.2 by executing the following command:

```
$ wget https://download.qemu.org/qemu-9.0.2.tar.xz
```

2. Execute the following command to decompress the archive:

```
$ tar xvf qemu-9.0.2.tar.xz
```

3. Navigate to the resulting directory by executing the following command:

```
$ cd qemu-9.0.2
```

4. Execute the following commands to build QEMU:

```
$ ./configure && make
```

> **Important note**
>
> I personally don't like installing applications or utilities directly from the source code since it can conflict with the installation from the package manager. However, if you want to install QEMU from the source code downloaded previously, you can simply execute `sudo make install`.
>
> If you execute the preceding commands and run into errors, it's most likely due to missing dependencies. You can navigate to this link to learn about the required dependencies for QEMU: `https://wiki.qemu.org/Hosts/Linux`.

Summary

In this chapter, we learned about the use cases where embedded Linux is appropriate for our system and the hardware requirements needed to run it adequately. Equally important, we learned when not to use embedded Linux. As we continue throughout the book, we will dive deeper into the subsystems covered in this chapter. Towards the middle of this book, we will see examples of applications that are perfectly suited for embedded Linux. As we learn about these applications in *Chapter 9, 10, and 11*, it's important to refer to the lessons learned in this chapter to understand which elements are relevant for embedded Linux. We also learned about and built QEMU to simulate an embedded Linux system in case we don't have access to the hardware used in the rest of the book, due to cost and availability in certain regions.

In the next chapter, we will learn about U-Boot.

Get this book's PDF version and more

Scan the QR code (or go to `packtpub.com/unlock`). Search for this book by name, confirm the edition, and then follow the steps on the page.

UNLOCK NOW

Note: Keep your invoice handy. Purchases made directly from Packt don't require an invoice.

2

Learning About U-Boot

As we learned in the previous chapter, the bootloader is one of the first pieces of software to be executed when an embedded Linux system is powered. We also discovered that U-Boot is one of the most popular bootloaders used in embedded Linux systems. In this chapter, we are going to learn about U-Boot in detail. First, we will review U-Boot's source code to understand its flow on a Raspberry Pi 5. Then, we will learn about other interesting directories in the source code and their purpose. For example, we will discover how U-Boot interacts with different hardware peripherals via device drivers.

Additionally, we will explore how U-Boot allows a user to set and save relevant information in persistent storage. Afterward, we will build U-Boot and run it on a Raspberry Pi 5 inside QEMU. However, before that, we will take a slight detour and build on our understanding of the cross-compilation process. Specifically, we will learn how to retrieve an appropriate toolchain and use it to compile an application, such as U-Boot, for execution on the Raspberry Pi 5. Then, we will explore U-Boot's console interface, learn about the commands we can execute, and see how we can implement our own. After that, we will discover the different boot options that U-Boot provides. Finally, we will learn how U-Boot can ensure that it only loads and executes trusted software during the boot process.

In this chapter, we are going to cover the following main topics:

- Understanding the boot process
- Learning about device drivers
- Exploring environment variables
- Executing commands
- Fetching and using the toolchain

- Building U-Boot
- Running U-Boot on a Raspberry Pi 5 and QEMU
- Exploring the console interface
- Implementing custom commands

Technical requirements

To be able to complete this chapter, you should be comfortable reading and writing C code and executing commands on the Linux Terminal. You should also be somewhat familiar with reading assembly code.

Understanding the boot process

In this section, we will walk through the U-Boot source code to understand the boot process. As we learned in *Chapter 1*, the U-Boot source code can be retrieved by following these steps:

1. Execute the following command to clone the repository containing the U-Boot source code:

```
$ git clone git://git.denx.de/u-boot.git
```

2. Navigate to the directory containing the retrieved source code by executing the following command:

```
$ cd u-boot
```

3. Execute the following command to retrieve U-Boot version `v2024.07`, which is the latest version at the time of writing:

```
$ git checkout tags/v2024.07
```

If we search the U-Boot source code, we will discover that there is no `main` function, which we typically expect to be called first in a C application. We can examine U-Boot's **linker script** to discover which function is executed first when U-Boot is launched. The linker script is responsible for placing functions and data structures in the final application binary. U-Boot's linker script, `arch/u-boot-elf.lds`, contains the following code:

```
ENTRY(CONFIG_PLATFORM_ELFENTRY)
SECTIONS
{
        . = CONFIG_PLATFORM_ELFENTRY;

        .data : {
                *(.data*)
```

```
        }
}
```

The ENTRY directive in the preceding linker script specifies that execution starts at the function dictated by the CONFIG_PLATFORM_ELFENTRY configuration option. The following entry can be found in the top-level Kconfig file:

```
config PLATFORM_ELFENTRY
        string
        default "__start" if MIPS
        default "_start"
```

This entry indicates that _start is the first function to be called when U-Boot is launched on the Raspberry Pi 5 (since the Raspberry Pi 5 doesn't contain a SoC with a MIPS architecture).

> Important note
>
> The CONFIG_PLATFORM_ELFENTRY configuration option and Kconfig file are part of the overall U-Boot configuration mechanism. This framework is borrowed from the Linux kernel, allowing us to configure different aspects of U-Boot. We can use predefined configuration files to configure U-Boot for our specific platform. Later, we'll learn how to use the appropriate file to configure U-Boot for the Raspberry Pi 5 before building and executing it.

The _start function is implemented in assembly instead of a C file. Specifically, it is implemented in start.S. We can execute the following command to discover that numerous start.S assembly files are located under the arch directory:

```
$ find -name start.S
./arch/mips/cpu/start.S
.
.
.
./arch/arm/cpu/armv7m/start.S
./arch/arm/cpu/armv8/start.S
.
.
.
```

We are interested in the `arch/arm/cpu/armv8/start.S` file since the BCM2712, the SoC used on the Raspberry Pi 5, contains ARM Cortex-A76 cores, which are based on the ARMv8 architecture. In this assembly file, we can see that the `_start` label ultimately jumps to the `_main` label, as shown here:

```
.global   _start
.
.
.
master_cpu:
          msr      SPSel, #1                 /* make sure we use SP_ELx */
          bl       _main
```

The `_main` label is implemented in the `arch/arm/lib/crt0_64.S` assembly file. After performing operations to initialize an appropriate environment for the remainder of U-Boot, such as initializing the stack, `_main` calls `board_init_f`. After `board_init_f` returns, `_main` finishes initializing the remainder of the environment and calls `board_init_r`, which is defined in `common/board.c` and does not return.

As shown in the following code, `board_init_r` calls `initcall_run_list` with an array of functions to call (`initcall_run_list` performs some checks before calling each function in the array):

```
static init_fnc_t init_sequence_r[] = {
          initr_trace,
          initr_reloc,
          event_init,
.
.
.
          INIT_FUNC_WATCHDOG_RESET
.
.
.
          run_main_loop,
};
```

As we can see, the last function in the array is `run_main_loop`, which essentially calls `main_loop`, found in `common/main.c`, and is the point where U-Boot can begin executing commands. These commands may be executed automatically, such as those responsible for launching the Linux kernel, or they may be executed by the user via the console interface.

In the next section, we will explore how device drivers work in U-Boot.

Learning about device drivers

Let's look at the **button GPIO** driver in U-Boot to understand how device drivers work. This driver is responsible for converting GPIO activity connected to a particular pin into key presses and is implemented in the `drivers/button/button-gpio.c` source file. Our analysis of the driver begins at the bottom of the source file, which contains the following definition:

```
U_BOOT_DRIVER(button_gpio) = {
        .name           = "button_gpio",
        .id             = UCLASS_BUTTON,
        .of_match       = button_gpio_ids,
        .ops            = &button_gpio_ops,
        .priv_auto      = sizeof(struct button_gpio_priv),
        .bind           = button_gpio_bind,
        .probe          = button_gpio_probe,
        .remove         = button_gpio_remove,
};
```

The preceding snippet registers the `button_gpio` driver with U-Boot with the following parameters:

- `name`: A string representing the driver's name—in this case, `button_gpio`. (Note that this is different from `button_gpio` inside the `U_BOOT_DRIVER(button_gpio)` declaration. The latter creates a C struct named `button_gpio`, whereas the former is the `name` element of the created C struct.)
- `id`: This element associates a driver with a particular **UCLASS**. In this case, the `button_gpio` driver belongs to `UCLASS_BUTTON`. We will examine the implementation of `UCLASS_BUTTON` later.
- `of_match`: This element defines a set of entries that must be present in the device tree to allow U-Boot to load the driver. In this instance, `of_match` is defined as follows:

```
static const struct udevice_id button_gpio_ids[] = {
        { .compatible = "gpio-keys" },
        { .compatible = "gpio-keys-polled" },
        { }
};
```

Thus, if either gpio-keys or gpio-keys-polled is present in the device tree, then U-Boot will load the button_gpio driver. We will cover the device tree in more detail in *Chapter 4*.

- ops: This element defines the set of functions that the button_gpio driver must implement. These functions are defined like so:

```
static const struct button_ops button_gpio_ops = {
        .get_state        = button_gpio_get_state,
        .get_code         = button_gpio_get_code,
};
```

  As we will see later, the UCLASS_BUTTON implementation uses the .get_state and .get_code callbacks to serve as an abstraction between the calling function and the underlying hardware driver.

- priv_auto: This element allocates memory for data that the driver strictly uses. In this instance, this refers to the button_gpio_priv C struct, which is defined at the top of the file.
- bind: This element defines a function pointer, which is called when U-Boot associates a driver with a node in the device tree, using the compatible string specified in the of_match element. This function allows the driver to perform some preliminary initialization.
- probe: This element defines a function pointer that is called to complete the initialization of the driver and, in turn, the device.
- remove: This element defines a function pointer that is called if a device is no longer needed, and the memory allocated by the driver during the probe can be freed. This may be necessary if we wish to set a device or peripheral back to its initial state for the Linux kernel.

As mentioned earlier, the button_gpio driver is associated with UCLASS_BUTTON, which is implemented in the drivers/button/button-uclass.c source file. Again, we can see the use of the UCLASS_BUTTON preprocessor macro at the bottom of that source file:

```
UCLASS_DRIVER(button) = {
        .id                     = UCLASS_BUTTON,
        .name                   = "button",
        .per_device_plat_auto    = sizeof(struct button_uc_plat),
};
```

The preceding macro creates a C struct called button with the following elements:

- id: This creates a specific UCLASS that specific drivers can register with. In this case, UCLASS_BUTTON is created, which the button_gpio driver registers with, as we saw earlier.

- `name`: This element is a string representation of the particular `UCLASS`.
- `per_device_plat_auto`: This element is used by U-Boot to allocate memory for `UCLASS` when a device belonging to that `UCLASS` is bound to the driver.

> Important note
>
> There is much more to explore regarding U-Boot device drivers than what's been covered in this section. The U-Boot Driver Model README, located at `https://github.com/dsd/u-boot/blob/master/doc/driver-model/README.txt`, provides much more detail about the different elements of the `U_BOOT_DRIVER` and `UCLASS_DRIVER` C structs.

In the next section, we will explore U-Boot environment variables, how they are used, and how the surrounding infrastructure is implemented.

Exploring environment variables

Environment variables are an important and valuable feature of U-Boot. They are represented by key-value pairs and are used to control U-Boot's behavior. Let's look at what behaviors can be controlled in U-Boot using environment variables:

- The `bootcmd` environment variable can be used to define U-Boot's default boot process. This environment variable can be complex or simple, depending on certain conditions. For example, if a device only has internal eMMC flash and no network connectivity, U-Boot may be configured to boot only using the internal flash. However, if the device has an SD card with a backup image, the `bootcmd` environment variable can be set to instruct U-Boot to boot from the SD card after determining that the internal flash is corrupt. Finally, if the device has network connectivity, the `bootcmd` environment variable can be set to instruct U-Boot to use the network as a final fallback if it fails to boot from the internal flash and the SD card.
- The `bootargs` environment variable is used to pass parameters to the Linux kernel during the boot process. These parameters typically consist of the following aspects:
    - The device and partition the Linux kernel should use as the root filesystem
    - Information about whether the root filesystem should be mounted with read and write permissions or read-only permissions

    - The serial port the Linux kernel should use to print messages during the boot process
    - Additional arguments that we haven't discussed here can be passed on to the Linux kernel. The following web page, which I encourage you to read, outlines more arguments that can be passed to the Linux kernel: `https://www.kernel.org/doc/html/v4.14/admin-guide/kernel-parameters.html`.
- The `bootdelay` environment variable controls how long, in seconds, U-Boot should wait for interaction from the user before loading and launching the Linux kernel.
- The `bootfile` environment variable informs U-Boot of the file that represents the Linux kernel.
- The `fdtfile` environment variable informs U-Boot of the file that represents the device tree.

We will see the values of these environment variables shortly, when we run U-Boot on the Raspberry Pi 5 and in QEMU. We will also explore other interesting environment variables.

For now, let's review the code base and understand the underlying mechanics of how U-Boot loads environment variables. The crux of the implementation is in the `env/` directory. The starting point for retrieving the environment variables is the `env_init` function, which is called from `board_init_f`. Similar to the `init_sequence_r` array used in `board_init_r`, `env_init` is part of the `init_sequence_f` array. As shown here, `board_init_f`, which is defined in `common/board_f.c`, iterates over the `init_sequence_f` array and calls each function in the array, one of which is `env_init`:

```
static const init_fnc_t init_sequence_f[] = {
    setup_mon_len,
          .
          .
          .
          env_init,               /* initialize environment */
          .
          .
          .
};

void board_init_f(ulong boot_flags)
{
.
.
```

```
.
        if (initcall_run_list(init_sequence_f))
                hang();
    .
    .
     .
}
```

As we can see, `env_init` iterates over the memory types where the environment variable can be stored, such as in EEPROM, external flash, or eMMC, and initializes them. A driver for each memory type registers itself with U-Boot, as shown here:

```
U_BOOT_ENV_LOCATION(fat) = {
        .location       = ENVL_FAT,
        ENV_NAME("FAT")
#ifdef LOADENV
        .load           = env_fat_load,
#endif
        .save           = ENV_SAVE_PTR(env_fat_save),
};
```

Here, the `U_BOOT_ENV_LOCATION` macro is the mechanism used by `env/fat.c` to register itself with U-Boot. Similar to the `U_BOOT_DRIVER` macro we saw in the previous section, it implements the functions required for interacting with environment variables.

The `env_load` function iterates over the memory types in an attempt to load the environment variables. Each driver reads the location within the specific memory where the environment variables are expected to be present. For example, in the case of the **FAT** driver, the driver checks for a `uboot.env` file. If the file exists, the driver calls `env_import` with the data contained in the file. Then, `env_import` checks the validity of the data by calculating the **Cyclic Redundancy Check (CRC)** code and comparing it to the value appended to the data. If the check passes, then environment variables are imported into U-Boot. If the process fails, U-Boot reverts to the set of default environment variables that have been compiled.

Beyond environment variables, executing commands is another valuable feature of U-Boot. As we've observed, certain environment variables, such as `bootcmd`, can perform relatively sophisticated operations. In the next section, we will learn about U-Boot **commands**. While commands can be executed similarly to certain environment variables, they cannot be modified. Rather, they are compiled in U-Boot. More specifically, we will explore how U-Boot supports command execution on the console.

Executing commands

The source code for commands supported in U-Boot is located under the `cmd` directory. Let's understand how commands are implemented in U-Boot by focusing on the **boot** command, which is implemented in `bootm.c`. The following snippet shows the implementation of the boot command:

```
int do_bootd(struct cmd_tbl *cmdtp, int flag, int argc, char *const argv[])
{
        return run_command(env_get("bootcmd"), flag);
}

U_BOOT_CMD(
        boot,   1,      1,      do_bootd,
        "boot default, i.e., run 'bootcmd'",
        ""
);
```

Similar to the `U_BOOT_DRIVER`, `UCLASS_DRIVER`, and `U_BOOT_ENV_LOCATION` macros we learned about in the previous sections, `U_BOOT_CMD` is also a macro that is used to register commands with U-Boot. The macro creates an entry in an internal table maintained by U-Boot with all supported commands. Each entry in the table is represented by a C structure, which is denoted as `struct cmd_tbl` and defined in `include/command.h`.

The following table describes the elements of the C structure and their settings for the `boot` command:

C Structure Element Name	Description	The boot Command Setting
`name`	The string that must be entered on the console interface to invoke the command	The boot string.
`maxargs`	The maximum number of arguments that the command can accept	1.
`cmd_rep`	Whether the command is repeatable or not (i.e., whether it can be invoked multiple times)	The command is repeatable.

C Structure Element Name	Description	The boot Command Setting
`cmd`	The function that will be executed when the command is invoked	The `do_bootd` function.
`usage`	A short message on how the command should be used	The default boot string (i.e., run `bootcmd`).
`help`	A more detailed message on how to use the command	An empty string.
`complete`	The function used to fill in the remainder of the command as a user begins to type	This function is `NULL` for the `boot` command. While not obvious from what we previously discussed, we can identify this by tracing the macros after the `U_BOOT_CMD` macro. The `U_BOOT_CMD_COMPLETE` macro is used when a complete function is present for a particular command.

Table 2.1 – struct cmd_tbl description

Here, we can see that the `boot` command invokes the `do_bootd` function, which executes the `bootcmd` environment variable as a command. Now that we have covered some of the main functionalities of U-Boot and learned how they work by analyzing the underlying source code, we can start building U-Boot. However, first, we'll take a slight detour and understand how to retrieve and use the toolchain.

Fetching and using the toolchain

In *Chapter 1*, we learned that the process for generating binaries targeting an ISA that is different from the one where the toolchain is invoked is called **cross-compilation**. Since U-Boot is a binary that will be executed on the Raspberry Pi 5, which contains a CPU running the ARM64 ISA, and we will be building it on our development PC, which contains a CPU running the x86-64 ISA, we will need to **cross-compile**. This is commonly accomplished with a toolchain.

Important note

When we use an IDE to develop embedded software for microcontrollers, we also cross-compile under the hood! However, the IDE usually contains the toolchain, so when we install the IDE, we also install the toolchain.

We can retrieve the toolchain by following these steps:

1. Execute the following command to retrieve a compressed version of the GNU toolchain that will run on our Linux development PC and generate binaries that can run on the Raspberry Pi 5:

```
$ wget https://developer.arm.com/-/media/Files/downloads/
gnu/13.3.rel1/binrel/arm-gnu-toolchain-13.3.rel1-x86_64-aarch64-
none-linux-gnu.tar.xz
```

2. Extract the compressed toolchain by executing the following command:

```
$ tar xvf arm-gnu-toolchain-13.3.rel1-x86_64-aarch64-none-linux-gnu.
tar.xz
```

After performing the extraction, we should see the following directory, which contains the toolchain:

```
$ ls
arm-gnu-toolchain-13.3.rel1-x86_64-aarch64-none-linux-gnu
```

The `bin` directory inside the `toolchain` directory contains the following applications. These can be executed throughout development and the debugging process:

```
$ cd arm-gnu-toolchain-13.3.rel1-x86_64-aarch64-none-linux-gnu/bin
$ ls
.
.
.
aarch64-none-linux-gnu-gcc
.
.
.
aarch64-none-linux-gnu-gdb
```

As we can see, the names of these applications contain three or four repeating components with dashes in between and a distinct final component:

```
aarch64-none-linux-gnu-gcc
```

Figure 2.1 – Toolchain "triple" specifics

The first four combined components are known as a toolchain **triple**. Generally speaking, a toolchain triple contains the following components in the name:

```
<Architecture>-<Vendor>-<Operating System>-<ABI>-<Application>
```

Figure 2.2 – Toolchain triple convention

> Important note
>
> You might be wondering why we call it a triple when there are four components. Sometimes, the **Application Binary Interface (ABI)** is omitted or combined with the operating system to form a single component. Other times, the vendor is omitted, and the operating system and ABI are left as distinct components of the triple.

Let's take a closer look at these components:

- **Architecture**: This is the architecture for which the binary will be compiled. In our case, we will compile binaries for the AArch64 ISA of the Raspberry Pi 5 CPU.
- **Vendor**: This is the organization that generated the toolchain. Although this is no longer used and is preserved for historical purposes, `none` or `unknown` may be used in its place, as is the case for our toolchain.
- **Operating System**: This is the target operating system for which the binary is compiled. Toolchains with an operating system designation of `none` in the triple are usually used for bare-metal application development.
- **ABI**: The ABI defines how applications interact with the underlying operating system.
- **Application**: This is not part of the triple and defines the eventual application executed. For example, **gcc** is used for compilation, **gdb** is used for debugging.

> Important note
>
> You might be wondering why we care about the **operating system** and **ABI** elements of the triple when compiling U-Boot since no operating system is present when we are running it. Commands in U-Boot have direct access to the underlying hardware without any protection afforded by a proper operating system, such as the Linux kernel. Thus, using the toolchain with the preceding triple doesn't adversely affect U-Boot during compilation.

Now that we have fetched the toolchain and understand some of the terminology surrounding it, we can start using it:

1. In a new Terminal, navigate to the toolchain's directory and execute the following command to add the toolchain to our `PATH`. Linux uses this `PATH` on our development PC to search for applications that we wish to execute from the command line:

```
$ export PATH=`pwd`:$PATH
```

> Note
>
> The updated `PATH` will not persist when a new Terminal is opened. You can find instructions online for automatically updating `PATH` whenever a new Terminal is opened.

2. Set the `CROSS_COMPILE` environment variable to the toolchain triple. This informs the U-Boot build system of the toolchain we wish to use. As we will see in *Chapter 3*, this environment variable is also used when compiling the Linux kernel:

```
$ export CROSS_COMPILE=aarch64-none-linux-gnu-
```

After setting these environment variables on our development PC, we should be able to use our toolchain to cross-compile U-Boot so that it can run on the Raspberry Pi 5 and QEMU. In the next section, we will learn how to compile U-Boot so that it can run on these two systems.

Building U-Boot

Before building U-Boot, you may need to install the appropriate dependencies to compile it successfully. You can find the necessary dependencies in `doc/build/gcc.rst`:

```
.
.
sudo apt-get install bc bison build-essential coccinelle \
      device-tree-compiler dfu-util efitools flex gdisk graphviz imagemagick \
      liblz4-tool libgnutls28-dev libguestfs-tools libncurses-dev \
      libpython3-dev libsdl2-dev libssl-dev lz4 lzma lzma-alone openssl \
      pkg-config python3 python3-asteval python3-coverage python3-filelock \
      python3-pkg-resources python3-pycryptodome python3-pyelftools \
      python3-pytest python3-pytest-xdist python3-sphinxcontrib.apidoc \
      python3-sphinx-rtd-theme python3-subunit python3-testtools \
      python3-virtualenv swig uuid-de
.
.
.
```

There are two main steps when building U-Boot. First, we must configure U-Boot for our target platform, enabling and disabling certain features. In the case of the Raspberry Pi 5, we need to execute the following command after navigating to the U-Boot source directory:

```
$ ARCH=arm64 make rpi_arm64_defconfig
```

The `rpi_arm64_defconfig` target in the preceding command configures U-Boot for the Raspberry Pi 5. The configuration specific to this platform is contained in `configs/rpi_arm64_defconfig`. It is important to note that this file does not contain the entire configuration for the target board. Instead, it contains specific features that should be configured for the target board. After executing the preceding command, a file containing the entire U-Boot configuration is generated. This file is `.config` and can be found at the root of the U-Boot source code.

Similarly, if we wish to configure U-Boot to execute in QEMU, we need to execute the following command:

```
$ ARCH=arm64 make qemu_arm64_defconfig
```

Similar to the previous `make` command, this command configures U-Boot for QEMU, simulating an ARM64 architecture.

After configuring U-Boot for either the Raspberry Pi 5 or QEMU, we can build U-Boot by executing the following command:

```
$ make
```

The preceding `make` command generates the `u-boot.bin` file, which contains the final U-Boot binary. The following files are also created during the build process:

- `u-boot`: This is the compiled U-Boot binary and contains debug information. This file can be useful for debugging U-Boot.
- `u-boot.bin`: This is a smaller, stripped-down version of the final U-Boot binary. This file is significantly smaller than the complete file; it contains debug information and is often used on the final embedded Linux system.
- `u-boot.sym`: This file contains a symbol table that's generated during the build process. It contains information about the names and addresses of functions and variables. This file can also be useful for debugging.
- `u-boot.map`: This file contains detailed information about the memory map of the final U-Boot binary. It contains the addresses and sizes of different U-Boot functions and variables and can also be valuable in debugging U-Boot.
- `System.map`: This file contains information similar to `u-boot.map`, but is presented differently.
- `u-boot.cfg`: This file contains the final configuration that's applied to U-Boot before it is compiled.
- `u-boot.dtb`: This file is a binary representation of the device tree, which describes the hardware on the board. U-Boot uses this file to execute the appropriate driver functions to initialize and interact with the hardware.
- `u-boot.srec`: This file is an **S-Record** (**SREC**) representation (a textual representation) of the final U-Boot binary. Each line contains the location in flash memory where a specific region should be stored, the binary data represented in textual format, and a checksum to ensure the data is valid. The SREC format is useful for systems that require specific addresses for each piece of data, such as embedded systems with segmented memory regions.

In the next section, we will learn how to run U-Boot on a Raspberry Pi 5 and in a simulated environment using QEMU.

Running U-Boot on a Raspberry Pi 5 and QEMU

In this section, we will learn how to run U-Boot on a Raspberry Pi 5 and in a simulated environment using QEMU.

Raspberry Pi 5

Follow these steps to get U-Boot running on a Raspberry Pi 5:

1. Connect a microSD card to your Linux development PC.
2. Download the Raspberry Pi Imager utility from `https://www.raspberrypi.com/software/` and install it on your Linux development PC.
3. Launch the Raspberry Pi Imager utility. Under **Operating System**, click on **CHOOSE OS** and select **Raspberry Pi OS (64-bit)**.
4. Under **Storage**, click **CHOOSE STORAGE** and select the option that matches the storage space of the microSD card connected to your PC.
5. Click on the **WRITE** button and confirm the prompts that follow.
6. Disconnect the microSD card from your Linux development PC and reconnect it. Two partitions should appear: one labeled **bootfs** and another labeled **rootfs**.
7. Execute the following command to copy the `u-boot.bin` binary to the first partition:

```
$ sudo cp u-boot.bin /media/mab/bootfs/
```

> Note
>
> Make sure you're using the U-Boot binary generated using the `rpi_arm64_defconfig` configuration. Also, make sure you replace the path to the microSD card with the appropriate location on your PC.

8. Open the `config.txt` file in the **bootfs** partition and make the following modification in bold:

```
# For more options and information see
# http://rptl.io/configtxt
# Some settings may impact device functionality. See link above for
details
kernel=u-boot.bin
```

9. Unmount the microSD card from your Linux development PC, disconnect it, and plug it into the Raspberry Pi 5.
10. Connect the ribbon cable to the port labeled **U** on the Raspberry Pi Debug Probe (which can be purchased from `https://www.raspberrypi.com/products/debug-probe/`). Plug a micro-USB cable into the corresponding Raspberry Pi Debug Probe port and the USB Type A end to your development PC. The resulting connections on the Raspberry Pi Debug Probe should mirror those shown here:

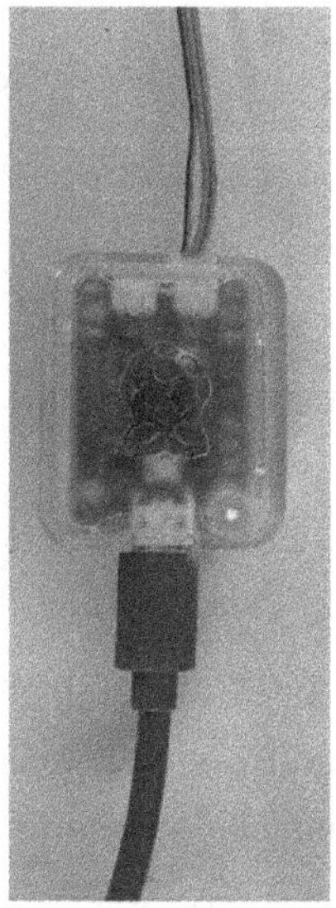

Figure 2.3 – Raspberry Pi Debug Probe

11. Connect the other end of the ribbon cable to the UART port on the Raspberry Pi 5, which can be found between the two HDMI ports:

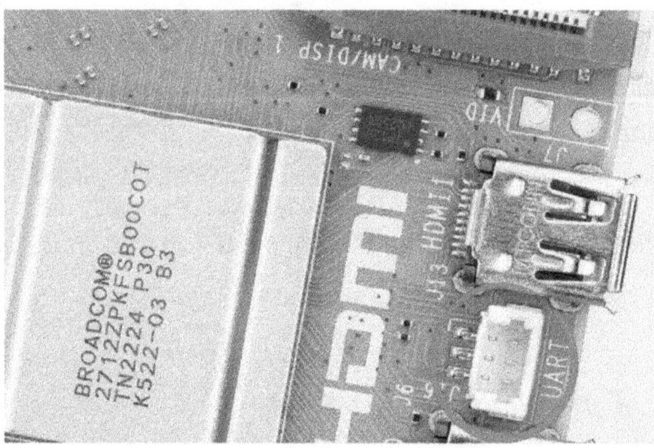

Figure 2.4 – UART port on the Raspberry Pi 5

12. Use your favorite Terminal emulator to open a connection to the serial port that appears.
13. Apply power to the Raspberry Pi 5. After a few seconds, you should see the following output on the console:

```
U-Boot 2024.07 (Sep 23 2024 - 14:08:40 -0400)

DRAM:  1020 MiB (effective 4 GiB)
mbox: Header response code invalid
RPI 5 Model B (0xc04170)
Core:  21 devices, 10 uclasses, devicetree: board
MMC:   mmc@fff000: 0, mmc@1100000: 1
Loading Environment from FAT... Unable to read "uboot.env" from mmc0:1...
In:    serial,usbkbd
Out:   serial,vidconsole
Err:   serial,vidconsole
mbox: Header response code invalid
bcm2835: Could not query MAC address
Net:   No ethernet found.

starting USB...
No USB controllers found
Hit any key to stop autoboot:  0
U-Boot>
```

Figure 2.5 – U-Boot console on the Raspberry Pi 5

> Note
>
> As we can see, U-Boot has detected the correct model of our Raspberry Pi 5.

QEMU

Follow these steps to launch U-Boot in QEMU:

> Note
>
> Make sure you're using the U-Boot binary that was generated using the `qemu_arm64_defconfig` configuration in the previous section.

1. From the root U-Boot directory, execute the following command to launch the ARM64 version of QEMU that was downloaded and built in *Chapter 1*:

```
$ ../qemu-9.0.2/build/qemu-system-aarch64 -M virt -cpu cortex-a76
-bios u-boot.bin -m 2G -nographic
```

2. The preceding invocation contains the following arguments:

    - `-M virt`: This argument instructs QEMU to use a virtualized target board
    - `-cpu cortex-a76`: This option instructs QEMU to use a Cortex A-76 CPU, which is the CPU in the SoC of the Raspberry Pi 5
    - `-bios u-boot.bin`: This option instructs QEMU to use the `u-boot.bin` binary we built in the previous section as the bootloader (or BIOS) for our simulated target
    - `-m 2G`: This option instructs QEMU to use 2 GB of memory in our simulated target
    - `-nographic`: This option instructs QEMU not to use a graphical interface and only provide a console

After executing this command on our Linux development PC, we should see the following output in the Terminal:

```
U-Boot 2024.07 (Sep 23 2024 - 15:39:02 -0400)

DRAM:  2 GiB
Core:  51 devices, 14 uclasses, devicetree: board
Flash: 64 MiB
Loading Environment from Flash... *** Warning - bad CRC, using default environment

In:    serial,usbkbd
Out:   serial,vidconsole
Err:   serial,vidconsole
No USB controllers found
Net:   eth0: virtio-net#32

starting USB...
No USB controllers found
Hit any key to stop autoboot:  0
=>
```

Figure 2.6 – U-Boot output in QEMU

We can exit QEMU by hitting *Ctrl* + *A* simultaneously, followed by *X*, on our keyboard.

In the next section, we will navigate the U-Boot console and explore some of its functionality.

Exploring the console interface

The console is an invaluable interface for interacting with U-Boot. Not only can we use it to execute U-Boot commands, but we can also observe messages printed by U-Boot to ensure that the commands performed the expected task successfully. In this section, we will learn how to navigate the U-Boot console interface and understand its value.

After booting the Raspberry Pi 5 or QEMU with U-Boot, we can hit any key to be presented with the U-Boot console interface:

```
starting USB...
No USB controllers found
Hit any key to stop autoboot:  0
=>
```

We can enter `help` in the console interface to view the available commands in U-Boot:

```
=> help
?         - alias for 'help'
base      - print or set address offset
bdinfo    - print Board Info structure
blkcache  - block cache diagnostics and control
boot      - boot default, i.e., run 'bootcmd'
.
.
.
```

As discussed in the previous section, we will see the `boot` command and the expected message that describes the command.

We can test the autocomplete feature of U-Boot by entering `boot` in the console, hitting the *Tab* key, and observing that U-Boot presents possible matches:

```
=> boot
  boot bootd bootdev bootefi bootelf bootflow booti bootm
  bootmeth bootp bootvx bootz
```

We can also enter the `printenv` command in the console and observe the available environment variables and their corresponding values:

```
=> printenv
arch=arm
baudrate=115200
board=qemu-arm
board_name=qemu-arm
.
.
.
```

Note

The environment variables will be different when running U-Boot on the Raspberry Pi 5.

Finally, we can set an environment variable using the `setenv` command and save the complete set of environment variables to persistent storage by executing the `saveenv` command. Use the `boot` command to start booting the board with the updated environment:

```
=> setenv hello packt
=> printenv hello
hello=packt
=> saveenv
Saving Environment to Flash... Un-Protected 2 sectors
Erasing Flash...
.. done
Erased 2 sectors
Writing to Flash... done
Protected 2 sectors
OK
```

Note

Since no disk is presented to QEMU as an argument, changes to environment variables will not persist across QEMU reboot. However, environment variables should persist across reboots on the Raspberry Pi 5.

In the next section, we will learn how to implement a custom U-Boot command and verify its functionality.

Implementing custom commands

In the previous section, we learned about U-Boot commands. To enhance our understanding, let's modify U-Boot with a custom command that will print **Hello Packt World** to the console. Let's get started:

1. Create a source file under the `cmd` directory called `packt.c` with the following content:

```
#include <common.h>
#include <command.h>
```

```
3 static int do_packt(struct cmd_tbl *cmd, int flag, int argc, char
*const argv[])
4 {
5         printf("Hello Packt World!\n");
6         return 0;
7 }

8 U_BOOT_CMD(packt, 1, 1, do_packt, "Simple Packt command", ""
);
```

Let's take a closer look at each line:

- Lines 1 and 2 include the header files necessary for the data types and macros used in the remainder of the source file.
- Lines 3 to 7 define the function that will be invoked when we execute the `packt` command on the U-Boot console.
- Line 8 uses the `U_BOOT_CMD` macro to register the `packt` command with U-Boot, with the following parameters:
    - `packt`: This is the command that needs to be executed on the U-Boot console to invoke the `do_packt` function.
    - 1: This is the `maxargs` parameter for the command. The command itself is considered an argument, which requires the maximum number of arguments to be at least 1.
    - 1: This informs U-Boot that the command is repeatable.
    - `"Simple Packt command"`: This is the informative message about the `packt` command that will be presented to the user.

2. Add the following line in bold to `cmd/Makefile` to ensure that our `packt.c` file is compiled with U-Boot:

```
# SPDX-License-Identifier: GPL-2.0+
#
# (C) Copyright 2004-2006
# Wolfgang Denk, DENX Software Engineering, wd@denx.de.

ifndef CONFIG_SPL_BUILD
obj-y += packt.o
```

> Note
>
> Ultimately, we would add `CONFIG_ option` to conditionally compile the source file if a particular feature is enabled.

After making these changes, we can recompile U-Boot and launch it on our Raspberry Pi 5 or QEMU. After being presented with the console, we can execute the `help` command and confirm that `packt` appears:

```
=> help
?          - alias for 'help'
.
.
.
nvme       - NVM Express sub-system
packt      - Simple Packt command
panic      - Panic with optional message
.
.
.
```

We can also execute `help packt` in U-Boot's console to verify the `help` message:

```
=> help packt
packt - Simple Packt command

Usage:
packt
```

Finally, we can execute `packt` on the console to confirm the expected output:

```
=> packt
Hello Packt World!
```

With that, we have confirmed the functionality of our custom command.

Summary

In this chapter, we briefly explored U-Boot. We navigated the source code to understand U-Boot's boot process and learned the importance of environment variables and how they are managed in U-Boot. Then, we discovered how device drivers and commands work in U-Boot. Finally, we transitioned to practically using U-Boot on a Raspberry Pi 5 and in a simulated environment using QEMU before implementing a custom command. The goal of the first few chapters is to dive deeper into each of the main components of an embedded Linux system.

In the next chapter, we will explore the Linux kernel.

Get this book's PDF version and more

Scan the QR code (or go to `packtpub.com/unlock`). Search for this book by name, confirm the edition, and then follow the steps on the page.

UNLOCK NOW

Note: Keep your invoice handy. Purchases made directly from Packt don't require an invoice.

Summary

Get this book's PDF version and more

3

Navigating the Linux Kernel

The Linux kernel is arguably the most run piece of software. Most servers, smartphones, tablets, networking equipment, and even modern-day smart appliances run the Linux kernel. Its ubiquity and complexity (recall from the previous chapter that it spans over 30 million lines of code) are insufficient to be covered in a single chapter. Rather, there have been countless books written exploring the Linux kernel in signicant detail along with its many subsystems. In this chapter, we will learn about the Linux kernel in the context of an embedded Linux system.

The Linux kernel is arguably the most important component in an embedded Linux system, and we will learn about it in this chapter. First, we will take a step back and understand the role of a kernel in an embedded system and why it's important. We will then learn about the different types of kernels and where the Linux kernel fits.

Then, we will focus on the Linux kernel and understand its structure. Luckily, the Linux kernel is organized quite nicely. Each directory in the kernel's code base has a specific responsibility. We will select a few interesting directories in the code base and go through the source files in each directory (I believe that navigating through code is a great way to learn about a particular topic). Since this book is not specifically dedicated to the Linux kernel, we won't go into excruciating detail about the entire code base.

Afterward, we will move from the theoretical to the practical. We will learn about the different mechanisms to configure the Linux kernel, and we will learn how to build it for both the Raspberry Pi 5 and for simulation using QEMU. We will explore the different build artifacts. Of course, to confirm our understanding, we will take a stab at modifying the Linux kernel to print an interesting message during boot. We will see how we can load the kernel and confirm our change.

Finally, we will learn how the modular nature of the Linux kernel facilitates support for new hardware. We will learn about device drivers and how they fit into the structure of the Linux kernel. We will see an example of a device driver that is an **out-of-tree** kernel module to understand the general structure of a device driver. We will also learn how to build the device driver and **load** it on our Raspberry Pi.

In this chapter, we are going to cover the following main topics:

- A kernel's value in an embedded system
- The different types of kernels
- Linux kernel features
- Configuring the Linux kernel
- Building and loading
- Linux kernel modules
- Linux device drivers

Technical requirements

You should have some experience with embedded software development. You should also be comfortable reading and writing C code and running scripts in different languages. You can follow the code for yourself by using the GitHub link here: `https://github.com/PacktPublishing/Embedded-Linux-Essentials-Handbook/tree/main/Chapter3`.

A kernel's value in an embedded system

As an embedded software engineer, you may be unfamiliar with a **kernel** if you are accustomed to bare-metal development. An operating system can be useful in embedded systems where the application must perform multiple tasks. If you have worked with a **real-time operating system** (**RTOS**), such as the **Zephyr Project RTOS**, **FreeRTOS**, **ThreadX**, or **NuttX**, you have most likely used an RTOS to launch different tasks or threads with certain responsibilities.

You may have wondered how the RTOS manages the execution of the different tasks in the application, the interactions across different tasks, and the execution of interrupt service routines within the context of tasks. The answer is the kernel.

As we continue to learn more about embedded Linux systems throughout this book, we will discover that the kernel is the most crucial component of the system. First, let's take a step back and understand the value a kernel brings in the context of an embedded system. A kernel provides the following capabilities that can be useful in an embedded system:

- **Scheduling**: As mentioned, one of the kernel's key responsibilities is managing the execution of the system's various tasks. This responsibility falls under the umbrella of scheduling, where the kernel ensures that each task gets sufficient CPU time when needed.
- **Real-time capabilities**: As we discussed in *Chapter 1, Exploring Embedded Linux's Architecture and Its Use Cases*, certain embedded systems have real-time requirements. Thus, the underlying kernel requires features to ensure tasks execute within a certain time limit.
- **Memory management**: The kernel ensures that each task only consumes, at most, the amount of memory that has been allocated to it. In the case of RTOS-based systems where a task has direct access to the underlying hardware, the kernel may still allow other tasks to execute even though one task may have exceeded its memory allocation. In the case of an embedded Linux system, where multiple applications are running, the kernel may terminate an application if it has exceeded its memory limit.
- **Hardware abstraction**: While RTOS-based embedded systems may allow application logic to directly access the underlying hardware, some RTOS variants have support for drivers and hardware abstraction. This allows application logic to interact with the underlying hardware using a standard API. In the case of embedded Linux systems, applications *must* use the kernel as an intermediary when accessing the hardware. Applications cannot directly interact with the underlying hardware.
- **Inter-task and inter-process communication**: The kernel offers mechanisms such as message queues, semaphores, and mutexes to enable different tasks to communicate with each other or to ensure that data structures are synchronized. In the case of embedded Linux systems, similar mechanisms exist to allow applications (or processes) to communicate with one another.
- **Power management**: In RTOS-based systems, the kernel may be responsible for ensuring that the CPU is in a low-power state when the application tasks are not performing any operations. Usually, the "idle task," which runs in the background, is responsible for putting the CPU in a low-power state.
- **Reliability**: A kernel can ensure that one particular task or application does not result in the entire system crashing by isolating memory between tasks and preventing one task from accessing the memory regions of another task. The kernel can have the infrastructure to provide some logging output during a catastrophic failure. This information can be stored in persistent memory so that developers can inspect and resolve the offending issue.

- **Filesystem management and networking**: The kernel may be responsible for managing files and networking on the system. While RTOS and bare-metal embedded systems usually implement these services outside of the core kernel, they are included in the kernel on embedded Linux systems.

Now that we understand the value a kernel brings to an embedded system, we can explore the different kernel types, which we will cover in the next section.

The different types of kernels

Size is one important metric used to classify kernels. Kernels can be categorized into the following categories based on their size.

Microkernel

A **microkernel** is the smallest of the two types of kernels. It provides only the essential services needed to run the system. Every other operating system component, such as memory management and device drivers, is kept out of the core kernel. These ancillary components are executed as applications with reduced privileges and interact with other components or the core kernel using a well-defined API. The advantages of a microkernel are as follows:

- **Stability and security**: Since most kernel services are executed with reduced privileges, any issues with these services will not bring down the entire system. Additionally, since the footprint of the core kernel is minimal and thus the attack surface area, it is relatively easier to ensure the security of a system that leverages a microkernel.
- **Modularity**: Since the core kernel isn't affected, it is easier to replace or upgrade core operating system functions without affecting the overall system. Depending on the architecture used, this may also be possible with monolithic kernels, but it is a key attribute of microkernels.
- **Ease of maintenance**: Since the core kernel is separate from different services, maintaining the core kernel can be easier. If there are issues in the core of a microkernel, developers don't need to consider the filesystem code base.

However, a microkernel has the following disadvantages:

- **Performance**: Since every operating system service needs to use a strict API to interact with another service, there may be overhead with this interaction. Thus, a system leveraging a microkernel may suffer from reduced performance.

- **Complexity**: While the core kernel may be simple, the overall system may be quite complex due to the number of services outside of the kernel that may be required. Additionally, each service requires the appropriate infrastructure for synchronization and message passing.

Monolithic kernel

Unlike a microkernel, a **monolithic kernel** allows all critical operating system features to operate with elevated privileges. Thus, all services, such as device drivers, memory management, and the network stack, access the same memory space as the core kernel. The advantages of a monolithic kernel are as follows:

- **Performance**: Since operating system services share the same address space as the core kernel, a monolithic kernel usually exhibits improved performance compared to microkernels.
- **Comprehensive**: A monolithic kernel usually includes core operating system features as part of the kernel, including device drivers, memory management, scheduling, and networking. These services operate at an elevated privilege, eliminating the need for ancillary services that are not part of the core kernel, as done with a microkernel.

However, a monolithic kernel has the following disadvantages:

- **Stability and security**: Since numerous services operate with elevated privileges inside the core kernel, an issue inside any of these services can crash the entire system. Additionally, if these services have security flaws, the entire system can be exposed to them.
- **Modularity**: Since operating systems are included in the kernel, adding or modifying functionality to these services requires recompiling and loading the entire kernel.

Modular kernel

Modularity is another important kernel classification. A kernel can be modular or not. A **modular kernel** allows portions of essential operating system services to be loaded during runtime instead of being compiled into the core kernel. This differs from traditional monolithic kernels, where all services are compiled with the core kernel.

Some of the advantages of a monolithic kernel are as follows:

- **Flexibility**: Since the operating system's features can be loaded and unloaded at runtime, the system can be updated without requiring a complete reboot.
- **Footprint**: Since operating system features are not compiled as part of the core kernel in a modular kernel, the core kernel can have a significantly reduced footprint.

- **Stability**: If modules loaded during runtime cause issues, the core kernel and the entire system do not need to encounter the same catastrophic issues. Instead, the kernel can unload the offending module and allow the system to function.

A modular kernel has the following disadvantages:

- **Performance**: Loading and unloading modules at runtime can incur a slight performance overhead briefly during runtime. However, once the modules are loaded, there is no additional performance overhead since the modules occupy the same memory space as the kernel and other modules.
- **Dependencies**: Modules may depend on other modules, and the modular kernel requires the necessary infrastructure to manage these dependencies. The infrastructure may be complex and require careful consideration in its implementation.

Now that we have learned about the different categories of kernels, we can identify how the Linux kernel fits within these categories in the next section.

Linux kernel features

The Linux kernel borrows features from a traditional monolithic and modular kernel. All operating system features in the Linux kernel operate with elevated privileges, as is the case with a monolithic kernel. Additionally, most of these features are compiled directly inside the kernel. For example, core subsystems such as the networking stack, filesystem, and device driver model are compiled directly inside the Linux kernel. However, specific elements of these implementations are compiled as loadable modules. For example, while the device driver model is compiled directly inside the Linux kernel, implementations of specific device drivers are compiled as modules. As another example, while the core filesystem infrastructure is compiled directly in the Linux kernel, specific filesystem implementations can be compiled as modules. They can be loaded dynamically during runtime.

The following is the terminology we need to review to further enhance future discussions surrounding the Linux kernel and embedded Linux systems in general:

- **Kernel space**: This term denotes the area where elements of the Linux kernel operate. Software that operates in kernel space has elevated privileges, such as direct access to the underlying hardware.

- **User space:** This term denotes the area where most of the software in an embedded Linux system operates. Applications that operate in user space have reduced privileges and rely on the Linux kernel for certain operations, such as accessing the underlying hardware or requesting additional memory for use.
- **Process:** This term denotes any application running on an embedded Linux system. Each process has an ID that can be used to reference it. A process operates in user space.
- **Kernel module:** This term denotes software that can be loaded onto the embedded Linux system during runtime to provide specific functionality. In a later section of this chapter, we will implement an example module, learn how to use it, and observe its behavior. A kernel module operates in kernel space.
- **Device driver:** This term denotes software used to interact with certain hardware. A device driver operates in kernel space and can be compiled directly as a feature of the Linux kernel or as a loadable kernel module. We will explore device drivers in more detail in a later section.

Now that we understand where the Linux kernel fits within the categories of different kernel types and have learned relevant jargon associated with embedded Linux systems, we can move to the hands-on portion of this chapter. In the next section, we will explore how to configure the Linux kernel for both the Raspberry Pi 5 and QEMU.

Configuring the Linux kernel

Similar to U-Boot, which we covered in *Chapter 2, Learning About U-Boot*, the Linux kernel must be configured before it can be compiled. The Linux kernel uses the same configuration infrastructure as U-Boot.

> Important note
>
> **Kconfig**, the name given to the configuration infrastructure, was first developed as part of the Linux kernel and later borrowed by U-Boot. While this chapter will not go into the details of Kconfig, you can explore the system in more detail in this article: `https://www.linux-magazine.com/Issues/2021/244/Kconfig-Deep-Dive`.

There are different ways we can configure the Linux kernel, as outlined here:

- `defconfig`: The Linux kernel can be configured using existing files that specify certain configuration options. We used this mechanism to configure U-Boot in *Chapter 2, Learning About U-Boot*, to run U-Boot on the Raspberry Pi 5 and QEMU.
- `config`: This mechanism prompts the user for every configuration option and allows them to set each option using the command line interface.
- `menuconfig`: This mechanism leverages a text-based menu to allow users to navigate throughout the configuration system of the Linux kernel and select the desired options.
- `gconfig`/`xconfig`: This is similar to `menuconfig` except that it uses a different graphical interface. `gconfig` uses GTK to display the user interface, whereas `xconfig` uses Qt.

Before we continue, we need to retrieve the Linux kernel source code. The Raspberry Pi has a *version*, or *fork*, of the Linux kernel. Although this kernel version is regularly updated with the *upstream*, or official, version, it is still different. Nonetheless, when targeting a particular hardware platform, it is advised to start with the version of the Linux kernel provided by the vendor. Let's start with a recent version of the Linux kernel, which can be retrieved by executing the following commands:

```
$ git clone https://github.com/raspberrypi/linux.git
$ cd linux
$ git checkout fbd8b3facb36ce888b1cdcf5f45a78475a8208f2
```

Additionally, we need to configure our environment to use the toolchain that we retrieved in *Chapter 2, Learning About U-Boot*, which can be accomplished by following the steps outlined here:

1. Navigate to the directory containing the toolchain by executing the following command:

   ```
   $ cd arm-gnu-toolchain-13.3.rel1-x86_64-aarch64-none-linux-gnu/bin
   ```

2. Execute the following command to add this directory to `PATH`:

   ```
   $ export PATH=`pwd`:$PATH
   ```

3. Set the `CROSS_COMPILE` environment variable to the toolchain triple by executing the following command:

   ```
   $ export CROSS_COMPILE=aarch64-none-linux-gnu-
   ```

In the next few subsections, we will configure the Linux kernel for the Raspberry Pi 5 and QEMU. Then, in the next section, we will compile the configured kernel and load it on each platform.

Raspberry Pi 5

We can configure the Linux kernel for the Raspberry Pi 5 by executing the following command from the directory containing the Linux kernel source code:

```
$ ARCH=arm64 make bcm2712_defconfig
```

A file named `.config` should appear in the root of the Linux kernel source directory, as shown here:

```
[linux]$ ls -a | grep config
.cocciconfig
.config
.config.old
Kconfig
```

`.config` contains the complete configuration of the Linux kernel. If we open it and compare it to the `bcm2712_defconfig` file, located under `arch/arm64/configs`, we can see that the configuration options specified in `bcm2712_defconfig` appear in `.config`. This is shown in the following figure, where the left-hand side is `bcm2712_defconfig`, the right-hand side is `.config`, and the relevant configuration options are highlighted in yellow:

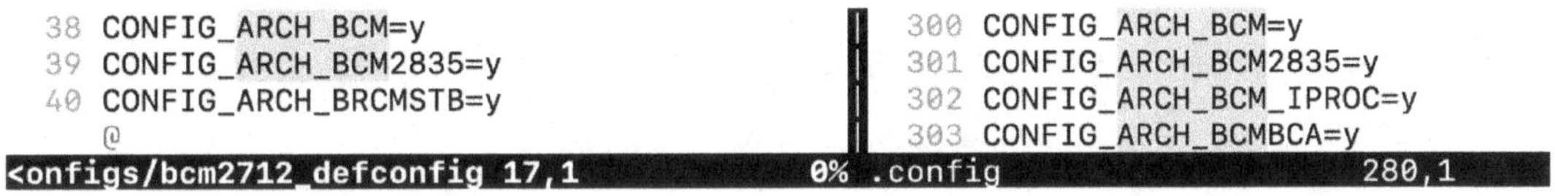

Figure 3.1 – Configuring the Linux kernel for the Raspberry Pi 5

We can also use the `menuconfig` and `xconfig` mechanisms to navigate around the Linux kernel's configuration. We can execute the following command to use `menuconfig`:

```
$ ARCH=arm64 make menuconfig
```

After executing the preceding command, we are presented with the screen shown in the following figure:

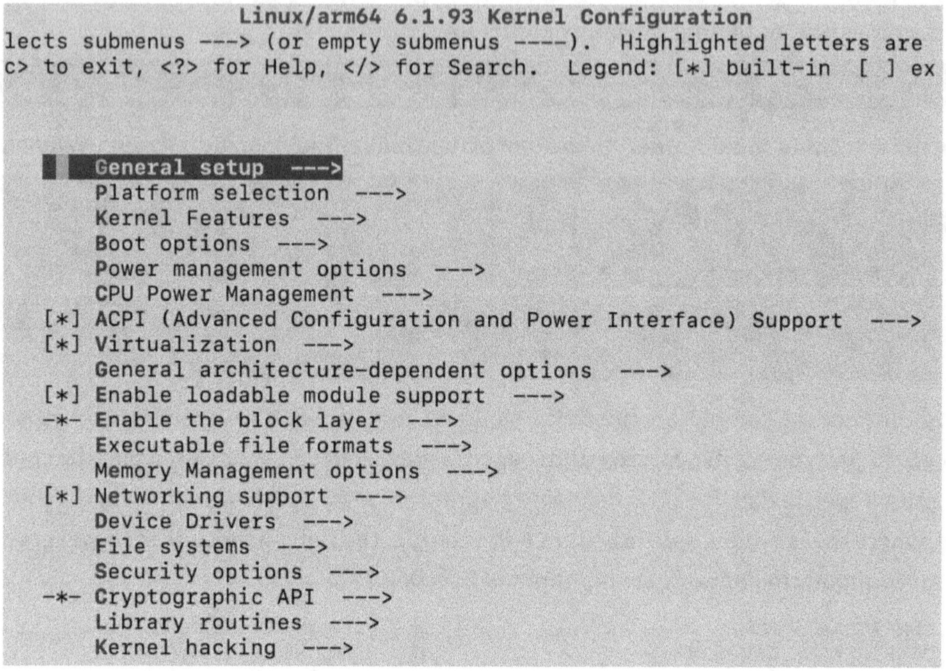

Figure 3.2 – The menuconfig interface

We can search for configuration options using the `menuconfig` interface by hitting the / key on our keyboard and being presented with the following search box:

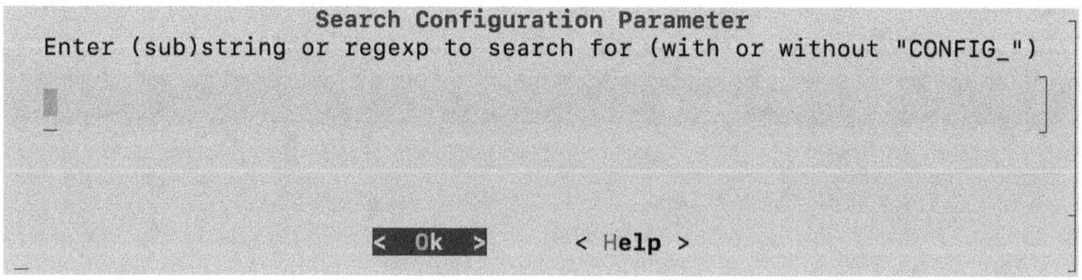

Figure 3.3 – Searching for a configuration option

We can enter a term in the search box, such as `BCM`, as shown here:

```
                     Search Configuration Parameter
Enter (sub)string or regexp to search for (with or without "CONFIG_")

BCM


                    < Ok >        < Help >
```

Figure 3.4 – Searching for a configuration option

After hitting the *Enter* key, we are presented with the configuration options that match our entry, as shown here:

```
Symbol: ARCH_BCM [=y]
Type  : bool
Defined at arch/arm64/Kconfig.platforms:36
  Prompt: Broadcom SoC Support
  Location:
    -> Platform selection
(1)   -> Broadcom SoC Support (ARCH_BCM [=y])


Symbol: ARCH_BCM2835 [=y]
Type  : bool
Defined at arch/arm64/Kconfig.platforms:41
  Prompt: Broadcom BCM2835 family
  Depends on: ARCH_BCM [=y]
  Location:
    -> Platform selection
      -> Broadcom SoC Support (ARCH_BCM [=y])
(2)     -> Broadcom BCM2835 family (ARCH_BCM2835 [=y])
Selects: TIMER_OF [=y] && GPIOLIB [=y] && MFD_CORE [=y]
```

Figure 3.5 – Results matching our search term

Each result that matches our search criteria contains the following details:

- `Symbol`: This is the name of the configuration option.
- `Type`: This is the data type defined by the configuration option. In the results shown in the preceding figure, the type is `bool`, which specifies whether the option can be enabled or disabled.
- `Prompt`: This is a brief message describing the purpose of the configuration option.
- `Depends on`: This describes which other configuration option this option depends on. This is helpful when understanding why a particular configuration option was not selected, even if we selected it.

- `Location`: This defines this option's location within the configuration hierarchy.
- `Selects`: This specifies which other options will be enabled if this particular option is enabled.

We can use a more sophisticated graphical interface to navigate throughout the Linux kernel configuration by executing the following command:

```
$ ARCH=arm64 make xconfig
```

After executing the preceding command, we are presented with the following window:

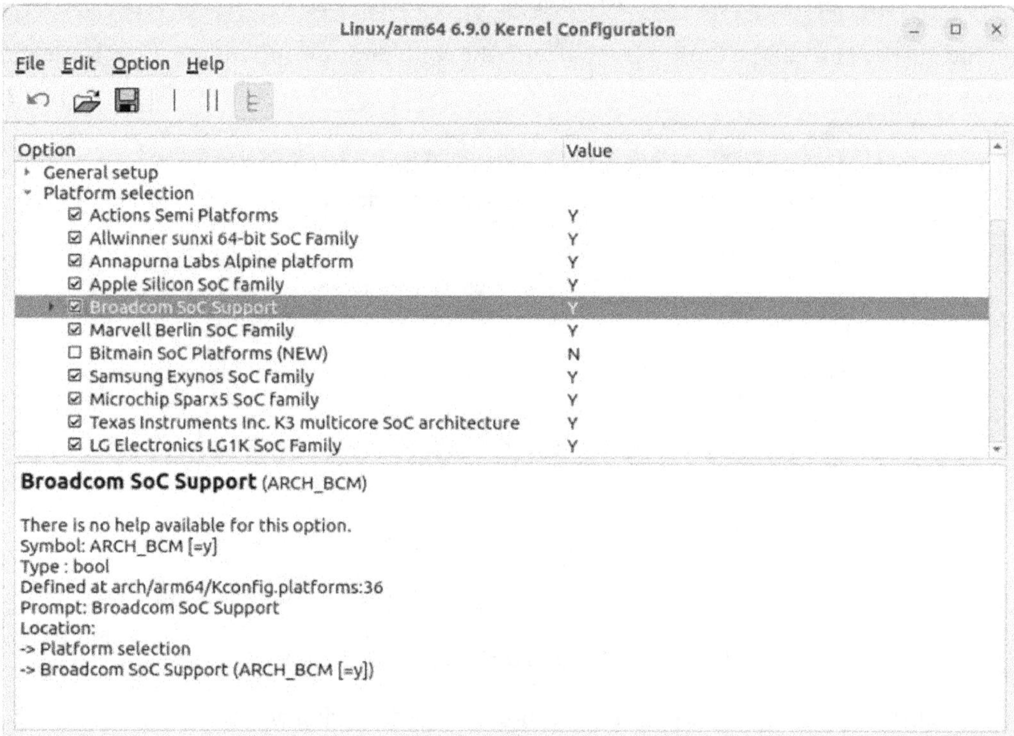

Figure 3.6 – The xconfig interface

We can see similarities between the `xconfig` interface and the `menuconfig` interface. They both present the same information about the overall Linux kernel configuration. As shown in the preceding figure, we can expand the **Platform selection** menu, click on **Broadcom SoC Support**, and we can see the same information as one of the results that were presented when we searched for `BCM` in the `menuconfig` interface.

We can search for configuration options in the `xconfig` interface by clicking on **Edit** and then clicking on **Find**, as shown in the following figure:

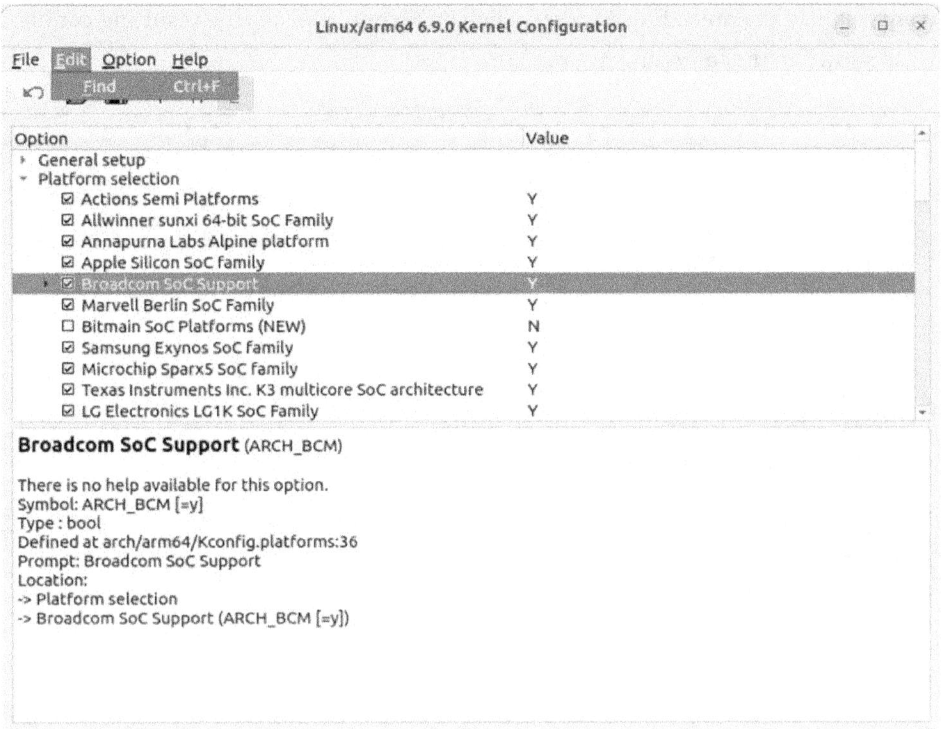

Figure 3.7 – Navigating the xconfig system

After clicking on **Find**, we are presented with the following window:

Figure 3.8 – Searching in xconfig

We can enter `BCM` in the preceding window, click on **Search**, and see the resulting configuration options, as shown in the following figure:

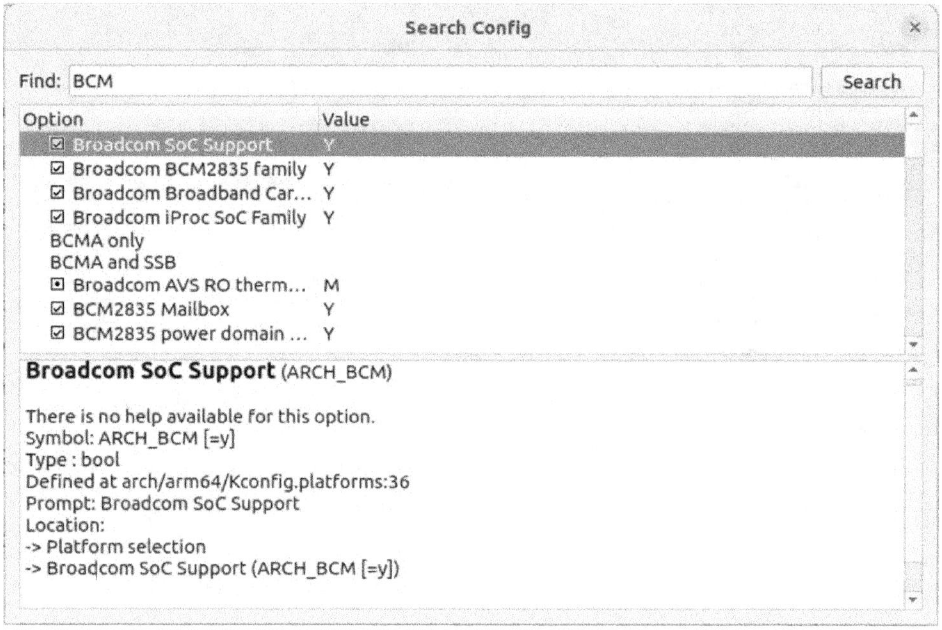

Figure 3.9 – Finding results in xconfig

We can see from the preceding figure that the search results and their corresponding details are identical to the search results when using the `menuconfig` interface. If we click on one of the options, we can see that the details are also identical. Essentially, the information that is presented is identical across both interfaces. The only difference is in the presentation. The `menuconfig` interface is a command-line interface and thus relies heavily on a keyboard for navigation and searching. The `xconfig` interface is a graphical user interface and thus relies on the mouse and keyboard for navigation.

QEMU

We can configure the Linux kernel for executing in QEMU by following a procedure similar to the one outlined previously for the Raspberry Pi 5. We can execute the following command to configure the Linux kernel for execution in QEMU:

```
$ ARCH=arm64 make defconfig
```

In the next section, we will learn how to compile the kernel for the Raspberry Pi 5 and QEMU and load it on the respective platforms.

Building and loading

Now that we have configured the Linux kernel, we can compile it and run it on the Raspberry Pi 5 and QEMU. The compilation process is identical to both. After configuring the Linux kernel using the steps described in the previous section, we can execute the following command to build it:

```
$ ARCH=arm64 make -j20
```

> Important note
>
> The number after the `-j` option in the preceding command instructs the build system to use 20 CPU cores to compile in parallel. This number depends on your system. I generally don't use all the CPU cores. Instead, I reserve a few CPU cores for other tasks on my development PC. Thus, in my case, where I have 24 CPU cores, I leave 4 CPU cores for other tasks.

Raspberry Pi 5

After compiling the Linux kernel configured for the Raspberry Pi 5, we can install it on the same micro-SD card that we installed U-Boot on in *Chapter 2, Learning About U-Boot*, by following the steps outlined here:

1. Insert the micro-SD card into your development PC.
2. Identify the location where Linux has placed the micro-SD card partitions. In my instance, where I was running Ubuntu 22.04, the first partition was placed under `/media/mab/bootfs` and the second partition under `/media/mab/rootfs`.
3. Execute the following command to copy the compiled Linux kernel to the first partition of the micro-SD card:

   ```
   $ cp arch/arm64/Image /media/mab/bootfs
   ```

4. Unmount the two partitions, and disconnect the micro-SD card from your development PC.
5. Insert the micro-SD card into the Raspberry Pi 5, ensure the Raspberry Pi debug probe is connected, and apply power to the Raspberry Pi 5. You should see the U-Boot prompt, as shown here:

   ```
   U-Boot>
   ```

6. Configure the address in RAM that U-Boot will use to store the Linux kernel by executing the following command:

```
U-Boot> setenv loadaddr 0x80000
```

7. Execute the following command to instruct U-Boot to load the Linux kernel from the micro-SD card into RAM:

```
U-Boot> fatload mmc 0:1 ${loadaddr} Image
23929344 bytes read in 998 ms (22.9 MiB/s)
```

8. Configure the address in RAM that U-Boot should use to store the Devicetree by executing the following command:

```
U-Boot> setenv fdtaddr 0x1F00000
```

9. Execute the following command to instruct U-Boot to load the Devicetree from the micro-SD card into RAM:

```
U-Boot> fatload mmc 0:1 ${fdtaddr} bcm2712-rpi-5-b.dtb
80218 bytes read in 5 ms (15.3 MiB/s)
```

10. Set the appropriate environment variable with the arguments that need to be passed to the kernel during boot by executing the following command with details of the arguments that follow:

```
U-Boot> setenv bootargs "console=ttyAMA0,115200 root=/dev/mmcblk0p2
rw rootwait earlycon"
```

- `console`: This argument informs the Linux kernel which device should be used for the console and its settings. Here, we use `ttyAMA0` as our console with a baud rate of `115200`.
- `root`: This argument specifies the device and partition that should be used for the root filesystem. Here, we are instructing the Linux kernel to use the second partition of the micro-SD card (`/dev/mmcblk0p2`) as the root filesystem.
- `rw`: This argument instructs the Linux kernel that the system can read and write to the root filesystem.
- `rootwait`: This argument instructs the Linux kernel to wait indefinitely until the device representing the root filesystem is ready before progressing with the boot process.

- `earlycon`: This argument enables early-stage console output from the Linux kernel. This can be useful for debugging purposes if we notice that the Linux kernel is not progressing during the boot process.

11. Execute the following command to instruct U-Boot to boot the Linux kernel we just loaded along with the Devicetree:

    ```
    U-Boot> booti ${loadaddr} - ${fdtaddr}
    ```

After following these steps, you should see the following output in the console:

```
U-Boot> booti ${loadaddr} - ${fdtaddr}
Moving Image from 0x80000 to 0x200000, end=1a20000
## Flattened Device Tree blob at 01f00000
   Booting using the fdt blob at 0x1f00000
Working FDT set to 1f00000
   Using Device Tree in place at 0000000001f00000, end 0000000001f16959
Working FDT set to 1f00000

Starting kernel ...

[    0.000000] Booting Linux on physical CPU 0x0000000000 [0x414fd0b1]
[    0.000000] Linux version 6.1.93-v8-16k+ (mab@system76-pc) (aarch64-
none-linux-gnu-gcc (Arm GNU Toolchain 13.3.Rel1 (Build arm-13.24))
13.3.1 20240614, GNU ld (Arm GNU Toolchain 13.3.Rel1 (Build arm-13.24))
2.42.0.20240614) #8 SMP PREEMPT Wed Oct  2 11:47:14 EDT 2024
[    0.000000] Machine model: Raspberry Pi 5 Model B Rev 1.0
[    0.000000] earlycon: pl11 at MMIO 0x000000107d001000 (options
'115200n8')
```

We have loaded the Linux kernel we just configured and compiled on our Raspberry Pi 5 from U-Boot!

Important note

At the time of writing, the Raspberry Pi 5 locked up while it was launching certain system services (well after the Linux kernel successfully launched), as shown here:

```
[    3.115540] systemd[1]: Starting systemd-modules-load.
service - Load Kernel Modules...
[    3.124768] systemd[1]: Starting systemd-remount-fs.
service - Remount Root and Kernel File Systems...
[    3.153430] systemd[1]: Starting systemd-udev-trigger.
service - Coldplug All udev Devices...
[    3.168267] systemd[1]: Started systemd-journald.service
- Journal Service.
```

Investigating and resolving this issue is outside the scope of this book. Nonetheless, plenty of advanced books and resources exist that can be used to debug and resolve the underlying issue.

QEMU

In the previous subsection, we used the root filesystem already present on the micro-SD card, which we flashed using the standard baseline Raspberry Pi image. However, that is not the case when we are using QEMU, and we need to create one for QEMU to use. Instead of creating a complete root filesystem, we can create a temporary filesystem that is stored in RAM and used by the Linux kernel during the initial stages of the boot process. This temporary filesystem is called `initramfs`. We will install **BusyBox** in `initramfs`, a lightweight application containing many common command-line utilities.

We can create `initramfs` by following the steps outlined here:

1. Download and extract BusyBox version 1.36.0 by executing the following commands:

```
$ wget https://github.com/mirror/busybox/archive/refs/tags/1_36_0.
tar.gz
$ tar -xvzf 1_36_0.tar.gz
```

2. Execute the following command to enter the BusyBox `menuconfig` interface:

```
$ cd busybox-1_36_0
$ make menuconfig
```

3. In the resulting interface, navigate to **Settings** and ensure that the **Build static binary (no shared libs)** option is selected.
4. Execute the following commands to build BusyBox:

```
$ make -j20
$ make install
```

5. Create a directory to store `initramfs` and create the appropriate subdirectories by executing the following commands:

```
$ mkdir initramfs
$ mkdir -p initramfs/bin initramfs/sbin initramfs/etc initramfs/proc
initramfs/sys initramfs/dev initramfs/usr/bin initramfs/usr/sbin
```

6. Execute the following command to copy the BusyBox binary and symbolic links:

```
$ cp -a busybox-1_36_0/_install/* ./initramfs
```

7. Create a file called `init` in the `initramfs` directory with the following contents, which mounts the appropriate filesystems that are needed to interact with the Linux kernel and launches a shell:

```
#!/bin/sh

mount -t devtmpfs devtmpfs /dev
mount -t proc none /proc
mount -t sysfs none /sys
exec /bin/sh
```

8. Execute the following command to give execute permissions to the `init` script:

```
$ chmod +x initramfs/init
```

9. Compress the directory into the final `initramfs` by executing the following commands:

```
$ cd initramfs
$ find . -print0 | cpio --null -ov --format=newc | gzip -9 > ../
initramfs.cpio.gz
```

Finally, we can launch the Linux kernel with the `initramfs` directory that we created in QEMU by executing the following commands:

```
$ cd linux/
$ ../../qemu-9.0.2/build/qemu-system-aarch64 -M virt -cpu cortex-a76
-nographic -smp 1 -kernel ./arch/arm64/boot/Image -append
"console=ttyAMA0" -m 2048 -initrd ../initramfs.cpio.gz
```

We should see the following output in QEMU, along with a shell at the end:

```
[linux]$ ../../qemu-9.0.2/build/qemu-system-aarch64 -M virt -cpu
cortex-a76 -nographic -smp 1 -kernel ./arch/arm64/boot/Image -append
"console=ttyAMA0" -m 2048 -initrd ../initramfs.cpio.gz
[    0.000000] Booting Linux on physical CPU 0x0000000000 [0x414fd0b1]
[    0.000000] Linux version 6.1.93-gfbd8b3facb36 (mab@system76-pc)
(aarch64-none-linux-gnu-gcc (Arm GNU Toolchain 13.3.Rel1 (Build arm-
13.24)) 13.3.1 20240614, GNU ld (Arm GNU Toolchain 13.3.Rel1 (Build arm-
13.24)) 2.42.0.20240614) #9 SMP PREEMPT Wed Oct  2 15:44:17 EDT 2024
[    0.000000] random: crng init done
[    0.000000] Machine model: linux,dummy-virt
[    0.000000] efi: UEFI not found.
.
.
.
[    0.520637] Run /init as init process
/bin/sh: can't access tty; job control turned off
~ #
```

In the next section, we will explore Linux kernel modules. We will learn how to implement and load a kernel module and observe the output.

Linux kernel modules

Kernel modules efficiently extend the functionality of the Linux kernel and are an integral part of its modular nature. Without kernel modules, we would need to integrate the relevant source code into the entire kernel, rebuild the Linux kernel, and reload it on our system to observe the impact of our addition. While this may be acceptable for a production environment, this long feedback loop would need to be more efficient for development. This would significantly impede the development of device drivers since any minor adjustment would require a rebuild of the entire Linux kernel and a reboot of the whole system. Kernel modules can shortcut this process by allowing code to be added to the Linux kernel during runtime. The development process can be described using the following diagram:

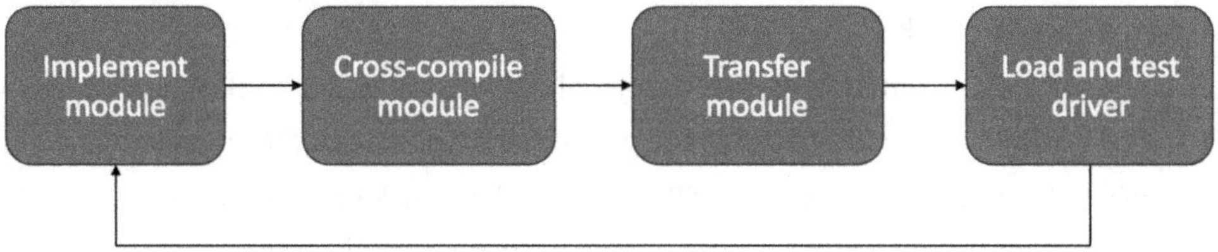

Figure 3.10 – Kernel module implementation workflow

First, we implement a particular feature as a kernel module. Second, we cross-compile it and transfer the binary file to our platform. Then, we load the driver and perform any needed tests to confirm functionality. If modifications are required, we go back to the first step and repeat the process until we are satisfied with the results.

Let's walk through an example to demonstrate the process shown in the preceding figure and briefly learn about some of the basic requirements of a kernel module. A simple kernel module is provided in the `kernel-module` directory of this book with the following source code:

```
#include <linux/init.h>
#include <linux/module.h>

static int __init test_init(void)
{
        printk(KERN_INFO "Hello World!\n");
        return 0;
}

static void __exit test_exit(void)
{
        printk(KERN_INFO "Goodbye World!\n");
}

module_init(test_init);
module_exit(test_exit);

MODULE_AUTHOR("Mohammed Billoo");
MODULE_DESCRIPTION("Hello World kernel module");
MODULE_LICENSE("GPL")
```

The following lists relevant portions of the preceding source code:

- Lines 1 and 2 are files we need to include that provide the prototypes for functions that will be used in the kernel module.
- Lines 3–7 define a function that will be called when the kernel module is loaded. This function prints `Hello World!` to the console and is registered with the Linux kernel on line 12.
- Lines 8–11 define a function that will be called when the kernel module is unloaded. This function prints `Goodbye World!` to the console and is registered with the Linux kernel on line 13.
- Lines 14–16 provide descriptions and licensing information associated with this kernel module.

We can compile the kernel module for execution in QEMU by following the steps outlined here:

1. Navigate to the directory corresponding to this chapter in the GitHub repository.
2. Configure and compile the Linux kernel for QEMU using the steps outlined in the previous section.
3. Navigate to the `kernel-module` directory and compile the kernel module by executing the following command:

```
$ ARCH=arm64 make
```

We need to update `initramfs` with the compiled kernel module. We can accomplish this by executing the following command to copy the compiled kernel module, `test-module.ko`, to the `usr/modules/` directory inside the `initramfs` directory:

```
$ cp test-module.ko ../initramfs/usr/modules/
```

Using the steps shown in the previous section, we can generate `initramfs` and launch QEMU with it and our Linux kernel. Finally, when we are presented with the prompt in QEMU, we can execute the `insmod` command to load the kernel module, as shown in the following snippet, and we should see the corresponding output, which is the `Hello World!` string that gets printed in the `test_init` function:

```
~ # insmod /usr/modules/test-module.ko
[    6.820838] test_module: loading out-of-tree module taints kernel.
[    6.824223] Hello World!
```

We can use the `lsmod` command to observe kernel modules loaded on our embedded Linux system. If we execute the `lsmod` command on our QEMU instance after installing the `test-module` kernel module, we will see the following output:

```
~ # lsmod
test_module 16384 0 - Live 0xffffbba7110b3000 (O)
```

Finally, we can execute the `rmmod` command to unload the kernel module, and we should see the output shown here, which is the `Goodbye World!` string printed in the `test_exit` function:

```
~ # rmmod test-module
[   10.599573] Goodbye World!
```

If we execute the `lsmod` command again, we can see that no kernel module is loaded, which is the expected output shown here:

```
~ # lsmod
~ #
```

In the next section, we will explore device drivers, which can be implemented as kernel modules.

Linux device drivers

A **device driver** is software meant to interact with a specific piece of hardware. Device drivers hide the underlying interactions with the hardware from the user.

The source code for device drivers supported in the Linux kernel is contained in the `drivers` directory. Device drivers constitute the majority of the Linux kernel. The `drivers` directory is the largest directory of the Linux kernel; it is nearly 69% of the entire Linux kernel source code.

Users can interact with device drivers using a few specific directories. For example, the `/dev` directory is a special filesystem that contains files corresponding to devices in the embedded Linux system. However, not all of the files in this directory are regular files we can read from and write to. Instead, these are **device files**. For example, if we plug a properly formatted flash drive into our embedded Linux system, the two partitions in the flash drive would appear under the `dev` directory as `sdX1` and `sdX2`, where `X` is a letter that the Linux kernel chooses. We can use the `mount` Linux command to interact with the filesystem on the flash drive partition.

We can write to certain files in the dev directory. For example, we can launch our QEMU instance and execute the following command to list the devices that are present on our system:

```
~ # ls /dev/
autofs           ptypb            tty31            tty63
console          ptypc            tty32            tty7
cpu_dma_latency  ptypd            tty33            tty8
full             ptype            tty34            tty9
gpiochip0        ptypf            tty35            ttyAMA0
```

We can write to the console file using the echo command and confirm the output to the console, as shown here:

```
~ # echo "hello packt" > /dev/console
hello packt
```

The /sys directory, also known as sysfs, is another interface that device drivers use to expose functionality and provide information to the user space about the underlying hardware. Similar to the /dev directory, sysfs is not a traditional directory. Instead, it is a virtual filesystem. Users can't create files in this directory. Device drivers follow a well-defined API in the Linux kernel to create files in this directory to support user space interaction.

For example, we can navigate to the /sys/class/mtd directory on our QEMU instance, which allows us to interact with the virtualized flash device. We can execute the ls command to discover the functionality exposed by the MTD driver in the Linux kernel, as shown here:

```
~ # ls /sys/class/mtd/
mtd0    mtd0ro
```

Here, mtd0 represents the read-write interface to the flash device. We can further explore the contents of the mtd0 directory by executing the ls command again, shown here:

```
~ # ls /sys/class/mtd/mtd0/
bad_blocks         ecc_step_size      name               size
bbt_blocks         ecc_strength       numeraseregions    subpagesize
bitflip_threshold  erasesize          of_node            subsystem
corrected_bits     flags              oobavail           type
dev                mtd0               oobsize            uevent
ecc_failures       mtdblock0          power              writesize
```

We can determine the size of the flash device by reading the `size` file using the command shown here:

```
~ # cat /sys/class/mtd/mtd0/size
134217728
```

With this, we have come to the end of the chapter.

Summary

In this chapter, we explored the Linux kernel in some detail. First, we took a step back and understood the relevance of kernels in embedded systems and the different types of kernels. Then, we learned where the Linux kernel fits within the categories we listed. Then, we discovered how to configure, compile, and run the Linux kernel on the Raspberry Pi 5 and in emulation using QEMU. Afterward, we explored Linux kernel modules, including implementing and loading a sample kernel module in QEMU. Finally, we briefly learned about device drivers. This chapter covered the Linux kernel, which is strictly one of the software components of an embedded Linux system. However, as we learned previously, hardware is essential in an embedded Linux system.

In the next chapter, we will explore the Devicetree and understand how it helps the Linux kernel learn about the hardware on our board.

4

Describing Hardware Using the Devicetree

The **Devicetree** is a data structure popularized by the Linux kernel to describe non-discoverable hardware on the system. The Linux kernel uses the Devicetree to know which device drivers to load and use during runtime. Most embedded software engineers new to Embedded Linux struggle with understanding the Ddevicetree. This chapter aims to provide a detailed review of the devicetree.

First, we will learn about the structure and format of the Devicetree and how the relevant source files can be converted into a format used by the Linux kernel. Second, we will understand how the Linux kernel uses the devicetree with the appropriate device drivers to configure the underlying hardware. Third, we will understand how devicetree overlays can be used to modify the devicetree while the system is running. Finally, we will work through some examples with actual hardware to gain hands-on experience with the device tree, enhancing our knowledge of how the devicetree can be used.

In this chapter, we are going to cover the following main topics:

- Using the Devicetree
- Interaction with the Linux Kernel
- Devicetree Overlay
- Example #1: Adding an Analog-to-Digital Converter (ADC)
- Example #2: Adding a Digital-to-Analog Converter (DAC)

- Example #3: Interacting with GPIO
- Example #4: Using Spidev to Interact With SPI Devices

Technical requirements

You should be comfortable reading and writing C code and executing commands on a terminal. You should also be comfortable writing and executing Python code. You can follow the examples in this chapter using the following Github link: `https://github.com/PacktPublishing/Embedded-Linux-Essentials-Handbook/tree/main/Chapter4`.

Using the Devicetree

In this section, we will learn how to use the devicetree. While the Linux kernel hides the details in compiling all of the devicetree files as a make target, it is helpful to understand the underlying process. We will learn about the utility that is ultimately used by the Linux kernel and how to use it. We will also learn about the structure and format of the devicetree. By the end of this section, we should be having a solid grasp of the devicetree structure; we will also know how to generate the devicetree binary from a source file and vice versa.

Creating the Devicetree

The following file types are relevant when working with devicetrees:

- `.dtb`: The binary representation of the devicetree. The Linux kernel ultimately uses this file to learn about the hardware present on the system.
- `.dts`: The *top-level* devicetree source file. This file is ultimately used to generate the devicetree binary file. The top-level devicetree source file can incorporate devicetree include files.
- `.dtsi`: Devicetree *include* files. The top-level devicetree files include these and define properties of a specific hardware portion.
- .dtbo: A compiled Devicetree overlay file. As we will learn in a later section, a Devicetree overlay allows us to make changes to the Devicetree used by the system during runtime.

The `dtc` utility converts the top-level devicetree source file into the devicetree binary. This utility is included in the Linux kernel codebase under the `scripts/dtc` directory. The dtc utility can be invoked using the following options, with the devicetree file for the Raspberry Pi 5 as an example:

```
$ ./scripts/dtc/dtc -I dts -O dtb -o rpi5.dtb arch/arm64/boot/dts/
broadcom/bcm2712-rpi-5-b.dts
```

The flags and options provided to the utility are described as follows:

- `-I`: This flag specifies the format of the source file. In this case, the dts argument indicates that we wish the utility to ingest a devicetree source file.
- `-O`: This flag specifies the format of the output file. In this instance, the dtb argument indicates that we wish the tool to generate a devicetree binary file.
- `-o`: This flag specifies the output file name we wish the utility to generate. In this case, we want the output in the rpi5.dtb file.
- Input file: The final argument is the input file, which is the Raspberry Pi 5 top-level devicetree file (e.g. `arch/arm64/boot/dts/broadcom/bcm2712-rpi-5-b.dts`).

If we execute the above command, we see the output below:

```
Error: arch/arm64/boot/dts/broadcom/bcm2712-rpi-5-b.dts:1.1-2 syntax error
FATAL ERROR: Unable to parse input tree
```

The above error points to the first line in the top-level devicetree file, which is the following:

```
#include "../../../../arm/boot/dts/bcm2712-rpi-5-b.dts"
```

The dtc utility does not know how to parse the `#include` statement. Instead, we must run the C preprocessor before running the dtc utility. We can convert the existing Raspberry Pi 5 top-level devicetree file to a file that can be consumed by the dtc utility with the following command:

```
$ cpp -nostdinc -I include -I arch  -undef -x assembler-with-cpp  arch/
arm64/boot/dts/broadcom/bcm2712-rpi-5-b.dts rpi5.dts.preprocessed
```

The above command creates the intermediate file named `rpi5.dts.preprocessed`. The file contains all the contents of the included devicetree files, as shown below:

```
# 0 "arch/arm64/boot/dts/broadcom/bcm2712-rpi-5-b.dts"
# 0 "<built-in>"
# 0 "<command-line>"
# 1 "arch/arm64/boot/dts/broadcom/bcm2712-rpi-5-b.dts"
# 1 "arch/arm64/boot/dts/broadcom/../../../../arm/boot/dts/bcm2712-rpi-
5-b.dts" 1

/dts-v1/;
.
.
/ {
```

```
    compatible = "brcm,bcm2712", "brcm,bcm2711";
    model = "BCM2712";
   .
   .
```

We can execute the original command to generate the devicetree binary file with the tweak to the input file as shown below:

```
$ ./scripts/dtc/dtc -I dts -O dtb -o rpi5.dtb rpi5.dts.preprocessed
```

Although the utility generates some warnings, it ultimately creates the devicetree binary file.

Devicetree Structure and Format

The devicetree is a text file with a collection of nodes. Each node can contain other nodes or can contain properties. A property is a key-value pair. Top-level devicetree files usually include devicetree include files to enable a hierarchical structure that reflects the underlying hardware.

"`bcm2712-rpi-5-b.dts`," located under the "`arch/arm/boot/dts`" directory in the Linux kernel codebase is the top-level devicetree file for the Raspberry Pi 5. This file includes the following intermediate devicetree files, as shown in the snippet below:

```
// SPDX-License-Identifier: GPL-2.0
/dts-v1/;
.
.
.
#include "bcm2712.dtsi"

#undef i2c0
#undef i2c3
.
.
.
i2c_rp1boot: &_i2c3 { };

#include "rp1.dtsi"
.
.
.
```

```
&rp1_usb1 {
        status = "okay";
};

#include "bcm2712-rpi.dtsi"
.
.
.
```

The organization of the devicetree reflects the hardware of the board itself, as follows:

- `bcm2712.dtsi`, which is the device tree file for the Broadcom 2712. The Broadcom 2712 is the SoC on the Raspberry Pi 5.
- `bcm2712-rpi.dtsi` contains the customizations of the Broadcom 2712 for the Raspberry Pi 5.
- `rpi1.dtsi` contains the peripheral specifications for the RP1 coprocessor.

The following image summarizes the devicetree files and the underlying hardware:

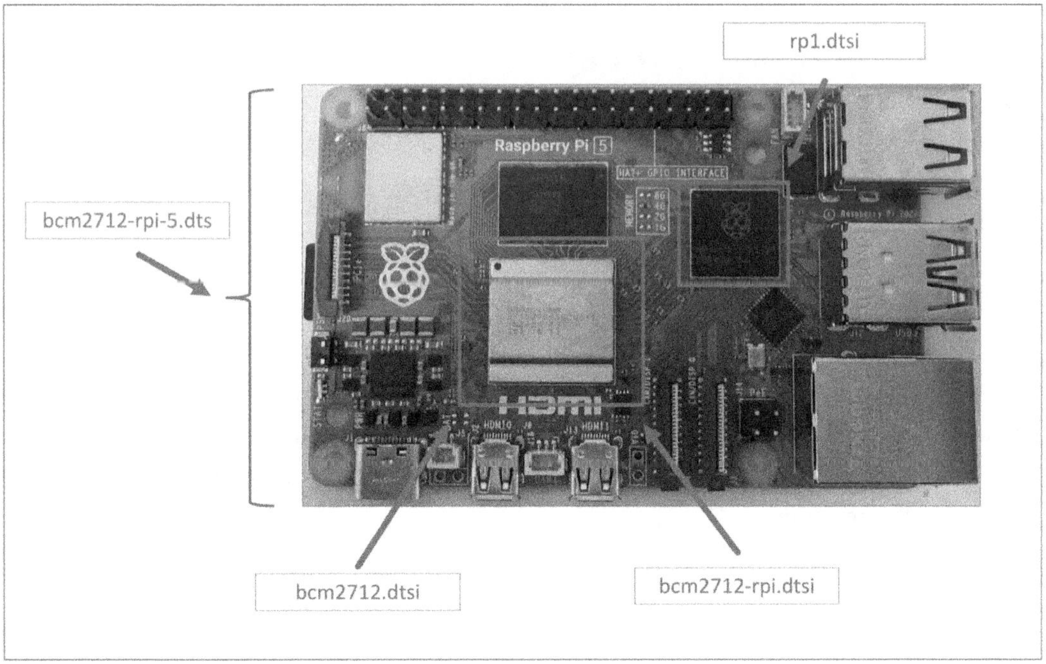

Figure 4.1 – Raspberry Pi 5 Hardware and Devicetree Files

We can see how devicetree files override properties specified in the underlying devicetree files. For example, the "soc" node is defined in the "bcm2712.dtsi" devicetree file. It defines the properties of the Broadcom 2712 System-on-Chip (SoC), as shown below:

```
soc: soc {
        compatible = "simple-bus";
        #address-cells = <1>;
        #size-cells = <1>;

        ranges     = <0x7c000000  0x10 0x7c000000  0x04000000>;
        /* Emulate a contiguous 30-bit address range for DMA */
        dma-ranges = <0xc0000000  0x00 0x00000000  0x40000000>,
                     <0x7c000000  0x10 0x7c000000  0x04000000>;
The "soc" node is customized in the "bcm2712-rpi.dtsi" devicetree file, as
shown below.
&soc {
        firmware: firmware {
                compatible = "raspberrypi,bcm2835-firmware", "simple-mfd";
                #address-cells = <1>;
                #size-cells = <1>;
.
.
.
        power: power {
                compatible = "raspberrypi,bcm2835-power";
                firmware = <&firmware>;
                #power-domain-cells = <1>;
        };
```

Devicetree nodes can be customized by prepending a & to a label followed by a curly brace, and then adding additional nodes and properties. In the above example, `firmware` and `power` nodes are added to the soc node.

> Important Note
>
> A Devicetree "**label**" is symbolic name given to a "**node**" in the Devicetree. Labels make it easier to reference specific nodes in the Devicetree, as we see above. The following shows the relationship between labels and nodes:
>
> ```
> label: node {
> }
> ```

A common practice is to enable a peripheral that is disabled by default. For example, as we can see in the "`rp1.dtsi`" devicetree file, the DMA controller of the RP1 controller is disabled by default:

```
rp1_dma: dma@188000 {
         reg = <0xc0 0x40188000  0x0 0x1000>;
         compatible = "snps,axi-dma-1.01a";
.
.
.
         snps,axi-max-burst-len = <8>;
         status = "disabled";
};
```

Then, the status property of the rp1_dma node is overridden in the "`bcm2712-rpi-5-b.dts`" devicetree file as shown below:

```
&rp1_dma  {
         status = "okay";
};
```

Now that we have a solid understanding of how the structure and organization of the devicetree help represent the underlying hardware, we will learn how the Linux kernel interacts with the devicetree to load the appropriate drivers. We will also see how device drivers load properties from the devicetree to configure the underlying hardware.

Interaction With the Linux Kernel

The devicetree alone is not helpful if there are no drivers to exercise the hardware described by the devicetree. In this section, we will understand how the kernel associates a node in the devicetree with a device driver.

Let's use the Raspberry Pi 5 devicetree entry corresponding to the power button as our example, which is shown below:

```
pwr_button {
compatible = "gpio-keys";

pinctrl-names = "default";
         pinctrl-0 = <&pwr_button_pins>;
         status = "okay";

         pwr_key: pwr {
            label = "pwr_button";
                // linux,code = <205>; // KEY_SUSPEND
                linux,code = <116>; // KEY_POWER
                 gpios = <&gio 20 GPIO_ACTIVE_LOW>;
                 debounce-interval = <50>; // ms
        };
};
```

Important Note

The Devicetree documentation is extensive and sits alongside the Linux kernel itself! We can find detailed explanations of the different Devicetree attributes of the "gpio-keys" device driver in `Documentation/devicetree/bindings/input/gpio-keys.yaml`.

For platform drivers, the key in the node is the `compatible` property, which the kernel uses to associate the node with the appropriate device driver. The kernel searches through all drivers that are part of the kernel or as part of loaded modules and finds an identical compatible property.

In this instance, the corresponding driver is the `gpio_keys.c` driver under the `drivers/input/keyboard` directory. The relevant portion is reproduced below:

```
static struct platform_driver gpio_keys_device_driver = {
        .probe          = gpio_keys_probe,
        .shutdown       = gpio_keys_shutdown,
        .driver         = {
```

```
                .name    = "gpio-keys",
                .pm      = &gpio_keys_pm_ops,
                .of_match_table = gpio_keys_of_match,
                .dev_groups     = gpio_keys_groups,
        }
};
```

The compatible string is in the `gpio_keys_of_match` data structure highlighted in bold above. This data structure contains the identical compatible property as that in the devicetree, as shown below:

```
static const struct of_device_id gpio_keys_of_match[] = {
        { .compatible = "gpio-keys", },
        { },
};
MODULE_DEVICE_TABLE(of, gpio_keys_of_match);
```

When the kernel identifies that this driver is associated with the `pwr_button` in the devicetree, it calls the `gpio_keys_probe` function in the `gpio_keys_device_driver` data structure above.

The `probe` function is usually the entry point for most drivers and is responsible for initializing the underlying hardware. The probe function may also establish files to facilitate userspace interaction using the kernel frameworks, such as `sysfs` or `debugfs`.

The device driver may also retrieve information from the devicetree and store it in a data structure for later use, using several functions the Linux kernel provides. For example, the "gpio_keys_get_devtree_pdata" function of the gpio_keys driver uses several functions to retrieve information from the devicetree, as shown below:

```
pdata->rep = device_property_read_bool(dev, "autorepeat");

device_property_read_string(dev, "label", &pdata->name);
.
.
.
if (fwnode_property_read_u32(child, "linux,code",
                                    &button->code)) {
          dev_err(dev, "Button without keycode\n");
                fwnode_handle_put(child);
              return ERR_PTR(-EINVAL);
        }
```

```
.
.
.
```

The `device_property_read_string` function reads the `label` property from the Devicetree and stores it in the `&pdata->name` variable; in this example, it is equal to `pwr_button`.

Similarly, `fwnode_property_read_u32` is another function that can be used to extract information from the devicetree. In this example, the "`linux,code`" property is extracted and stored in the `&button->code` variable and will be equal to `116`.

> Important Note
>
> The "116" value and other key codes are defined in the **`include/uapi/linux/input-event-codes.h`** header file in the Linux kernel source repository.

In the next few sections, we will walk through examples of using the devicetree to add hardware to our Raspberry Pi 5. We will see how the device ultimately appears in Linux and how we can interact with it from Linux.

Example #1: Adding an Analog-to-Digital Converter (ADC)

In this section, we will learn how we can enable support for a specific analog-to-digital converter (ADC) in the devicetree. We will learn how to confirm that the device appeared in Linux and how we can confirm its functionality. Specifically, we will use a Texas Instruments ADS1115. A development board can be purchased from Adafruit using this link: `https://www.adafruit.com/product/1085`.

Connecting the Hardware

After soldering the headers to the ADS1115 development board, we can connect it to the Raspberry Pi 5 using the connections shown in the following image:

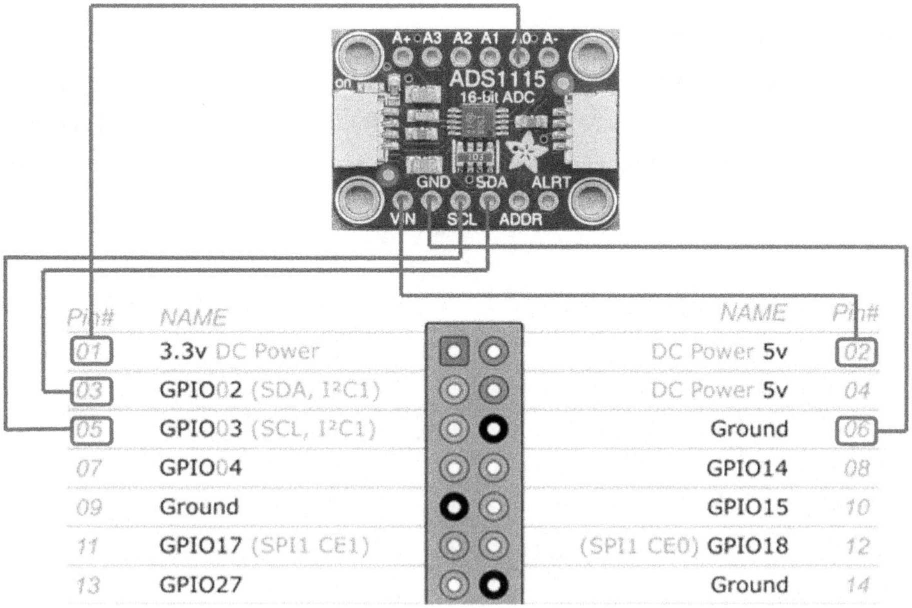

Figure 4.2 – Raspberry Pi 5 onnections to ADS1115 development board

The following table describes the connections:

ADS1115 Pin	Raspberry Pi 5 Pin	Notes
Vin	Pin #2	Connect to +5V on the Raspberry Pi 5 for power to the board.
GND	Pin #6	Connect ground on the board to the ground of the Raspberry Pi 5.
SCL	Pin #5	Connect to the default SCL pin on the Raspberry Pi 5.
SDA	Pin #3	Connect to the default SDA pin on the Raspberry Pi 5.
A0	Pin #1	Connect channel 0 analog input on the ADS1115 to the 3.3-volt output on the Raspberry Pi 5.

Table 4.1 – Connections Between Raspberry Pi 5 and ADS1115 Development Board

Modifying the Devicetree

After connecting the ADS1115 to the Raspberry Pi 5, we must enable it in the devicetree so that we can interact with the ADC in Linux. We need to add the following lines to the end of the top-level devicetree file, which is located at "`arch/arm/boot/dts/bcm2712-rpi-5-b.dts`" as shown below:

```
&rp1_i2c1 {
    ads1115@48 {
        compatible = "ti,ads1115";
        reg = <0x48>;

        channel@0 {
            reg = <0>;
            ti,gain = <1>;
        };
    };
```

The `rp1_i2c1` label is defined in the `rpi1.dtsi` intermediate Devicetree file. The label represents one of the I2C controllers on the RP1 silicon chip on the Raspberry Pi 5.

The specific controller represented by the `rp1_i2c1` label is connected to the SCL and SDA lines on pins 5 and 3 of the header. Thus, we need to add the node representing the ADS1115 ADC under this node. The following list describes each line above:

- `&rp1_i2c1 {`: A reference to the relevant I2C controller.
- `ads1115@48 {`: A node representing the ADS1115. The typical convention in the devicetree for I2C devices is to specify the I2C device address after the '@' symbol in the node name.
- `compatible = "ti,ads1115"`: The "compatible" property is used by the Linux kernel to know which driver corresponds to this device.
- `reg = <0x48>`: This property specifies the device I2C address.
- `channel@0 {`: This node represents the configuration for channel 0 on the ADC itself, which is the "A0" pin on the development board. Again, the typical convention is to specify the channel number after the '@' symbol in the node name.
- `'reg = <0>'`: The channel number corresponding to this configuration.
- `'ti,gain = <1>'`: The voltage range configuration.

The `ti,gain` parameter is ultimately used to set the `Programmable gain amplifier configuration` bits in the `Config Register` of the ADS1115. As shown in the screenshot of the datasheet, a value of 1 indicates a voltage range of **+/- 4.096 V**.

Table 8. Config Register Field Descriptions

Bit	Field	Type	Reset	Description
15	OS	R/W	1h	**Operational status or single-shot conversion start** This bit determines the operational status of the device. OS can only be written when in power-down state and has no effect when a conversion is ongoing. When writing: 0 : No effect 1 : Start a single conversion (when in power-down state) When reading: 0 : Device is currently performing a conversion 1 : Device is not currently performing a conversion
14:12	MUX[2:0]	R/W	0h	**Input multiplexer configuration (ADS1115 only)** These bits configure the input multiplexer. These bits serve no function on the ADS1113 and ADS1114. 000 : AIN_P = AIN0 and AIN_N = AIN1 (default) 001 : AIN_P = AIN0 and AIN_N = AIN3 010 : AIN_P = AIN1 and AIN_N = AIN3 011 : AIN_P = AIN2 and AIN_N = AIN3 100 : AIN_P = AIN0 and AIN_N = GND 101 : AIN_P = AIN1 and AIN_N = GND 110 : AIN_P = AIN2 and AIN_N = GND 111 : AIN_P = AIN3 and AIN_N = GND
11:9	PGA[2:0]	R/W	2h	**Programmable gain amplifier configuration** These bits set the FSR of the programmable gain amplifier. These bits serve no function on the ADS1113. 000 : FSR = ±6.144 V(1) 001 : FSR = ±4.096 V(1) 010 : FSR = ±2.048 V (default) 011 : FSR = ±1.024 V 100 : FSR = ±0.512 V 101 : FSR = ±0.256 V 110 : FSR = ±0.256 V 111 : FSR = ±0.256 V

Figure 4.3 – ADS1115 PGA Configuration

The default setting of 2 will result in a voltage range of **+/- 2.048** volts. Since we are connecting the A0 analog input to the 3.3-volt output of the Raspberry Pi, we can't use the default setting of 2 ("010").

The properties that can be passed to the driver via the devicetree to configure the hardware are specified in the "bindings," which are documented in the Linux kernel. The bindings for the ADS1115 are located in `Documentation/devicetree/bindings/iio/adc/ti,ads1015.yaml`. As shown in the snippet below, we can see the mapping from the `ti,gain` setting to the PGA index, and ultimately the voltage range of the ADC:

```
ti,gain:
  $ref: /schemas/types.yaml#/definitions/uint32
  minimum: 0
  maximum: 5
```

```
    description: |
      pga is the programmable gain amplifier (values are full scale)
      0: +/- 6.144 V
      1: +/- 4.096 V
      2: +/- 2.048 V (default)
      3: +/- 1.024 V
      4: +/- 0.512 V
      5: +/- 0.256 V
```

As we can see in the above documentation, setting the `ti,gain` property in the node to 1 will configure the ADC to sense voltages between +/- 4.096 volts.

Compiling and Loading the Devicetree

Once we've modified the devicetree, we will need to compile it and load it on the Raspberry Pi 5 to interact with the ADC. We can compile the devicetree by executing the following command at the root of the Linux kernel codebase:

```
$ ARCH=arm64 make dtbs
```

Then, we can transfer the compiled devicetree binary, located at `arch/arm64/boot/dts/broadcom/bcm2712-rpi-5-b.dtb` to the user's home directory on the Raspberry Pi 5. Then, on the Raspberry Pi 5, we can copy the devicetree binary to `/boot/firmware/`, which is where the Raspberry Pi 5 bootloader looks for all of the devicetree binary files, by executing the following command:

```
$ sudo cp bcm2712-rpi-5-b.dtb /boot/firmware
```

Finally, we can ensure the changes have been committed to the underlying Flash storage, and we can reboot by executing the following commands:

```
$ sync && sudo reboot
```

Confirming Behavior

> Important Note
>
> The "`bcm2712_defconfig`" configuration that we have been using to configure the Linux kernel for the Raspberry Pi 5 already has support for this device as a kernel module. Thus, we only need to add the device in our Devicetree.

After rebooting the Raspberry Pi 5, we can confirm that the Linux kernel has detected our change and successfully loaded the driver for the ADS1115 ADC by confirming the presence of the "`/sys/bus/iio/devices/iio:device0/`" directory. If this directory exists, we can navigate to it and confirm the name of the device corresponding to this directory bye executing the following commands:

```
$ cd "/sys/bus/iio/devices/iio:device0"
$ cat name
ads1015
```

We can see that the device's name corresponds to the driver that was loaded.

Important Note:

A single driver is used for both the ADS1015 and ADS1115 variants of the ADC. Since this driver was originally meant for the ADS1015, that is why we see its name here. We can confirm that our devicetree changes have been applied by executing the following command:

```
$ cat of_node/name
ads1115
```

Which is more in line with our expectations (recall that we defined the node name to be "`ads1115`" in our Devicetree modification)!

The ADC count for A0 input can be read from the `in_voltage0_raw` file, and the scale factor from the `in_voltage0_scale` file. If we have A0 connected to the 3.3-volt output of the Raspberry Pi 5, we can see the count value and scale factor by executing the following commands:

```
$ cat in_voltage0_raw
17631
$ cat in_voltage0_scale
0.1875
```

If we multiply the two numbers and divide by 1000, we can see that the result is 3.305 volts, which is what we expected!

If we connect the A0 input to any one of the ground connections on the Raspberry Pi 5 header and rerun the same command above, we get the following output:

```
$ cat in_voltage0_raw
-1
```

If we multiply the raw output to the scale factor and divide by 1000, we get a result of -0.0001875 volts, close to 0 volts!

In the next section, we will learn about an alternative mechanism to modify the devicetree, which allows for better organization.

Devicetree Overlays

In the previous section, we learned how to modify the top-level devicetree of the Raspberry Pi 5 to add support for the TI ADS1115 ADC. There are several disadvantages to directly modifying the devicetree. Some of these include:

- **Ownership**: Since we don't own the Raspberry Pi 5 Linux kernel repository, any change we make to the top-level devicetree file (or any other devicetree file) in this repository will not persist. Our modifications to the devicetree to account for our hardware are specific to our use case and cannot be generalized for inclusion into the overall repository. Instead, we would have to fork the repository to incorporate our modifications.
- **Maintenance**: If we fork the "upstream" repository, which the maintainers at Raspberry Pi own, we would need to incorporate any upstream changes to our fork. This requires additional work regularly and can be catastrophic if a critical update is missed.
- **Sustainability**: If we want to add new hardware or remove existing hardware, we would need to make changes to the top-level devicetree file. It may not be ideal to stack changes in the top-level devicetree file as we did in the previous section since it can become messy. The top-level devicetree file may not be the best location to apply these changes and it can become cumbersome to identify the ideal location.

Instead of making changes to the existing devicetree files, we can leverage Devicetree overlays to make specific changes to the devicetree.

Devicetree overlays are fragments of the devicetree that override a configuration in the final devicetree loaded by the system. A devicetree overlay can be compiled and transferred to the system. Then, during boot, the system can be instructed to load a specific overlay and the result will be as if the main devicetree file has been modified.

In this section, we will cover the syntax of a devicetree overlay.

The syntax of a devicetree overlay is similar to that of the devicetree itself. We need the devicetree version and any relevant include statements. However, for an overlay, we also need a special directive, noted by `/plugin/` to instruct Linux that this is an overlay. The following snippet shows a sample implementation:

```
/dts-v1/;
/plugin/;

#include <dt-bindings/gpio/gpio.h>
.
.
.
```

Once we've written the devicetree overlay, we can compile it with the command we learned previously when compiling the devicetree. We can use the `dtc` script in the Linux kernel repository, as shown below:

```
$ ./scripts/dtc/dtc -O dtb -o <output_overlay> <input_overlay>
```

The parameters in the above command are as follows:

- `output_overlay`: This is the filename of the compiled devicetree overlay. This parameter should match the filename specified in the `input_overlay` parameter, except the extension needs to be "`dtbo`."
- `Input_overlay`: This is the filename of the devicetree overlay we wish to compile.

Once we have compiled the devicetree file, we can transfer it to the Raspberry Pi 5. After transferring it to the Raspberry Pi 5, we need to copy it to the `/boot/firmware/overlays` directory.

Finally, we need to update the `config.txt` file in the `/boot/firmware` directory and an entry for the device tree overlay, in bold in the snippet below:

```
# Additional overlays and parameters are documented
# /boot/firmware/overlays/README
dtoverlay=<output_overlay>
```

In the next section, we will see an example of compiling a Devicetree overlay to add support for a peripheral on our system.

Example #2: Adding a Digital-to-Analog Converter (DAC)

In this section, we will learn how to enable support for a digital-to-analog converter (DAC) using a devicetree overlay. Specifically, we will use a Microchip MCP4725. A development board can be purchased from Adafruit using this link: `https://www.adafruit.com/product/935`.

We will need to enable the drivers in the kernel for the MCP4725, since the standard Raspberry Pi 5 kernel doesn't enable them by default.

Connecting the Hardware

After soldering the headers to the MCP4725 development board, we can connect it to the Raspberry Pi 5 using the connections shown in the following image:

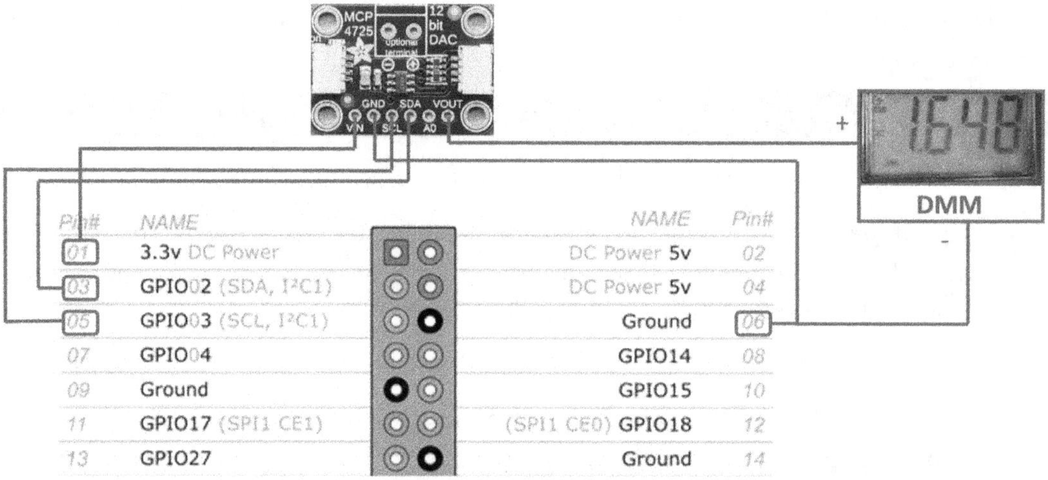

Figure 4.4 – Connections between Raspberry Pi 5 and MCP4725 development board

The following table describes the connections:

MCP4725Pin	Raspberry Pi 5 Pin	Notes
Vin	Pin #1	Connect to +3.3V on the Raspberry Pi 5 for power to the board.
GND	Pin #6	Connect ground on the board to the ground of the Raspberry Pi 5.
SCL	Pin #5	Connect to the default SCL pin on the Raspberry Pi 5.

MCP4725Pin	Raspberry Pi 5 Pin	Notes
SDA	Pin #3	Connect to the default SDA pin on the Raspberry Pi 5.
Vout	N/A	Connect to a multimeter (i.e. DMM) to monitor the analog voltage from the DAC

Table 4.2 - Connections between Raspberry Pi 5 and MCP4725 development board

Adding Support in the Kernel

The standard Raspberry Pi 5 Linux kernel does not have the MCP4725 driver enabled by default. We will need to enable this driver before we can add it to a devicetree overlay, which can be accomplished with the following steps:

1. Open the Raspberry Pi 5 Linux configuration, which is located at "`arch/arm64/boot/configs/bcm2712_defconfig`," and add the following line in bold:

```
CONFIG_MCP3422=m
CONFIG_TI_ADS1015=m
CONFIG_MCP4725=m
CONFIG_BME680=m
```

2. Reconfigure the Linux kernel using the following command:

```
$ ARCH=arm64 make bcm2712_defconfig
```

3. Compile the kernel modules by executing the following command:

```
$ ARCH=arm64 make modules
```

4. Execute the following commands, which will create a directory and then instruct the Linux kernel to *install* the kernel modules in this directory. This step is critical because it defines the order in which kernel modules are loaded on our system on boot.

```
$ mkdir output
$ export INSTALL_MOD_PATH=$PWD/output
$ export CROSS_COMPILE=aarch64-buildroot-linux-gnu-
$ ARCH=arm64 make modules_install
```

5. Upload the directory `output/lib/modules/6.1.69-v8-16k+` (at the time of writing) to the Raspberry Pi to the location `/lib/modules`.

Creating a Devicetree Overlay

The last step is to create a devicetree overlay to instruct the Linux kernel that we have connected the MCP4725 to the Raspberry Pi 5. The following snippet shows this can be done:

```
/dts-v1/;
/plugin/;

&rp1_i2c1 {
    mcp4725@62 {
        compatible = "microchip,mcp4725";
        reg = <0x62>;
        vdd-supply = <&rp1_vdd_3v3>;
    };
};
```

The following list describes each line above:

- `&rp1_i2c1 {`: A reference to the I2C controller that is connected to the MCP4725.
- `mcp4725@62 {`: A node representing the MCP4725. As we saw in the previous section, the convention is to add the I2C address after the '@' symbol.
- `compatible = "microchip,mcp4725"`: The compatible property allows the Linux kernel to associate the MCP4725 driver with this particular device.
- `reg = <0x62>`: The reg property, under a I2C node, specifies the device I2C address.
- `vdd-supply`: A property specific to the MCP4725 device driver, allowing it to inform the underlying hardware of the analog reference to use for output generation.

Compiling and Loading the Devicetree Overlay

Before testing the hardware, we need to compile and load the devicetree overlay onto the Raspberry Pi 5 by following these steps:

1. Execute the command we learned above, making sure to include the filenames, as shown below:

```
$ ./scripts/dtc/dtc -O dtb -o add-mcp4725.dtbo add-mcp4725.dts
```

2. Transfer `add-mcp4725.dtbo` to the directory `/boot/firmware/overlays` on the Raspberry Pi 5. Finally, we can add the following line to the file "`/boot/firmare/configs.txt`."

```
# Additional overlays and parameters are documented
# /boot/firmware/overlays/README
dtoverlay=add-mcp4725.dtbo
```

Now we should have support for the MCP4725 DAC in our Embedded Linux image.

Testing the Devicetree Overlay

After rebooting the Raspberry Pi 5, we can confirm that the Linux kernel successfully detected the MCP4725, and the driver initialized the device.

We can execute the following command to confirm that the device is indeed the MCP4275:

```
$ cat /sys/bus/iio/devices/iio\:device0/of_node/name
mcp4725
```

We can check the default binary value of the DAC by executing the following command:

```
$ cat /sys/bus/iio/devices/iio\:device0/out_voltage0_raw
2048
```

Since this is a 12-bit DAC, the maximum digital value we can specify to the DAC is 4095 (i.e. 2^{12} - 1). Thus, the default digital value is half of the maximum. Since we are using 3.3 volts as our reference voltage, our output should be approximately 1.64 volts.

If we observe the voltage reported by our multimeter, which should be connected to the analog output pin on the MCP4725 development board (i.e. Vout), we see just that!

Figure 4.5 – Analog voltage out from MSP4725 on boot

We can instruct the DAC to use full-scale output by executing the following command:

```
$ echo 4095 > /sys/bus/iio/devices/iio\:device0/out_voltage0_raw
```

If we observe the value reported by our multimeter, we see that it reports 3.3 volts as shown below:

Figure 4.6 – Full-scale output reported from MSP4725

This is the result we expect!

In the next section, we will learn how to interact with general-purpose input-output (**GPIO**) using the Linux **sysfs** and **pinctrl** interfaces.

Example #3: Interacting with GPIO

In this section, we will learn how we can use the Linux pinctrl and sysfs interfaces to control GPIO pins on our Raspberry Pi 5 header. Specifically, we will be using **GPIO3** in this section, which is connected to pin 5 on the header, as shown below:

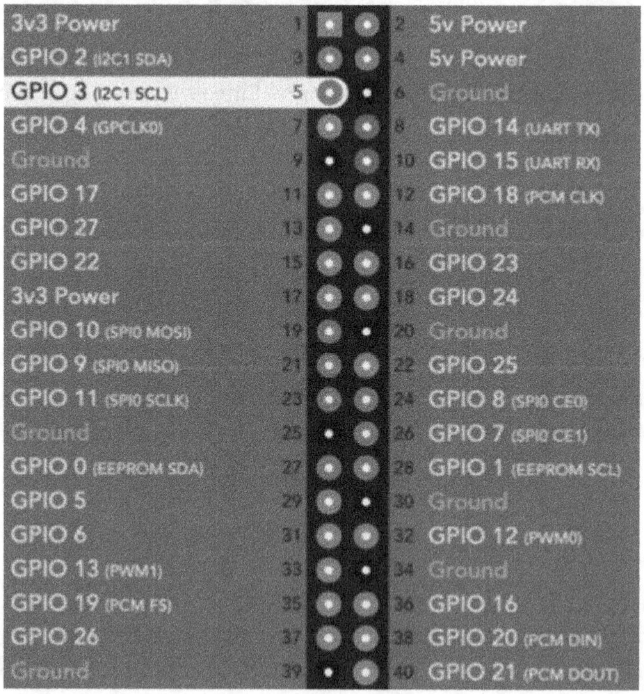

Figure 4.7 – Raspberry Pi 5 GPIO header pinout

> Important Note
>
> GPIO3 is referenced in the Raspberry Pi 5 Devicetree file as an "alias", which is a reference to a Devicetree label, as shown below:
>
> ```
> / {
>     aliases: aliases {
>       .
>       .
>       .
>       gpio3 = &pinctrl;
> };
> ```

The **pinctrl** subsystem and corresponding application are one mechanism that can be used to control a GPIO on the header. We can execute the following command to get a list of the GPIOs that are available on the header:

```
$ pinctrl
.
.
.
3: no    pu | -- // PIN5/GPIO3 = none
```

> Important Note
>
> The **pinctrl** tool is specific to the Raspberry Pi and may not be readily available for other platforms.

We can execute the following command to configure GPIO3 as an input:

```
$ pinctrl set 3 ip
```

We can execute the following command to confirm the configuration (**ip** confirms that GPIO3 is configured as an input):

```
$ pinctrl get 3
 3: ip    pu | lo // PIN5/GPIO3 = input
```

We can connect pin 5 on the header to 3.3 volts (which is supplied by pin 1 on the header), and execute the following command to confirm the input state:

```
$ pinctrl get 3
 3: ip    pu | hi // PIN5/GPIO3 = input
```

`hi` confirms that the pin is logic high.

To use the **sysctrl** interface to perform the same experiment as above, we need to first identify the GPIO controller that is connected to GPIO3. We can do so by executing the following command:

```
$ gpioinfo | grep -B4 PIN5
gpiochip4 - 54 lines:
        line   0:      "ID_SD"       unused   input  active-high
        line   1:      "ID_SC"       unused   input  active-high
        line   2:       "PIN3"       unused   input  active-high
        line   3:       "PIN5"       unused   input  active-high
```

As seen in the above output, **gpiochip4** is the controller that is connected to GPIO3. We can execute the following command to determine the available controllers on our Raspberry Pi 5:

```
$ ls /sys/class/gpio/
export  gpiochip399  gpiochip453  gpiochip459  gpiochip476  gpiochip480
unexport
```

If we execute the following command, we can see that gpiochip399 is an alias of gpiochip4:

```
$ ls /sys/class/gpio/gpiochip399/device
.
.
.
gpiochip4
```

We will need to *export* a particular GPIO number to be able to interact with it. The specific number will be 402, which is the base number for the gpio controller (i.e. "399") added with "3", which is the offset based on the output of the following command:

```
$ gpioinfo | grep -B4 PIN5
gpiochip4 - 54 lines:
        line   0:      "ID_SD"       unused   input  active-high
        line   1:      "ID_SC"       unused   input  active-high
        line   2:       "PIN3"       unused   input  active-high
        line   3:       "PIN5"       unused   input  active-high
```

We can execute the following commands to make the GPIO available to us:

```
$ cd /sys/class/gpio
$ echo 402 > export
```

We can execute the following command to configure GPIO3 as an input:

```
$ cd gpio402
$ echo in > direction
```

Finally, we can connect GPIO3/PIN5 to 3.3 volts (i.e. pin 1 on the Raspberry Pi 5 header), and execute the following command to confirm that a logical high is present on the GPIO:

```
$ cat value
1
```

In the next section, we will learn how to interact with a peripheral that is connected over the SPI bus by writing a Python application.

Example #4: Using Spidev to Interact with SPI Devices

In this section, we will be communicating with a peripheral that is connected to our Raspberry Pi 5 over the SPI bus. Specifically, we will be using the BME280, which is a humidity, barometric, and temperature sensor. A breakout board can be purchased from Adafruit by using the following link: `https://learn.adafruit.com/adafruit-bme280-humidity-barometric-pressure-temperature-sensor-breakout`. The following diagram shows the connections between the Raspberry Pi 5 and the BME280 breakout board:

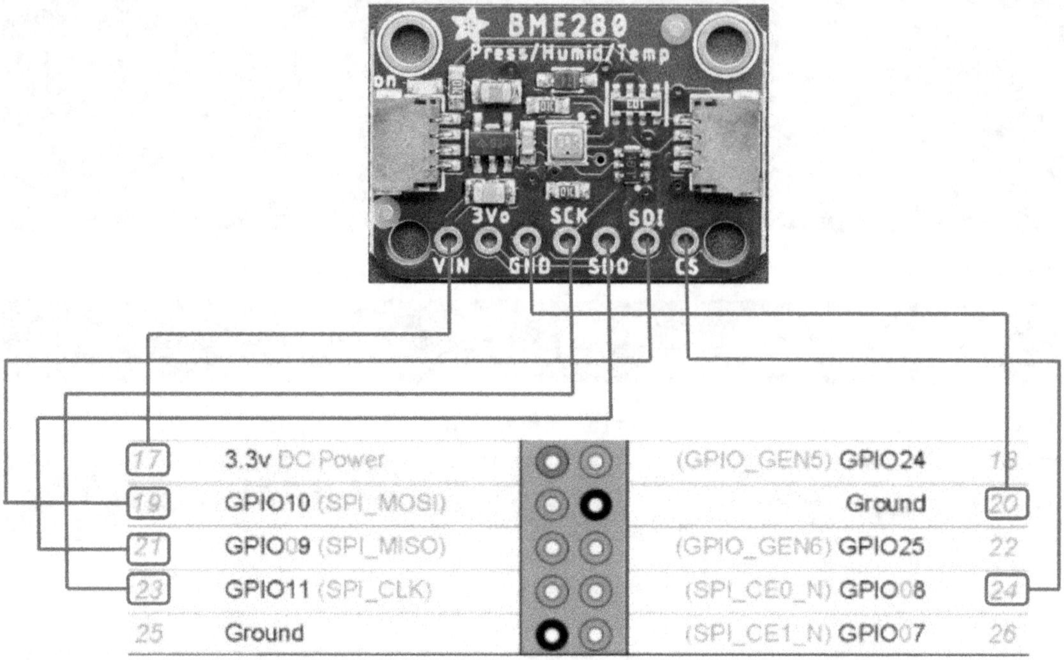

Figure 4.8 – Connection between BME280 and Raspberry Pi 5

The connections are listed below:

1. **VIN** on the BME280 should be connected to 3.3 volts on the Raspberry Pi 5, such as pin 17.
2. **GND** on the BME280 should be connected to a Ground pin on the Raspberry Pi 5, such as pin 20.
3. **SCK** on the BME280 should be connected to pin 23 on the Raspberry Pi 5, which is the clock line for the SPI interface.
4. **SDO** on the BME280 should be connected to pin 21 on the Raspberry Pi 5, which is the MISO line for the SPI interface.
5. **SDI** on the BME280 should be connected to pin 19 on the Raspberry Pi 5, which is the MOSI line for the SPI interface.
6. **CS** on the BME280 should be connected to pin 24 on the Raspberry Pi 5, which is the chip select line of the SPI interface.

After connecting the BME280 to the Raspberry Pi 5, we need to enable the SPI interface on the Raspberry Pi 5 by using the `raspi-config` utility, selecting the `Interface Options` menu, selecting the `SPI` menu, and selecting `Yes`, as shown below:

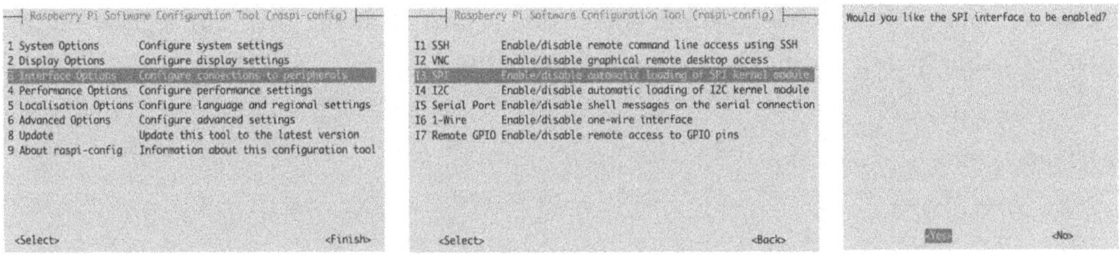

Figure 4.9 – Enabling the SPI bus on the Raspberry Pi 5

In this example, we use `spidev`, an interface that allows userspace applications to interact with devices over the SPI bus. Spidev exposes a SPI device as a file under `/dev`, usually called `spidevX.Y`, where `X` refers to the specific SPI bus and `Y` represents the chipselect used to control the device. We can enable Spidev in the Linux kernel by enabling the corresponding Kconfig option. As shown below, we can see that for the Raspberry Pi 5, the default kernel configuration uses Spidev as a kernel module:

```
CONFIG_SPI_GPIO=m
CONFIG_SPI_SPIDEV=m
CONFIG_SPI_SLAVE=y
```

We also need to ensure that Spidev is associated with a particular SPI bus, which is accomplished using the Devicetree. For the Raspberry Pi 5, we can see that the Spidev is defined in the `bcm2712-rpi-5-b.dts`, as shown below:

```
&spi10 {
        pinctrl-names = "default";
        cs-gpios = <&gio 1 1>;
        pinctrl-0 = <&spi10_pins &spi10_cs_pins>;

        spidev10: spidev@0 {
                compatible = "spidev";
                reg = <0>;      /* CE0 */
                #address-cells = <1>;
                #size-cells = <0>;
                spi-max-frequency = <20000000>;
                status = "okay";
        };
};
```

Then, we can run the following Python application, which reads the `chip_id:` register on the BME280 using Spidev, which is located at address 0xD0.

```
import time
import spidev

spi_ch = 0

# Enable SPI
spi = spidev.SpiDev(0, spi_ch)
spi.max_speed_hz = 1200000

reply = spi.xfer([208, 0]) # 0xD0 to retrieve chip_id

print("chip_id: ", reply)
```

The relevant portions of the application are as follows:

- `spidev.SpiDev`: This line initiates and creates an instance of the SpiDev class using bus 0 and device 0.
- `spi.max_speed_hz = 1200000`: This line sets the maximum speed that the underlying driver should use.
- `reply = spi.xfer([208, 0])`: This line performs the SPI transfer, transmitting 0xD0, followed by 0x0, and returns the response from the BME280.

After executing the above application, we get the following output:

```
$ python3 bme280_version.py
chip_id:  [255, 96]
```

The value of the "CHIP_ID" register, which is the second element in the list is "96", which is "0x60" in hexadecimal. According to the BME280 datasheet, which can be retrieved from `https://cdn-learn.adafruit.com/assets/assets/000/115/588/original/bst-bme280-ds002.pdf?1664822559` and is reproduced below, the CHIP_ID register for the BME280 should be 0x60!

Register	Bits	Content	BMP280	BME280
0xD0 "*id*"	7:0	*chip_id*	Read value is 0x56 / 0x57 (samples) 0x58 (mass production)	Read value is 0x60

Figure 4.10 – CHIP_ID register value

Summary

In this chapter, we learned about the structure and format of the devicetree and its interaction with the Linux kernel and relevant device drivers. We also learned how devicetree overlays can be used to modify the devicetree while the system is running. Finally, we worked through some examples with actual hardware using different peripheral buses.

In the next chapter, we will transition from understanding Embedded Linux internals to learning how to build complete, bootable Linux images using frameworks like Buildroot and the Yocto Project.

Summary

Get this book's PDF version and more

Part 2

Building an Embedded Linux Image

In this part, you will gain an in-depth understanding of the different frameworks that can be used to build a complete Embedded Linux image and how to use frameworks on Raspberry Pi.

This part has the following chapters:

- *Chapter 5, Exploring Frameworks to Build an Image*
- *Chapter 6, Building an Image Using the Yocto Project*
- *Chapter 7, Building an Image Using Buildroot*

5

Exploring Frameworks to Build an Image

In *Part 1*, we built a foundation for understanding how embedded Linux systems operate at their core. We learned about the different software components that make a complete embedded Linux system and briefly learned about these components in detail. For example, we learned about the responsibilities of a bootloader and the Linux kernel, and how the devicetree describes the underlying hardware. With this understanding, we're now ready to move from Linux internals to creating complete, bootable images that bring embedded systems to life. In *Part 2*, we'll learn how to assemble complete, customized embedded Linux images using two key frameworks: Buildroot and The Yocto Project. We'll gain hands-on experience in flashing, testing, and troubleshooting real images on the Raspberry Pi 5.

This chapter will serve as an overview of the remaining topics covered in this part of the book. We will learn about how the different components of an embedded Linux image, which was covered in *Chapter 1, Exploring Embedded Linux's Architecture and Its Use Cases,* can be combined to form a cohesive image. This image can then be flashed onto a target hardware platform, such as our Raspberry Pi 5. In this chapter, we will briefly review the two popular frameworks to build an embedded Linux image: Buildroot and The Yocto Project. Finally, we will compare and contrast these two frameworks and understand when to select one of these frameworks.

We are going to cover the following main topics in this chapter:

- Creating an embedded Linux image
- The Yocto Project
- Buildroot
- Which one to choose

Technical requirements

You should be comfortable with executing commands on a terminal. You should also be familiar with running Python applications and reading Python code. You can also follow along with the examples in this chapter by using the following GitHub link: `https://github.com/PacktPublishing/Embedded-Linux-Essentials-Handbook/tree/main/Chapter5`.

Creating an embedded Linux image

In this section, we will learn about the different components of an embedded Linux image. We will also understand the general process of creating an embedded Linux image. As mentioned in *Chapter 1, Exploring Embedded Linux's Architecture and Its Use Cases*, an embedded Linux system contains the following software components:

- **Bootloader**: The bootloader is responsible for initializing the CPU and necessary peripherals before launching the kernel
- **Linux kernel**: The kernel is the crux of the embedded Linux operating system and is responsible for launching applications and ensuring they can safely access the necessary hardware
- **Devicetree**: The devicetree describes the hardware on the system
- **Root filesystem**: The **root filesystem**, or **RFS**, contains all the files present on the system
- **Toolchain**: The toolchain is used to convert source code into binaries and applications that can be executed on the target embedded Linux system

Before diving into specific frameworks, it's important to understand the underlying workflow common to all of them. Regardless of the framework, building an embedded Linux image follows the same fundamental process, as outlined here:

1. Retrieve or generate the toolchain for the target processor.
2. Retrieve the source code for the bootloader and build it using the retrieved toolchain.
3. Retrieve the source code for the Linux kernel.

4. Configure and build the Linux kernel for the target device.
5. Compile the appropriate devicetree for the target device.
6. Retrieve the source code for the desired applications and services to be installed on the final embedded Linux image.
7. Compile the applications and services into their final binaries.
8. Combine the bootloader, Linux kernel, devicetree, applications, and services into a final image that can be installed on the device.

We can "boil down" the process for creating an embedded Linux image into the following:

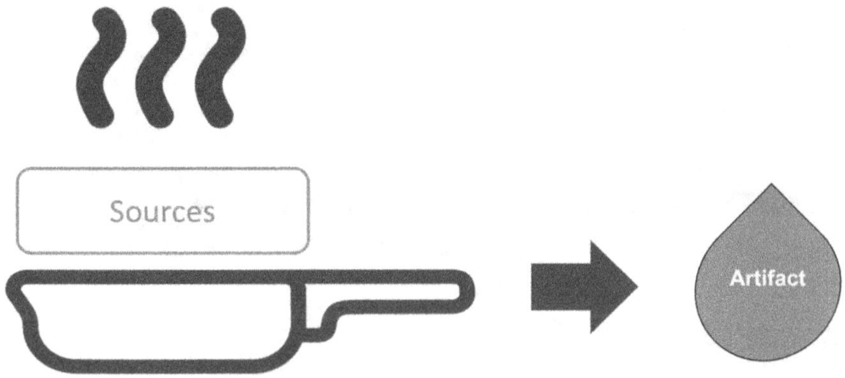

Figure 5.1 – Compiling component sources

Figure 5.1 shows an analogy of cooking that I like to use when thinking about the process of creating an embedded Linux image. As we will see, this analogy works well for one of the popular frameworks used to generate an embedded Linux image. However, the general process is identical for both Buildroot and The Yocto Project. For each of the components, the bootloader, the Linux kernel, the devicetree, and the applications in the RFS, the process involves the following:

- Retrieving the source code for each component. This is akin to retrieving the ingredients when cooking.
- Using the toolchain, each component is compiled into a final binary that can be executed or used on the embedded Linux system. This is similar to preparing each ingredient.

However, just having compiled components is not sufficient, similar to how having the ingredients alone is not sufficient in cooking. We still need to combine the compiled elements into a cohesive image that can be used to boot the embedded Linux system, just as we need to combine the prepared ingredients into the final dish.

The following figure shows the general process of combining the different components into a final embedded Linux image. In this case, instead of using the toolchain, other Linux tools are used to combine the binaries into the final embedded Linux image.

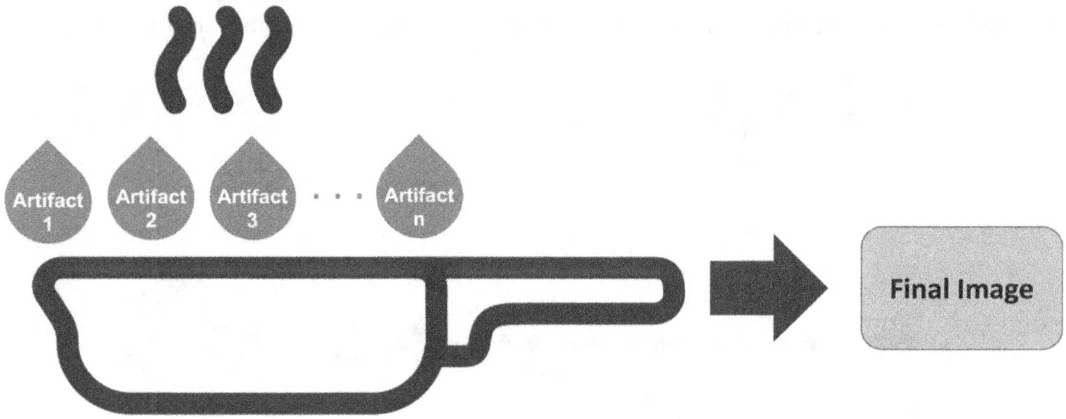

Figure 5.2 – Creating an embedded Linux image

Once the embedded Linux image has been generated, it can be flashed onto the final system. During the development stage, the image is usually flashed onto an SD card. This makes it easy for developers to make quick changes to the image and try them out on the target system. After development, once the image is finalized, it is usually flashed onto the boot storage of the target system.

In the next section, we will review **The Yocto Project**, a popular framework used to create embedded Linux images.

The Yocto Project

In this section, we will learn about The Yocto Project's paradigm, infrastructure, and tools. This chapter is meant to serve as an overview of The Yocto Project and to allow us to get comfortable with the background and terminology. In *Chapter 6, Building an Image Using The Yocto Project*, we will cover the framework in more detail and see examples of performing common tasks when using The Yocto Project.

> Important note
>
> It is important to note that The Yocto Project is closely related to and relies on **OpenEmbedded**. OpenEmbedded is the underlying project that provides the necessary tooling for other frameworks to create custom embedded Linux images. The Yocto Project leverages the tooling and infrastructure offered by OpenEmbedded to create embedded Linux images. Because The Yocto Project is tightly coupled with OpenEmbedded, the appropriate designation for the framework is The Yocto Project/OpenEmbedded. However, for the sake of brevity, the rest of the chapter and book will refer to the framework simply as The Yocto Project.

Paradigm

We will first understand the paradigm behind The Yocto Project. Understanding The Yocto Project's paradigm helps us ensure we are in the proper mindset when using it to create an embedded Linux image, which allows us to achieve the following:

- Remember the steps necessary to accomplish trivial tasks
- Troubleshoot and resolve esoteric errors
- Troubleshoot and resolve anomalous behavior when creating an embedded Linux image, with no errors being reported

As we will learn in the *Which one to choose* section, the decision to use The Yocto Project or Buildroot is usually driven by the vendor of the CPU platform we are using. However, the vendor may deviate from The Yocto Project's best practices. Thus, if we encounter issues when customizing or creating the embedded Linux image, understanding the paradigm of The Yocto Project will help us understand and make the necessary modifications to resolve these issues.

BitBake

The paradigm of The Yocto Project is akin to *baking*. The *baking* analogy is used extensively throughout The Yocto Project. For example, the core tool used in The Yocto Project is **BitBake**. BitBake has the following characteristics:

> Important note
>
> BitBake technically falls under the umbrella of OpenEmbedded.

- It is the application used to build almost everything in The Yocto Project.
- It creates an **artifact**, the binary output of each component, by following a **recipe**.
- At a minimum, each recipe provides instructions on generating the artifact corresponding to the recipe. The steps contained in the recipe are known as **tasks**.
- Each recipe has a strict format and structure that BitBake parses for correctness. BitBake's infrastructure tracks dependencies across tasks. If a task in a particular recipe depends on a task in another recipe, it first **bakes** the dependent recipe before baking the original target recipe.
- BitBake's infrastructure allows for building a recipe for both the host PC and the target embedded system. If a recipe is intended to be built for the host PC, the artifact will also be included in the **SDK**. We will learn more about the SDK generated by The Yocto Project in *Chapter 6, Building an Image Using the Yocto Project*.

Recipes

As mentioned earlier, each recipe is a set of instructions that BitBake uses to create a particular artifact. BitBake parses each recipe before applying the steps outlined to ensure correctness. The following shows an example of perhaps the simplest recipe, which consists of installing a shell script to the root filesystem:

```
SUMMARY = "Simple Bitbake recipe"
LICENSE = "CLOSED"

SRC_URI = "\
```

```
    file://test_script.sh \
"

do_install() {
    install -d ${D}{bindir}
    install -m 0755 ${WORKDIR}/test_script.sh ${D}{bindir}/test_script.sh
}

FILES_${PN} = " ${bindir}/test_script.sh"
```

Important note

The preceding source code listing is shown only to give you a taste of the unique structure of a recipe, which is radically different from what you, as an embedded software engineer, may be accustomed to. Don't worry about understanding what each line means at the moment. We will dive into the details of the structure of a recipe and understand different types of recipes in *Chapter 6, Building an Image Using The Yocto Project.*

The following listing shows the shell script:

```
#!/bin/bash

echo "Hello World"
```

A BitBake recipe is a file that ends with a .bb extension. A special type of recipe, called an **append** recipe, can add to or override the functionality of a proper recipe. Other types of files are also used by The Yocto Project, which we will cover in more detail in *Chapter 6, Building an Image Using The Yocto Project.*

BitBake recipes are usually organized into a directory structure, such as the one shown in the following diagram:

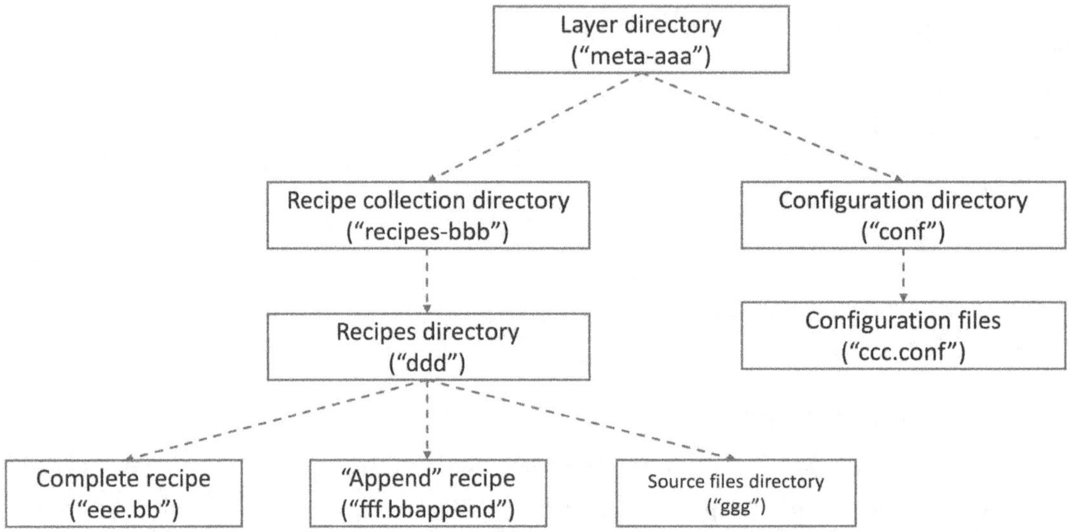

Figure 5.3 – Recipe organization

The following are some important points about the organization shown in *Figure 5.3*:

- The top-level directory is called the **layer**. A layer consists of recipes specific to an organization or framework. For example (as we will see in *Chapter 6, Building an Image Using The Yocto Project*), the following are common layers used in embedded Linux systems that are based on The Yocto Project:
    - `meta-raspberrypi`: This layer, maintained at `https://github.com/agherzan/meta-raspberrypi`, contains recipes that can be used to create an embedded Linux image using The Yocto Project for the Raspberry Pi.
    - `meta-swupdate`: This layer, maintained at `https://github.com/sbabic/meta-swupdate`, contains recipes to support SWUpdate, a framework that adds support for remote updates.
- Each layer contains the following:
    - A `conf` directory that contains relevant configuration files.

- A directory with different types of recipes. In the preceding image, this directory is called `recipes-bbb`. This directory contains multiple sub-directories, where each sub-directory can contain multiple recipes. Each directory can have the following:
  - A complete recipe with a `.bb` extension, as we saw earlier.
  - An append recipe that overrides or adds functionality to a recipe in another directory. The append recipe may even add or override the functionality of a recipe implemented in another layer.
  - A directory containing relevant source files that are used by the recipe.

In the next section, we will review **Buildroot**, another popular framework used to create embedded Linux images. We will cover Buildroot in more detail in *Chapter 7, Building an Image Using Buildroot.*

Buildroot

In this section, we will learn about Buildroot's paradigm, infrastructure, and tooling. Remember, this chapter is meant to introduce these two frameworks. We will dive into more detail on Buildroot in *Chapter 7, Building an Image Using Buildroot.*

Differences from The Yocto Project

Since we covered The Yocto Project first, let's understand the main differences between it and Buildroot, listed next:

- **Recipes versus Makefiles**: While The Yocto Project uses recipes to compile and assemble applications, Buildroot uses Makefiles.
- **Artifacts versus binaries**: The Yocto Project generates **artifacts**, which can be contained in popular packaging file formats, such as **.rpm**, **.deb**, or **.ipk**. These artifacts contain the applications, scripts, and configuration files that will ultimately be placed in the root filesystem. On the other hand, Buildroot places the final applications, scripts, and configuration files directly in the root filesystem without any additional packaging.
- **Learning curve**: As we will see later, Buildroot uses systems, such as **Kconfig** and **make**, that an embedded software engineer may already be familiar with. However, The Yocto Project uses mechanisms that embedded software engineers may not be familiar with and require time to understand. Thus, Buildroot is usually easier for embedded software engineers to pick up, whereas The Yocto Project has a steeper learning curve.

Paradigm and process

As with The Yocto Project, we will first understand the paradigm behind using Buildroot to create an embedded Linux image. As mentioned earlier, Buildroot is much simpler than The Yocto Project. Nonetheless, Buildroot's overall process for creating an embedded Linux image is nearly identical to The Yocto Project, which is listed next:

1. It retrieves the source code for the toolchain and compiles it for later use. Buildroot can also be instructed to use an **external** toolchain, which is a toolchain that has been retrieved or compiled outside of Buildroot. This can be important or helpful in the following cases:
    - Buildroot doesn't support the target architecture
    - The toolchain generated by Buildroot does not natively support certain features that the user needs
2. It identifies the applications that are needed for the final embedded Linux image.
3. It retrieves the source code corresponding to the desired application.
4. It compiles the application using the cross-compiler into a binary that can be executed on the final system.
5. It uses install scripts to determine where and how to install the target application into the final image.

The process is summarized in the following figure:

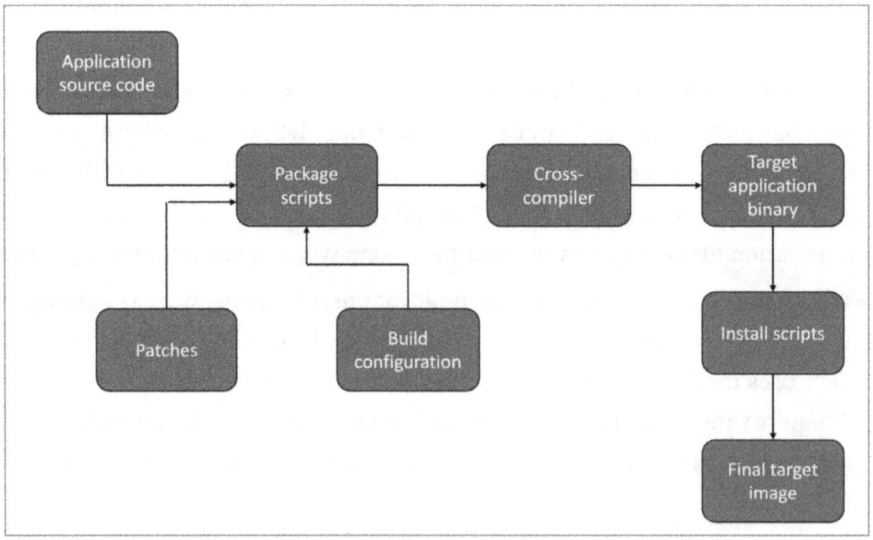

Figure 5.4 – Buildroot process

As mentioned earlier, Buildroot uses the same Kconfig system from the Linux kernel to allow a user to configure it. Thus, we can use the process we learned in *Chapter 3, Navigating the Linux Kernel*, to configure Buildroot:

1. We can retrieve the latest Buildroot release candidate at the time of writing by executing the following command:

```
$ wget https://buildroot.org/downloads/buildroot-2024.02-rc2.tar.gz
```

2. Next, we can decompress the tarball by executing the following command:

```
$ tar xzvf buildroot-2024.02-rc2.tar.gz
```

3. Then, we can change into the resulting directory and enter the Buildroot configuration by executing the following commands:

```
$ cd buildroot-2024.02-rc2
$ make menuconfig
```

4. Finally, we will be presented with the following window, which we will be familiar with from our experience of configuring the Linux kernel:

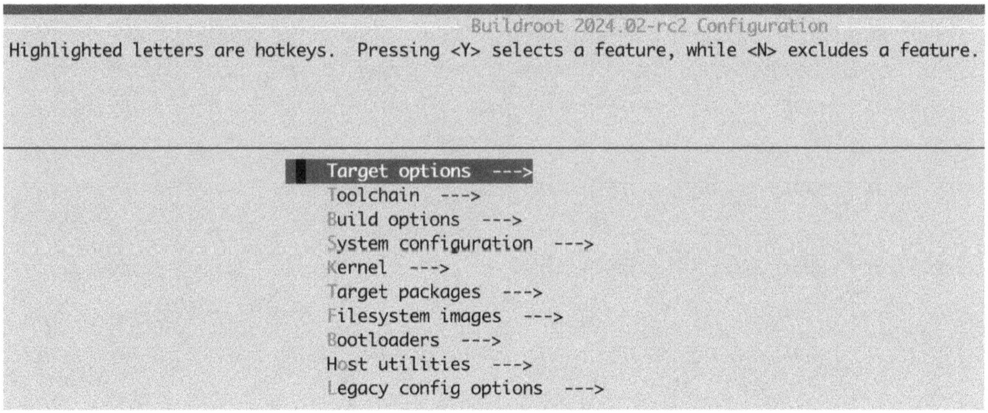

Figure 5.5 – Buildroot configuration interface

Important note

Remember, this chapter is meant to introduce Buildroot. The preceding figure is presented to make you comfortable with the Kconfig interface. We will go through each option in *Chapter 7, Building an Image Using Buildroot,* where we will learn about Buildroot in more detail.

As mentioned earlier, Buildroot uses `make` as its fundamental tool. `make` uses **Makefiles** as a set of procedures that it needs to follow to build and manage an application. The following is an example Makefile that creates a Buildroot package:

> Note
>
> **elehbr**, which stands for **Embedded Linux Essentials Handbook Buildroot**, is a simple application that prints "Hello World" to the console.

```
################################################################################
#
# elehbr package
#
################################################################################

ELEHBR_VERSION = 1.0
ELEHBR_SITE = $(BR2_EXTERNAL_ELEHBR_PATH)/package/elehbr/src
ELEHBR_SITE_METHOD = local

define ELEHBR_BUILD_CMDS
    $(MAKE) CC="$(TARGET_CC)" LD="$(TARGET_LD)" -C $(@D)
endef

ELEHBR_INSTALL_TARGET = YES

define ELEHBR_INSTALL_TARGET_CMDS
    $(INSTALL) -D -m 0755 $(@D)/elehbr  $(TARGET_DIR)/usr/bin
endef

$(eval $(generic-package))
```

> Important note
>
> The preceding listing is shown only to give you a taste of a typical Makefile used in Buildroot. If you have used `make` in the past and are familiar with Makefiles, you probably understand what the listing is doing. If you haven't used `make` before, don't fret! We will dive into the details of Buildroot and cover Makefiles in more detail in *Chapter 7, Building an Image Using Buildroot*.

While we covered some of the major differences between The Yocto Project and Buildroot earlier in this section, we didn't learn about how to decide which ones to use. In the next section, we will understand the advantages and disadvantages of The Yocto Project and Buildroot, as well as how to decide which framework to use when creating our embedded Linux image.

Which one to choose

In the previous two sections, we learned about two popular frameworks used to create embedded Linux images: The Yocto Project and Buildroot. In this section, we will understand the advantages and disadvantages of each framework. Finally, we will review some general principles to decide which framework to use.

To recap, the following are the advantages of using Buildroot:

- Embedded software engineers can quickly get started with Buildroot. As we saw in the previous section, Buildroot is based on Makefiles and uses mechanisms such as Kconfig that are borrowed from the Linux kernel. Thus, we can use the lessons we learned when working with the Linux kernel and other Makefile-based applications to understand and navigate Buildroot.
- Buildroot has an active developer community with many contributors and active maintainers.
- Buildroot supports a wide variety of boards and different CPU architectures.
- The resulting embedded Linux image can be smaller due to the minimal set of components and applications needed to create a bootable image.

An initial build based on Buildroot is typically faster than an initial build based on The Yocto Project.

The main disadvantage of Buildroot is that it may require a full build after a configuration change. Buildroot's main directive is to be as simple as possible. Thus, it doesn't attempt to be smart when identifying configuration changes. Instead, it relies heavily on `make` to identify dependencies. When a particular application's source code changes, Buildroot does not have any mechanisms on top of `make` to identify dependencies. Thus, there may be instances where a certain package needed to be rebuilt but was not. Instead, an embedded software engineer may need to initiate a complete Buildroot build as a solution.

The following are the advantages of using The Yocto Project to create an embedded Linux system:

- It supports a wider variety of boards and architectures. The Yocto Project has gained tremendous support from board and silicon vendors in the recent past.
- The Yocto Project's layered architecture makes it easy to customize an embedded Linux image for our own hardware and software needs.
- It supports a wide variety of different application frameworks and update mechanisms.
- It is mostly self-contained. The Yocto Project contains all of the tools necessary to create an embedded Linux image using it. For example, BitBake, which we covered previously, is a part of OpenEmbedded, which is included by default in The Yocto Project.

The Yocto Project's **shared state cache** usually makes successive builds much faster than Buildroot.

The following are the main disadvantages of The Yocto Project:

- Out-of-the-box builds are generally larger than Buildroot. Significant customization may be required to achieve an image comparable in size to Buildroot.
- Creating an embedded Linux image using The Yocto Project requires significantly more resources than Buildroot. Generally, a powerful development PC is required to generate builds from scratch in a time that is comparable to Buildroot.
- Similarly, The Yocto Project artifacts may occupy more disk space than the packages and binaries generated by Buildroot.
- The learning curve of The Yocto Project is much steeper when compared to Buildroot. Since The Yocto Project's paradigm is a radical departure from Buildroot's Makefile-based system, it takes novice and even advanced embedded software engineers time to get comfortable with the framework.

How do we decide whether to choose Buildroot or The Yocto Project? Ultimately, choosing between The Yocto Project and Buildroot depends on our overall goals, team expertise, and project requirements. Here are examples:

- If we require a small root filesystem (typically less than 8 MB in size), we should use Buildroot. Although it is possible to reduce the final image size when using The Yocto Project, it can require significant time and effort.
- If we have novice embedded software engineers, or don't have time to understand the nuances of The Yocto Project, we should use Buildroot. Buildroot is generally more friendly to novice embedded software engineers easier to learn.

- If our final embedded Linux image needs specific frameworks or many software components, we should use The Yocto Project. There are many third-party layers available that can add certain applications and services to our embedded Linux image. On the other hand, if we wish to add an application to an embedded Linux image created from Buildroot, we generally have to create the appropriate Buildroot tooling ourselves.

However, the overarching principle I use when selecting the appropriate framework is to let my hardware vendor's choice guide me. If the vendor of our board or silicon uses a framework for their **Board Support Package (BSP)**, we should use the framework that they selected. It would incur a significant amount of time and cost if we switched frameworks. Thus, if the vendor uses Buildroot, we should also use Buildroot. Similarly, if the vendor uses The Yocto Project, we should also use The Yocto Project. However, if the vendor hasn't selected a particular framework, or the board is supported on both frameworks, we can use the preceding guidelines in our determination.

Summary

In this chapter, we learned about Buildroot and The Yocto Project, the two most popular frameworks used to create embedded Linux images. These frameworks are tremendously valuable in streamlining the process to create a cohesive and comprehensive embedded Linux image. Otherwise, we would have to manually go through the process of retrieving the source code for each component, compiling each component, and combining all the components into an image. We briefly understood the mindset and paradigm between these frameworks and some key principles we can use to help us select the appropriate framework. In the next few chapters, we will dive deeper into these frameworks and create an embedded Linux image using them.

In the next chapter, we will learn more about The Yocto Project.

6

Building an Image Using the Yocto Project

In the previous chapter, we learned the value of frameworks such as the Yocto Project and Buildroot in streamlining the process of generating complete embedded Linux images. Without these frameworks, we would have to manually create our images.

This chapter focuses on the Yocto Project. While the previous chapter provided an overview of the framework, here we will explore it in detail. We will begin with the background information, including terminology and the related projects and frameworks that the Yocto Project builds upon. Then, we will dive into how to use the Yocto Project, learning about the mechanics of creating an embedded Linux image: setting up our environment, executing the required commands, and implementing common customizations for our system. We'll apply these steps to run our image on both a Raspberry Pi 5 and a virtualized environment using QEMU.

We are going to cover the following main topics in this chapter:

- Overview
- Creating an embedded Linux image
- Adding custom applications
- Customizing the final image
- Customizing the Linux kernel
- Customizing U-Boot
- Validating our customizations

Technical requirements

You should be comfortable executing commands on a terminal. You should also be familiar with running Python applications and reading Python code. You can follow the examples in this chapter using the following Github link: `https://github.com/PacktPublishing/Embedded-Linux-Essentials-Handbook/tree/main/Chapter6`.

Overview

As we learned in *Chapter 5, Exploring Frameworks to Build an Image*, the Yocto Project is a framework designed to help us build an embedded Linux image. However, the Yocto Project relies on another framework, called **OpenEmbedded**. OpenEmbedded provides the underlying data structures and mechanisms that the Yocto Project uses to make sense of recipes and how to combine them to formulate a cohesive embedded Linux image. OpenEmbedded is such an integral component that the Yocto Project is technically called **The Yocto Project/OpenEmbedded**. The latter is usually dropped for the sake of brevity.

The following figure depicts how the different components of the Yocto Project fit together:

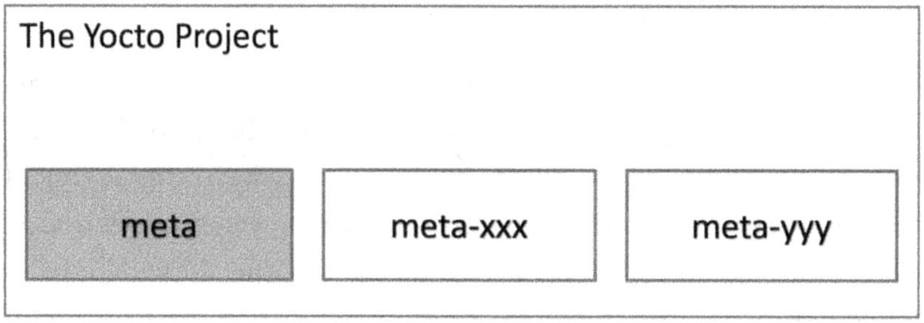

Figure 6.1 – OpenEmbedded and the Yocto Project

The box labeled **meta**, highlighted in red, represents the primary OpenEmbedded **layer**. A layer is a collection of **metadata** that defines how embedded Linux components are configured, compiled, and incorporated into the final image. Metadata consists of the following:

- **Recipe files**: Files with a `.bb` extension define how to retrieve, patch, configure, compile, and install a specific software component in the final embedded Linux image.
- **Recipe append files**: Files with a `.bbappend` extension extend or override operations defined in a recipe from another layer. Recipe append files are useful for modifying the behavior of a recipe defined in another layer that we may not have access to. We'll see the efficacy of recipe append files in a later section, when we modify an existing embedded Linux recipe and patch the Linux kernel.

- **Class files**: Files with a `.bbclass` extension contain reusable logic that can be used by multiple recipes to accomplish similar behavior.
- **Include files**: Files with a `.inc` extension contain configuration fragments that can be shared across similar recipes. Include files are useful for recipes in the same layer, whereas class files are usually used by multiple recipes across different layers.
- **Configuration files**: Files with a `.conf` extension configure global and layer-specific properties. For example, **MACHINE** and **DISTRO** are common configuration options for creating an embedded Linux image. A MACHINE or DISTRO configuration has its own file, and further specifies details of the embedded Linux image. Differentiating MACHINE and DISTRO configurations can be confusing for novices, and their differences are outlined next:
    - **MACHINE**: The MACHINE configuration defines the hardware platform of the embedded Linux system. For example, the architecture of the target CPU, the devicetree to use, and any specific kernel command-line arguments are options that can be defined in a MACHINE configuration.
    - **DISTRO**: The DISTRO configuration specifies the overall system configuration and policies. For example, the DISTRO can specify which package management system, such as RPM or DEB, will be used to install software packages. The DISTRO can also define the backend graphics system, if any, and which initialization system to use.

One of the disadvantages of using the core `meta` layer of OpenEmbedded when creating an embedded Linux image using the Yocto Project is that we need to pull in other essential layers. We would also need to incorporate the `Bitbake` binary to build our image.

Luckily for us, the Yocto Project provides a reference implementation called **Poky**. Poky serves as a starting point that we can use to build a baseline embedded Linux distribution and then customize it. It includes the core `meta` layer from OpenEmbedded, `Bitbake`, and other valuable and essential layers.

The following figure shows how Poky fits within the Yocto Project, and how we can incorporate other layers for our final custom embedded Linux image:

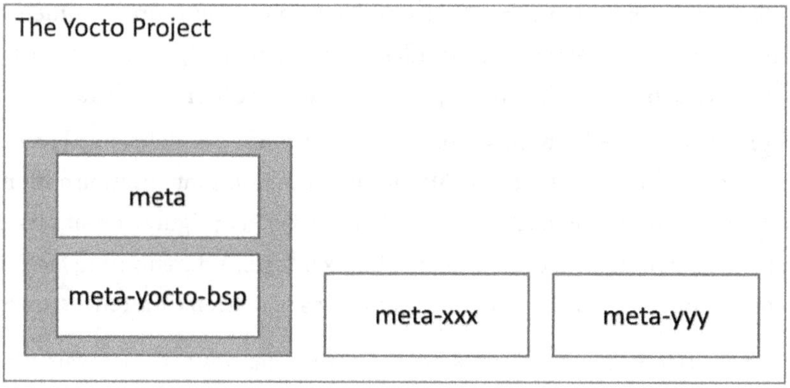

Figure 6.2 – Poky and the Yocto Project

In the preceding figure, the red box represents the Poky reference distribution. It contains the core `meta` layer of OpenEmbedded and other valuable layers, such as the `meta-yocto-bsp` layer. Similar to the previous figure, we can incorporate other layers that are important for our embedded Linux image, whether they be our own or from third parties, and build on top of the Poky reference distribution.

In the next section, we will understand how to practically use the Yocto Project to create an embedded Linux image and apply customizations. We will learn how to accomplish these tasks for a Raspberry Pi 5 and a virtual environment in QEMU.

Creating an embedded Linux image

In this section, we will learn how to create a complete embedded Linux image using the Yocto Project. We will take a deeper dive into the framework before walking through the mechanics of performing the operations.

Identifying and retrieving layers

As we learned in the previous chapter, the top-level entity in the Yocto Project is called a **layer**, with each layer containing multiple directories to manage different recipes, as shown in the following figure:

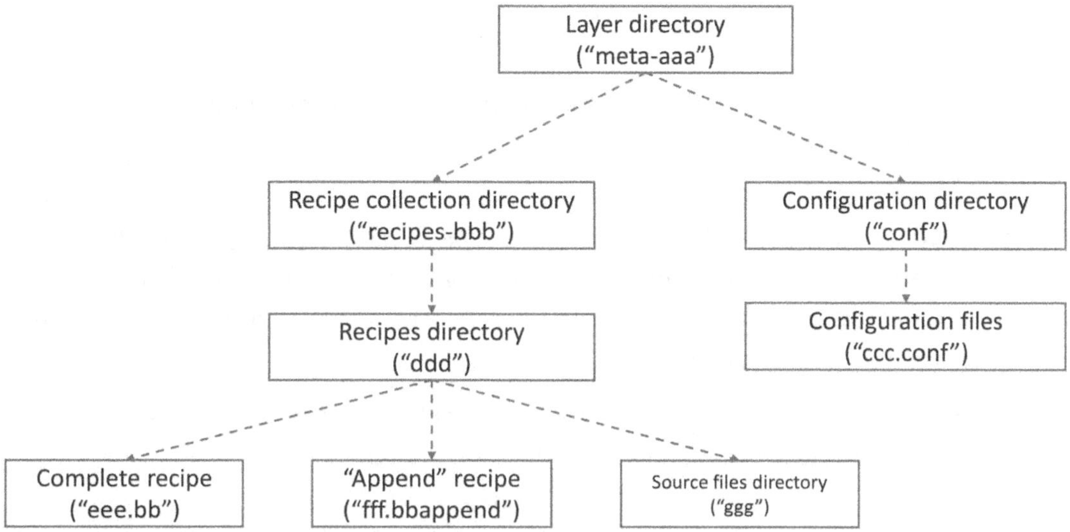

Figure 6.3 – Individual layer directory structure

If we zoom out from the preceding figure, we can see the directory structure shown here:

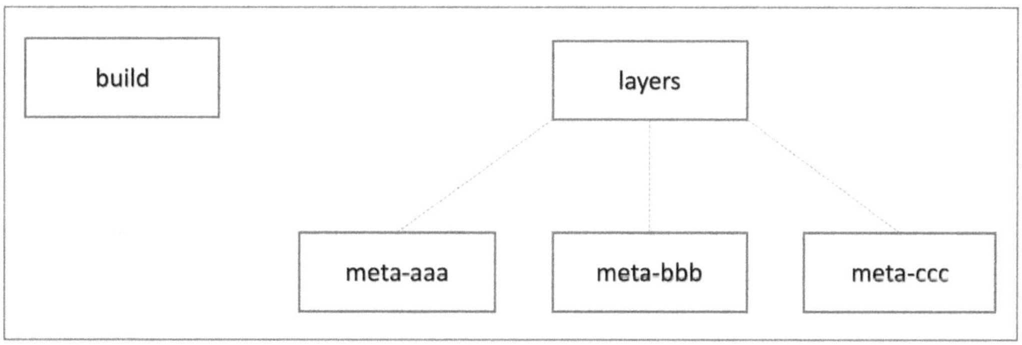

Figure 6.4 – Multiple-layer directory structure

We need to emulate the directory structure shown, which contains the following two directories:

- **build**: This directory contains the build configuration, artifacts, and temporary artifacts used to speed up subsequent builds and debug issues
- **layers**: This directory contains the layers needed to create the embedded Linux image

We can emulate this directory structure by creating the layers directories by executing the following command:

```
$ mkdir layers
```

> Important note
>
> We don't *have* to create the build directory. It will be automatically created for us in the future.

We then need to change to the `layers` directory and retrieve the necessary layers. How do we determine these necessary layers? Since we are targeting a Raspberry Pi 5, we will need to determine whether a layer exists that can generate an image for the Raspberry Pi. We can make this determination by doing the following:

1. Navigating to `https://layers.openembedded.org/layerindex/branch/master/layers/`, which is a listing of layers provided by the Yocto Project.
2. Typing `raspberrypi` in the search bar at the top, as shown in the following screenshot:

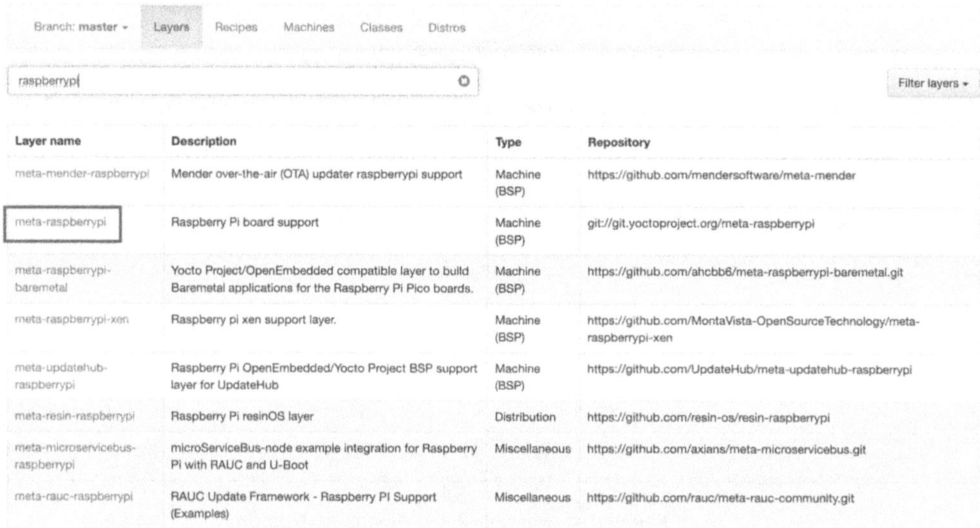

Layer name	Description	Type	Repository
meta-mender-raspberrypi	Mender over-the-air (OTA) updater raspberrypi support	Machine (BSP)	https://github.com/mendersoftware/meta-mender
meta-raspberrypi	Raspberry Pi board support	Machine (BSP)	git://git.yoctoproject.org/meta-raspberrypi
meta-raspberrypi-baremetal	Yocto Project/OpenEmbedded compatible layer to build Baremetal applications for the Raspberry Pi Pico boards.	Machine (BSP)	https://github.com/ahcbb6/meta-raspberrypi-baremetal.git
meta-raspberrypi-xen	Raspberry pi xen support layer.	Machine (BSP)	https://github.com/MontaVista-OpenSourceTechnology/meta-raspberrypi-xen
meta-updatehub-raspberrypi	Raspberry Pi OpenEmbedded/Yocto Project BSP support layer for UpdateHub	Machine (BSP)	https://github.com/UpdateHub/meta-updatehub-raspberrypi
meta-resin-raspberrypi	Raspberry Pi resinOS layer	Distribution	https://github.com/resin-os/resin-raspberrypi
meta-microservicebus-raspberrypi	microServiceBus-node example integration for Raspberry Pi with RAUC and U-Boot	Miscellaneous	https://github.com/axians/meta-microservicebus.git
meta-rauc-raspberrypi	RAUC Update Framework - Raspberry PI Support (Examples)	Miscellaneous	https://github.com/rauc/meta-rauc-community.git

Figure 6.5 – Searching for a Raspberry Pi layer

3. Clicking on **meta-raspberrypi** and taking note of the Git repo associated with this layer, as shown in the following screenshot:

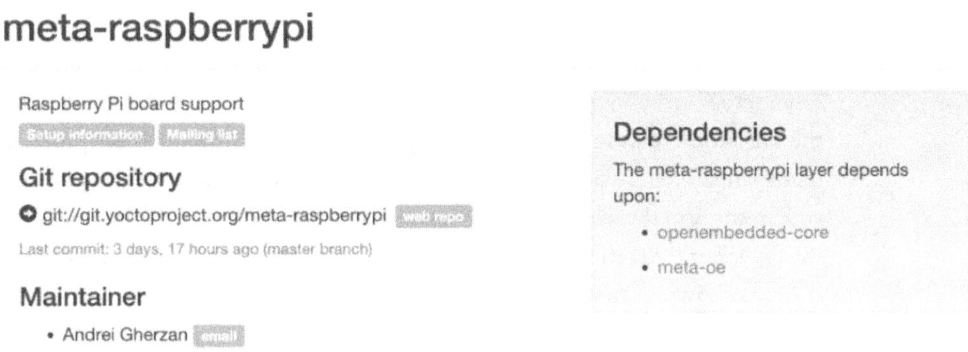

Figure 6.6 – meta-raspberrypi layer repository

We can retrieve the layer by executing the following command:

```
$ cd layers
$ git clone git://git.yoctoproject.org/meta-raspberrypi
```

If we click on the **web repo** button in *Figure 6.6*, we will see the following (as of the publication date):

Figure 6.7 – Web interface of the meta-raspberrypi layer

The preceding screenshot shows that the **kirkstone** branch added support for the Raspberry Pi 5. We can switch to this branch by executing the following command:

```
$ cd meta-raspberrypi/
$ git checkout---track remotes/origin/kirkstone
```

Important note

The Yocto Project has code names for certain releases. In this instance, we are using the **kirkstone** release of the **meta-raspberrypi** layer. Although best practice is to name the branch associated with the release, this is not always the case. Instead, we can confirm the version of the Yocto Project that the layer supports by looking at the **layer configuration file**, which is located at `meta-raspberrypi/conf/layer.conf`, as shown in the following snippet:

```
# We have a conf and classes directory, append to BBPATH
BBPATH .= ":${LAYERDIR}"

# We have a recipes directory containing .bb and .bbappend
files, add to BBFILES
BBFILES += "${LAYERDIR}/recipes*/*/*.bb \
    ${LAYERDIR}/recipes*/*/*.bbappend"

BBFILE_COLLECTIONS += "raspberrypi"
BBFILE_PATTERN_raspberrypi := "^${LAYERDIR}/"
BBFILE_PRIORITY_raspberrypi = "9"

LAYERSERIES_COMPAT_raspberrypi = "kirkstone"
LAYERDEPENDS_raspberrypi = "core"\
```

Versions of all layers within the BSP must support the same release of the Yocto Project. Thus, we must also use versions of other layers on the **kirkstone** release.

It can be beneficial to include **poky** as a layer. Poky is a reference distribution and implementation of OpenEmbedded/the Yocto Project. It includes commonly used recipes, including recipes to form baseline images. These recipes usually serve as the basis of custom image recipes. We can retrieve poky by executing the following command:

```
$ cd ../
$ git clone https://git.yoctoproject.org/poky
```

Again, we have to check out the **kirkstone** branch by executing the following command:

```
$ git checkout --track remotes/origin/kirkstone
```

We can confirm that our branch supports the kirkstone branch by inspecting the layer configuration file, which is `layers/poky/meta-poky/conf/layer.conf`, and is reproduced partially here:

```
# We have a conf and classes directory, add to BBPATH
BBPATH =. "${LAYERDIR}:"

# We have recipes-* directories, add to BBFILES
BBFILES += "${LAYERDIR}/recipes-*/*/*.bb \
    ${LAYERDIR}/recipes-*/*/*.bbappend"

BBFILE_COLLECTIONS += "yocto"
BBFILE_PATTERN_yocto = "^${LAYERDIR}/"
BBFILE_PRIORITY_yocto = "5"

LAYERSERIES_COMPAT_yocto = "kirkstone"
```

In the next section, we will learn how to create an embedded Linux image.

Setting up and creating a build

In this section, we will walk through the necessary steps to create a complete embedded Linux image. First, we will learn how to create an image for a Raspberry Pi 5, and then we will learn how to do the same for an emulated target using QEMU. Recall that QEMU is a valuable tool to learn about embedded Linux systems when hardware may not be available or accessible.

Targeting the Raspberry Pi 5

Fortunately, the Yocto Project provides a script that we can **source** and make the necessary utilities, such as `Bitbake` and its derivative utilities, available to us. We can do so by executing the following command from the base directory of the Yocto environment:

```
$ cd ../
$ source ./layers/poky/oe-init-build-env
```

Executing the preceding command will create the build directory and change us to that directory.

Important note

"Sourcing" a script (or any file) is different from executing a script. When we source a file, we apply any environment variables defined in that script in our own terminal instance. For example, if we view the definition of our **PATH** variable, we can see that a few entries have been made by sourcing the preceding script, as shown here:

```
[build]$ echo $PATH
/home/dev/src/layers/poky/scripts:/home/dev/src/layers/poky/
bitbake/bin:/usr/local/sbin:/usr/local/bin:/usr/sbin:/usr/
bin:/sbin:/bin
```

We need to now instruct the Yocto Project infrastructure of the `meta-raspberrypi` layer, since it is only aware of the layers under the poky directory; we will use the **bitbake-layers** utility to do so. We can change to the build directory and execute the following command to notify the Yocto Project infrastructure of the `meta-raspberrypi` layer:

```
$ bitbake-layers add-layer ../layers/meta-raspberrypi/
```

We can use the same utility to list the layers that the Yocto Project infrastructure is aware of by executing the following command:

```
$ bitbake-layers show-layers
NOTE: Starting bitbake server...
layer                 path                                      priority
==========================================================================
meta                  /home/dev/src/layers/poky/meta            5
meta-poky             /home/dev/src/layers/poky/meta-poky       5
meta-yocto-bsp        /home/dev/src/layers/poky/meta-yocto-bsp  5
meta-raspberrypi      /home/dev/src/layers/meta-raspberrypi     9
```

The output of the `bitbake-layers show-layers` command has the following format:

```
<layer name>        <layer path>      <layer priority>
```

Finally, we can execute the following command to create the final embedded Linux image:

```
$ MACHINE="raspberrypi5" bitbake rpi-test-image
```

The preceding command instructs the Yocto Project to use `rpi-test-image` to create an embedded Linux image for the Raspberry Pi 5 **machine**. The machine indicates a particular hardware platform for our embedded Linux image. After executing the preceding command, the `build` directory has the following contents:

- `downloads`: This directory contains all the source code and other files that Bitbake needs to create packages from recipes.
- `cache`: This directory primarily contains parsed recipe metadata. This includes information about variables, tasks, and dependencies defined in recipes. This allows Bitbake to avoid re-parsing recipes and re-evaluating dependencies, and speeds up subsequent builds.
- `sstate-cache`: This directory contains the shared state cache of the Yocto Project, which is arguably one of its important features. Bitbake uses this directory to store the results of building a particular recipe. Thus, when Bitbake needs to build the same recipe without any changes, since it may be dependent on a recipe that has changed, Bitbake extracts the artifacts stored in the shared state cache. This prevents Bitbake from having to rebuild the same recipe from scratch.
- `tmp`: This directory stores intermediate and final build artifacts. For example, the following are relevant directories within `tmp`:
    - `work`: This directory contains the build outputs for each recipe.
    - `work-shared`: This directory is used to store recipe outputs that are shared with other recipes.
    - `deploy`: This directory contains the final outputs from the build process. For example, `images/raspberrypi5/` contains the final outputs of the build process, including the Linux kernel binary, Devicetree binary, and root filesystem.
    - `conf`: This directory contains the relevant configuration that the build system uses – for example:
        - `local.conf`: This file contains all the local user configuration. Poky, the reference distribution we mentioned earlier, contains `oe-init-build-env`, a script that OpenEmbedded provides for a minimal configuration. This script creates the minimal `local.conf` file found in the `conf` directory. We can create our own configuration and set the `MACHINE` variable to `raspberrypi5` and use that for future builds. This would allow us to omit specifying `MACHINE` in future `bitbake` invocations.

- `bblayers.conf`: This file contains the layers that Bitbake will use to scan for recipes. If we open this file, we can see that it contains the `meta-raspberrypi` layer (in bold) we added using the `bitbake-layers` tool:

```
# POKY_BBLAYERS_CONF_VERSION is increased each time
build/conf/bblayers.conf
# changes incompatibly
POKY_BBLAYERS_CONF_VERSION = "2"

BBPATH = "${TOPDIR}"
BBFILES ?= ""

BBLAYERS ?= " \
  /home/dev/src/layers/poky/meta \
  /home/dev/src/layers/poky/meta-poky \
  /home/dev/src/layers/poky/meta-yocto-bsp \
  /home/dev/src/layers/meta-raspberrypi \
  "
```

After executing the preceding command, we will have an embedded Linux image that we can flash onto an SD card and boot on our Raspberry Pi 5. We will learn how to do so in detail in a subsequent section.

Targeting QEMU

We can also create an embedded Linux image designed to run in a virtualized environment using QEMU. We don't need to incorporate the `meta-raspberrypi` layer, since the Yocto Project already supports creating such an image. We can create an embedded Linux image for QEMU by executing the following command:

```
$ MACHINE=qemuarm64 bitbake core-image-minimal
```

The `core-image-minimal` embedded Linux image is a basic image that the Yocto Project can generate. It allows us to boot into an embedded Linux system with console output and a simple login prompt. Similar to the Raspberry Pi 5, we will learn how to launch the image using QEMU in a later section.

In the next section, we will learn a strategy for managing layers with the Yocto Project.

Managing layers

As we have seen, retrieving the necessary layers and ensuring they are aligned can be tedious. The previous subsection demonstrated the extensive series of operations with only two layers. The process can be further extended with many more layers, which is usually the case with a production-ready image. **Repo** is a tool created by Google to manage the different repositories in Android. We can use it to manage the different layers and eliminate most manual steps during layer setup.

Repo uses a **manifest** file to describe the required repositories. We can install the Repo tool by executing the following command (if we're running an Ubuntu-based Linux distribution):

```
$ sudo apt-get install -y repo
```

We can retrieve the baseline Repo manifest file used in this chapter by executing the following command:

```
$ repo init -u https://github.com/PacktPublishing/Embedded-Linux-
Essentials-Handbook.git -m Chapter6/base-default.xml -b main
$ repo sync
```

The first command retrieves and parses the manifest file, and the second command retrieves the repositories specified in the manifest file. The following describes the options specified in the `repo init` command:

- `-u https://github.com:PacktPublishing/Embedded-Linux-Essentials-Handbook.gitgit@github.com:PacktPublishing/Embedded-Linux-Essentials-Handbook.git`: Specifies the URL of the repository that contains the manifest file.
- `-m Chapter6/base default.xml`: Specifies the location of the repo manifest file in the repository.
- `-b main`: Instructs the repo tool to use the `main` branch in the repository to locate the manifest file.

Once we have executed the preceding commands, the `layer` directory will be present. However, we still have to add the `meta-raspberrypi` layer using the `bitbake-layers` command shown previously.

In the next section, we will also see how we can eliminate this step. In the next section, we will learn how to create a set of recipes to add a custom application to the base image in our custom layer.

Creating a custom application

In this section, we will learn how to create and add a custom application to our embedded Linux image.

First, we'll have to create a layer that contains the recipe for our custom application. We can do so by navigating to the `layers` directory and executing the following command (and remembering to source the setup script from earlier):

```
$ bitbake-layers create-layer meta-packt
```

It is important to note that the preceding command only creates our custom layer. It doesn't add it to the Yocto Project framework. We can confirm this by looking at the contents of the `bblayers.conf` file, which is located at `build/conf` and is reproduced here:

```
$ cat build/conf/bblayers.conf
# POKY_BBLAYERS_CONF_VERSION is increased each time build/conf/bblayers.
conf
# changes incompatibly
POKY_BBLAYERS_CONF_VERSION = "2"

BBPATH = "${TOPDIR}"
BBFILES ?= ""

BBLAYERS ?= " \
  /media/mab/mab_home/packt/embeddedlinux/rpi5/Embedded-Linux-Essentials-
Handbook/yocto/layers/poky/meta \
  /media/mab/mab_home/packt/embeddedlinux/rpi5/Embedded-Linux-Essentials-
Handbook/yocto/layers/poky/meta-poky \
  /media/mab/mab_home/packt/embeddedlinux/rpi5/Embedded-Linux-Essentials-
Handbook/yocto/layers/poky/meta-yocto-bsp \
  /media/mab/mab_home/packt/embeddedlinux/rpi5/Embedded-Linux-Essentials-
Handbook/yocto/layers/meta-raspberrypi \
```

We need to execute the following command to add our custom layer:

```
$ bitbake-layers add-layer ../layers/meta-packt/
```

We can confirm that the layer was added by viewing the contents of `build/conf/bblayers.conf` by executing the following command:

```
$ cat build/conf/bblayers.conf
# POKY_BBLAYERS_CONF_VERSION is increased each time build/conf/bblayers.
conf
# changes incompatibly
POKY_BBLAYERS_CONF_VERSION = "2"

BBPATH = "${TOPDIR}"
BBFILES ?= ""

BBLAYERS ?= " \
  /media/mab/mab_home/packt/embeddedlinux/rpi5/Embedded-Linux-Essentials-
Handbook/yocto/layers/poky/meta \
  /media/mab/mab_home/packt/embeddedlinux/rpi5/Embedded-Linux-Essentials-
Handbook/yocto/layers/poky/meta-poky \
  /media/mab/mab_home/packt/embeddedlinux/rpi5/Embedded-Linux-Essentials-
Handbook/yocto/layers/poky/meta-yocto-bsp \
  /media/mab/mab_home/packt/embeddedlinux/rpi5/Embedded-Linux-Essentials-
Handbook/yocto/layers/meta-raspberrypi \
  /media/mab/mab_home/packt/embeddedlinux/rpi5/Embedded-Linux-Essentials-
Handbook/yocto/layers/meta-packt \
```

Now that we have our layer, we can create a recipe that compiles a simple "Hello World" application. The following listing shows the source file:

```
#include <stdio.h>

int main(int argc, char** argv)
{
    printf("hello world\n");
    return 0;
}
```

The following listing shows the Makefile:

```
hello-world:
	${CC} -o hello-world hello-world.c -Wl,--hash-style=gnu
install:
	install -d ${DESTDIR}/usr/bin/
	install -m 0755 hello-world ${DESTDIR}/usr/bin/hello-world
```

The first Makefile target compiles our "Hello World" application. The second `install` target installs our application to the appropriate location in the final root filesystem.

We can create a `hello-world` directory in our layer under the `recipes-example` directory by executing the following command:

```
$ mkdir layers/meta-packt/recipes-example/hello-world
```

> Important note
>
> Ideally, we would want to place this directory in a more sensible directory than the recipes example (we are only using this directory because it was created when we created the layer).

This directory will contain the `hello-world` recipe. We can create another directory inside the `hello-world` directory called `hello-world`, which will contain the source file and Makefile. We can perform these operations using the following commands:

```
$ mkdir hello-world
$ cp ~/hello-world.c hello-world/
$ cp ~/Makefile hello-world
```

Thus, our directory will be as follows:

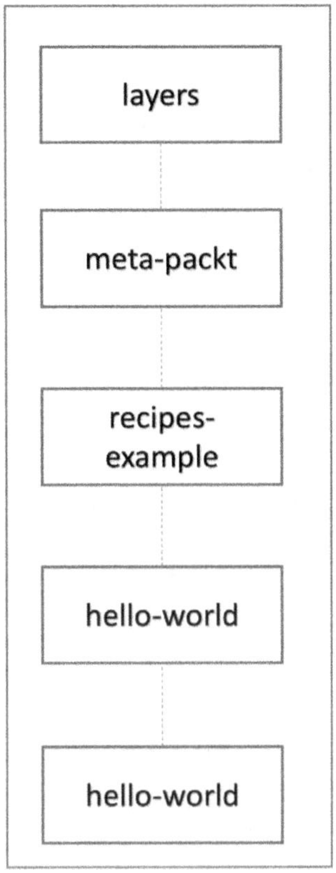

Figure 6.8 – Layer directory structure

We can use the `recipetool` command to create an initial version of the `hello-world` recipe by executing the following command in the top-level `hello-world` directory:

```
$ cd layers/meta-packt/recipes-example/hello-world
$ recipetool create -N hello-world hello-world/
```

After executing the preceding command, a recipe file called `hello-world.bb` is created as a template. We will need to make the changes in bold:

```
SRC_URI = "\
        file://hello-world.c \
        file://Makefile \
"
```

```
S = "${WORKDIR}"
# NOTE: this is a Makefile-only piece of software, so we cannot generate
much of the
# recipe automatically - you will need to examine the Makefile yourself
and ensure
# that the appropriate arguments are passed in.

do_configure () {
        # Specify any needed configure commands here
        :
}

do_compile () {
        # You will almost certainly need to add additional arguments here
        oe_runmake hello-world
}

do_install () {
        # This is a guess; additional arguments may be required
        oe_runmake install 'DESTDIR=${D}'
}

FILES_${PN} += "/usr/bin/hello-world"
```

We can confirm that our recipe is correct by building the recipe using the following command and seeing the corresponding output:

```
$ bitbake hello-world
.
.
.
NOTE: Tasks Summary: Attempted 638 tasks of which 638 didn't need to be
rerun and all succeeded.
```

In the next section, we will learn how to customize an existing recipe.

Customizing the final image

In this section, we will learn how to customize the final image, which is necessary when creating a custom application, as we did in the previous section, and we wish to add it to the final image.

Raspberry Pi 5

As mentioned previously, the final image using this version of the Yocto Project distribution for the Raspberry Pi 5 uses the `rpi-test-image` recipe to create the final embedded Linux.

When customizing an existing recipe in the Yocto recipe, we need to create an **append** recipe. An append recipe can either add or override functionality in an existing recipe.

Normally, we could use **devtool** to customize an existing recipe, but we can't do so because `rpi-test-image` is an image recipe. We have to create the append recipe manually by following these steps:

1. Create a `recipes-core/images` directory tree inside our layer by executing the following command:

```
$ mkdir -p recipes-core/images
```

2. Create a file called `rpi-test-image.bbappend` and add the following content to it:

```
IMAGE_INSTALL:append = " hello-world"
```

We can confirm that our custom application is added to the image by following these steps:

1. Build the final `rpi-test-image` by executing the following command:

```
$ MACHINE="raspberrypi5" bitbake rpi-test-image
```

2. Navigate to the `build/tmp/work/raspberrypi5-poky-linux/rpi-test-image/1.0-r0/rootfs/usr/bin/` directory and confirm the presence of the `hello-world` binary.

In a later section, we will see how we can confirm that our application was added to our final embedded Linux image.

QEMU

We can add our custom application to an embedded Linux image for QEMU in two ways. As we discussed in a previous section, we can Bitbake the `core-image-minimal` recipe to generate a minimal bootable embedded Linux image that we can use with QEMU. The first way to add our custom "Hello World" application to our QEMU-based image is similar to the technique we applied for the Raspberry Pi 5. We can create a recipe append file that adds our "Hello World" application to the `core-image-minimal` recipe, similar to the previous subsection, by following the steps outlined here:

1. Create a file called `core-image-minimal.bbappend` and add the following content to it:

   ```
   IMAGE_INSTALL:append = " hello-world"
   ```

2. Build the `core-image-minimal` recipe by executing the following command:

   ```
   $ MACHINE="qemuarm64" bitbake core-image-minimal
   ```

3. Confirm the presence of the `hello-world` binary under `build/tmp/work/qemuarm64-poky-linux/core-image-minimal/1.0-r0/rootfs/usr/bin/`.

In a later section, we will see how we can confirm that our application was added to our final embedded Linux image.

In the next section, we will learn how to customize the Linux kernel in the Yocto Project.

Customizing the Linux kernel

In this section, we will learn how to customize the Linux kernel in the Yocto Project. We are going to heavily use the `devtool` utility mentioned earlier to do the following:

- Modify the Raspberry Pi 5's Linux kernel
- Test that the Linux kernel builds successfully
- Create an append recipe with our change
- Perform the same steps for the Linux kernel that will run in QEMU

Raspberry Pi 5

We can execute the following command to create a sandbox to play around with the Linux kernel used on the Raspberry Pi 5:

```
$ MACHINE="raspberrypi5" devtool modify virtual/kernel
```

The preceding command creates a directory located at `build/workspace/sources/linux-raspberrypi/`, which is the sandbox for us to modify the existing source code and recipe associated with the Linux kernel. We can make the same modification to the Linux kernel that we made in *Chapter 2, Learning About U-Boot*. Recall that we modified `init/main.c` with the following change in bold:

```
        do_sysctl_args();

        printk("Packt embedded Linux!\n");
        if (ramdisk_execute_command) {
                ret = run_init_process(ramdisk_execute_command);
                if (!ret)
```

We can execute the following command to build the recipe with our modification to make sure that the Linux kernel still builds:

```
$ MACHINE="raspberrypi5" devtool build linux-raspberrypi
```

We then need to commit our change using the following commands:

```
$ git add .
$ git commit -m "Test change"
```

Finally, we can execute the following command to generate the append recipe and store it in our custom layer:

```
$ MACHINE="raspberrypi5" devtool update-recipe -a ../../../../layers/meta-
packt/ linux-raspberrypi
```

After executing the preceding command, we can confirm that the append recipe was generated by examining the contents of our layer using the tree command, as shown here:

```
[meta-packt]$ tree
.
├── conf
│   └── layer.conf
├── COPYING.MIT
├── README
├── recipes-core
│   └── images
│       └── rpi-test-image.bbappend
├── recipes-example
│   ├── example
│   │   └── example_0.1.bb
│   └── hello-world
│       ├── hello-world
│       │   ├── hello-world.c
│       │   └── Makefile
│       └── hello-world.bb
├── recipes-kernel
│   └── linux
│       ├── linux-raspberrypi
│       │   └── 0001-Test-modification.patch
│       └── linux-raspberrypi_6.1.bbappend
└── recipes-recipetool

11 directories, 10 files
```

Figure 6.9 – Contents of our custom layer

The `linux-raspberrypi_6.1.bbappend` file under `recipes-kernel/linux` has the following content:

```
FILESEXTRAPATHS:prepend := "${THISDIR}/${PN}:"

SRC_URI += file://0001-Test-modification.patch
```

If we examine the patch file referenced in the append recipe, we see it contains the following:

```
From: Mohammed Billoo <mab@mab-labs.com>
Date: Tue, 26 Mar 2024 12:37:00 -0400
Subject: [PATCH] Test modification
```

```
---
 init/main.c | 1 +
 1 file changed, 1 insertion(+)

diff --git a/init/main.c b/init/main.c
index fe378351e8a9..5a2c5f19ac55 100644
--- a/init/main.c
+++ b/init/main.c
@@ -1530,6 +1530,7 @@ static int __ref kernel_init(void *unused)

        do_sysctl_args();

+       printk("Packt Embedded Linux!\n");
        if (ramdisk_execute_command) {
                ret = run_init_process(ramdisk_execute_command);
                if (!ret)
```

As we can see, the patch file has our change! In the next section, we will confirm that our change manifested when we ran the modified kernel on our Raspberry Pi.

QEMU

We can perform steps similar to those in the previous section to customize the Linux kernel used in QEMU. For QEMU, we first need to execute the following command:

```
$ MACHINE="qemuarm64" devtool modify virtual/kernel
```

For QEMU, unlike the Raspberry Pi, the preceding command creates a directory located at `build/workspace/sources/linux-yocto/`.

> **Important note**
>
> Unlike the Raspberry Pi, which uses the `linux-raspberrypi` recipe for the Linux kernel, QEMU uses the `linux-yocto` recipe for the Linux kernel.

We can apply the same modification for the QEMU Linux kernel that we did for the Raspberry Pi Linux kernel. Then, we can execute the following command to build the recipe with our modification to make sure that the Linux kernel still builds:

```
$ MACHINE="qemuarm64" devtool build linux-yocto
```

We can commit the change to the QEMU Linux kernel in exactly the same way we did for the Raspberry Pi Linux kernel.

Finally, we can execute the following command to generate the append recipe and store it in our custom layer:

```
$ MACHINE=" qemuarm64" devtool update-recipe -a ../../../../layers/meta-
packt/ linux-yocto
```

In the next section, we will learn how to follow a similar process to modify **U-Boot**.

Customizing U-Boot

In this section, we will walk through the steps to customize U-Boot using the Yocto Project. Recall that U-Boot is one of the most popular bootloaders used in embedded Linux systems.

> Important note
>
> When this chapter was written, U-Boot support for the Raspberry Pi 5 was still a work in progress. Thus, this section will focus on the Raspberry Pi 4 as a valid alternative.

We will use **devtool** to perform the same steps we followed to modify the Linux kernel:

1. We can create a sandbox for us to make changes to U-Boot by executing the following command:

   ```
   $ MACHINE="raspberrypi4" devtool modify virtual/bootloader
   ```

2. A working directory is created under `build/workspace/sources/u-boot`. We can navigate to this directory and make the following change (in bold) to `common/main.c`:

   ```
           if (IS_ENABLED(CONFIG_VERSION_VARIABLE))
                   env_set("ver", version_string);  /* set version
   variable */

           printf("Packt Embedded Linux!\n");
           cli_init();

           if (IS_ENABLED(CONFIG_USE_PREBOOT))
   ```

3. We can ensure that our change still allows U-Boot to be compiled successfully by executing the following command:

```
$ MACHINE="raspberrypi4" devtool build u-boot
```

4. We can commit our change by executing the following commands:

```
$ git add .
$ git commit -m "Test change"
```

5. We can create an append recipe with our modification to U-Boot by executing the following command:

```
$ MACHINE="raspberrypi4" devtool update-recipe -a ../../../../
layers/meta-packt/ u-boot
```

We can confirm that the append recipe was created and added to our layer:

```
[meta-packt]$ tree
.
├── conf
│   └── layer.conf
├── COPYING.MIT
├── README
├── recipes-bsp
│   └── u-boot
│       ├── u-boot
│       │   └── 0001-Test-change.patch
│       └── u-boot_2022.01.bbappend
├── recipes-core
│   └── images
│       └── rpi-test-image.bbappend
├── recipes-example
│   ├── example
│   │   └── example_0.1.bb
│   └── hello-world
│       ├── hello-world
│       │   ├── hello-world.c
│       │   └── Makefile
│       └── hello-world.bb
├── recipes-kernel
│   └── linux
│       ├── linux-raspberrypi
│       │   └── 0001-Test-modification.patch
│       └── linux-raspberrypi_6.1.bbappend
└── recipes-recipetool

14 directories, 12 files
```

Figure 6.10 – Layer directory structure with U-Boot changes

As we can see from the preceding screenshot, our U-Boot append recipe was added in our layer under `recipes-bsp/u-boot`.

Validating our customizations

In this section, we will learn how to validate the customizations we made in the previous sections.

Flashing a Raspberry Pi 5

We can create and flash an embedded Linux image built using the Yocto Project for the Raspberry Pi 5 by following the steps outlined here:

1. As described in the section titled *Customizing the final image*, build the final `rpi-test-image` by executing the following command:

```
$ MACHINE="raspberrypi5" bitbake rpi-test-image
```

2. The final image is located at `build/tmp/deploy/images/raspberrypi5/rpi-test-image-raspberrypi5.wic.bz2`.
3. Plug in the SD card into a Linux PC.
4. Execute the following command to determine the device associated with the SD card (and enter the `sudo` password if prompted):

```
$ sudo dmesg -w
```

5. Note the drive letter associated with the SD card, as shown in the following screenshot:

```
[4747440.162891] usb-storage 5-2.4.4:1.0: USB Mass Storage device
detected
[4747440.163045] scsi host13: usb-storage 5-2.4.4:1.0
[4747441.168476] scsi 13:0:0:0: Direct-Access  Mass  Storage Device
1.00 PQ: 0 ANSI: 0 CCS
[4747441.168919] sd 13:0:0:0: Attached scsi generic sg1 type 0
[4747441.489023] sd 13:0:0:0: [sdb] 124735488 512-byte logical blocks:
[4747441.489023] sd 13:0:0:0: (63.9 GB/59.5 GiB)
[4747441.489143] sd 13:0:0:0: [sdb] Write Protect is off
[4747441.489145] sd 13:0:0:0: [sdb] Write Protect is off
[4747441.489145] sd 13:0:0:0: [sdb] Mode Sense: 03 00 00 00
[4747441.489244] sd 13:0:0:0: [sdb] No Caching mode page found
[4747441.489245] sd 13:0:0:0: [sdb]
[4747441.489245] sd 13:0:0:0: [sdb] Assuming drive cache: write through
[4747441.499245] sd 13:0:0:0: [sdb]
[4747441.490900] sdb: sdb1 sdb2
[4747441.490997] sd 13:0:0:0:[sdb] Attached SCSI removable disk
```

Figure 6.11 – Identifying the SD card

6. Execute the following command to write the image to the SD card (making sure to replace `/dev/sdX` with the appropriate drive associated with the SD card):

```
$ bzcat tmp/deploy/images/raspberrypi5/rpi-test-image-raspberrypi5.
wic.bz2 | sudo dd status=progress of=/dev/sdX
```

We will learn how to interact with the Raspberry Pi 5 using a console interface in the next subsection.

Accessing a console interface

We can follow these steps to get a console interface to the Raspberry Pi 5:

1. Plug in the SD card to the bottom of the Raspberry Pi 5, as shown in the following figure:

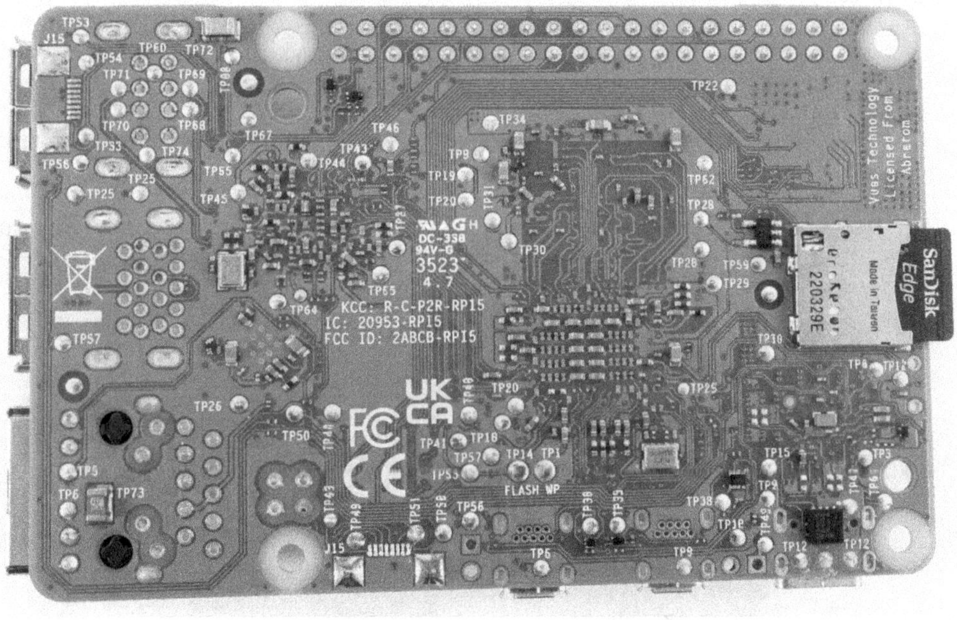

Figure 6.12 – Plugging in the SD card to the Raspberry Pi 5

2. Plug in the ribbon cable to the side marked **U** on the Raspberry Pi debug probe (`https://www.raspberrypi.com/products/debug-probe/`) and plug in a micro-USB cable to the corresponding port on the debug probe, as shown here:

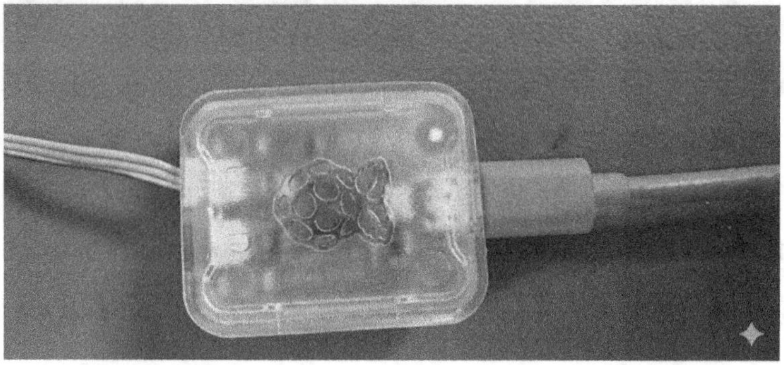

Figure 6.13 – Appropriate connections to Raspberry Pi debug probe

3. Plug in the other side of the micro-USB cable to the development PC.
4. Open a terminal application on the development PC and connect to the enumerated COM port with a baud of 115,200, 8 data bits, no flow control, and 1 start bit.
5. Plug in a USB-C power cable (with +5 V input voltage) to the corresponding port of the Raspberry Pi 5. All the connections to the Raspberry Pi 5 are shown here:

Figure 6.14 – Necessary Raspberry Pi 5 connections

6. The terminal application should show the output in the following figure (note the reference to **Poky (Yocto Project Reference Distro)** and **raspberrypi5**):

```
[   10.099143] Bluetooth: BNEP (Ethernet Emulation) ver 1.3
[   10.104587] Bluetooth: BNEP filters: protocol multicast
[   10.109958] Bluetooth: BNEP socket layer initialized
[   10.117084] Bluetooth: MGMT ver 1.22
[   10.124431] NET: Registered PF_ALG protocol family
[   10.159539] nfc: nfc_init: NFC Core ver 0.1
[   10.163926] NET: Registered PF_NFC protocol family
[   10.184893] Bluetooth: RFCOMM TTY layer initialized
[   10.189815] Bluetooth: RFCOMM socket layer initialized
[   10.195107] Bluetooth: RFCOMM ver 1.11

Poky (Yocto Project Reference Distro) 4.0.17 raspberrypi5 /dev/ttyAMA10

raspberrypi5 login: root
root@raspberrypi5:~# 
```

Figure 6.15 – Console output on Raspberry Pi 5

We will see how to verify the custom application we created earlier in the next subsection.

Custom application verification

We can confirm that our custom application is included in the embedded Linux image by following these steps:

1. Ensure that the `layers/meta-packt/recipes-core/images/rpi-test-image.bbappend` file is present and has the following line:

```
IMAGE_INSTALL:append = " hello-world"
```

2. Build the embedded Linux and flash it to the SD card using the steps outlined in the previous section.
3. Plug the SD card into the Raspberry Pi, connect the debug probe, and apply power to the Raspberry Pi.
4. Ensure that a console is available on the Raspberry Pi.
5. Execute the following command with the corresponding output to confirm the presence of the *Hello World* application, represented by the `hello-world` binary:

```
root@raspberrypi5:~# ls -l /usr/bin/ | grep hello
-rwxr-xr-x    1 root     root          6224 Mar  9 12:34 hello-world
```

6. Execute the following command to run the `Hello World` application with the corresponding output:

```
root@raspberrypi5:~# hello-world
hello world
```

We will learn how to verify our Linux kernel customization in the next subsection.

Linux kernel customization verification

We can verify that our Linux kernel customization from earlier was successful by following these steps:

1. Build the embedded Linux image using the Yocto Project, flash it on the SD card, plug the SD card into the Raspberry Pi 5, and apply power to the Raspberry Pi 5.
2. Confirm that a console interface to the Raspberry Pi 5 is present.
3. Execute the following command, which filters the kernel logs for the `Packt Embedded Linux` string, and ensure the corresponding output to confirm the customization to the Linux kernel:

```
root@raspberrypi5:~# dmesg | grep Packt
[    2.640392] Packt Embedded Linux
root@raspberrypi5:~#
```

Summary

While the previous chapter helped us understand the motivation behind creating a complete embedded Linux image and how frameworks can help us create these images, this chapter walked us through the mechanics when using the Yocto Project.

In this chapter, we learned how to create an embedded Linux image using the Yocto Project. We learned about the overall process and how to perform tasks that are common when developing a specific product. For example, we learned how to create custom applications and add them to our embedded Linux system using the Yocto Project. Then, we learned about the steps needed to customize the Linux kernel and U-Boot.

In the next chapter, we will learn how to perform similar operations using Buildroot, the other popular framework used to create embedded Linux images.

Get this book's PDF version and more

Scan the QR code (or go to `packtpub.com/unlock`). Search for this book by name, confirm the edition, and then follow the steps on the page.

UNLOCK NOW

Note: Keep your invoice handy. Purchases made directly from Packt don't require an invoice.

7

Building an Image Using Buildroot

Chapter 5, *Exploring Frameworks to Build an Image*, provided an overview of The Yocto Project and Buildroot, two popular frameworks for creating embedded Linux images.

This chapter will focus on Buildroot, expanding on the overview from *Chapter 5* by diving into the framework's practical details. We will learn about the mechanics of creating an embedded Linux image, set up our environment, execute the required commands, and implement common customizations for our system.

We are going to cover the following main topics in this chapter:

- Creating an embedded Linux image
- Creating a custom application
- Customizing the final image
- Customizing the Linux kernel
- Customizing U Boot
- Validating our customizations

Technical requirements

You should be comfortable with executing commands on a terminal and navigating and editing text files in an editor. You can follow along with the samples in this chapter by referring to the GitHub repository located here: `https://github.com/PacktPublishing/Embedded-Linux-Essentials-Handbook/tree/main/Chapter7`.

Creating an embedded Linux image

We will learn how to create a complete embedded Linux image using Buildroot and take a deeper dive into the framework before walking through the mechanics of performing the operations.

> Important note
>
> At the time of writing this chapter, Buildroot doesn't officially support the Raspberry Pi 5. Although variants, or "forks," of Buildroot claim to support the Raspberry Pi 5, they are in the context of other applications. Thus, for this chapter, we decided to focus on the Raspberry Pi 4 to give you a thorough understanding of Buildroot without worrying about hardware support. However, at the end of the first section, we use a product that supports the Raspberry Pi 5 and use Buildroot to create an embedded Linux image using Buildroot for the Raspberry Pi 5. The lessons learned from this exercise help us expand our knowledge of Buildroot and understand how to customize it.

Raspberry Pi 4

In this section, we will learn the mechanics of creating a standard embedded Linux image for the Raspberry Pi 4 using Buildroot.

As we learned in *Chapter 5, Exploring Frameworks to Build an Image*, Buildroot's infrastructure is much simpler than the infrastructure of The Yocto Project. Buildroot is self-contained and has everything needed to build a bootable minimal image. One strategy to include Buildroot in a larger repo is to include it as a **Git submodule**. A Git submodule is a Fit repository contained inside another repository. We've already added Buildroot as a Git submodule to the book's overall repository on GitHub. We can retrieve Buildroot by executing the following commands:

```
$ git clone https://github.com/PacktPublishing/Embedded-Linux-Essentials-
Handbook.git
$ cd Embedded-Linux-Essentials-Handbook
$ git submodule update --init Chapter7/buildroot
```

We can create a complete Linux image for the Raspberry Pi 4 by following these steps:

1. Navigate to the Buildroot directory by executing the command below:

   ```
   $ cd Chapter7/buildroot
   ```

2. Execute the following command to configure Buildroot for the Raspberry Pi 4:

```
$ make raspberrypi4_defconfig
```

3. Create the final image by executing the following command:

```
$ make all
```

After waiting some time, the final image will be ready and located at `output/images/sdcard.img`.

Raspberry Pi 5

As mentioned earlier, when writing this chapter, the official version of Buildroot (located here: `https://github.com/buildroot/buildroot`) does not support the Raspberry Pi 5. However, Home Assistant (`https://www.home-assistant.io/`) can be used, which is an open source home automation ecosystem and framework that is community-driven. Home Assistant emphasizes local control and privacy. The following steps outline the process of building the embedded Linux operating system for the Raspberry Pi 5:

1. We can clone the repository for the Home Assistant embedded Linux operating system, including the Buildroot submodule, by executing the following command:

```
$ git clone --recurse-submodules https://github.com/home-assistant/
operating-system.git
```

2. Home Assistant has a Docker container to facilitate the build process. The embedded Linux image can be built for the Raspberry Pi 5 by executing the following command:

```
$ sudo scripts/enter.sh make rpi5_64
```

3. The final image is located at `output/images/haos_rpi5-64-12.3.dev0.img.xz`.
4. Plug an SD card into your Linux development PC, and identify the drive that it is enumerated as. For example, the SD card might appear as `/dev/mmcblk0`.
5. This file can be extracted into a `.img` file, which can be written to an SD card, using the following command:

```
$ xz -decompress output/images/haos_rpi5-64-12.3.dev0.img.xz | sudo
dd of=/dev/mmcblk0
```

Home Assistant achieves this by using the `br2-external` mechanism in Buildroot. The `br2-external` mechanism provides a convenient way to customize project-specific configuration files and packages outside the official Buildroot tree. This can be achieved by setting the `BR2_EXTERNAL` environment variable.

Specifically, in the case of Home Assistant, we see that the BUILDROOT_EXTERNAL environment variable, which points to the buildroot-external directory, is set at the top-level Makefile, which is reproduced in the following snippet:

```
BUILDDIR:=$(shell pwd)

BUILDROOT=$(BUILDDIR)/buildroot
BUILDROOT_EXTERNAL=$(BUILDDIR)/buildroot-external
```

Subsequently, we see that each of the make targets specifies the BR2_EXTERNAL environment variable to the BUILDROOT_EXTERNAL environment variable, as shown in the following snippet:

```
all: $(TARGETS)

savedefconfig:
	@echo "config $*"
	$(MAKE) -C $(BUILDROOT) O=$(O) BR2_EXTERNAL=$(BUILDROOT_EXTERNAL)
"savedefconfig"

$(TARGETS_CONFIG): %-config:
	@echo "config $*"
	$(MAKE) -C $(BUILDROOT) O=$(O) BR2_EXTERNAL=$(BUILDROOT_EXTERNAL)
"$*_defconfig"

$(TARGETS): %: %-config
	@echo "build $@"
	$(MAKE) -C $(BUILDROOT) O=$(O) BR2_EXTERNAL=$(BUILDROOT_EXTERNAL)

	# Do not clean when building for one target
ifneq ($(words $(filter $(TARGETS),$(MAKECMDGOALS))), 1)
	@echo "clean $@"
	$(MAKE) -C $(BUILDROOT) O=$(O) BR2_EXTERNAL=$(BUILDROOT_EXTERNAL)
clean
endif
```

As specified in the relevant section of the Buildroot user manual (`https://buildroot.org/downloads/manual/customize-outside-br.txt`), a `br2-external` tree must contain at least the following three files:

- `external.desc`: This file provides a human-readable description of the external tree. We can see that this file, which is reproduced next, in the Home Assistant external tree, is brief and describes Home Assistant:

```
name: HASSOS
desc: HassOS Buildroot tree
```

- `external.mk`: This file adds custom package recipes that are visible and can be invoked by the official Buildroot tree. As shown in the following snippet, this file adds all of the recipes in the external tree and customizes the Buildroot customization:

```
include $(sort $(wildcard $(BR2_EXTERNAL_HASSOS_PATH)/package/*/*.
mk))

.PHONY: linux-check-dotconfig
linux-check-dotconfig: linux-check-configuration-done
        CC=$(TARGET_CC) LD=$(TARGET_LD) srctree=$(LINUX_SRCDIR) \
        ARCH=$(if $(BR2_x86_64),x86,$(if $(BR2_
aarch64),arm64,$(ARCH))) \
        SRCARCH=$(if $(BR2_x86_64),x86,$(if $(BR2_
aarch64),arm64,$(ARCH))) \
         $(BR2_EXTERNAL_HASSOS_PATH)/scripts/check-dotconfig.py \
                $(BR2_CHECK_DOTCONFIG_OPTS) \
                --src-kconfig $(LINUX_SRCDIR)Kconfig \
                --actual-config $(LINUX_SRCDIR).config \
                $(shell echo $(BR2_LINUX_KERNEL_CUSTOM_CONFIG_FILE)
$(BR2_LINUX_KERNEL_CONFIG_FRAGMENT_FILES))
```

- `Config.in`: This file references other configuration files inside the external tree, allowing Buildroot to add additional packages provided by the external tree. For example, the following snippet shows that the external buildroot tree provided by Home Assistant adds support for the RTL8723 Bluetooth chipset:

```
source "$BR2_EXTERNAL_HASSOS_PATH/package/bluetooth-rtl8723/Config.
in"
```

If we open package/bluetooth-rtl8723/Config.in, we see the following information, which describes the bluetooth-rtl8723 package:

```
config BR2_PACKAGE_BLUETOOTH_RTL8723
        bool "bluetooth rtl8723"
        depends on BR2_PACKAGE_BLUEZ5_UTILS_CLIENT
        help
          Install bluetooth for rtl8723.
```

We can see for ourselves that this feature is part of the official Buildroot tree by following these steps:

1. Launch the Docker container provided by the Home Assistant source by executing the following command:

```
$ sudo scripts/enter.sh
```

2. Set the BR2_EXTERNAL environment variable to the buildroot-external directory by executing the following commands:

```
/build# cd buildroot-external
/build/buildroot-external# export BR2_EXTERNAL=`pwd`
```

3. Instruct Buildroot to use the rpi5_64 configuration offered by Home Assistant's external Buildroot tree by executing the following commands:

```
/build/buildroot-external# cd ../buildroot
/build/buildroot# make rpi5_64_defconfig
```

4. Launch Buildroot's interactive configuration menu by executing the following command:

```
#/build/buildroot# make menuconfig
```

The following menu should appear after executing the preceding command:

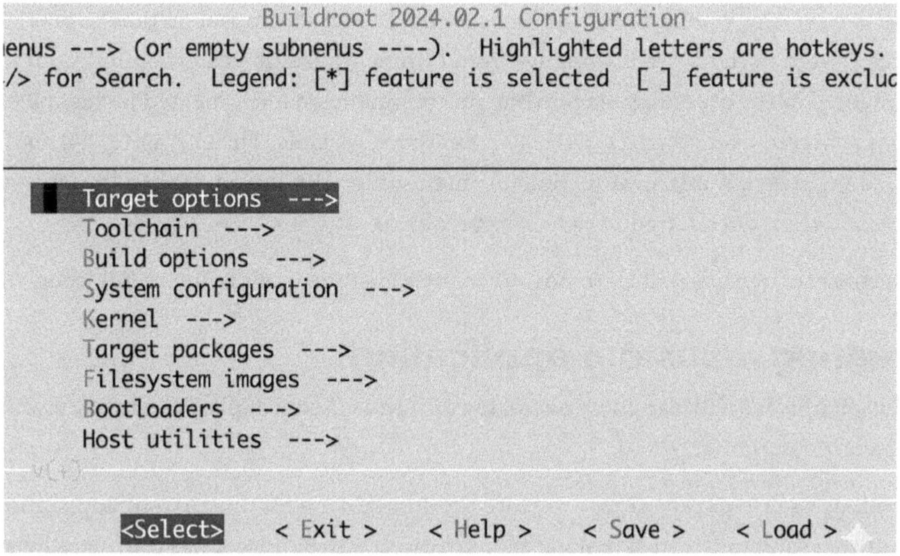

Figure 7.1 – Buildroot configuration menu with Home Assistant's external tree

5. Hit the / key and type **BLUETOOTH** in the menu that appears, as shown in the following screenshot:

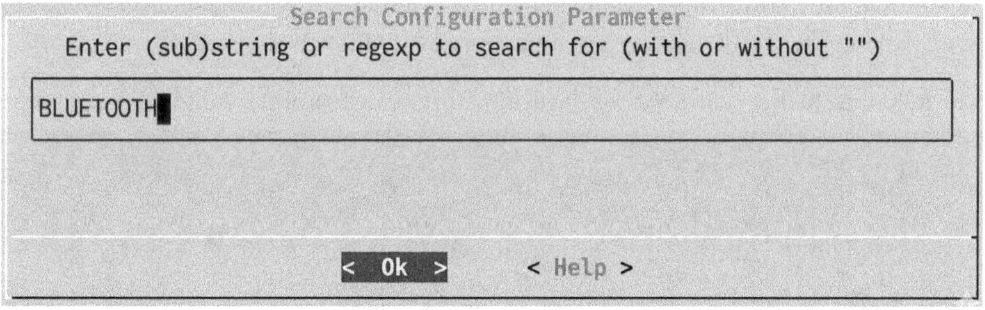

Figure 7.2 – Searching for BLUETOOTH in Buildroot

6. Hit *Enter*, and the following should appear:

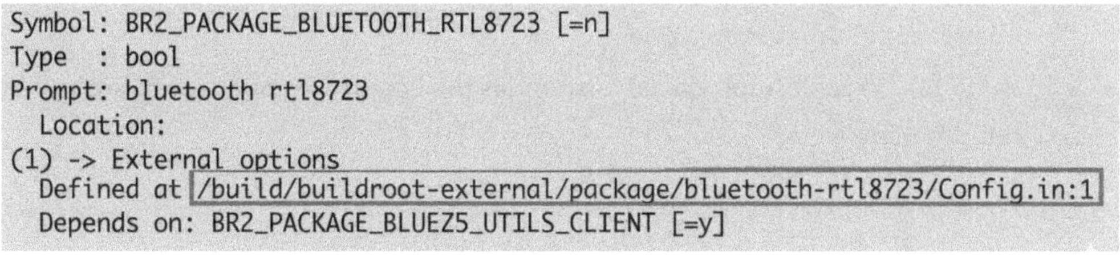

Figure 7.3 – RTL8723 Bluetooth chipset referred to by Home Assistant's external tree

As we can see, this configuration option is for the Bluetooth chipset on the Raspberry Pi 5, which we referred to in the overall configuration of Home Assistant's external Buildroot tree. Also, as highlighted in the preceding screenshot, its configuration file is located inside the external tree. This is achieved using the `BR2_EXTERNAL` Buildroot variable. The `BR2_EXTERNAL` variable can be used to augment any missing functionality in the official Buildroot tree or add our customizations. These additions are referred to as `br2-external` trees.

In the next section, we will learn how to create a custom application in Buildroot.

Creating a custom application

In this section, we will learn how to create and add a custom application to our embedded Linux image using Buildroot.

We will use a `br2-external` tree to store the source code for our custom application. Using an out-of-tree source instead of making changes directly to Buildroot has the following advantages:

- We don't have to fork Buildroot. If we were to include our custom application inside the main Buildroot source tree, we would have to fork Buildroot and incorporate any updates to Buildroot into our fork.
- Similarly, we can operate independently of Buildroot. We can remain focused on just our changes most of the time and only update Buildroot as needed.

The following listing shows the top-level directory structure of our Buildroot configuration:

```
[Chapter7]$ ls -l
total 12
drwxrwxr-x 16 mab mab    4096 Apr 20  2024 buildroot
drwxrwxr-x  5 mab mab    4096 Apr  8  2024 external
-rw-rw-r--  1 mab mab     261 Apr  8  2024 Makefile
```

Each directory and file shown in the preceding figure is described next:

- `buildroot`: This directory, stored as a Git submodule in our repository, contains the upstream Buildroot source tree
- `Makefile`: This file, reproduced next, hides the detailed steps to configure and build our Buildroot image:

```
config:
        make -C buildroot BR2_EXTERNAL=`pwd`/external
raspberrypi4_64_defconfig
```

```
elehbr:
	make -C buildroot BR2_EXTERNAL=`pwd`/external elehbr

show-info:
	make -C buildroot BR2_EXTERNAL=`pwd`/external show-info

all:
	make -C buildroot BR2_EXTERNAL=`pwd`/external all
```

Instead, we can invoke the following commands from the top level of this chapter's repository:

- `make config`: This command instructs Buildroot to use the Raspberry Pi 4 configuration. The Makefile specifies the `BR2_EXTERNAL` variable to inform Buildroot of our external tree.
- `make elehbr`: This command instructs Buildroot only to compile our custom `elehbr` application. The application's name is derived from the title of the book and Buildroot: Embedded **L**inux **E**ssentials **H**andbook **B**uild**r**oot. This application prints `Hello Embedded Linux World` to standard out. We will review the implementation of the application in a later bullet point.
- `make show-info`: This command instructs Buildroot to show all the packages enabled in the Buildroot build.
- `make all`: This command instructs Buildroot to build our final embedded Linux image for the Raspberry Pi 4.

- `external`: This directory contains our external Buildroot tree.

The following listing shows the structure of the `external` directory:

```
[Chapter7]$ tree external
external
├── Config.in
├── external.desc
├── external.mk
├── package
│   └── elehbr
│       ├── Config.in
```

```
|       ├── elehbr.mk
|       └── src
|           ├── eleh_br.c
|           └── Makefile
```

- `Config.in`: This file contains references to the underlying recipes that Buildroot ultimately needs to be aware of. The content of this file, shown next, references the configuration file in the package directory, which contains all of our custom applications and configurations. The `$BR2_EXTERNAL_ELEHBR_PATH` variable is defined by Buildroot using the `BR2_EXTERNAL` variable that we have specified:

```
source "$BR2_EXTERNAL_ELEHBR_PATH/package/elehbr/Config.in"
```

- `external.desc`: This file, shown next, contains a description of our external Buildroot tree:

```
name: ELEHBR
desc: Buildroot examples for Embedded Linux Essentials Handbook
```

- `external.mk`: This file, reproduced next, references all of the Makefiles in our custom applications and configurations for inclusion in Buildroot:

```
include $(sort $(wildcard $(BR2_EXTERNAL_ELEHBR_PATH)/package/*/*.
mk))
```

- `package`: This directory contains all our Buildroot customizations beyond any custom, compiled applications. This may include patches, scripts, and configurations.
- `elehbr`: This directory contains the necessary files to build our custom application:
    - `Config.in`: This file contains the configuration settings for our custom application. As shown, this file defines the following:
        - A configuration option for our custom application, which will be visible in Buildroot's configuration UI
        - The type of configuration option, which is a Boolean in this case, since we want to enable or disable whether our custom application gets built
        - A string, which describes additional information about our custom application, which will also be visible from Buildroot's configuration UI

- `eleh-br.mk`: This file, shown next, informs Buildroot about certain details about our application, including instructions on how to build our custom application:

```
##############################################################
############
#
# eleh-br package
#
##############################################################
############

ELEHBR_VERSION = 1.0
ELEHBR_SITE = package/elehbr/src
ELEHBR_SITE_METHOD = local

define ELEHBR_BUILD_CMDS
    $(MAKE) CC="$(TARGET_CC)" LD="$(TARGET_LD)" -C $(@D)
endef

define ELEHBR_INSTALL_TARGET_CMDS
    $(INSTALL) -D -m 0755 $(@D)/eleh-br  $(TARGET_DIR)/usr/
bin
endef

$(eval $(generic-package))
```

The variables specified in the preceding file are described here:

- `ELEHBR_VERSION`: This variable contains the versioning information associated with our custom application.
- `ELEHBR_SITE`: This variable contains the location of the source code for our custom application.
- `ELEHBR_SITE_METHOD`: This variable informs Buildroot how to retrieve the source code for our custom application. The `local` option informs Buildroot that the source code is located on the relative path pointed to by the `ELEHBR_SITE` variable.

    - `ELEHBR_BUILD_CMDS`: This variable informs Buildroot how to compile our application. In this instance, we've instructed Buildroot to use `make`.
    - `ELEHBR_INSTALL_TARGET_CMDS`: This variable informs Buildroot how to install the final application to our final embedded Linux image.
- `src`: This directory contains our application's source code:
    - `eleh_br.c`: This file, which is reproduced next, contains the source code of our simple `Hello World` application:

```
#include <stdio.h>

int main(void)
{
        printf("Hello Embedded Linux World!\n");
        return 0;
}
```

    - `Makefile`: This file, reproduced next, contains the instructions used by Buildroot to compile our application:

```
.PHONY: clean
.PHONY: eleh-br

eleh-br: eleh_br.c
        $(CC) -o $@ $^

clean:
        rm eleh-br
```

To confirm that Buildroot can detect our custom application, we can perform the following steps:

1. From the top-level location of this chapter's repository, execute the following command to configure Buildroot for the Raspberry Pi 4:

```
$ make config
```

2. Execute the following command to enter Buildroot's configuration menu:

```
$ make -C buildroot menuconfig
```

The following window should appear:

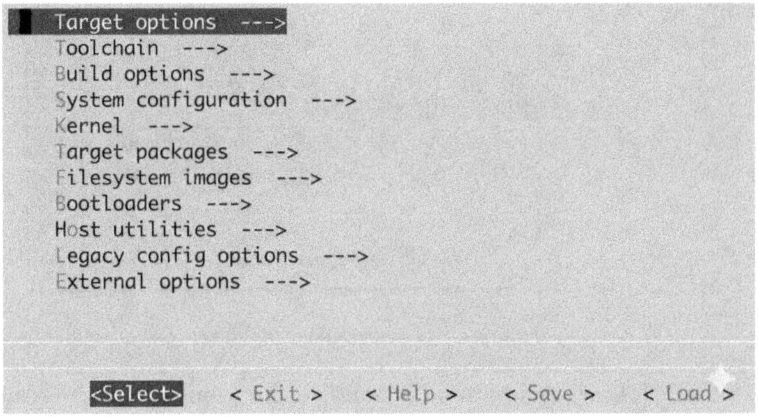

Figure 7.4 – Buildroot's configuration menu

3. In the resulting window, hit the / key on your keyboard, and type `elehbr` in the resulting dialog box. The following search results should appear:

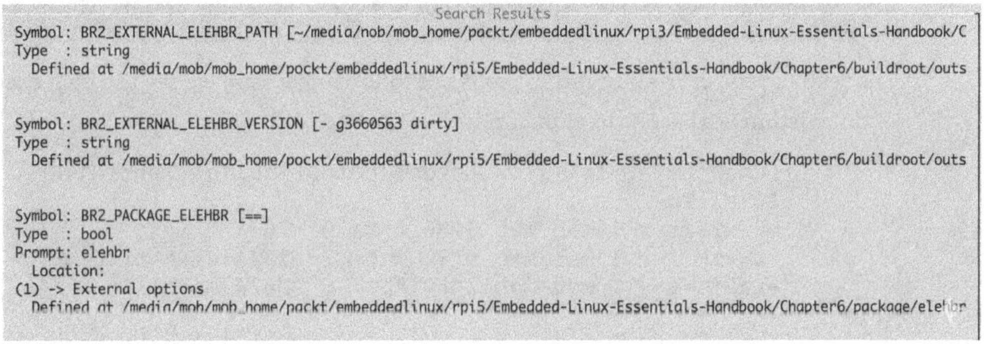

Figure 7.5 – Our custom application in Buildroot

4. Hit the *1* key on your keyboard, and hit the spacebar key in the resulting window:

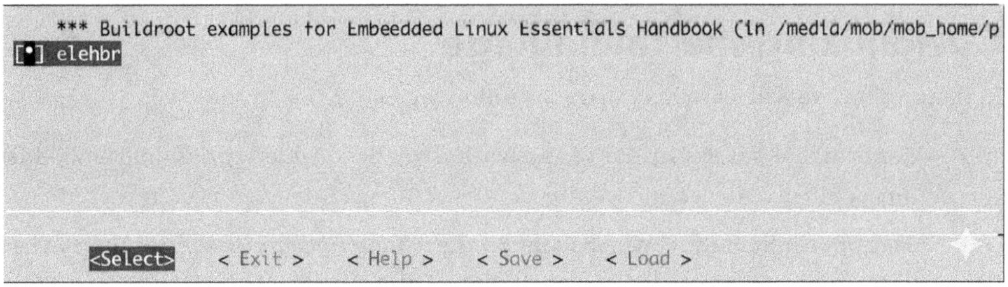

Figure 7.6 – Selecting our custom application in Buildroot

5. Hit the *Esc* key a few times, and then select **Yes** and hit the *Enter* key when the following window appears:

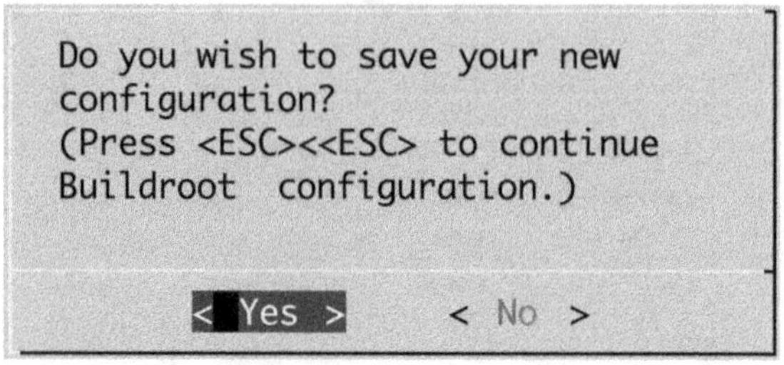

Figure 7.7 – Finalizing our Buildroot configuration

6. Execute the following command to build our final embedded Linux image:

```
$ make elehbr
```

We can confirm that our custom application was indeed compiled by executing the following command:

```
$ ls -l buildroot/output/build/elehbr-1.0/
```

The result of the preceding command is the following, where we see the final executable of our custom `Hello World` application:

```
[Chapter7]$ ls -l buildroot/output/build/elehbr-1.0/
total 20
-rwxr-xr-x 1 mab mab 8936 Apr 20  2024 elehbr
-rw-r--r-- 1 mab mab   92 Apr  8  2024 eleh_br.c
-rw-r--r-- 1 mab mab   69 Apr  8  2024 Makefile
```

Figure 7.8 – Confirming the compilation of our custom Buildroot application

In the next section, we will learn how to customize the final image by adding our custom application.

Customizing the final image

In this section, we will learn how to do the following:

- Confirm that our `Hello World` application has been added to our final embedded Linux image
- Save our configuration, which includes the default options for the Raspberry Pi 4 and our `Hello World` application
- Apply our saved configuration to a clean checkout of our entire Buildroot configuration

We can confirm that our `Hello World` application has been added to our final image by doing the following:

1. Build the entire Buildroot embedded Linux image by executing the following command:

   ```
   $ make all
   ```

2. Create a directory called `rfs` in the current working directory and mount the Buildroot root filesystem to this directory by executing the following commands:

   ```
   $ mkdir rfs
   $ sudo mount -o loop buildroot/output/images/rootfs.ext4 rfs
   ```

3. Use the `ls` and `file` commands to confirm the existence of the `elehbr` executable in the root filesystem by executing the following commands with the corresponding results:

   ```
   [Chapter7]$ ls rfs/usr/bin/elehbr
   rfs/usr/bin/elehbr
   [Chapter7]$ file rfs/usr/bin/elehbr
   rfs/usr/bin/elehbr: ELF 64-bit LSB pie executable, ARM aarch64,
   version 1 (SYSV), dynamically linked, interpreter /lib/ld-linux-
   aarch64.so.1, for GNU/Linux 6.1.0, stripped
   ```

We can save the final configuration of our embedded Linux image, which contains the default configuration for the Raspberry Pi 4 and also includes our custom application, by executing the following command:

```
$ make -C buildroot/ savedefconfig BR2_DEFCONFIG=../external/configs/
elehbr_defconfig
```

> Important note
>
> Since this file has already been checked into this chapter's repository, it is unnecessary to check it in again. However, if this were the first time we were saving the configuration, we would want to check in the configuration for reuse later (as we will see in the next step).

We can see that the `elehbr_defconfig` file has been created in the `external/configs` directory:

```
[Chapter7]$ ls external/configs/
elehbr_defconfig
```

We can use our saved configuration in future builds without going through the manual process of enabling our Hello World application via the ELEHBR configuration option by executing the following command:

```
$ make -C buildroot BR2_EXTERNAL=`pwd`/external elehbr_defconfig
```

We can confirm that our custom application has been included in the Buildroot configuration by opening buildroot/.config and confirming the existence of the following lines:

```
BR2_EXTERNAL_NAMES="ELEHBR"
BR2_EXTERNAL_ELEHBR_PATH="/media/mab/mab_home/packt/embeddedlinux/rpi5/
Embedded-Linux-Essentials-Handbook/Chapter7/external"
BR2_EXTERNAL_ELEHBR_VERSION="-g51152e3-dirty"
.
.
.
BR2_PACKAGE_ELEHBR=y
```

We can follow the steps outlined earlier to build our embedded Linux image and confirm the presence of our custom application.

> Important note
>
> Saving a configuration to a custom defconfig and then using the custom configuration as we did previously for future builds is a best practice for modifying a vendor-provided Buildroot configuration to use with our custom hardware or system.

In the next section, we will learn how to modify the Linux kernel in Buildroot.

Customizing the Linux kernel

In this section, we will learn how to customize the Linux kernel using Buildroot. We will use quilt, which is a tool to create and manage patches.

> Important note
>
> Buildroot downloads and extracts the source code for the Linux kernel on the Raspberry Pi as a **tarball**, which is a compressed collection of source files. This is why we have opted to use `quilt` instead of using the Git workflow demonstrated in *Chapter 6, Building an Image Using the Yocto Project*, to manage patches. On an Ubuntu-based Linux distribution, `quilt` can be installed by executing the following command:
>
> ```
> $ sudo apt-get install quilt
> ```

The following steps outline this procedure:

1. Retrieve and build the Linux kernel for the Raspberry Pi 4 using Buildroot by executing the following command:

   ```
   $ make -C buildroot linux
   ```

2. Navigate to the `buildroot/output/build/linux-custom` directory.
3. Execute the following command to create a directory that will contain our patch:

   ```
   $ mkdir patches
   ```

4. Execute the following command to start a patch series using `quilt`:

   ```
   $ quilt new linux-mab.patch
   ```

5. Execute the following command to edit `init/main.c` in the Linux kernel:

   ```
   $ quilt edit init/main.c
   ```

6. Make the same modification to the Linux kernel that we made in *Chapter 3, Navigating the Linux Kernel*. Recall that we modified `init/main.c` with the following change highlighted in bold:

   ```
           printk("Packg Embedded Linux\n");
           do_sysctl_args();

           if (ramdisk_execute_command) {
                   ret = run_init_process(ramdisk_execute_command);
                   if (!ret)
   ```

7. Execute the following command to finalize our patch file:

```
$ quilt refresh
```

There should be a patch file located at `patches/linux-mab.patch`.

8. Navigate to the top-level directory of this chapter in the repository and execute the following command to create the appropriate directory to store our patch:

```
$ mkdir -p external/patches/linux
```

9. Execute the following command to copy our patch file to this directory (this is a best practice to add *any* patch to a Buildroot recipe):

```
$ cp buildroot/output/build/linux-custom/patches/linux-mab.patch
external/patches/linux/
```

10. Add the following line to our Buildroot config file, located at `external/configs/elehbr_config`:

```
BR2_GLOBAL_PATCH_DIR="$(BR2_EXTERNAL_ELEHBR_PATH)/patches"
```

We can confirm that the customization via our patch actually works by following these steps:

1. Remove the Linux kernel build artifacts from the Buildroot build by executing the following command:

```
$ rm -fr buildroot/output/build/linux-*
```

2. Rebuild only the Linux kernel by executing the following command:

```
$ make -c buildroot/ linux
```

3. Navigate to the location of the Linux kernel source code downloaded and extracted by Buildroot by executing the following command:

```
$ cd buildroot/output/build/linux-custom
```

4. Open `init/main.c` and confirm that the line we added is present:

```
        printk("Packt Embedded Linux\n");
        do_sysctl_args();

        if (ramdisk_execute_command) {
                ret = run_init_process(ramdisk_execute_command);
                if (!ret)
```

Now that we have understood the process of customizing the Linux kernel in Buildroot and verifying the customization, we will learn how to customize U-Boot.

Customizing U-Boot

In this section, we will learn how to customize U-Boot. Before we can get started, we will need to configure Buildroot to build and use U-Boot as part of our embedded Linux image by following these steps:

1. Enter Buildroot's configuration menu by executing the following command:

```
$ make -C buildroot menuconfig
```

2. Enter the **Bootloaders** menu as shown in the following figure:

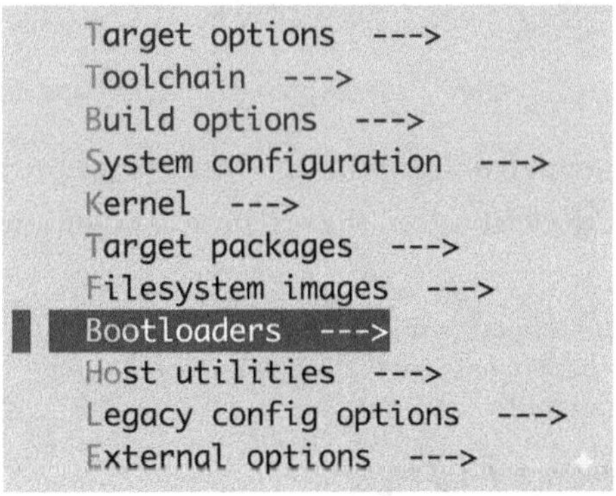

Figure 7.9 – Buildroot Bootloaders menu

3. Enable the **U-Boot** option in the **Bootloaders** menu, as shown in the following figure:

```
[ ] ARM Trusted Firmware (ATF)
[ ] Barebox
[ ] binaries-marvell
[ ] boot-wrapper-aarch64
[ ] EDK2
[ ] grub2
[ ] mv-ddr-marvell
[ ] optee_os
[ ] shim
[ ] ti-k3-boot-firmware
[ ] ti-k3-r5-loader
[*] U-Boot
      Build system (Kconfig)  --->
      U-Boot Version (2024.01)  --->
()    Custom U-Boot patches
      U-Boot configuration (Using an in-tree board defconfig file)  --->
()    Board defconfig
()    Additional configuration fragment files
[ ]   U-Boot needs dtc
[ ]   U-Boot needs host python 3.x
[ ]   U-Boot needs pylibfdt
[ ]   U-Boot needs pyelftools
[ ]   U-Boot needs OpenSSL
[ ]   U-Boot needs lzop
[ ]   U-Boot needs gnutls
[ ]   U-Boot needs util-linux
[ ]   U-Boot needs xxd
      U-Boot binary format  --->
[ ]   Install U-Boot SPL binary image
[ ]   Install u-boot-initial-env
[ ]   Boot on the Xilinx ZynqMP SoCs
()    Device Tree Source file paths
```

Figure 7.10 – Enabling U-Boot for the Raspberry Pi

4. Highlight the **Board defconfig** option, hit the *Enter* key, type `rpi_4` in the resulting window, and hit *Enter* over the **Ok** button. The resulting configuration should look like the following:

```
[*] U-Boot
      Build system (Kconfig)  --->
      U-Boot Version (2024.01)  --->
()    Custom U-Boot patches
      U-Boot configuration (Using an in-tree board defconfig file)
(rpi_4) Board defconfig
()    Additional configuration fragment files
```

Figure 7.11 – Setting the U-Boot board type

Next, we can customize U-Boot by following these steps:

1. Download, extract, and build U-Boot by executing the following command:

```
$ make -C buildroot/ uboot
```

2. Navigate to the U-Boot source directory by executing the following command:

```
$ cd buildroot/output/build/uboot-2024.01/
```

3. Begin the process of creating a patch file by executing the following commands:

```
$ mkdir patches
$ quilt new uboot-mab.patch
```

4. Add `common/main.c` to the patch by executing the following command:

```
$ quilt edit common/main.c
```

5. Add the following line (in bold) to `common/main.c`.

```
        if (IS_ENABLED(CONFIG_VERSION_VARIABLE))
                env_set("ver", version_string);  /* set version
variable */

        printf("Packt Embedded Linux\n");
        cli_init();

        if (IS_ENABLED(CONFIG_USE_PREBOOT))
```

6. Save the file, exit, and execute the following command to finalize the patch:

```
$ quilt refresh
```

7. Navigate back to the top-level directory of this chapter in the repository and execute the following commands to make the appropriate directory in our external Buildroot tree and copy the patch file over:

```
$ mkdir external/patches/uboot
$ cp buildroot/output/build/uboot-2024.01/patches/uboot-mab.patch
external/patches/uboot/
```

The following steps describe how to confirm that our patch applies the expected change:

1. Remove the existing U-Boot source code by executing the following command:

```
$ rm -fr buildroot/output/build/uboot-2024.01
```

2. Rebuild U-Boot by executing the following command:

```
$ make -C buildroot/ uboot
```

3. Confirm that the `common/main.c` file has the following line (in bold):

```
	if (IS_ENABLED(CONFIG_VERSION_VARIABLE))
		env_set("ver", version_string);  /* set version variable */

	printf("Packt Embedded Linux\n");
	cli_init();

	if (IS_ENABLED(CONFIG_USE_PREBOOT))
```

In this section, we learned how to customize U-Boot in Buildroot. We will learn how to verify our customizations in the next section.

Validating our customizations

In this section, we will learn how to verify the customizations we made to a standard Buildroot image on a Raspberry Pi 4 (ensure that you have followed the steps outlined in the *Creating an embedded Linux image* section).

Flashing a Raspberry Pi 4

There are two distinct mechanisms we can use to write the final image to the SD card, depending on the operating system of the development PC. Each mechanism is outlined next.

Flashing an image on Windows

The embedded Linux image for the Raspberry Pi 4 can be written to the SD card on a Windows PC by following these steps:

1. Navigate to `https://www.raspberrypi.com/software/` and click on the **Download for Windows** button to download the Raspberry Pi Imager application:

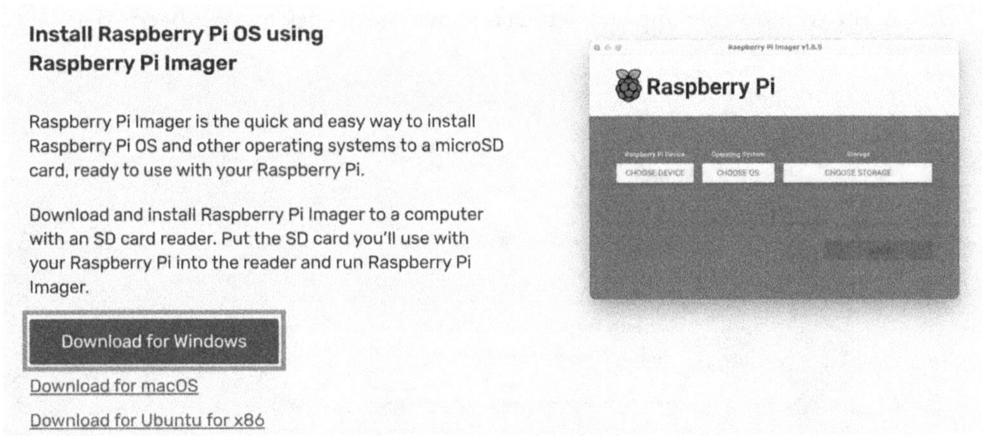

Figure 7.12 – Downloading Raspberry Pi Imager

2. Install the Raspberry Pi Imager application on the Windows PC.
3. Plug in a blank SD card to the Windows PC.
4. Launch the Raspberry Pi Imager application and click on **CHOOSE DEVICE**, as shown in the following screenshot:

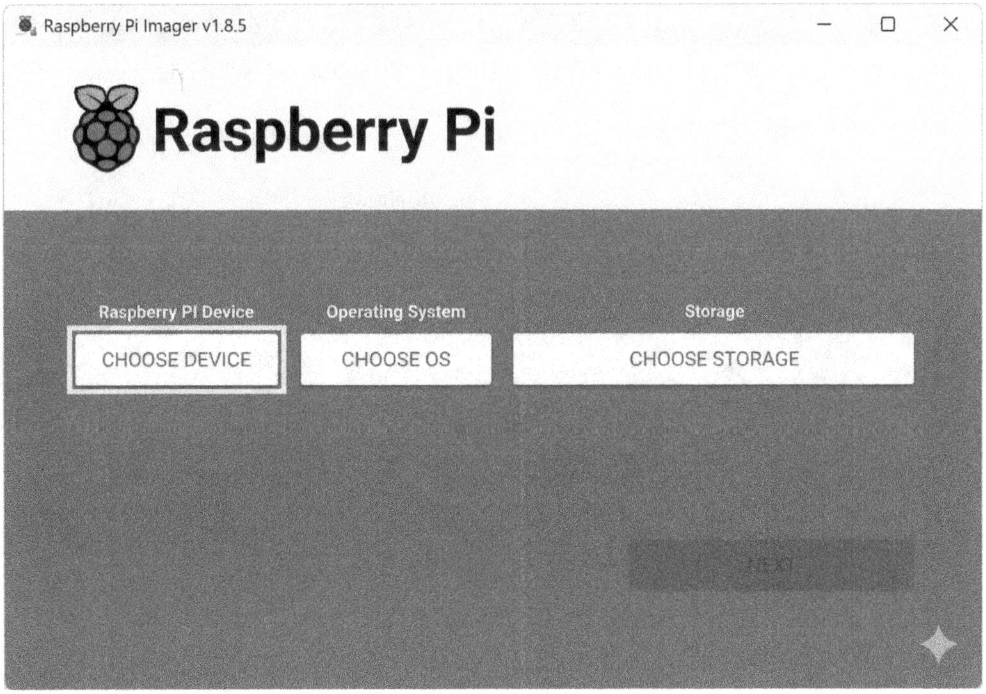

Figure 7.13 – Selecting the appropriate device

5. In the window that appears, which is shown next, click on **Raspberry Pi 4**:

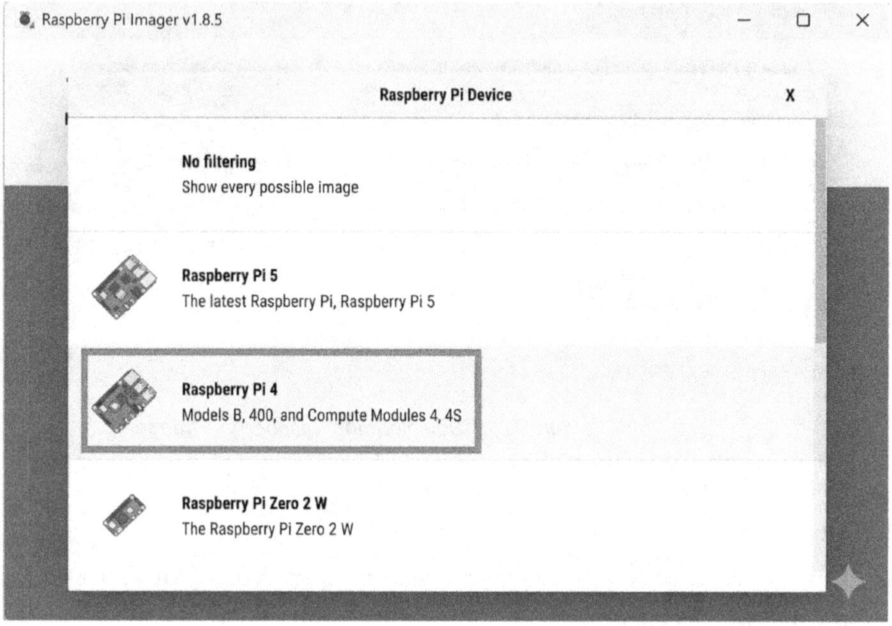

Figure 7.14 – Selecting the Raspberry Pi 4

6. In the original application window, click on **CHOOSE OS**, which is shown next:

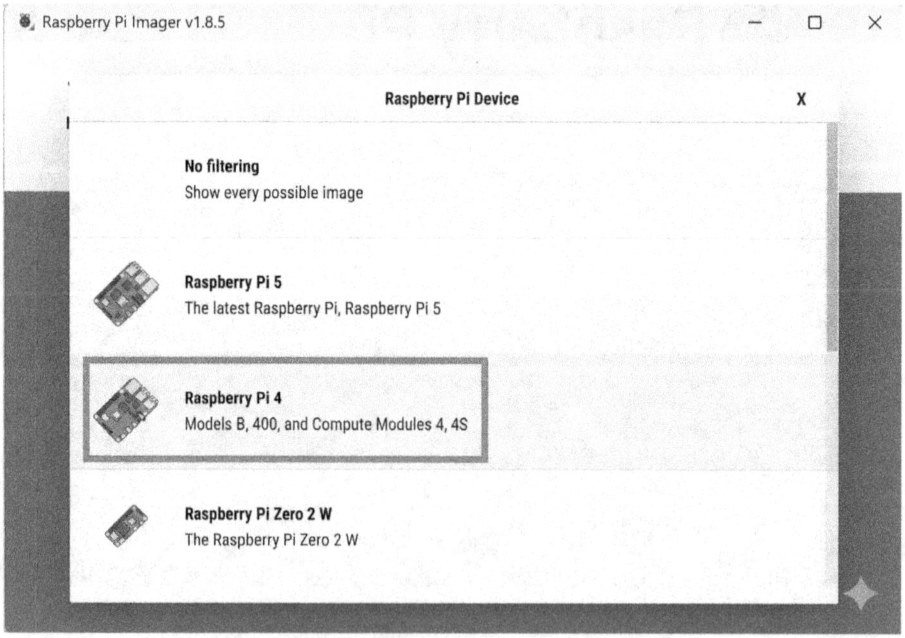

Figure 7.15 – Selecting the appropriate operating system

7. In the resulting window, click on **Use custom**, as shown in the following screenshot:

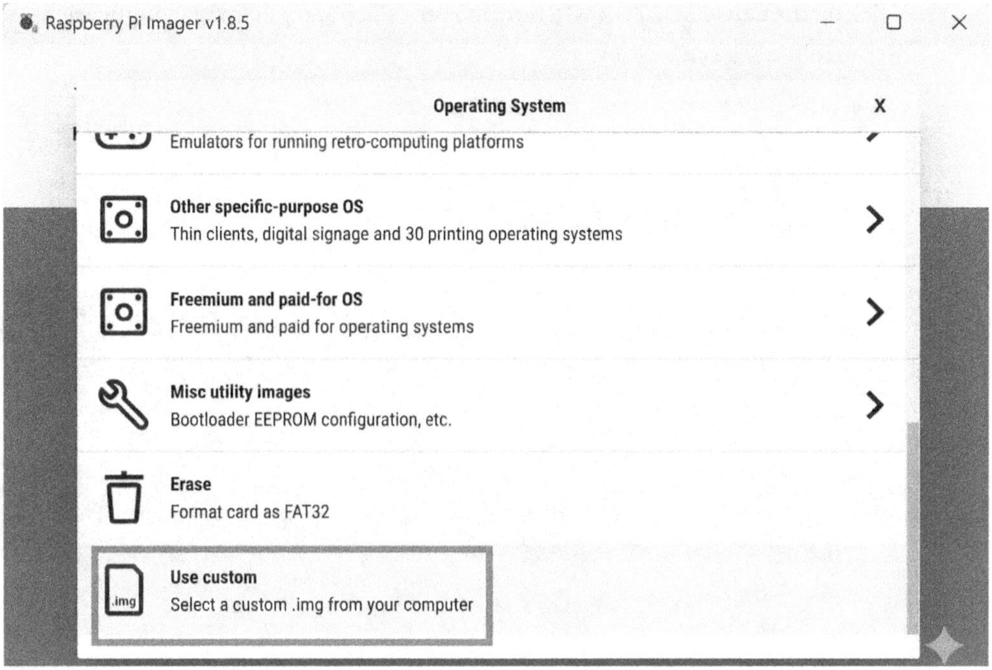

Figure 7.16 – Using a custom operating system to flash

8. In the resulting window, navigate to the location of the `sdcard.img` file, select the file, and click **Open**, as shown in the following screenshot:

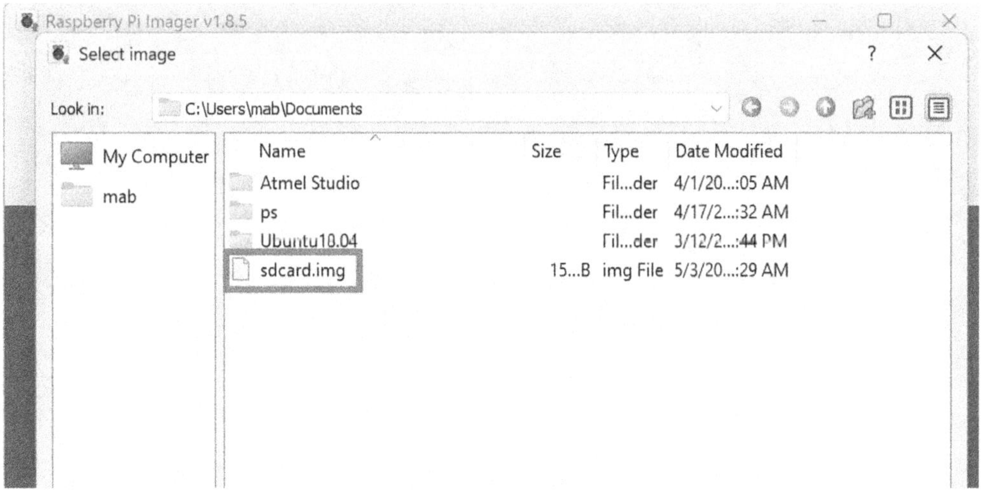

Figure 7.17 – Selecting the image to flash

9. Plug the SD card into your Windows PC.
10. Click on the **CHOOSE STORAGE** button in the Raspberry Pi Imager application, as shown in the following screenshot:

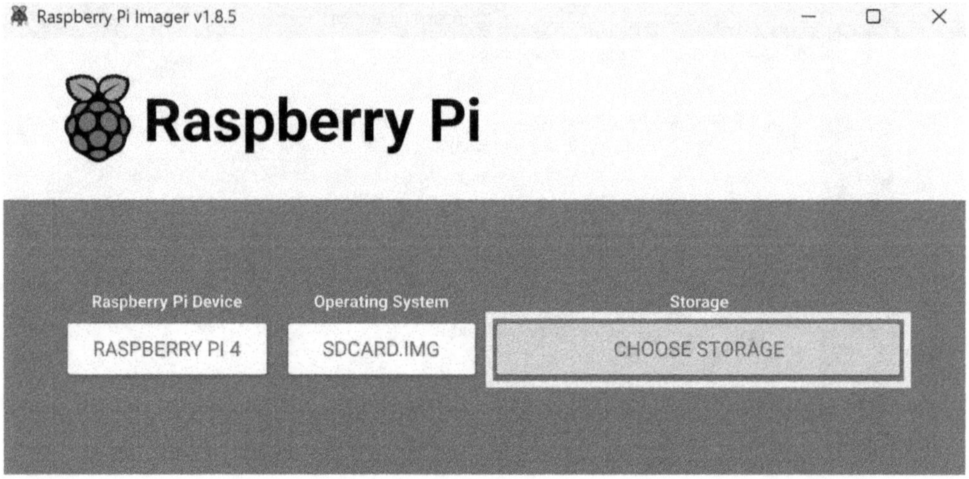

Figure 7.18 – Selecting storage option

11. In the resulting window, select the entry corresponding to the SD card that was just plugged in. For example, in the following screenshot, a 64 GB SD card was plugged into the Windows PC:

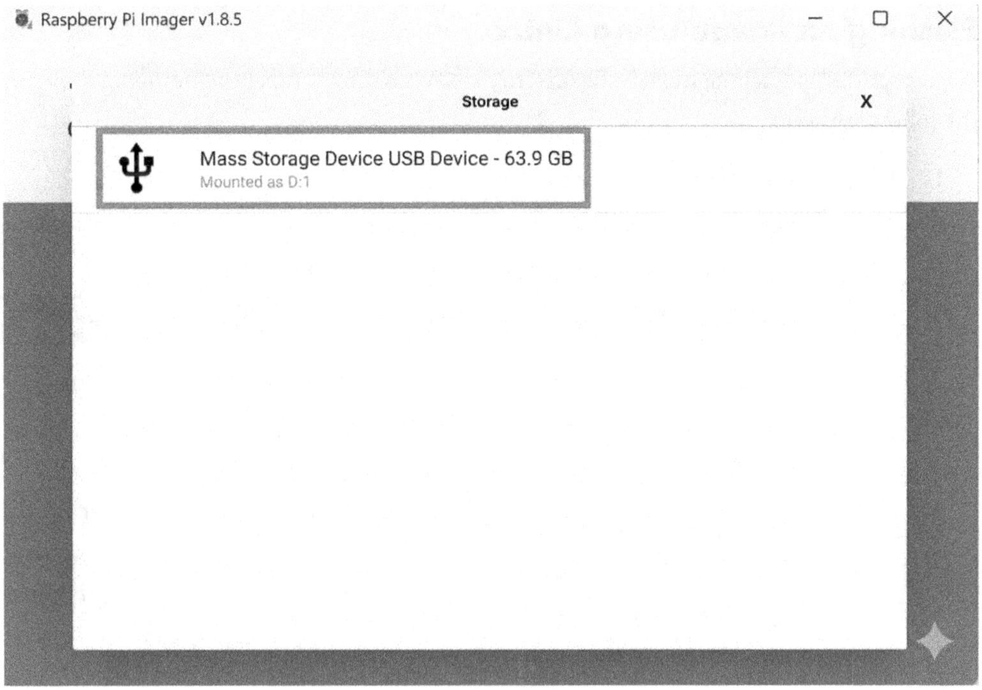

Figure 7.19 – Choosing the appropriate SD card

12. Click **Next** in the main window, as shown in the following screenshot:

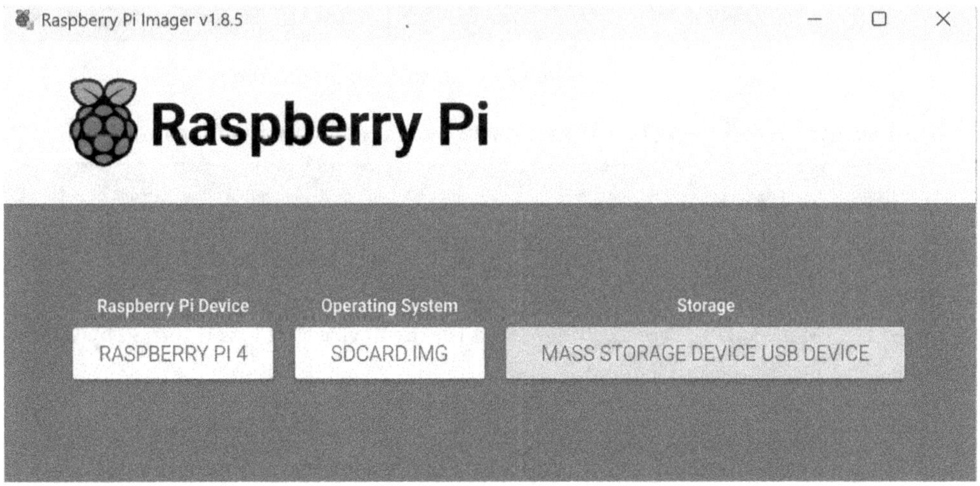

Figure 7.20 – Progressing with image flashing

Flashing an image using Linux

The embedded Linux image can be flashed to the SD card on a Linux development PC by completing the following steps:

1. Plug the SD card into the Linux PC.
2. Execute the following command to determine the device associated with the SD card (and enter the sudo password if prompted):

```
$ sudo dmesg -w
```

3. Note the drive letter associated with the SD card, as shown in the following screenshot:

```
[4747440.162891] usb-storage 5-2.4.4:1.0: USB Mass Storage device
detected
[4747441.163845] scsi host13: usb-storage 5-2.4.4:1.0
[4747441.168476] scsi 13:0:0:0: Direct-Access    Mass   Storage De
ice 1.00 PQ: 0 ANSI: 0 CCS
[4747441.168919] sd 13:0:0:0: Attached scsi generic sgl type 0
[4747441.489823] sd 13:0:0:0: [sdb] 124735488 512-byte logical b
locks: (63.9 GB/59.5 GiB)
[4747441.489143] sd 13:0:0:0: [sdb] Write Protect is off
[4747441.489143] sd 13:0:0:0: [sdb] Mode Sense: 03 00 00 00
[4747441.489244] sd 13:0:0:0: [sdb]
[4747441.489245] sd 13:0:0:0: [sdb] No Caching modepage found
[4747441.489245] sd 13:0:0:0: Assuming drive cache: write through
[4747441.499246] sd 13:0:0:0: [sdb]
[4747441.490900] sdb: sdb1 sdb2
[4747441.490997] sd 13:0:0:0: [sdb] Attached SCSI removable disk
```

Figure 7.21 – Identifying the SD card

4. Execute the following command to write `sdcard.img` to the SD card:

```
$ sudo dd stats=progress if output/images/sdcard.img of=/dev/sdb
```

> Important note
>
> Make sure to replace `/dev/sdb` with the device that was returned by Linux in the previous line of code.

The SD card should now contain the embedded Linux operating system that we will run on the Raspberry Pi. We will see how to gain access to a console interface to the Raspberry Pi 4 in the next subsection.

Accessing a console interface

We can follow the steps outlined next to get to a console on the Raspberry Pi 4:

1. Connect a USB-to-UART adapter (such as one from Adafruit: `https://www.adafruit.com/product/954`) to the Raspberry Pi 4, using the following diagram as a reference:

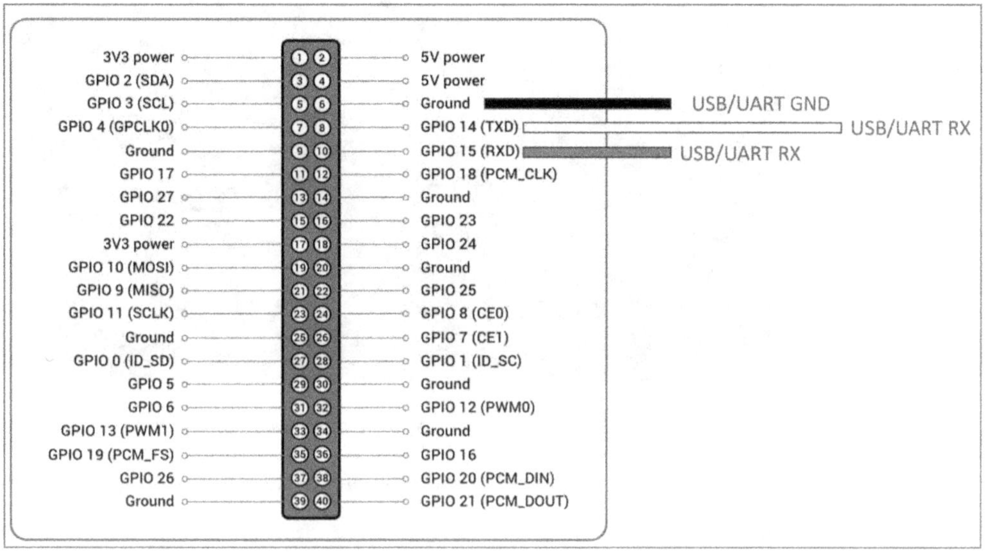

Figure 7.22 – Console connections to the Raspberry Pi 4

2. Plug in the USB side of the USB-to-UART adapter to a USB port on your PC and open a terminal program (such as **PuTTY** on Windows or **Minicom** on Linux).
3. Connect a +5V power adapter to the USB-C port of the Raspberry Pi 4. The complete connections should mimic that shown in the following figure:

Figure 7.23 – Raspberry Pi 4 console and power connections

4. Plug in the SD card to the micro-SD card slot of the Raspberry Pi 4, as shown in the following figure:

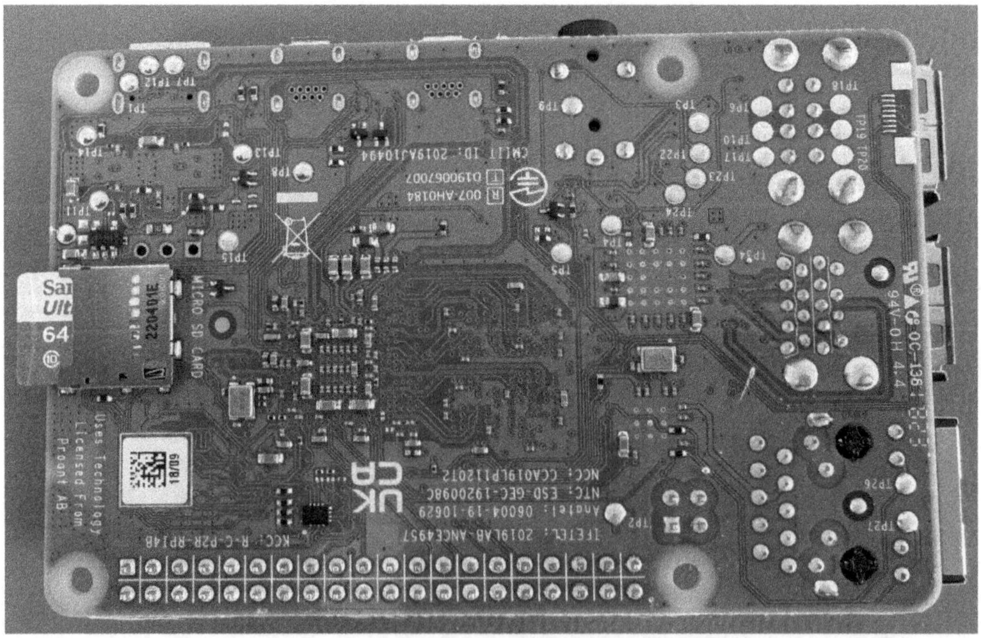

Figure 7.24 – Raspberry Pi 4 SD card connection

5. You should see output similar to that shown in the following figure in the terminal application (notice the text **Welcome to Buildroot**):

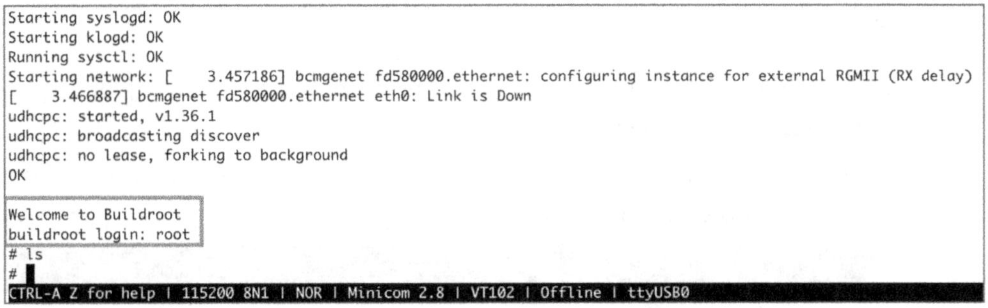

Figure 7.25 – Console output from the Raspberry Pi 4 using a Buildroot image

The username to log in to the Raspberry Pi 4 is `root`, with no password. We will learn how to verify that our custom application exists on our embedded Linux image and functions as expected in the next subsection.

Custom application verification

We can confirm the presence of our custom application on a Raspberry Pi 4 using Buildroot by following these steps:

1. Make sure that you have followed the steps outlined in the *Creating a custom application* and *Flashing a Raspberry Pi 4* sections.
2. Open a terminal application for a console interface to the Raspberry Pi 4.
3. Log in to the Raspberry Pi 4 using `root` as the username and no password.
4. Execute the following command to confirm the presence of our `Hello World` application (recall that we named the application `elehbr`):

```
$ ls -l | grep elehbr
-rwxr-xr-x    1 root     root          5920 May  5  2024 elehbr
```

5. Execute the following command to run the application and confirm its output:

```
# elehbr
Hello Embedded Linux World!
```

We will see how to confirm our U-Boot customization in the next subsection.

U-Boot customization verification

We can validate the U-Boot customization from an embedded Linux image created using Buildroot by following these steps:

1. Ensure that the U-Boot customization has been applied by following the steps outlined in the *Customizing U-Boot* section.
2. Execute the following command on a Linux PC to see which drive is associated with the SD card (enter the sudo password when prompted):

```
$ sudo dmesg -w
```

3. Plug the SD card into the Linux PC.
4. Note the drive associated with the SD card (as shown in the following code block, it is /dev/sda):

```
[4942876.502132] usb-storage 5-2.4.4:1.0: USB Mass Storage device
detected
[4942876.502533] scsi host12: usb-storage 5-2.4.4:1.0
[4942877.535867] scsi 12:0:0:0: Direct-Access     Mass     Storage
Device   1.00 PQ: 0 ANSI: 0 CCS
[4942877.536159] sd 12:0:0:0: Attached scsi generic sg0 type 0
[4942877.862485] sd 12:0:0:0: [sda] 124735488 512-byte logical
blocks: (63.9 GB/59.5 GiB)
[4942877.862648] sd 12:0:0:0: [sda] Write Protect is off
[4942877.862655] sd 12:0:0:0: [sda] Mode Sense: 03 00 00 00
[4942877.862813] sd 12:0:0:0: [sda] No Caching mode page found
[4942877.862819] sd 12:0:0:0: [sda] Assuming drive cache: write
through
[4942877.864713]  sda: sda1 sda2
```

5. Execute the following command to create a directory to store the contents of the first partition on the SD card:

```
$ mkdir ./sdcard_part1
```

6. Execute the following command to mount the first partition of the SD card (replace /dev/sda with the drive reported by Linux):

```
$ sudo mount /dev/sda1 ./sdcard_part1
```

7. Copy the U-Boot binary to the first partition on the SD card by executing the following command:

```
$ cp buildroot/output/images/u-boot.bin ./sdcard_part1
```

8. Open the `config.txt` file in the `sdcard_part1` directory and make the following change (in bold):

```
start_file=start4.elf
fixup_file=fixup4.dat

kernel=u-boot.bin
```

9. Unmount the SD card by executing the following command:

```
$ sudo umount ./sdcard_part1
```

10. Plug the SD card into the Raspberry Pi, and you should see the following output on the console interface (taking note of the items in bold that correspond to our change):

```
U-Boot 2024.01 (May 05 2024 - 17:03:57 -0400)

DRAM:  924 MiB (effective 3.8 GiB)
RPI 4 Model B (0xc03115)
Core:  211 devices, 16 uclasses, devicetree: board
MMC:   mmcnr@7e300000: 1, mmc@7e340000: 0
Loading Environment from FAT... Unable to read "uboot.env" from
mmc0:1...
In:    serial,usbkbd
Out:   serial,vidconsole
Err:   serial,vidconsole
Net:   eth0: ethernet@7d580000
Packt Embedded Linux
PCIe BRCM: link up, 5.0 Gbps x1 (SSC)
starting USB...
```

> Important note
>
> There are additional steps necessary in U-Boot to successfully boot into Linux from U-Boot. These additional steps are out of the scope of this book. You are encouraged to use `https://ltekieli.com/buildroot-with-raspberry-pi-u-boot/` as a starting point to boot the Linux kernel from U-Boot.

We will see how to verify our Linux kernel customization in the next subsection.

Linux kernel customization verification

We can verify our Linux kernel customization by following the steps outlined here:

1. Flash the custom Buildroot image to the SD card by following the steps in the *Flashing a Raspberry Pi 4* section.
2. Plug the SD card into the Raspberry Pi 4 and apply power to the Raspberry Pi 4.
3. Ensure that a console interface to the Raspberry Pi 4 is available.
4. Execute the following command, which filters the kernel logs for the `Packt Embedded Linux` string, and ensure the corresponding output to confirm the customization to the Linux kernel:

```
Welcome to Buildroot
buildroot login: root
# dmesg | grep Packt Embedded Linux
[    3.139434] Packt Embedded Linux
```

Summary

In this chapter, we learned how to create an embedded Linux image using Buildroot. We learned about the overall process and how to perform common tasks when developing a specific product. For example, we learned how to create custom applications and add them to our embedded Linux system using Buildroot. Then, we learned about the steps needed to customize the Linux kernel and U-Boot.

The past few chapters have helped us understand the value of the frameworks used to create complete and cohesive embedded Linux images. We learned about two popular frameworks that can be used to create embedded Linux images and how to choose between the two. Armed with this information, we can now confidently build a complete embedded Linux image. In the next few chapters, we will learn about meaningful applications that can be deployed on embedded Linux systems.

Get this book's PDF version and more

Scan the QR code (or go to `packtpub.com/unlock`). Search for this book by name, confirm the edition, and then follow the steps on the page.

UNLOCK NOW

Note: Keep your invoice handy. Purchases made directly from Packt don't require an invoice.

Part 3

Developing Applications

In this part, you will learn about the different phases of application development targeting an Embedded Linux system. This part will cover implementation, loading, testing, debugging, and launching applications on startup. This part will cover popular frameworks used in developing applications in Embedded Linux, along with hands-on projects.

This part has the following chapters:

8

Building, Debugging, and Launching Applications on Startup

In *Part 2*, we built on the lessons learned from *Part 1* and learned how to build a complete embedded Linux image using popular frameworks. We learned how to incorporate bootloader and kernel customizations into our embedded Linux image and how to add custom applications. We will now move up the embedded software "stack" and focus on application development.

In *Part 3*, we will learn how applications can be implemented and built for execution on an embedded Linux system. We will cover, in detail, how to compile, execute, and efficiently debug embedded Linux applications. We will learn how to use popular programming languages to implement specific application types across different verticals.

This chapter will lay the foundation for the remaining chapters in this part. We will learn about the mechanics associated with common application development tasks. Specifically, we will learn how to retrieve the toolchain from Buildroot or the Yocto Project, depending on which framework was used to create our embedded Linux image. We will learn how to use the compiler to build our application. Then, we will learn how to use common tools to debug our application and verify its performance.

We are going to cover the following main topics in this chapter:

- Setting up the toolchain and compiling applications
- `gdbserver`: remote debugging on a device
- Valgrind: identifying memory leaks
- `systemd`: launching applications on boot

Technical requirements

You should be comfortable executing commands on a terminal. You can follow the examples in this chapter using the following Github link: `https://github.com/PacktPublishing/Embedded-Linux-Essentials-Handbook/tree/main/Chapter8`.

Setting up the toolchain and compiling applications

Recall from *Chapter 1, Exploring Embedded Linux's Architecture and Its Use Cases,* that the toolchain is one of the key components of an embedded Linux system. The toolchain converts source code representing the other components (i.e., bootloader, kernel, and applications) into their binary form for execution on the target platform. We didn't explicitly interact with the toolchain or observe it in action in *Part 2* because its retrieval and use are hidden by the Yocto Project and Buildroot frameworks. However, including an application in our **board support package** (**BSP**) and reflashing our board solely for testing an application is time-consuming and unnecessary. Instead, the application development process for an embedded Linux system consists of the following steps:

1. Retrieve the toolchain for our target platform.
2. Write the application.
3. Build the application using the retrieved toolchain.
4. Transfer the application to our target platform (using a file transfer mechanism such as File Transfer Protocol (FTP) or Secure Copy Protocol (SCP)).
5. Test the application on our target platform.

Usually, *steps 2* to *5* are repeated as we update our application based on testing. In this section, we will learn how to retrieve the toolchain from the BSP and use it to build applications. Recall from *Part 2* that the **Yocto Project** and **Buildroot** are two popular frameworks that can be used to generate the BSP. Since Buildroot and the Yocto Project are quite disparate, the process for retrieving the toolchain differs for each framework. Thus, we will focus on each in the following subsections.

> Important note
>
> The toolchain is everything beyond just the compiler necessary to build applications to run on the embedded Linux system. It also includes the linker and relevant libraries, which have been compiled for the target embedded Linux system and are present there.

Buildroot

The following steps outline how to retrieve the toolchain from the Buildroot framework:

1. Navigate to the `Chapter7` folder in the GitHub repository directory by executing the following command from the root of the Git repository associated with this book:

```
$ cd Chapter7/
```

2. Configure the Buildroot framework for our specific platform by executing the following command:

```
$ make config
```

3. Execute the following command to enter Buildroot's configuration UI:

```
$ make -C buildroot menuconfig
```

4. Hit the / slash key on your keyboard, and type `HOST_ENVIRONMENT_SETUP`, as shown here:

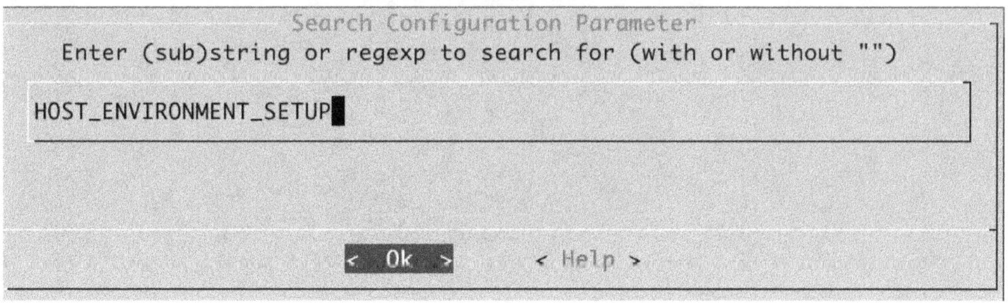

Figure 8.1 – Searching for the Buildroot toolchain

5. Hit the *Enter* key on the keyboard, and the following window will be displayed:

```
Symbol: BR2_PACKAGE_HOST_ENVIRONMENT_SETUP [=n]
Type  : bool
Prompt: host environment-setup
  Location:
(1) -> Host utilities
  Defined at package/environment-setup/Config.in.host:1
```

Figure 8.2 – Searching for the appropriate toolchain option

6. Hit the *1* key on the keyboard, and the following should be displayed:

```
[ ] host cramfs
[ ] host crudini
[ ] host cryptsetup
[ ] host dbus-python
[ ] host delve
[ ] host depot-tools
[ ] host dfu-util
[ ] host dos2unix
[*] host dosfstools
[ ] host doxygen
[ ] host dtc
-*- host e2fsprogs
[ ] host e2tools
[ ] host environment-setup
[ ] host erofs-utils
[ ] host exfatprogs
[ ] host f2fs-tools
[ ] host faketime
[ ] host fatcat
[ ] host firmware-utils
[ ] host flutter-sdk-bin
[ ] host fwup
[ ] host genext2fs
[*] host genimage
[ ] host genpart
[ ] host gnupg
```

Figure 8.3 – Searching for the appropriate toolchain configuration

7. Hit the *spacebar* key on the keyboard and highlight the *Enter* key, as shown in the following window:

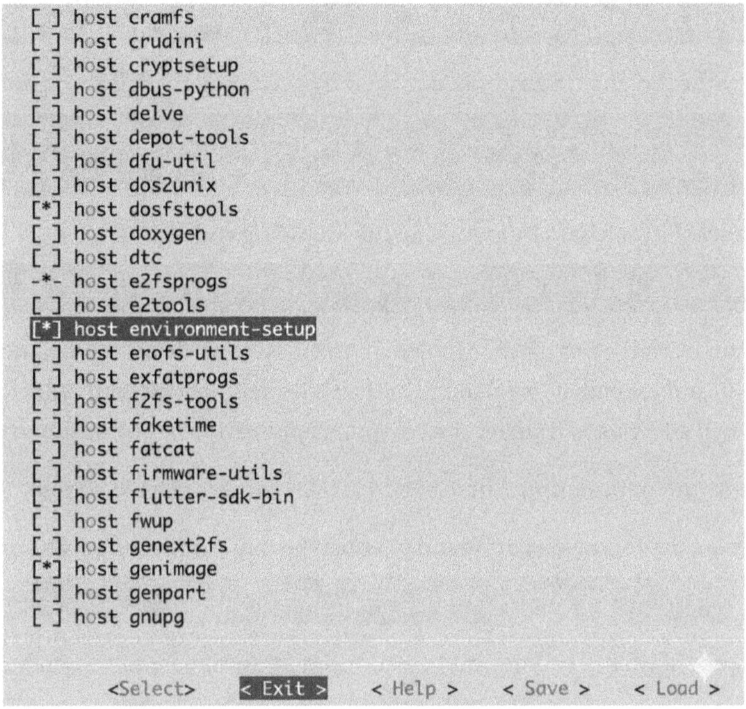

Figure 8.4 – Enabling the appropriate toolchain option

8. Continue to back out of the subsequent menus. At the final menu, highlight **Yes** and click the *Enter* key on the keyboard, as shown here:

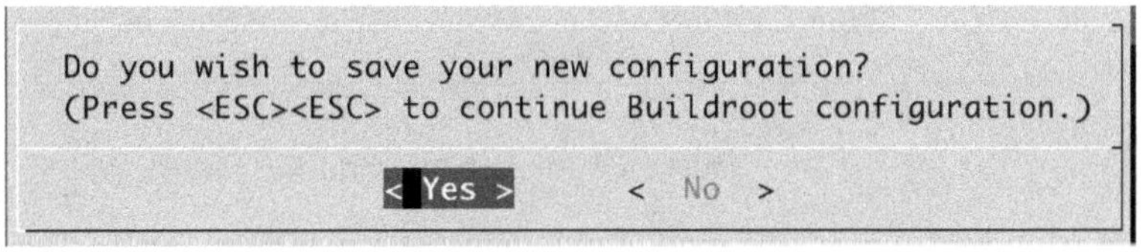

Figure 8.5 – Saving the final configuration

9. Execute the following command to create the toolchain:

```
$ make -C buildroot sdk
```

The toolchain is located at `buildroot/output/images/aarch64-buildroot-linux-gnu_sdk-buildroot.tar.gz`.

10. Create a directory called `sdk` that will contain the toolchain by executing the following command:

```
$ mkdir sdk
```

11. Copy the toolchain to the `sdk` directory by executing the following command:

```
$ cp buildroot/output/images/aarch64-buildroot-linux-gnu_sdk-
buildroot.tar.gz sdk/
```

12. Extract the toolchain by executing the following command:

```
$ tar aarch64-buildroot-linux-gnu_sdk-buildroot.tar.gz
```

Before we can learn how to use our toolchain to cross-compile our application, deploy it to the Raspberry Pi, and execute it, we need to add an **SSH** server to our embedded Linux image. The SSH server will allow us to transfer the compiled application to our Raspberry Pi.

We can follow the steps outlined here to add an SSH server to the Raspberry Pi:

1. Execute the following command to enter the Buildroot configuration menu:

```
$ make -C buildroot menuconfig
```

2. Hit the / slash key on your keyboard, and type `dropbear`, as shown here:

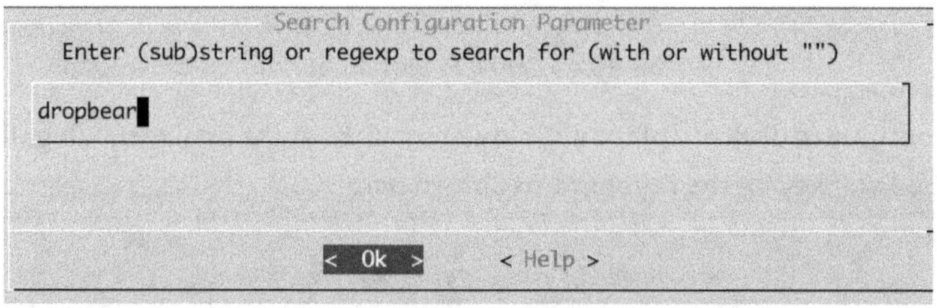

Figure 8.6 – Searching for an SSH server

> Important note
>
> **Dropbear** is one variant of SSH that can be installed on an embedded Linux system. **OpenSSH** is an alternative. While Dropbear is less resource-intensive than OpenSSH, it is not as resource-rich as OpenSSH. However, due to its size, Dropbear is usually the preferred choice in most production embedded Linux systems.

3. Hit the *Enter* key on the keyboard, and the following window will be displayed:

```
Symbol: BR2_PACKAGE_DROPBEAR [=y]
Type  : bool
Prompt: dropbear
  Location:
    -> Target packages
(1)   -> Networking applications
  Defined at package/dropbear/Config.in:1
  Selects: BR2_PACKAGE_ZLIB [=n] && BR2_PACKAGE_LIBTOMCRYPT [=n]
```

Figure 8.7 – Finding available Dropbear options

4. Hit the *1* key on the keyboard, and the following should be displayed:

```
[ ] dhcpdump
[ ] dnsmasq
[ ] drbd-utils
[ ] dropbear
[ ] easyframes
[ ] ebtables
    *** ejabberd needs erlang, toolchain w/ C++ ***
[ ] ethtool
[ ] faifa
```

Figure 8.8 – Available Dropbear options

5. Hit the *spacebar* key on the keyboard and highlight the *Enter* key, as shown in the following window:

```
[*] dropbear
[*]   client programs (NEW)
[ ]   disable reverse DNS lookups (NEW)
[*]   optimize for size (NEW)
[ ]   log dropbear access to wtmp (NEW)
[ ]   log dropbear access to lastlog (NEW)
[ ]   enable legacy crypto (NEW)
()    path to custom localoptions.h definitions file (NEW)
[ ] easyframes
[ ] ebtables

     <Select>    < Exit >    < Help >    < Save >    < Load >
```

Figure 8.9 – Enabling Dropbear

6. Continue to back out of the subsequent menus. At the final menu, highlight **Yes** and click the *Enter* key on the keyboard, as shown here:

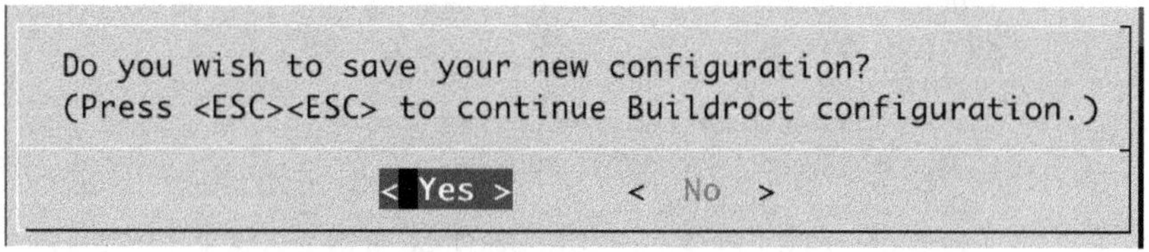

Figure 8.10 – Saving the final configuration

7. Execute the following command to build the embedded Linux image:

```
$ make all
```

8. Follow the steps outlined in *Chapter 7, Building an Image Using Buildroot*, to flash the resulting image to the Raspberry Pi 4.

To remotely access the Raspberry Pi over SSH, we will need to follow the steps outlined here:

1. Generate an SSH key on your Linux development machine by executing the following command (you may choose the default options when presented in the subsequent prompts):

```
$ ssh-keygen
```

2. Execute the following command to view the public portion of the SSH key:

```
$ cat ~/.ssh/id_rsa.pub
```

3. Create the `.ssh` directory on the Raspberry Pi by executing the following command:

```
$ mkdir ~/.ssh/
```

4. Copy the public portion of the SSH key to the `authorized_keys` file under the `.ssh` directory on the Raspberry Pi.
5. Execute the following command on your Linux PC to remotely log in to the Raspberry Pi (replace `Raspberry Pi IP address` with the IP address of your Raspberry Pi):

```
$ ssh -i ~/.ssh/id_rsa root@<Raspberry Pi IP address>
```

Now that we can remotely log in to the Raspberry Pi, we can follow the steps outlined here to use our toolchain:

1. Navigate to the `sdk` directory by executing the following command from the root of the Git repository:

```
$ cd Chapter8/sdk
```

2. Execute the following commands to configure our environment to be able to use the toolchain:

```
$ cd aarch64-buildroot-linux-gnu_sdk-buildroot
$ source environment-setup
 _           _ _     _                 _
| |__  _   _(_) | __| |_ __ ___   ___ | |_
| '_ \| | | | | |/ _` | '__/ _ \ / _ \| __|
| |_) | |_| | | | (_| | | | (_) | (_) | |_
|_.__/ \__,_|_|_|\__,_|_|  \___/ \___/ \__|

       Making embedded Linux easy!

Some tips:
* PATH now contains the SDK utilities
* Standard autotools variables (CC, LD, CFLAGS) are exported
* Kernel compilation variables (ARCH, CROSS_COMPILE, KERNELDIR) are exported
* To configure do "./configure $CONFIGURE_FLAGS" or use
  the "configure" alias
* To build CMake-based projects, use the "cmake" alias
```

3. Navigate to the location of our custom application from *Chapter 7, Building an Image Using Buildroot*, by executing the following command from the root of the Git repository:

```
$ cd Chapter7/external/package/elehbr/src/
```

4. Execute the following command to compile the application using the generated toolchain:

> Note
>
> The command executed by the Makefile is prepended with `aarch64-buildroot-linux-gnu-`. This indicates that this compiler is intended to generate applications that can be executed on a 64-bit ARM system, such as the Raspberry Pi.

```
$ make elehbr
aarch64-buildroot-linux-gnu-gcc -o elehbr eleh_br.c
```

5. The file type of the compiled application can be confirmed by executing the following command:

> Note
>
> `ARM aarch64` in the output is further validation that the application is intended to be executed on the Raspberry Pi.

```
$ file elehbr
elehbr: ELF 64-bit LSB pie executable, ARM aarch64, version 1
(SYSV), dynamically linked, interpreter /lib/ld-linux-aarch64.so.1,
for GNU/Linux 6.1.0, not stripped
```

Finally, we can transfer and execute the compiled application by following the steps outlined here:

1. Transfer the compiled application to the Raspberry Pi by executing the following command (replace `Raspberry Pi IP address` with the IP address of your Raspberry Pi):

```
$ scp -i ~/.ssh/id_rsa elehbr root@<Raspberry Pi IP address>:~/
```

2. Execute the following command to remotely log in to the Raspberry Pi:

```
$ ssh -i ~/.ssh/id_rsa root@<Raspberry Pi IP address>
```

3. Finally, execute the compiled application, as shown here:

```
# ./elehbr
Hello Embedded Linux World
```

Next, we will learn how to generate a toolchain using the Yocto Project and use it to cross-compile a similar application for execution on the Raspberry Pi.

The Yocto Project

The following steps outline how to retrieve the toolchain from the Yocto Project:

1. Navigate to the location of the Yocto Project directory created in *Chapter 7, Building an Image Using Buildroot.*
2. Execute the following command to set up the environment for image creation:

```
$ source layers/poky/oe-init-build-env
```

3. Generate the toolchain by executing the following command:

```
$ MACHINE="raspberrypi5" bitbake -c populate_sdk rpi-test-image
```

4. After executing the preceding command, the toolchain installer is located at `tmp/deploy/sdk/poky-glibc-x86_64-rpi-test-image-cortexa76-raspberrypi5-toolchain-4.0.17.sh`.
5. Create a directory to house the toolchain by executing the following command:

```
$ mkdir sdk
```

6. Navigate to the newly created directory and execute the installer script by executing the following commands:

```
$ cd sdk
$ ~/yocto/build/tmp/deploy/sdk/ poky-glibc-x86_64-rpi-test-image-
cortexa76-raspberrypi5-toolchain-4.0.17.sh
```

7. Enter `./` in the subsequent prompt and `Y` in the following prompt, as shown here:

```
$ ../tmp/deploy/sdk/poky-glibc-x86_64-rpi-test-image-cortexa76-
raspberrypi5-toolchain-4.0.17.sh
Poky (Yocto Project Reference Distro) SDK installer version 4.0.17
=================================================================
Enter target directory for SDK (default: /opt/poky/4.0.17): ./
You are about to install the SDK to "/media/mab/mab_home/packt/
embeddedlinux/rpi5/Embedded-Linux-Essentials-Handbook/yocto/build/
sdk". Proceed [Y/n]? Y
Extracting SDK
```

As we did in the previous subsection, we will need to add Dropbear to the embedded Linux image to transfer our application to the Raspberry Pi and execute it there. We can add Dropbear using the Yocto Project by following the steps outlined here:

1. Add the following line to `build/conf/local.conf`:

```
IMAGE_INSTALL:append = " dropbear"
```

2. Rebuild the embedded Linux image as shown in *Chapter 6, Building an Image Using the Yocto Project*, and flash it to the SD card.
3. To copy the public portion of your SSH key from your Linux PC to the Raspberry Pi, repeat the steps outlined in the previous subsection.
4. Confirm that you can log in to the Raspberry Pi using SSH.

We can compile the custom application we created in *Chapter 6, Building an Image Using the Yocto Project*, by following the steps outlined here:

1. Navigate to the `sdk` directory that was created previously.
2. Set up your compilation environment by executing the following command:

```
$ source environment-setup-cortexa76-poky-linux
```

3. Assuming that the `sdk` directory is located inside the `build` directory of the Yocto Project environment, execute the following command to navigate to the location of the custom application's source code:

```
$ cd ../../layers/meta-packt/recipes-example/hello-world/hello-
world/
```

4. Execute the following command to compile the application:

> Note
>
> The compiler is again prepended with `aarch64-poky-linux`, indicating that `make` is using the toolchain generated from the Yocto Project.

```
$ make
aarch64-poky-linux-gcc  -mcpu=cortex-a76 -march=armv8.2-a+crypto
-mbranch-protection=standard -fstack-protector-strong  -O2 -D_
FORTIFY_SOURCE=2 -Wformat -Wformat-security -Werror=format-security
--sysroot=/media/mab/mab_home/packt/embeddedlinux/rpi5/Embedded-
Linux-Essentials-Handbook/yocto/build/sdk/sysroots/cortexa76-poky-
linux -o hello-world hello-world.c
```

5. Confirm that the application is meant for execution on the Raspberry Pi by executing the following command:

   > Note
   >
   > The mention of `ARM aarch64` is further validation that the application is intended for the Raspberry Pi.

   ```
   $ file hello-world
   hello-world: ELF 64-bit LSB pie executable, ARM aarch64, version 1
   (SYSV), dynamically linked, interpreter /lib/ld-linux-aarch64.so.1,
   BuildID[sha1]=a0b3a67d4b0fc685b3342e1b11036e3a12121970, for GNU/
   Linux 3.14.0, with debug_info, not stripped
   ```

6. Transfer the application to the Raspberry Pi using the steps outlined in the previous section.
7. Execute the following command to run the application on the Raspberry Pi and confirm the output:

   ```
   root@raspberrypi5:~# ./hello-world
   hello world
   ```

In this section, we observed how having an independent toolchain can quicken our development environment. We can use the toolchain to compile our application, transfer it to the target platform, and execute it there for verification. When we are finally satisfied with the execution of the application, we can include the final version in our baseline embedded Linux image using the steps outlined in *Chapter 6, Building an Image Using the Yocto Project*, and *Chapter 7, Building an Image Using Buildroot*. In the next section, we will learn how to remotely debug our applications.

gdbserver: remote debugging on a device

Debugging is a critical task that must be performed when developing embedded software. Software developers use **gdb**, which is a popular open source debugging tool, when they write applications on their desktop PC. While using `gdb` on an embedded Linux system is possible, it is not advised. Due to the resource constraints of an embedded Linux system, running `gdb` on a target system can be cumbersome. Instead, we can install and run **gdbserver** on the embedded Linux system. `gdbserver` is a comparatively lightweight application that serves as a relay between `gdb` running on the Linux development PC and the application on the embedded Linux system, as shown in the following figure:

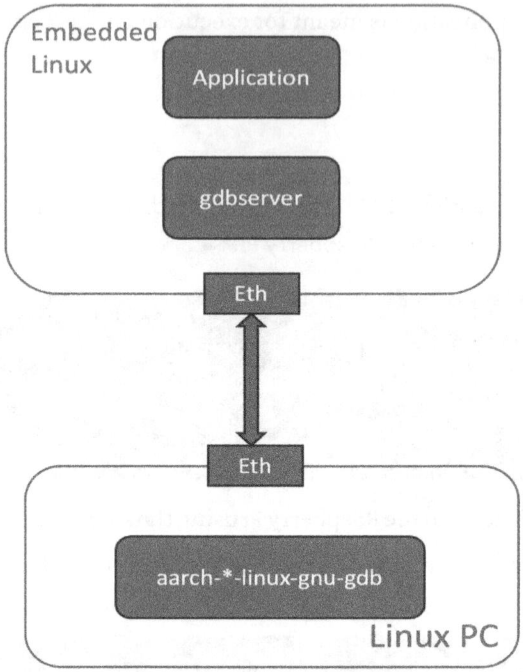

Figure 8.11 – Remote debugging

As shown in *Figure 8.11*, the variant of `gdb` provided in the toolchain generated from Buildroot or the Yocto Project is used on the Linux development PC. This is indicated by the `aarch*-linux-gnu-gdb` application in the figure.

In the following subsections, we will see how to install `gdbserver` using Buildroot and the Yocto Project. Finally, we will learn how to use `gdbserver` on the embedded Linux system and `gdb` on the development PC to perform step-through debugging of our *Hello World!* application.

The Yocto Project

`gdbserver` can be installed on the final embedded Linux image using the Yocto Project by following the steps outlined here:

1. Navigate to the location of the Yocto Project directory created in *Chapter 7, Building an Image Using Buildroot.*
2. Execute the following command to set up the environment for image creation:

```
$ source layers/poky/oe-init-build-env
```

3. Add the following line to `build/conf/local.conf`:

```
IMAGE_INSTALL:append = " gdbserver"
```

4. Rebuild the embedded Linux image, as shown in *Chapter 6, Building an Image Using the Yocto Project*, and flash it to the SD card.

Buildroot

`gdbserver` can be installed on the final embedded Linux image using Buildroot by following the steps outlined here:

1. Navigate to the `Chapter7` directory from the root of the GitHub repository by executing the following command:

```
$ cd Chapter7
```

2. Execute the following command to perform a baseline configuration of the embedded Linux image from *Chapter 7, Building an Image Using Buildroot*:

```
$ make config
```

3. Enter the Buildroot configuration menu by executing the following command:

```
$ make -C buildroot menuconfig
```

4. Hit the / key on the keyboard, type `host_gdb`, and hit the *Enter* key to list the search results, as shown here:

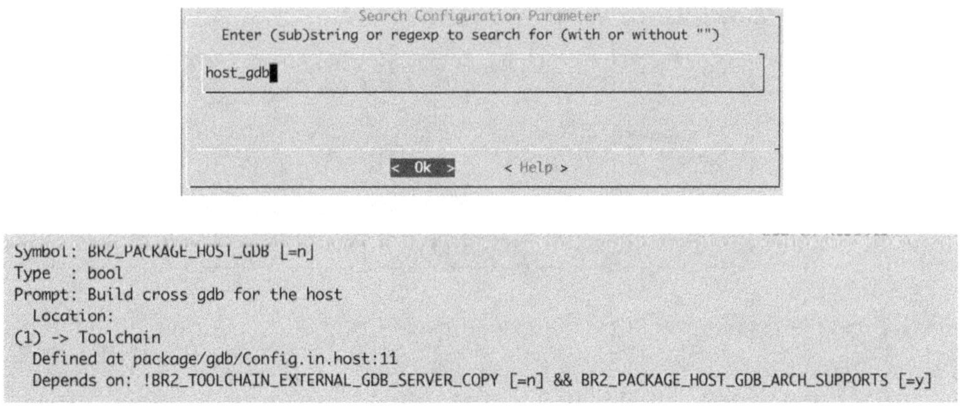

Figure 8.12 – Searching for host_gdb in Buildroot

5. Hit the *1* key on the keyboard, hit the *spacebar* to select the **Build cross gdb for the host** option, highlight the Enter option in the menu, and hit the *Enter* key, as shown here:

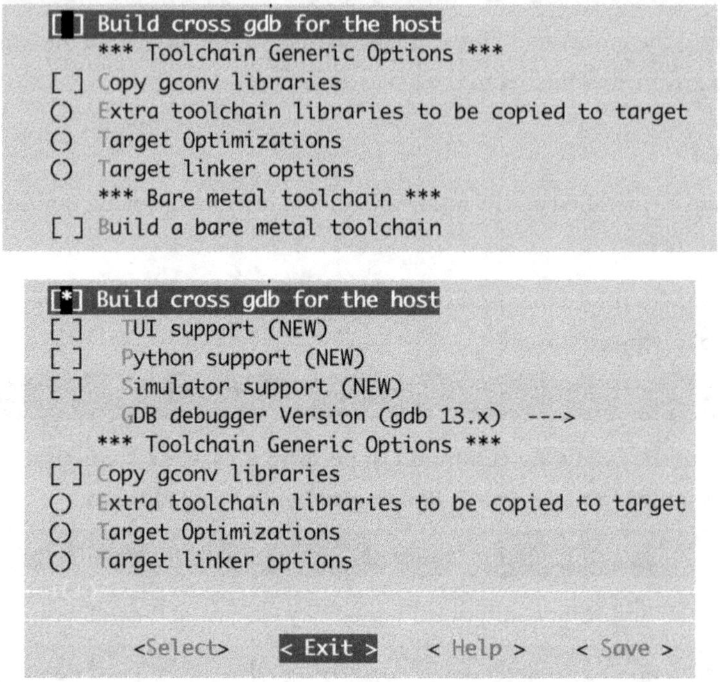

Figure 8.13 – Enabling gdb that will run on the development PC

6. Hit the / key on the keyboard, type package_gdb, and hit the *Enter* key to list the search results, as shown here:

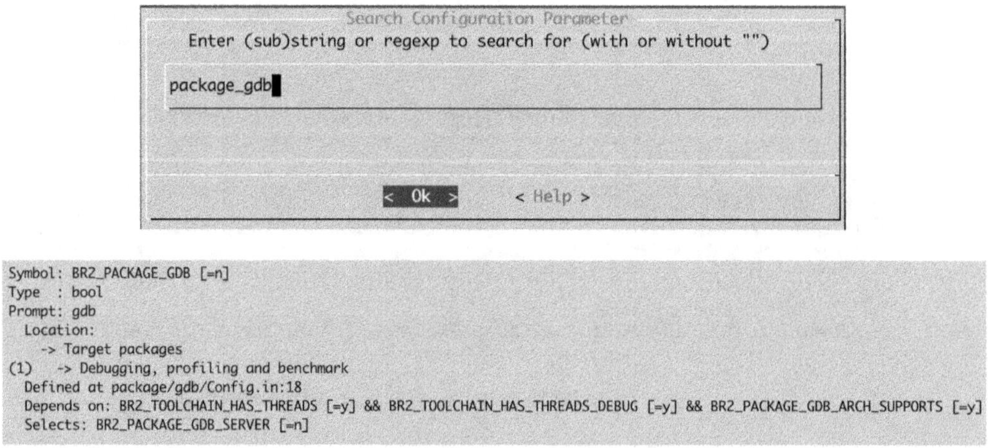

Figure 8.14 – Searching for package_gdb in Buildroot

7. Hit the *1* key on the keyboard, hit the *spacebar* to select the **gdb** option, highlight the `Enter` option in the menu, and hit the *Enter* key, as shown here:

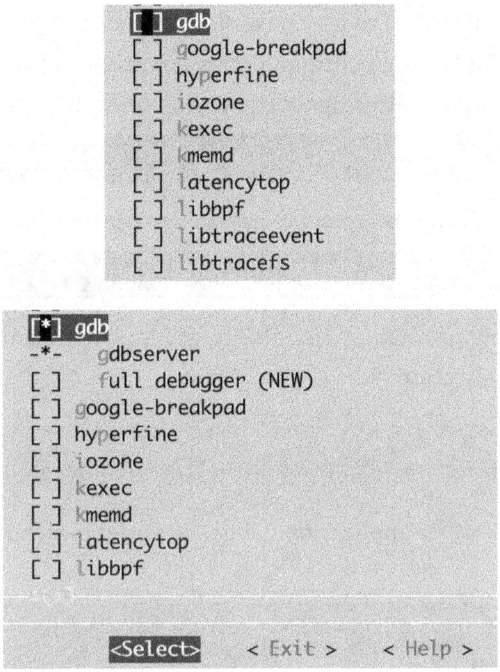

Figure 8.15 – Enabling gdb and gdbserver on the embedded Linux system

8. Follow the steps outlined in *Chapter 7, Building an Image Using Buildroot*, to flash the resulting image to the Raspberry Pi 4.

Testing

We will now learn how to use `gdbserver` to remotely debug our custom application; we will focus on the embedded Linux system created by the Yocto Project, running on the Raspberry Pi 5.

> Important note
>
> The subsection assumes that we have configured Dropbear from the previous section and have noted the IP address from the console interface. It also assumes we have followed the previous steps to generate the SDK.

The following steps describe how to use `gdbserver` to perform step-through debugging of our *Hello World* application:

1. Configure your terminal to use the toolchain created by the Yocto Project framework by executing the following command (this command assumes that we have started the terminal in the `build` directory of the Yocto Project framework):

```
$ source sdk/environment-setup-cortexa76-poky-linux
```

2. Execute the following command to navigate to the location of the *Hello World* application:

```
$ cd ../layers/meta-packt/recipes-example/hello-world/hello-world/
```

3. Make the following change (in bold) to the Makefile to add debugging symbols to the *Hello World* application:

```
hello-world:
        ${CC} -o hello-world hello-world.c -g
```

4. Build the *Hello World* application using the target toolchain by executing the following command:

```
$ make
aarch64-poky-linux-gcc  -mcpu=cortex-a76 -march=armv8.2-a+crypto
-mbranch-protection=standard -fstack-protector-strong  -O2 -D_
FORTIFY_SOURCE=2 -Wformat -Wformat-security -Werror=format-security
--sysroot=/media/mab/mab_home/packt/embeddedlinux/rpi5/Embedded-
Linux-Essentials-Handbook/yocto/build/sdk/sysroots/cortexa76-poky-
linux -o hello-world hello-world.c
```

5. Execute the following command to transfer the compiled application to the Raspberry Pi 5:

```
$ scp -i ~/.ssh/id_rsa hello-world root@<IP address>:~/
```

6. Remotely log in to the Raspberry Pi 5 using SSH by executing the following command:

```
$ ssh root@<IP address>
```

7. Execute the following command to launch `gdbserver` on the Raspberry Pi 5:

```
oot@raspberrypi5:~# gdbserver localhost:12345 ./hello-world
Process /home/root/hello-world created; pid = 594
Listening on port 1234
```

8. Launch the gdb debugger generated from the toolchain by executing the following command, with the corresponding output:

```
$ aarch64-poky-linux-gdb hello-world
.
.
.
Reading symbols from hello-world...
(gdb)
```

9. Execute the following command in the gdb terminal to connect to the server running on the Raspberry Pi 5:

```
(gdb) target remote <IP address>:12345
```

10. Add a breakpoint at the first line of the main function by executing the following command in the gdb terminal:

```
(gdb) break main
Breakpoint 1 at 0x700: file hello-world.c, line 4.
```

11. Execute the following to begin the debug session (we can see that gdb has stopped at our breakpoint):

```
(gdb) c
Continuing.
Reading /lib/libc.so.6 from remote target...
Reading /lib/.debug/libc.so.6 from remote target...
Reading /lib/.debug/libc.so.6 from remote target...

B Breakpoint 1, main (argc=1) at hello-world.c:4
4       {
```

12. We can retrieve a listing of the call stack during the breakpoint by entering the following command (we can also enter bt, which is short for *backtrace*):

```
(gdb) backtrace
#0  main (argc=1) at hello-world.c:4
```

Since the version of gdb from the generated toolchain doesn't have **TUI** support, we can use an alternative by following the steps outlined here:

1. Execute the following command to install a version of gdb that can support popular architectures, such as ARM64, which is the architecture of the CPU running on the Raspberry Pi 5:

```
$ sudo apt-get install gdb-multiarch
```

2. Start a gdbserver session on the Raspberry Pi 5 by executing the following command:

```
root@raspberrypi5:~# gdbserver localhost:12345 ./hello-world
```

3. Execute the following command to start a gdb session on the Linux PC:

```
$ gdb-multiarch hello-world
.
.
.
Reading symbols from hello-world...
```

4. Connect to the gdbserver instance running on the Raspberry Pi 5 by executing the following command:

```
(gdb) target remote <IP address>:12345
```

5. Execute the following command to add a breakpoint at the first line of the `main` function:

```
(gdb) break main
Breakpoint 1 at 0x555555550700: file hello-world.c, line 4.
```

6. Start the application by executing the following command:

```
(gdb) c
Continuing.
Reading /lib/libc.so.6 from remote target...
Reading /usr/lib/debug/.build-id/89/
ee7a046ed4706a137921ff3be155b37f085e72.debug from remote target...
Reading /lib/.debug/libc.so.6 from remote target...
Reading /lib/.debug/libc.so.6 from remote target...

Breakpoint 1, main (argc=1) at hello-world.c:4
4       {
```

7. After gdb stops at the breakpoint, we can hit the *Ctrl* + *X* key combination followed by the *a* key, and we should see the following screen:

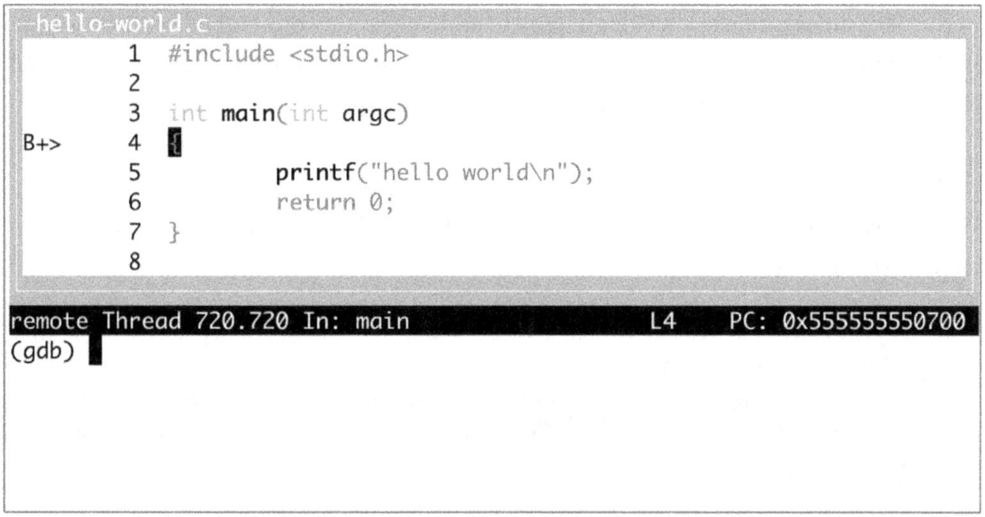

Figure 8.16 – gdb with a primitive user interface

8. We can see that the highlighted line, prepended with B+>, is the location of our breakpoint. We can use the *up* and *down* arrow keys to navigate inside the source file. Finally, we also have a gdb console interface underneath the TUI interface, which we can use to enter commands to help us debug our application.

> Important note
>
> **TUI** stands for **text user interface**. As we can see, TUI is a primitive user interface with all textual and graphical elements. Nonetheless, it is a powerful mechanism to help us navigate the code base around a breakpoint.

In the next section, we will learn how to use **Valgrind** to identify memory leaks in our application.

Valgrind: identifying memory leaks

While using gdb can be valuable to ensure that an application functions correctly, identifying and resolving performance issues is also a critical step in application development. Memory leaks can be detrimental to the performance of applications. A memory leak occurs when memory is dynamically allocated by an application but not freed. An unresolved memory leak in an application may result in the embedded Linux kernel prematurely terminating the application to ensure that the application doesn't consume all system memory and halt the entire system. Valgrind is a utility that can identify and locate memory leaks.

In the next subsections, we will learn how to add Valgrind to our embedded Linux system using Buildroot and the Yocto Project. Finally, we will create a contrived memory leak in our *Hello World* application. We will learn how to use Valgrind to identify and locate the memory leak.

Buildroot

Valgrind can be installed on the final embedded Linux image using Buildroot by following the steps outlined here:

1. Navigate to the `Chapter7` directory from the root of this book's Git repository by executing the following command:

```
$ cd Chapter8
```

2. Execute the following command to perform a baseline configuration of the embedded Linux image from *Chapter 7, Building an Image Using Buildroot*:

```
$ make config
```

3. Enter the Buildroot configuration menu by executing the following command:

```
$ make -C buildroot menuconfig
```

4. Hit the / key on the keyboard, type `valgrind`, and hit the *Enter* key to list the search results, as shown here:

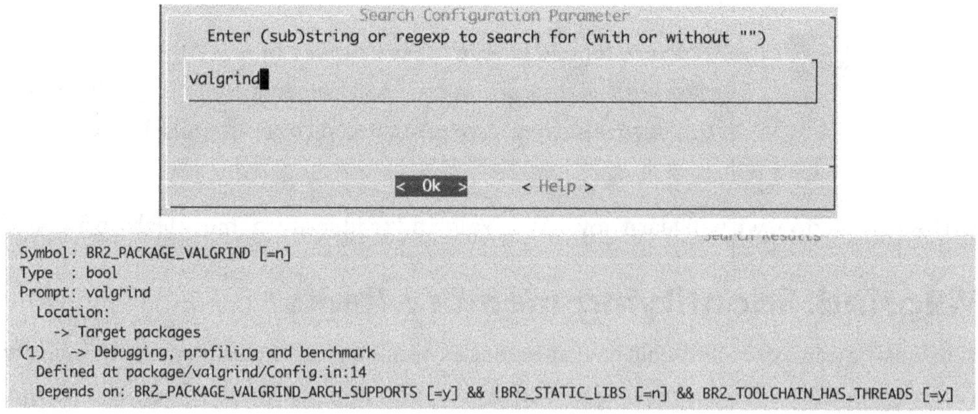

Figure 8.17 – Searching for Valgrind in Buildroot

5. Hit the *1* key on the keyboard, hit the *spacebar* to select the `valgrind` option, highlight the `Enter` option in the menu, and hit the *Enter* key, as shown here:

```
[*] valgrind
[*]   Memcheck: a memory error detector (NEW)
[*]   Cachegrind: a cache and branch-prediction profiler (NEW)
[*]   Callgrind: a call-graph generating cache and branch prediction profiler (NEW)
[*]   Helgrind: a thread error detector (NEW)
[*]   DRD: a thread error detector (NEW)
[*]   Massif: a heap profiler (NEW)
[*]   DHAT: a dynamic heap analysis tool (NEW)
[ ]   SGCheck: an experimental stack and global array overrun detector (NEW)
[ ]   BBV: an experimental basic block vector generation tool (NEW)
[ ]   Lackey: an example tool (NEW)
[ ]   Nulgrind: the minimal Valgrind tool (NEW)
```

Figure 8.18 – Enabling Valgrind in Buildroot

6. Follow the steps outlined in *Chapter 9, Project 1: Using Python to Build a Web Server to Display Sensor Data*, to flash the resulting image to the Raspberry Pi 4.

The Yocto Project

Valgrind can be installed on the final embedded Linux image using the Yocto Project by following the steps outlined here:

1. Navigate to the location of the Yocto Project directory created in *Chapter 6, Building an Image Using the Yocto Project.*
2. Execute the following command to set up the environment for image creation:

```
$ source layers/poky/oe-init-build-env
```

3. Add the following line to `build/conf/local.conf`:

```
IMAGE_INSTALL:append = " valgrind"
```

4. Rebuild the embedded Linux image as shown in *Chapter 6, Building an Image Using the Yocto Project*, and flash it to the SD card.

Testing

Next, we will see how Valgrind can help us identify memory leaks. We will use the modified version of the *Hello World* application, which is reproduced here and can be retrieved from the `Chapter8` directory of the Git repository:

```
#include <stdlib.h>
#include <stdio.h>
#include <string.h>

char *ptr;

int main(int argc, char *argv[])
{
        printf("Hello World!\n");
        ptr = malloc(20);
        strcpy(ptr, "Hello World");
        return 0;
}
```

In the preceding example, we have a global variable of the `char` pointer type called `ptr`. Then, in the `main` function, we do the following:

1. Print `Hello World!` as we did previously.
2. Use the `malloc` function to allocate 20 bytes and assign the memory to the `ptr` variable.
3. Copy the `Hello World` string to the `ptr` variable.
4. Exit out of the `main` function.

The memory leak in the application will result in the use of the `malloc` function without a corresponding call to the `free` function.

We can source the toolchain environment as shown previously and compile the application by executing the following command:

```
${CC} -o hello-world-memory-leak hello-world-memory-leak.c -ggdb3
```

The options in the invocation are as follows:

- `-o`: This option produces an executable named `hello-world-memory-leak`
- `-ggdb3`: This option generates debugging information within the executable that Valgrind will use

We can transfer the application to the Raspberry Pi 5 and run Valgrind against the application by executing the following command with the corresponding output:

```
root@raspberrypi5:~# valgrind --leak-check=full --show-leak-kinds=all ./
hello-world-memory-leak
==2114== Memcheck, a memory error detector
==2114== Copyright (C) 2002-2017, and GNU GPL'd, by Julian Seward et al.
==2114== Using Valgrind-3.18.1 and LibVEX; rerun with -h for copyright
info
==2114== Command: ./hello-world-memory-leak
==2114==
Hello World!
==2114==
==2114== HEAP SUMMARY:
==2114==     in use at exit: 20 bytes in 1 blocks
==2114==   total heap usage: 2 allocs, 1 frees, 1,044 bytes allocated
==2114==
==2114== 20 bytes in 1 blocks are still reachable in loss record 1 of 1
==2114==    at 0x486552C: malloc (vg_replace_malloc.c:381)
==2114==    by 0x120763: main (hello-world-memory-leak.c:10)
==2114==
==2114== LEAK SUMMARY:
==2114==    definitely lost: 0 bytes in 0 blocks
==2114==    indirectly lost: 0 bytes in 0 blocks
==2114==      possibly lost: 0 bytes in 0 blocks
==2114==    still reachable: 20 bytes in 1 blocks
==2114==         suppressed: 0 bytes in 0 blocks
==2114==
==2114== For lists of detected and suppressed errors, rerun with: -s
==2114== ERROR SUMMARY: 0 errors from 0 contexts (suppressed: 0 from 0)
```

Here, `--leak-check=full` and `--show-leak-kinds=all` instruct Valgrind to provide comprehensive information on possible memory leaks detected in the target application.

The following portion shows any dynamically allocated memory that wasn't properly cleared:

```
==2114== HEAP SUMMARY:
==2114==     in use at exit: 20 bytes in 1 blocks
==2114==   total heap usage: 2 allocs, 1 frees, 1,044 bytes allocated
```

We can see in the preceding output that Valgrind is reporting that the 20 bytes we assigned to the `ptr` variable were allocated twice but freed only once.

Similarly, the following output shows that the 20 bytes are still accessible after the application has terminated:

```
==2114== 20 bytes in 1 blocks are still reachable in loss record 1 of 1
==2114==    at 0x486552C: malloc (vg_replace_malloc.c:381)
==2114==    by 0x120763: main (hello-world-memory-leak.c:10)
```

Additionally, the preceding output shows exactly which line in our application contains the invocation of the `malloc` function without a corresponding call to the `free` function.

Finally, the following output shows a summary of all leaks in the application:

```
==2114== LEAK SUMMARY:
==2114==    definitely lost: 0 bytes in 0 blocks
==2114==    indirectly lost: 0 bytes in 0 blocks
==2114==      possibly lost: 0 bytes in 0 blocks
==2114==    still reachable: 20 bytes in 1 blocks
==2114==         suppressed: 0 bytes in 0 blocks
```

In the preceding output, we can see that Valgrind is informing us that the 20 bytes we allocated are still reachable upon application termination since we didn't free them.

In the next section, we will learn about **systemd** and how it can be used to help us launch applications automatically on boot.

systemd: launching applications on boot

In this section, we will learn how `systemd` can help us launch applications on boot.

> Important note
>
> `systemd` is a complex topic and cannot be covered in significant detail in one chapter, let alone a section of a chapter. Readers seeking a deeper understanding of `systemd` are encouraged to consult the book titled *Linux Service Management Made Easy with systemd: Advanced techniques to effectively manage, control, and monitor Linux Systems and Services*, which can be retrieved using the following link: `https://www.packtpub.com/en-us/product/linux-service-management-made-easy-with-systemd-9781801811644`.

Previously, we implemented and executed a simple *Hello World* application on our Raspberry Pi 5. While transferring the application using SCP and executing it on the Raspberry Pi 5 is sufficient for testing, it is not acceptable for deployment. Instead, we need a mechanism to execute the application automatically when the system starts. `systemd` is one such framework that we can use to accomplish this task.

SysVInit has traditionally served this purpose. The following list outlines the main differences between SysVInit and `systemd`:

- **Application management**: SysVInit uses a simple tiered directory structure. Scripts to manage application execution are stored in `/etc/init.d`. SysVInit has different directories, which contain symbolic links to the scripts contained in `/etc/init.d`. Each of the scripts in these directories, which follow the `/etc/rcX.d/` naming convention, are executed when Linux achieves a particular **run level**, `d`. Each script has directives to start, stop, and restart an application. On the other hand, `systemd` uses a more complex approach. Application execution is defined in files with a `.service` extension, known as a **service unit**. Each service unit supports many directives that control when and how a particular application should be executed.
- **Dependency management**: SysVInit has a primitive mechanism for dependency management. Each script is prepended with `S` and a number. The scripts are executed in order of increasing number. For example, if `S01appA`, `S02appB`, and `S03appC` are present, `S01appA` is executed first, `S02appB` is executed second, and `S03appC` is executed last. `systemd` manages dependencies differently. Each service unit can contain multiple directives that describe the application's dependencies.

We can create a service unit for the `hello-world` application we implemented in *Chapter 6, Building an Image Using the Yocto Project*, by following the steps outlined here:

1. Ensure that the `hello-world` application is located at `/usr/bin` on the Raspberry Pi.
2. Create a file called `hello-world.service` located at `/etc/systemd/system/` and add the following contents to it:

```
[Unit]
Description=Hello World system

[Service]
ExecStart=/usr/bin/hello-world
```

```
[Install]
WantedBy=multi-user.target
```

3. The following describes the lines in the preceding service unit:

    - Each section starts with the name of the section enclosed in brackets. For example, `[Unit]` specifies options for the `Unit` section, which contains generic information about the service. In this instance, `Description` is a short human-readable title of the unit, and is set to `Hello World system`.
    - The `[Service]` section provides instructions on controlling the service. The only line under the `Service` section is the `ExecStart` command, which specifies the command that should be executed when the service is started.
    - The `[Install]` section defines the installation details associated with our service. The `WantedBy` entry defines when our service should be started during the boot cycle. In this instance, we have specified that our service will be run when the system has reached `multi-user` state, or the run level where users can log in to the system.

4. We can load our service by executing the following command:

```
$ sudo systemctl daemon-reload
```

5. We can instruct `systemd` to load our service whenever the system boots by executing the following command. This also instructs `systemd` to start the service immediately:

```
$ sudo systemctl --now enable hello-world
Created symlink /etc/systemd/system/multi-user.target.wants/hello-
world.service → /etc/systemd/system/hello-world.service.
```

6. We can confirm that our service was successfully started by executing the following command, which prints the logging associated with our `hello-world` service:

```
$ journalctl -u hello-world
Jul 15 14:00:51 raspberrypi systemd[1]: Started hello-world.service
- Hello World system.
Jul 15 14:00:51 raspberrypi hello-world[493183]: hello world
Jul 15 14:00:51 raspberrypi systemd[1]: hello-world.service:
Deactivated
successfully.
```

We can see from the line in bold in the output that our service was successfully started, and it printed `hello world`.

Summary

In this chapter, we learned about application development. Specifically, we gained valuable insight into how to set up our toolchain and cross-compile applications for development. This way, we don't need to regenerate our entire embedded Linux image to only test certain applications.

We also learned how to debug applications on our Raspberry Pi using `gdbserver` and a local version of `gdb` running on our development machine. These tools enable us to efficiently debug our target embedded system.

We explored how to use Valgrind to identify memory leaks in our application and ensure that it is performant. Finally, we demonstrated how `systemd` can be used as a framework to automatically launch applications on boot.

With the lessons learned in this chapter, we are armed with the appropriate tools to develop sophisticated and performant applications and incorporate them into our final embedded Linux image.

In the next chapter, we'll build a complete Python-based project that reads real sensor data on the Raspberry Pi, stores it, and serves it through a lightweight web interface.

Get this book's PDF version and more

Scan the QR code (or go to `packtpub.com/unlock`). Search for this book by name, confirm the edition, and then follow the steps on the page.

UNLOCK NOW

Note: Keep your invoice handy. Purchases made directly from Packt don't require an invoice.

9

Project 1: Using Python to Build a Web Server to Display Sensor Data

In the next three chapters, we will learn how to create and run applications on the Raspberry Pi 5 Embedded Linux system. Each chapter will provide a detailed walkthrough of an application targeting a distinct objective, using a unique framework. In this chapter, we will create an application that will perform the following tasks:

- Collect temperature data from a sensor
- Store the temperature data in a local database
- Reports the temperature data on a web server

The application will be developed in Python on the Raspberry Pi 5 and will be collecting light data from a sensor, storing it in a database, and presenting it for display using a web interface.

We are going to cover the following main topics in this chapter:

- Project overview and system architecture
- Collecting sensor data
- Storing sensor data using InfluxDB
- Creating a web server using Flask

Technical requirements

You should be comfortable executing commands on a terminal. You should be comfortable reading, writing, and executing Python applications. Finally, you should also ensure that you have downloaded the Git repository associated with this book, located at `https://github.com/PacktPublishing/Embedded-Linux-Essentials-Handbook/tree/main/Chapter9`.

Project overview and system architecture

In this section, we will learn about the project covered in this chapter. We will understand the details of the project via a system architecture diagram. As mentioned, there are three main components of this project, as follows:

1. **Collecting sensor data:** The first task that our application needs to accomplish is to collect sensor data. Specifically, it collects the amount of light perceived by the corresponding sensor. The application targets the AMS TSL2591 light sensor, which can be found here: `https://www.digikey.com/en/products/detail/ams-osram-usa-inc/TSL25911FN/4211515`. Adafruit sells an evaluation board for easy use of the TSL2591. It can be purchased from `https://www.adafruit.com/product/1980` and is shown in the following figure:

Figure 9.1 – Adafrauit TSL2591 light sensor

The steps outlined next need to be followed to successfully collect sensor data:

    1. Enable the appropriate Kconfig in the Linux kernel to add support for the AMS TSL2591 light sensor driver.
    2. Add a devicetree overlay to inform the AMS TSL2591 driver of the I2C bus that the sensor is connected.
    3. Create a Python application to periodically collect data reported by the AMS TSL2591 light sensor via the **Industrial I/O** (**IIO**) interface of the Linux kernel.

2. **Storing sensor data**: After collecting light data from the AMS TSL2591 sensor, the application needs to store it in a database. We will use InfluxDB as our database (`https://github.com/influxdata/influxdb`). InfluxDB is designed for data collected over consistent periods of time, known as **time series** data. The Python application developed in the first bullet point will be expanded to add this functionality.
3. **Presenting sensor data**: The final task will be to present the sensor data to the outside world using a web server that responds to queries to a few endpoints.

The following figure shows the connections between the Adafruit TSL2591 evaluation board and the Raspberry Pi 5:

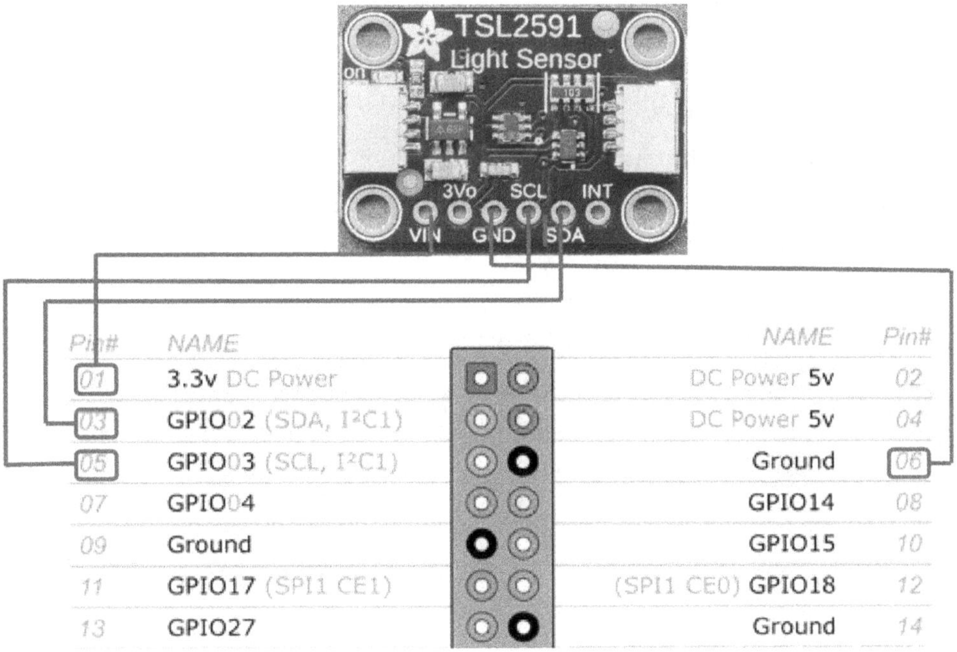

Figure 9.2 – Connections between the Adafruit TSL2591 and Raspberry Pi 5

The connections between the boards are outlined as follows:

- **VIN** on the Adafruit TSL2591 is connected to pin 1 on the Raspberry Pi 5, which supplies 3.3 volts
- **GND** on the Adafruit TSL2591 is connected to pin 6 on the Raspberry Pi 5, which is one of the ground points
- **SCL** on the Adafruit TSL2591 is connected to pin 5 on the Raspberry Pi 5, which is the SCL line of the I2C1 controller on the Raspberry Pi 5
- **SDA** on the Adafruit TSL2591 is connected to pin 3 on the Raspberry Pi 5, which is the SDA line of the I2C1 controller on the Raspberry Pi 5

In the next section, we will understand the steps required to periodically collect data from the AMS TSL2591 sensor.

Collecting sensor data

In this section, we will learn the steps required to collect data from the AMS TSL2591 sensor periodically. We will walk through the steps outlined here:

1. Flash Raspbian on the Raspberry Pi 5.
2. Add support for I2C on the Raspberry Pi 5.
3. Customize the Linux kernel.
4. Add a device tree overlay.
5. Confirm data using the terminal interface.
6. Implement a simple Python application that periodically queries the sensor for the perceived light intensity.

> Important note
>
> The steps described in this section are similar to the steps outlined in *Chapter 3, Navigating the Linux Kernel*. Recall that in this chapter, we learned how to add support for different peripherals connected to the Raspberry Pi 5 via the I2C and SPI buses.

Flashing Raspbian on the Raspberry Pi 5

First, we need to flash the stock Raspbian OS on the Raspberry Pi 5 by following the steps outlined here:

1. Plug a micro-SD card into your PC.
2. Open the **Raspberry Pi Imager** application and click on **CHOOSE DEVICE**, as shown here:

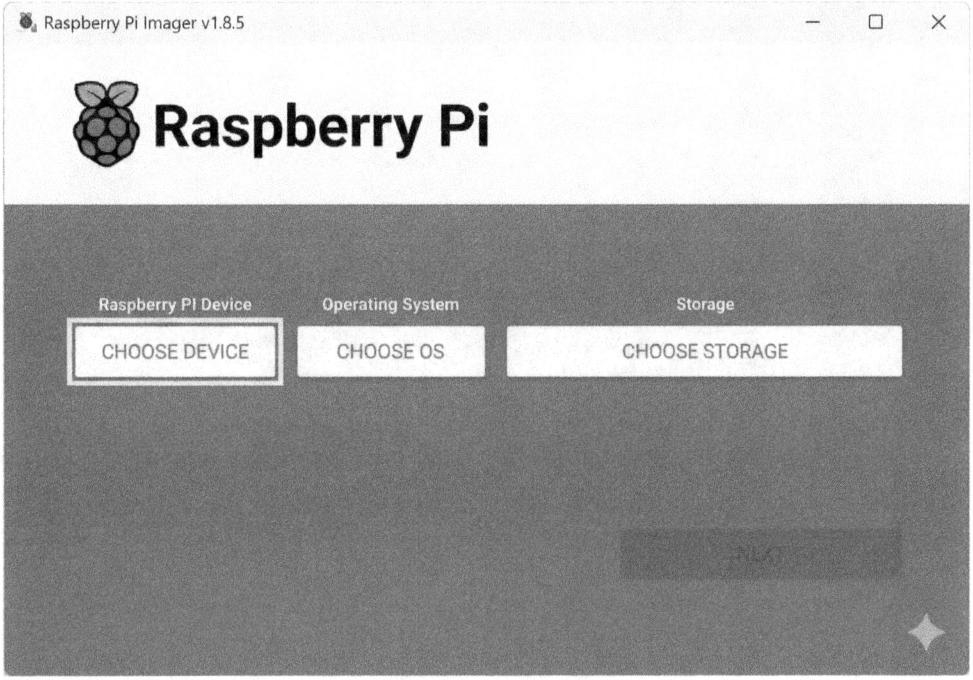

Figure 9.3 – Selecting the device to flash

3. In the resulting popup, click on the **Raspberry Pi 5** option, as shown here:

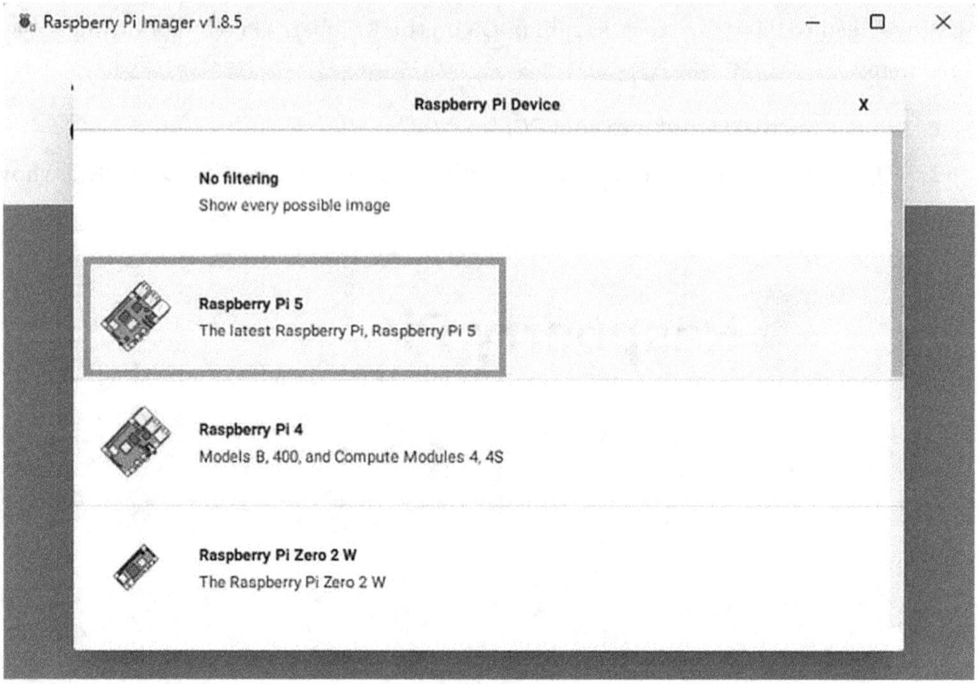

Figure 9.4 – Selecting the Raspberry Pi 5

4. Click on **CHOOSE OS** in the main window, as shown here:

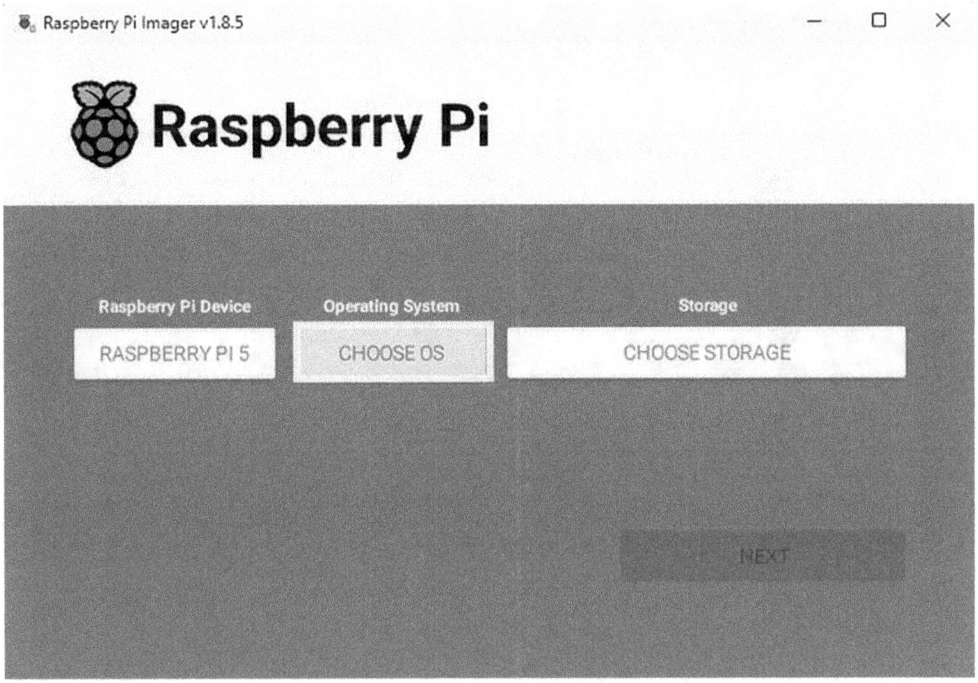

Figure 9.5 – Selecting the operating system to flash

5. In the resulting window, click on **Raspberry Pi OS (64-bit)**, as shown here:

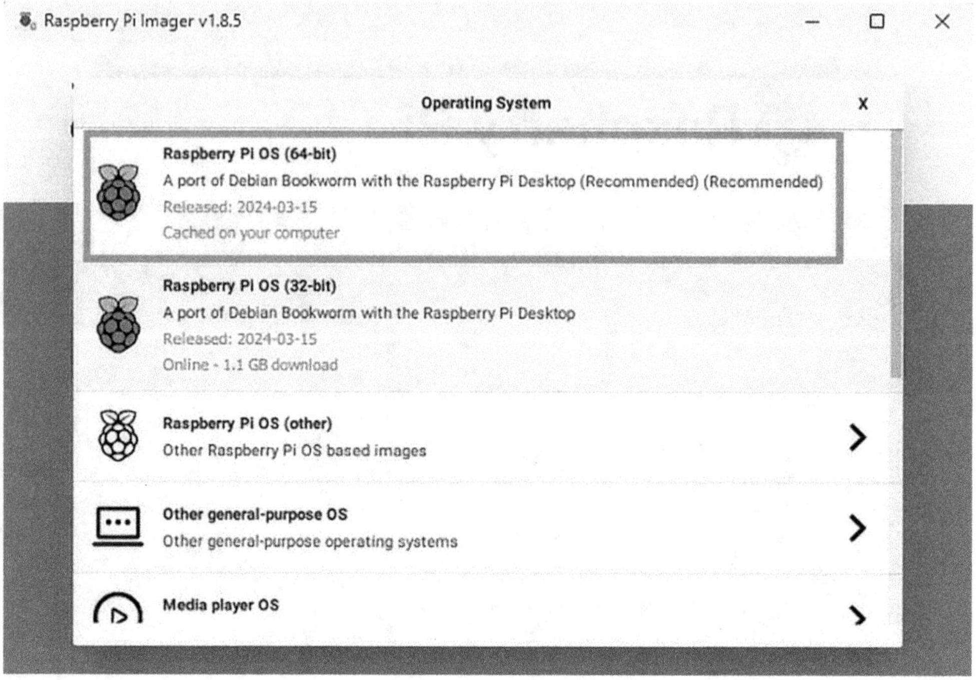

Figure 9.6 – Choosing to flash Raspberry Pi OS

6. After the window closes, click on **CHOOSE STORAGE**, as shown next, and click on the SD card in the resulting window:

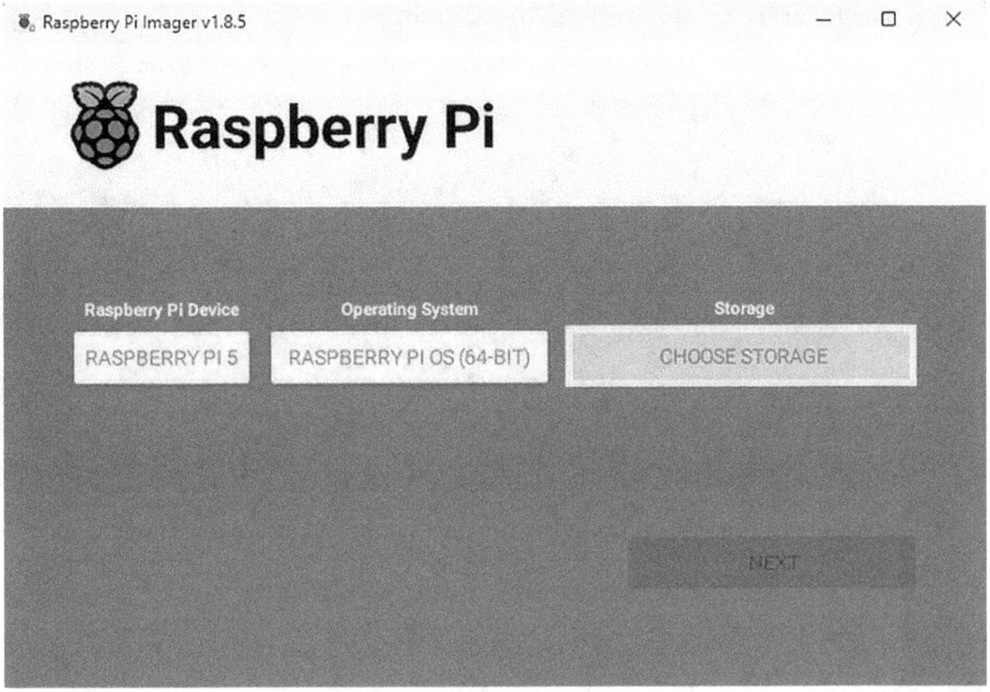

Figure 9.7 – Selecting the micro-SD card

7. Click on **Next** and wait for the process to finish.

Our SD card now contains the stock Raspberry Pi OS image. Next, we will add support for I2C.

Adding support for I2C on the Raspberry Pi 5

After flashing the micro-SD card, plugging it into the Raspberry Pi 5, and powering up the Raspberry Pi 5, we need to enable support for the I2C bus by following the steps outlined here:

1. Remotely log in to the Raspberry Pi 5.
2. Open the Raspberry Pi configuration tool by executing the following command:

```
$ sudo raspi-config
```

3. In the resulting window, use the arrow keys to highlight **3 Interface Options** and hit the *Enter* key.

4. In the resulting menu, highlight **I4 I2C** using the arrow keys and hit the *Enter* key.
5. In the final window, highlight **Yes** and hit the *Enter* key.
6. Finally, hit the *Esc* key to exit the application.
7. Execute the following command to confirm that the Raspberry Pi 5 can detect the TSL2591:

```
~$ i2cdetect -y 1
     0  1  2  3  4  5  6  7  8  9  a  b  c  d  e  f
00:                         -- -- -- -- -- -- -- --
10: -- -- -- -- -- -- -- -- -- -- -- -- -- -- -- --
20: -- -- -- -- -- -- -- -- -- 29 -- -- -- -- -- --
30: -- -- -- -- -- -- -- -- -- -- -- -- -- -- -- --
40: -- -- -- -- -- -- -- -- -- -- -- -- -- -- -- --
50: -- -- -- -- -- -- -- -- -- -- -- -- -- -- -- --
60: -- -- -- -- -- -- -- -- -- -- -- -- -- -- -- --
70: -- -- -- -- -- -- -- --
```

8. Based on the preceding output, we can see that the TSL2591 sensor is observed at address `0x29`!

Next, we will customize the Linux kernel to add support for the TSL2591 sensor.

Customizing the Linux kernel

The Linux kernel has a driver available for the AMS TSL2591 (and, in turn, the Adafruit TSL2591 evaluation board).

We can follow the steps outlined here to install a version of the Linux kernel that has support for the Adafruit TSL2591 evaluation board:

1. Execute the following command to navigate to the SDK that was generated using the Yocto Project:

```
$ cd <path to yocto>/build/sdk
```

2. Configure the environment to use the toolchain generated from the Yocto Project by executing the following command:

```
$ source environment-setup-cortexa76-poky-linux
```

3. Clone the repository that contains the Raspberry Pi version of the Linux kernel by executing the following command:

```
$ git clone https://github.com/raspberrypi/linux
```

4. Modify the `arch/arm64/configs/bcm2712_defconfig` file with the following addition:

```
diff --git a/arch/arm64/configs/bcm2712_defconfig b/arch/arm64/
configs/bcm2712_defconfig
index 76effcbc199b..7c5cb573a0aa 100644
--- a/arch/arm64/configs/bcm2712_defconfig
+++ b/arch/arm64/configs/bcm2712_defconfig
@@ -1472,7 +1472,7 @@ CONFIG_MAILBOX=y
 CONFIG_BCM2835_MBOX=y
 CONFIG_BCM2712_IOMMU=y
 CONFIG_RASPBERRYPI_POWER=y
-CONFIG_IIO=m
+CONFIG_IIO=y
 CONFIG_IIO_BUFFER_CB=m
 CONFIG_IIO_SW_TRIGGER=m
 CONFIG_MCP320X=m
@@ -1492,6 +1492,7 @@ CONFIG_INV_MPU6050_I2C=m
 CONFIG_APDS9960=m
 CONFIG_BH1750=m
 CONFIG_TSL4531=m
+CONFIG_TSL2591=y
 CONFIG_VEML6070=m
 CONFIG_IIO_HRTIMER_TRIGGER=m
 CONFIG_IIO_INTERRUPT_TRIGGER=m
```

5. Execute the following command to configure the Linux kernel for the Raspberry Pi 5 (along with my modifications):

```
$ ARCH=arm64 make bcm2712_defconfig
```

6. Compile the Linux kernel by executing the following command:

```
$ ARCH=arm make -j10
```

7. Execute the following command to compile the kernel modules:

```
$ ARCH=arm make modules
```

8. Inform the Linux kernel build system to install the kernel modules to the current directory by executing the following command:

```
$ export INSTALL_MOD_PATH=`pwd`
```

9. Execute the following command to install the kernel modules in the current directory:

```
$ ARCH=arm64 make modules_install
```

The kernel modules will be installed in the current directory under `lib/modules/6.1.69-v8-16k+`.

10. Compress the directory with the kernel modules by executing the following command:

```
$ tar cvzf modules.tar.gz ./lib/modules/6.1.69-v8-16k+/
```

11. Execute the following command to transfer the compiled kernel to the Raspberry Pi 5 (make sure to replace `<user name>` and `<IP address>` with the username and IP address of the Raspberry Pi 5, respectively):

```
$ scp arch/arm64/boot/Image.gz <user name>@<IP address>:~/
```

12. Transfer the compressed archive of the kernel modules by executing the following command:

```
$ scp modules.tar.gz <user name>@<IP address>:~/
```

13. Log in to the Raspberry Pi 5, and copy the compiled kernel to the first partition by executing the following commands:

```
~$ cd /boot/firmware/
/boot/firmware$ sudo cp ~/Image.gz ./kernel-mab.img
```

14. Modify `config.txt` to point to the newly compiled kernel, as shown here (in bold):

```
# For more options and information see
# http://rptl.io/configtxt
# Some settings may impact device functionality. See link above for details

kernel=kernel-mab.img
```

15. Execute the following commands to extract the kernel modules from the compressed archive:

```
$ cd ~/
~$ tar xzvf modules.tar.gz
```

16. Copy the compiled kernel modules to the appropriate location on the Embedded Linux system by executing the following command:

```
$ cd /lib/modules/
$ sudo cp -r ~/lib/modules/6.1.69-v8-16k+/ ./
```

Next, we're going to add the TSL2591 sensor as part of a devicetree overlay on the Raspberry Pi 5.

Adding a devicetree overlay

Now that we have added support in the Linux kernel for the TSL2591 sensor, we need to inform the kernel of the sensor's location on the Raspberry Pi 5. We can achieve this by creating and loading a device tree overlay by following the steps outlined here:

1. Create a text file named `add-tsl2591.dts` with the following content:

```
/dts-v1/;
/plugin/;

&rp1_i2c1 {
    tsl2591@28 {
        compatible = "amstaos,tsl2591";
        reg = <0x29>;
    };
};
```

The file informs the Linux kernel that our TSL2591 sensor is connected to the I2C1 bus on the Raspberry Pi 5, at address `0x29`.

2. Compile the devicetree overlay by executing the following command (replace `<path to Raspberry Pi Linux>` with the location of Raspberry Pi's fork of the Linux kernel):

```
$ <path to Raspberry Pi Linux>/scripts/dtc/dtc -O dtb -o add-tsl2591.dtbo add-tsl2591.dts
```

3. Execute the following command to transfer the compiled devicetree overlay to the Raspberry Pi 5:

```
$ scp add-tsl2591.dtbo <user name>@<IP address>:~/
```

4. Log in to the Raspberry Pi 5.
5. Copy the compiled devicetree overlay to the `overlays` directory on the first partition of the Raspberry Pi by executing the following commands:

```
$ cd /boot/firmware
$ sudo cp ~/add-tsl2591.dtbo ./overlays/
```

6. Inform the Raspberry Pi 5 to load the compiled overlay by adding the following line to `config.txt` (in bold):

```
# Run as fast as firmware / board allows
arm_boost=1

# Add TSL2591 device
dtoverlay=add-tsl2591.dtbo
```

7. Reboot the Raspberry Pi 5.

After rebooting, the Raspberry Pi should have support for the TSL2591 sensor. We will confirm support by viewing the data output on a terminal interface.

Confirming data on a terminal interface

Follow the steps outlined here to confirm data from the TSL2591 sensor:

1. Confirm that the TSL2591 driver has successfully initialized the TSL2591 sensor and added it to the IIO subsystem by executing the following command:

```
$ cat /sys/bus/iio/devices/iio\:device0/of_node/name
tsl2591
```

2. Under ambient lighting conditions, execute the following command to view the intensity reported by the TSL2591 sensor:

```
$ cat /sys/bus/iio/devices/iio\:device0/in_illuminance_input
65.426000
```

3. Place an object over the TSL2591 sensor to emulate darker lighting conditions.

4. Execute the following command to view the intensity reported by the TSL2591 sensor under these darker conditions:

```
$ cat /sys/bus/iio/devices/iio\:device0/in_illuminance_input
4.293000
```

We can see that the reported intensity is much lower under darker lighting conditions than under brighter lighting conditions, which is expected!

Installing the IIO library

Before we can implement the Python application, we need to install the IIO library. This library allows us to interface with the TSL2591 device driver from userspace. We can install this library by following the steps here:

1. Execute the following command to install the required packages:

```
$ sudo apt-get install build-essential libxml2 libzstd-dev libxml2-
dev bison flex libcdk5-dev cmake libaio-dev libusb-1.0-0-dev
libserialport-dev libxml2-dev libavahi-client-dev doxygen graphviz
```

2. Download the source code for the IIO library and navigate to the source code directory by executing the following command:

```
$ git clone https://github.com/analogdevicesinc/libiio.git
$ cd libiio
```

3. Execute the following command to check out the tag associated with version 0.25 (this is the version of the Python "bindings" that will be installed later, and it is important to keep the same versions):

```
$ git checkout tags/v0.25
```

4. Compile the IIO library by executing the following commands:

```
$ mkdir build
$ cd build
$ cmake ../
$ make
```

5. Execute the following command to install the compiled library:

```
$ sudo make install
```

Next, we will implement a simple Python application to query the TSL2591 sensor and print the output periodically.

Implementing a simple Python application

Finally, we can implement a simple Python application to query the TSL2591 sensor for observed light intensity periodically. We can accomplish this by following the steps outlined here:

1. Create a Python virtual environment by executing the following command:

```
$ python -m venv .env
```

> Important note
>
> A **virtual environment** (venv) in Python allows us to maintain organization across different applications. Since different Python applications may have different dependencies, a virtual environment allows us to avoid mixing different dependencies together or, worse, having all of the dependencies across all Python applications installed globally on our platform.

2. Execute the following command to activate the environment that was just created:

```
$ source .env/bin/activate
```

3. Install the Python bindings for the IIO library by executing the following command:

```
(.env) pi@rpi5:~ $ pip install pylibiio
Looking in indexes: https://pypi.org/simple, https://www.piwheels.
org/simple
Collecting pylibiio
  Downloading pylibiio-0.25-py3-none-any.whl (11 kB)
Installing collected packages: pylibiio
Successfully installed pylibiio-0.25
```

> Important note
>
> **Bindings** are thin wrappers that allow applications implemented using one programming language, such as Python, to access functions from a library implemented in another language, such as C/C++. As was mentioned earlier, and as we can see from the preceding output, the version of the Python bindings is 0.25.

4. Create a text file called `get-sensor-data.py` and add the following lines of source code:

```
1 from time import sleep
2 import iio

3 ctx = iio.LocalContext()
4 ctrl = ctx.find_device('tsl2591')

5 chan = ctrl.find_channel('illuminance')

6 while True:
7     intensity = chan.attrs['input'].value
8     print(intensity)
9     sleep(0.1)
```

The application performs the following tasks:

1. Line 1 imports the `sleep` symbol from the `time` module.
2. Line 2 imports the `iio` module that was just installed.
3. Line 3 creates an `iio` context, which is used to access the values reported by an IIO device safely.
4. Line 4 finds the TSL2591 device and creates an object representing the device in the Python application.
5. Line 5 finds the IIO channel that represents the light intensity reported by the sensor. An **IIO channel** is a mechanism the IIO subsystem uses to report values reported by the underlying device.
6. Line 6 creates an infinite loop.
7. Line 7 extracts the light intensity perceived by the TSL2591 device.
8. Line 8 prints the intensity.
9. Line 9 puts the application to sleep for 100 milliseconds.

We can run the preceding Python application by executing the following command, and see the results that are printed:

```
$ python get-sensor-data.py
14.446000
14.401000
14.274000
```

```
14.152000
14.050000
13.974000
13.876000
```

In this section, we used the lessons learned from previous chapters to configure our Raspberry Pi 5 to interface with an AMS TSL2591 digital light sensor. We also learned how to implement a Python application to safely retrieve and print this sensor data periodically.

In the next section, we will build on the Python application and store the data collected in a database.

Storing sensor data using InfluxDB

In this section, we will learn how to store the light intensity data from the TSL2591 sensor in an InfluxDB (`https://www.influxdata.com/`) database. InfluxDB is an open source database whose architecture is ideal for time series data. Time series data is data that is recorded over regular time intervals, such as sensor data.

We need to perform the following steps to ultimately implement a Python application to store data collected from the TSL2591 in an InfluxDB database:

1. Install and start the InfluxDB service.
2. Configure the InfluxDB service.
3. Implement a Python application to store data retrieved from the TSL2591 sensor into the InfluxDB database.

Installing and starting the InfluxDB service

We need to perform the following steps to install and start the InfluxDB service:

1. Execute the following command to download the InfluxDB package for the Raspberry Pi:

   ```
   $ curl -LO https://download.influxdata.com/influxdb/releases/
   influxdb2_2.7.6-1_arm64.deb
   ```

2. Install the InfluxDB package by executing the following command:

   ```
   $ sudo dpkg -i influxdb2_2.7.6-1_arm64.deb
   ```

3. Finally, execute the following command to start the InfluxDB service:

   ```
   $ sudo service influxdb start
   ```

Configuring the InfluxDB service

Before we can use the InfluxDB service, we need to configure it using the InfluxDB **command-line interface (CLI)** by following the steps outlined here:

1. Execute the following command to download the compressed archive containing the InfluxDB CLI:

   ```
   $ wget https://download.influxdata.com/influxdb/releases/influxdb2-
   client-$ 2.7.5-linux-arm64.tar.gz
   ```

2. Extract the InfluxDB CLI from the compressed archive by executing the following command:

   ```
   $ tar xvzf ./influxdb2-client-2.7.5-linux-amd64.tar.gz
   ```

3. Execute the following command to place the InfluxDB CLI in a sensible location:

   ```
   $ sudo cp ./influx /usr/local/bin/
   ```

4. Begin the setup process by executing the following command:

   ```
   $ influx setup
   ```

5. After executing the preceding command, the following prompts will be presented, and the following responses should be given:

   - **Please type your primary username:** `pi-packt`
   - **Please type your password:** `pi-packt`
   - **Please type your password again:** `pi-packt`
   - **Please type your primary organization name:** `packt`
   - **Please type your primary bucket name:** `ch12`
   - **Please type your retention period in hours, or 0 for infinite:** `12`
   - **Setup with these parameters?** `Yes`

Implementing a Python application

Finally, we can extend the Python application we wrote previously to store sensor data retrieved from the TSL2591 sensor by following the steps outlined here:

1. Create a **bucket** in the InfluxDB database to store the sensor data by executing the following command:

   ```
   $ influx bucket create -n packt-ch12
   ```

2. Navigate to the location where we created our environment previously and execute the following command to activate it:

```
$ source .env/bin/activate
```

3. Install the library required by our Python application to interact with the InfluxDB database by executing the following command:

```
(.env) $ pip install 'influxdb-client[ciso]'
```

4. Retrieve the token associated with the user that we created previously by executing the following command:

```
$ influx auth list
ID                        Description               Token
User Name       User ID                 Permissions
0d27dac785d82000        pi-packt's Token        3563QrhOmUNToC_
zA_ALsfqaN9LlBFk9B2r3nqSTtZoa32PdfB1xz7_
SbQu5vLsH7AxJAfj4QXVYsmIKMnP2EQ==        pi-packt
0d27dac753582000        [read:/authorizations write:/authorizations
read:/buckets write:/buckets read:/dashboards write:/dashboards
read:/orgs write:/orgs read:/sources write:/sources read:/
tasks write:/tasks read:/telegrafs write:/telegrafs read:/
users write:/users read:/variables write:/variables read:/
scrapers write:/scrapers read:/secrets write:/secrets read:/labels
write:/labels read:/views write:/views read:/documents write:/
documents read:/notificationRules write:/notificationRules read:/
notificationEndpoints write:/notificationEndpoints read:/checks
write:/checks read:/dbrp write:/dbrp read:/notebooks write:/
notebooks read:/annotations write:/annotations read:/remotes write:/
remotes read:/replications write:/replications]
```

5. The `3563QrhOmUNToC_zA_ALsfqaN9LlBFk9B2r3nqSTtZoa32PdfB1xz7_SbQu5vLsH7AxJAfj4QXVYsmIKMnP2EQ==` token will be used in our Python application.

6. Extend the Python application that we created previously with the following additions (the implementation is also present in the `get-and-store-sensor-data.py` file in the `Chapter12` directory of the book's Git repository):

```
from influxdb_client import InfluxDBClient, Point
from influxdb_client.client.write_api import SYNCHRONOUS

from time import sleep
```

```
4 import iio

5 ctx = iio.LocalContext()
6 ctrl = ctx.find_device('tsl2591')

7 chan = ctrl.find_channel('illuminance')
8 bucket = "ch9"

9 client = InfluxDBClient(url="http://localhost:8086",
token="3563QrhOmUNToC_zA_ALsfqaN9L1BFk9B2r3nqSTtZoa32PdfB1xz7_
SbQu5vLsH7AxJAfj4QXVYsmIKMnP2EQ==", org="packt")
10 write_api = client.write_api(write_options=SYNCHRONOUS)

11 while True:
12     intensity = chan.attrs['input'].value
13     p = Point("measurement").tag("location", "office").
field("intensity", intensity)
14     write_api.write(bucket=bucket, record=p)
    sleep(0.1)
```

The additions to the application are responsible for the following tasks:

1. Line 1 retrieves the `InfluxDBClient` symbol from the `influxdb_client` Python module we installed, which will interact with the InfluxDB server. It also retrieves the `Point` symbol from the same module to generate data to write to the InfluxDB database.
2. Line 2 retrieves the `SYNCHRONOUS` symbol, which allows us to perform **synchronous** writes to the database. A synchronous write ensures we get immediate feedback on whether the write succeeded.
3. Line 8 creates the `bucket` variable, set to `ch12`.
4. Line 9 creates an instance of `InfluxDBClient` to interact with the InfluxDB database. We pass the following arguments:
    - `url`: Set to `http://localhost:8086`, the address and port of the InfluxDB running locally on our Raspberry Pi

- token: Set to 3563QrhOmUNToC_zA_ALsfqaN9L1BFk9B2r3nqSTtZoa32PdfB1xz7_SbQu5vLsH7AxJAfj4QXVYsmIKMnP2EQ==, the token associated with the packt organization we created previously
- org: Set to packt, the organization we created previously

5. Line 10 creates an object we can use to write to the InfluxDB database. We set write_options to SYNCHRONOUS so we get immediate feedback on the database operation.
6. Line 13 creates a point in our time series data with the following parameters:
   - measurement: The name given to our point in the time series data.
   - tag: We can use a tag to specify additional information associated with a point in the time series data. In this instance, we have specified a location point, set to office.
   - field: We specify an intensity field with the reading retrieved from the TSL2591 sensor.
7. Finally, line 14 writes the data point we created to the ch12 bucket.

We can confirm that our application has been implemented correctly by following the steps outlined here:

1. Run the Python application by executing the following command:

```
$ python get-and-store-sensor-data.py
```

2. After a few seconds, hit the *Ctrl* + *C* key combination to terminate the application.
3. Execute the following command to retrieve the most recent measurement from the ch12 bucket, captured within 10 minutes of the current time:

```
$ influx query 'from(bucket:"ch12") |> range(start: -10m) |> last()'
```

The preceding command generates the output captured in the following figure:

```
                        _start:time                      _stop:time
  ------------------------------  ------------------------------
  2024-06-08T12:36:41.055137562Z  2024-06-08T12:46:41.055137562Z

                      _field:string     _measurement:string
             ----------------------  ----------------------
                          intensity             measurement

        location:string                       _time:time          _value:string
  ----------------------  ------------------------------  ----------------------
                  office  2024-06-08T12:45:24.535125030Z                9.365000
```

Figure 9.8 – Most recent light intensity reading

We can make the following observations from the output:

- The `_field:string` key contains the `intensity` value, which aligns with our implementation
- Similarly, the `_measurement:string` key contains the `measurement` value, which is what we passed to the `Point` data structure in our Python application
- The `location:string` key, a tag we specified, contains the `office` value, which is expected
- Finally, the `_value:string` key contains the reading retrieved from the TSL2591 sensor

In this section, we learned how to expand our Python application to store readings from the TSL2591 sensor in the InfluxDB database for later retrieval. In the next section, we will learn how to build a Python application to provide the most recent sensor reading when queried by a remote entity via an HTTP endpoint.

Creating a web server using Flask

In this section, we will learn how to create a web server in Python to report the readings from the TSL2591 sensor in response to an HTTP query. We will use **Flask**, which is a lightweight Python library used to host a web server. We can accomplish this task by following the steps outlined here:

1. Open a new terminal, remotely log in to the Raspberry Pi 5, navigate to the directory where we created our environment previously, and execute the following command to activate the environment:

```
$ source .env/bin/activate
```

2. Install Flask by executing the following command:

```
$ pip install flask
```

3. Add the following code to a Python source file (the implementation is also present as the `flask-sensor-data.py` file in the `Chapter12` directory of the book's Git repository):

```
1 from influxdb_client import InfluxDBClient
2 from flask import Flask

3 app = Flask(__name__)

4 bucket = "ch9"
5 client = InfluxDBClient(url="http://localhost:8086",
token="3563QrhOmUNToC_zA_ALsfqaN9LlBFk9B2r3nqSTtZoa32PdfB1xz7_
SbQu5vLsH7AxJAfj4QXVYsmIKMnP2EQ==", org="packt")

6 query_api = client.query_api()

7 @app.route('/')
8 def get_last_reading():
9     result = query_api.query('from(bucket:"ch12") |> range(start:
-10m) |> last()')
10    results = []

11    for table in result:
12          for record in table.records:
13                 results.append((record.get_field(), record.get_
value()))

14    final_result = results[0]
15    return final_result[1]
```

The Python application performs the following tasks:

1. Line 1 imports `InfluxDBClient` from the `influxdb_client` module, which will be used to interact with the InfluxDB database.
2. Line 2 imports the `Flask` symbol from the `flask` module, which will be used to implement the web server.

3. Line 3 instantiates the Flask web server (the `__name__` directive in Python equates to the name of our source file).
4. Lines 4 and 5 are used to interact with the appropriate bucket in the InfluxDB database.
5. Line 6 creates an instance of an object to read data from the InfluxDB database.
6. Line 7 is a mechanism typically used in Flask applications to define endpoints. In this particular instance, we have defined a single endpoint, which is the base of our web server. Thus, when another application performs a `GET` operation on the / endpoint, it will be directed to the endpoint defined on line 7.
7. Line 8 defines a function that implements the specific endpoint, which will be called by the Flask library when an application performs a `GET` operation on the / endpoint.
8. Line 9 performs a query on the InfluxDB database to retrieve the most recent measurement captured at least 10 minutes ago.
9. Line 10 creates an empty Python list.
10. Lines 11 to 13 iterate over the results from the query to the InfluxDB database and add them to our empty list (since we have queried for a single result (the last result), the results will contain a single element).
11. Line 14 retrieves the first (and only) element in our list, which is the `('intensity', '7.053000')` tuple.
12. Finally, line 15 returns the second element of the tuple to the application performing the query. Since we only require the value itself, we return the second element of the tuple.

We can test the implementation by following the steps outlined here:

1. Open three separate terminals. In two of the three terminals (let's call them terminal A and B), navigate to the directory where we created our environment and activate it. The third terminal (let's call it terminal C) does not require the environment to be activated.
2. In terminal A, run the Python application that retrieves the reading from the TSL2591 sensor and stores it in the InfluxDB by executing the following command:

```
$ python get-and-store-sensor-data.py
```

3. In terminal B, execute the following commands to run our web server application:

```
$ export FLASK_APP=flask-sensor-data
$ export FLASK_ENV=development
$ flask run
```

4. In terminal C, query the Python web server by executing the following command with the corresponding output:

```
$ curl http://localhost:5000/
6.043000
```

As we can see in the output, we successfully retrieved the reading from the TSL2591 sensor that was stored in the InfluxDB database.

> Try it for yourself!
>
> Try different lighting conditions and execute the preceding command to see whether the value changes!

Summary

In this chapter, we implemented an end-to-end solution to retrieve readings from a digital light sensor in a Python application, store them in an appropriate database, and then present them to a remote entity using a web interface. We learned how to combine several different components of the embedded Linux stack into a cohesive application. The application we developed in this chapter used a web browser as the main interface. In the next few chapters, we will learn how to develop a GUI that can be used without a web browser and run completely locally on the Raspberry Pi.

In the next chapter, we will learn how to build GUI applications using a framework called **Qt**.

Scan the QR code to join instantly!

Get this book's PDF version and more

Scan the QR code (or go to `packtpub.com/unlock`). Search for this book by name, confirm the edition, and then follow the steps on the page.

UNLOCK NOW

Note: Keep your invoice handy. Purchases made directly from Packt don't require an invoice.

10

Project 2: Using Qt to Build a Scientific Instrument

In this chapter, we will use a popular GUI framework, called **Qt**, to see how we can create a scientific instrument. This application will use the same TSL2591 sensor as used in *Chapter 9, Project 1: Using Python to Build a Web Server to Display Sensor Data*. However, the application in this chapter will periodically collect and store data from the TSL2591 sensor in the background whenever instructed by the GUI. The GUI will also include buttons to start and stop this background collection task. Finally, the GUI will feature a separate button to capture a single sensor reading of the TSL2591 sensor and display the reading in a box in the GUI.

We are going to cover the following main topics in this chapter:

- Qt basics and application overview
- Generating the Qt toolchain
- Installing Qt Creator and creating our kit
- Attaching a display to the Raspberry Pi 5
- Installing Qt on the Raspberry Pi 5
- Hello Qt World!
- Adding UI elements
- Backend implementation using C++
- Interacting with hardware asynchronously
- Implementing timing

Technical requirements

You should be comfortable with executing commands on a terminal. You should also be comfortable with reading, writing, and executing C++ applications. Finally, you should ensure that you have downloaded the Git repository associated with this book, located at `https://github.com/PacktPublishing/Embedded-Linux-Essentials-Handbook`.

Qt basics and application overview

In this section, we will review the basics of Qt and provide an overview of the application created later in this chapter.

> Important note
>
> Although Qt 6 is the latest version of Qt, developing applications based on Qt 6 to run on an embedded Linux system is not streamlined at the time of writing. Thus, we will focus on using Qt 5 in the next two chapters. Qt 6 provides enhancements over Qt 5. For example, it offers improved graphics handling with better support for modern graphics APIs such as Vulkan, Metal, and Direct3D 12. Additionally, it uses more modern features of C++17 and uses CMake as its default build system (instead of qmake). Finally, Qt 6 has dropped support for some older operating systems, focusing on modern platforms and improved hardware acceleration support.

Qt is a framework for developing GUI applications that can run across different platforms. For example, if we create an application using Qt that runs on our desktop PC, we can use the same source code to run the application on the Raspberry Pi. Qt supports popular programming languages such as C++ and Python.

Being a framework with a focus on developing sophisticated GUIs, Qt offers the following two mechanisms for developing UIs:

- **Qt Quick**: Qt Quick interfaces are fluid, dynamic, and best for touch interfaces. Qt Quick interfaces can be created using **Qt Quick Controls**. Qt Quick Controls is a module that supplies graphical elements using **QML**, a custom UI specification and programming language developed by Qt. QML supports using JavaScript to implement the logic behind the UI. The application developed in this chapter will use Qt Quick.

- **Qt widgets**: Qt widgets are UI elements in typical desktop environments. Qt widgets integrate seamlessly into the underlying platform, providing a look native to the underlying operating system. While Qt widgets are intended for applications leveraging large UI components on desktop PCs, they can also be used for touch interfaces. The application we will create in *Chapter 14, Rust in Embedded Linux: The Kernel and Applications*, will use Qt widgets.

The following are used to create Qt applications:

- **Qt Creator**: Qt Creator is the main IDE that developers should use to create Qt applications. It has the following features:
    - It allows us to write software in C++, QML, JavaScript, Python, and other languages.
    - It integrates with most popular version control systems, such as Git.
    - It supports native CMake and cross-compiling with CMake.
    - It allows us to build and run our Qt application on desktop, mobile, and embedded platforms.
    - It supports debugging applications in an emulated environment.
    - It contains a native Qt Quick compiler, which allows us to convert QML and JavaScript into native machine code. Native machine code is most efficient for execution on the target platform.
- **Qt Design Studio**: Qt Design Studio targets graphic designers to help them create sophisticated GUIs. It can import designs from popular graphic design software, such as Figma, and generate source code that can be used by developers in Qt Creator. We will not be using Qt Design Studio in this book.

Our application will consist of one screen, which has the following GUI elements:

- A **Start** button, which will start a background task that will query the TSL2591 sensor every 500 milliseconds. When the **Start** button is pressed, the text of the button will change to **Stop**.
- A text box that will display the latest reading from the TSL2591 sensor.
- A **Now** button to take one reading from the TSL2591 sensor and display it in the text box. This button will be hidden if the background task is running.

The GUI elements on the second screen are shown in the following figure:

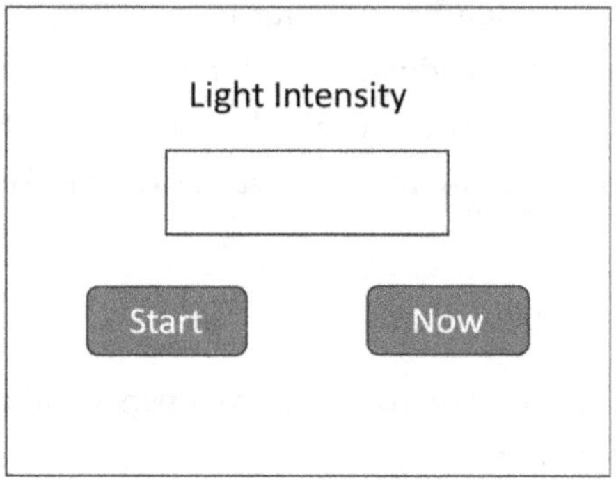

Figure 10.1 – GUI layout

In the next section, we will learn how to generate the toolchain we will use as part of our Qt development workflow in Qt Creator.

> Important note
>
> Although we will be running our Qt application on the Raspberry Pi 5, we will be using the tools on our Linux development PC to create and compile the Qt application. Additionally, we will be using our Linux development PC to deploy our Qt application to the Raspberry Pi 5.

Generating the Qt toolchain

In this section, we will learn how to generate the toolchain necessary to compile Qt applications. This section assumes that you have followed the instructions outlined in *Chapter 7, Building an Image Using Buildroot,* to set up and create our Board Support Package (BSP) based on The Yocto Project. We can generate the toolchain needed to compile our Qt application by following these steps:

1. We need to retrieve and add the `meta-qt5` layer by first cloning the `kirkstone` branch of the `meta-qt5` repository. Execute the following command:

```
$ cd yocto/layers
$ git clone --branch kirkstone https://github.com/meta-qt5/meta-qt5.
git
```

2. Then, execute the following command to set up The Yocto Project environment:

```
$ cd ../
$ source layers/poky/oe-init-build-env
```

   Add the `meta-qt5` layer to the BSP by executing the following command:

```
$ bitbake-layers add-layer ../layers/meta-qt5/
```

3. Execute the following command to generate the toolchain we can use to create applications based on Qt5:

```
$ MACHINE="raspberrypi5" bitbake meta-toolchain-qt5
```

4. We can install the Qt 5 toolchain by executing the following commands:

```
$ mkdir qt5-sdk
$ cd qt5-sdk
$ ../tmp/deploy/sdk/poky-glibc-x86_64-meta-toolchain-qt5-cortexa76-
raspberrypi5-toolchain-4.0.17.sh
```

Make sure to instruct the shell script to install the toolchain in the current directory by entering `./` when prompted for the installation location, as shown here:

```
Poky (Yocto Project Reference Distro) SDK installer version 4.0.17
==================================================================
Enter target directory for SDK (default: /opt/poky/4.0.17): ./
```

In the next section, we will learn how to install Qt 5 and Qt Creator on our Linux development PC and add our toolchain to Qt Creator.

Installing Qt Creator and configuring our kit

In this section, we will learn how to install Qt Creator on our Linux development PC and add our toolchain to Qt Creator.

> Important note
>
> This section uses the open source version of Qt. Using this version of Qt has certain implications and requirements. Ensure that you (or your organization) meet these requirements and are satisfied with the implications. Otherwise, you will have to use the commercial version of Qt.

Follow these steps to download the appropriate Qt installer:

1. Navigate to `https://www.qt.io` and click on **Download. Try.**, as shown in the following screenshot:

Figure 10.2 – Downloading the Qt installer

2. On the following page, click on **Explore Qt Community Edition**, as shown in the following screenshot:

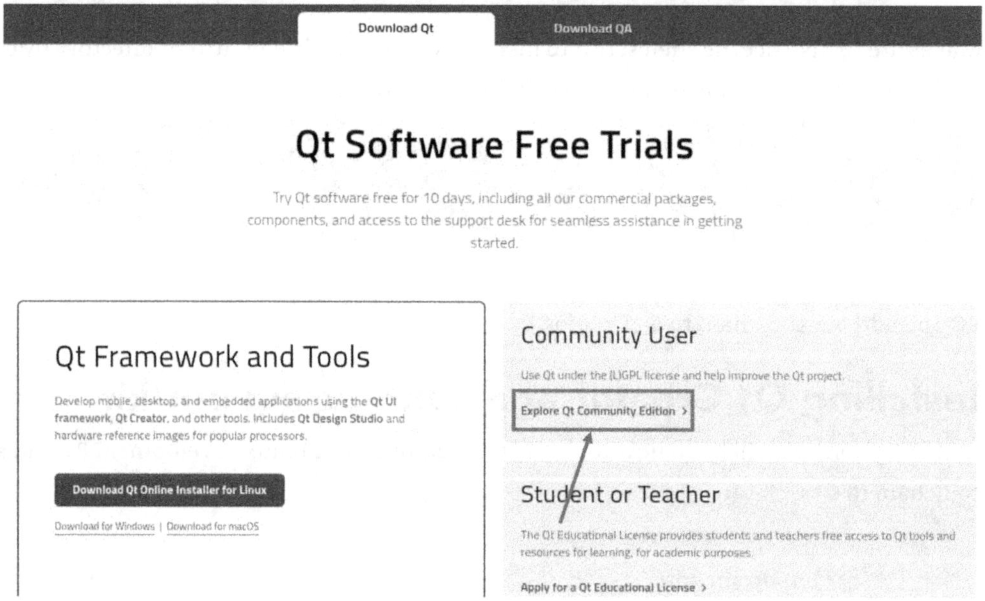

Figure 10.3 – Downloading open source Qt

3. On the following page, ensure that you read the stipulations outlined by Qt when using the open source version. Afterward, scroll down to the bottom of the page and click on **Qt Online Installer**, as shown in the following screenshot:

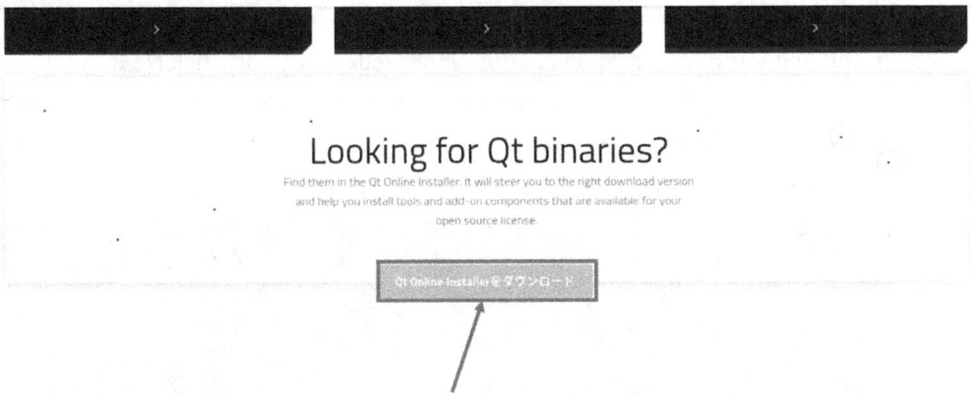

Figure 10.4 – Downloading Qt Online Installer

4. Then, click on **Linux x64** and then on **Qt Online Installer for Linux (64-bit)**, as shown in the following figure:

Figure 10.5 – Downloading Qt Online Installer for Linux

Next, follow these steps to install Qt and Qt Creator:

1. Run the installer as a super user by executing the following command:

```
$ sudo ./qt-online-installer-linux-x64-4.8.0.run
```

2. In the first window that opens, enter your credentials and click **Next**, as shown in the following screenshot (note: if you have not already, please register with Qt to obtain your credentials):

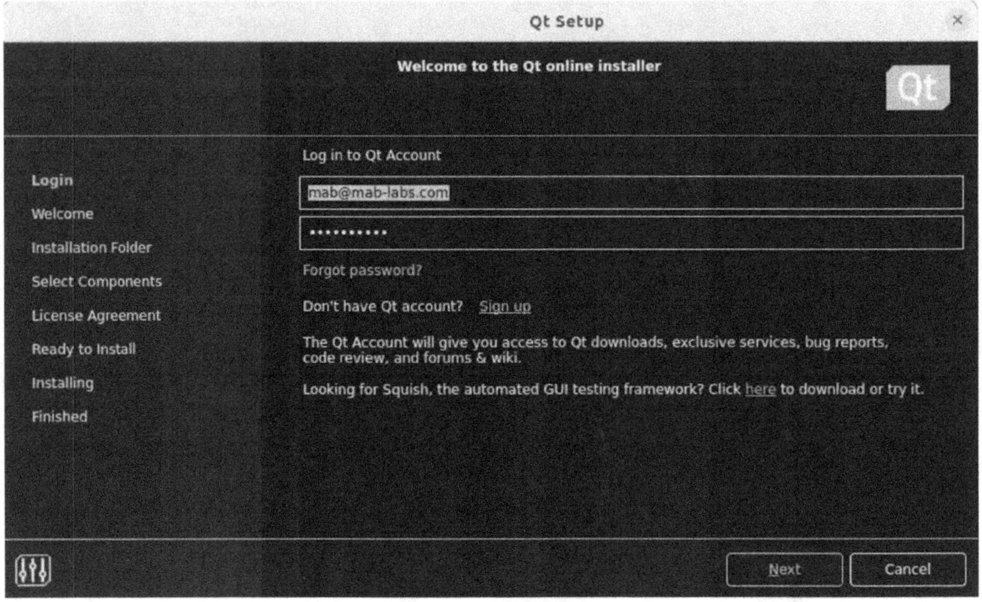

Figure 10.6 – Logging in to Qt

3. In the subsequent window, check the box next to **I have read and agreed to the terms and conditions of using Open Source Qt** and click **Next**, as shown in the following screenshot:

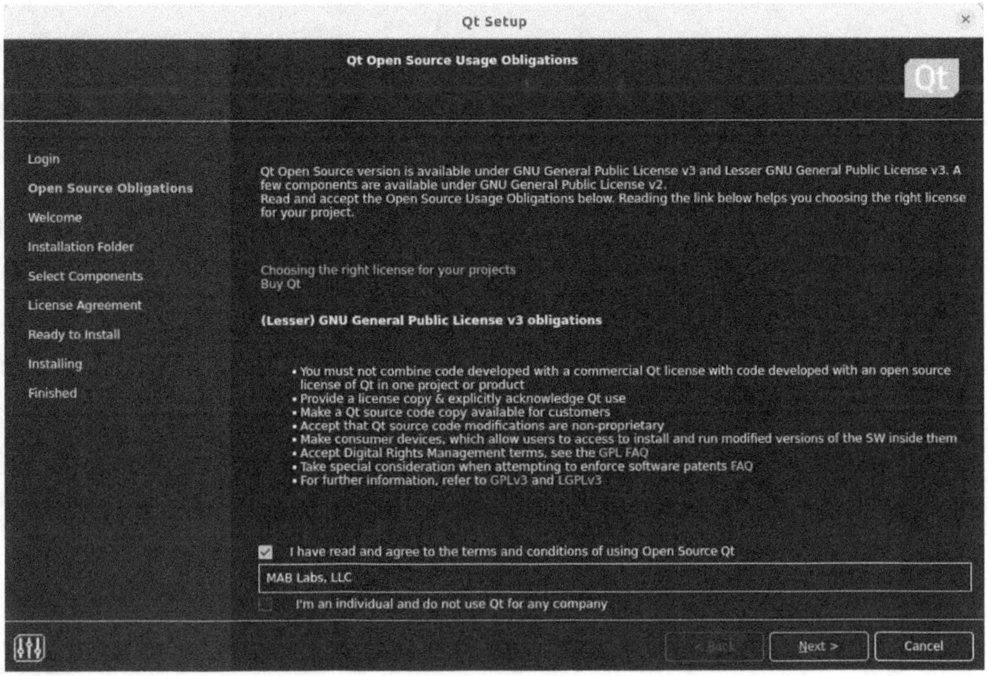

Figure 10.7 – Agreeing to the open source conditions

4. Click **Next** in the two subsequent windows that appear.

5. In the following window, choose the appropriate installation location, ensure that **Custom Installation** is selected, and click **Next**, as shown in the following screenshot:

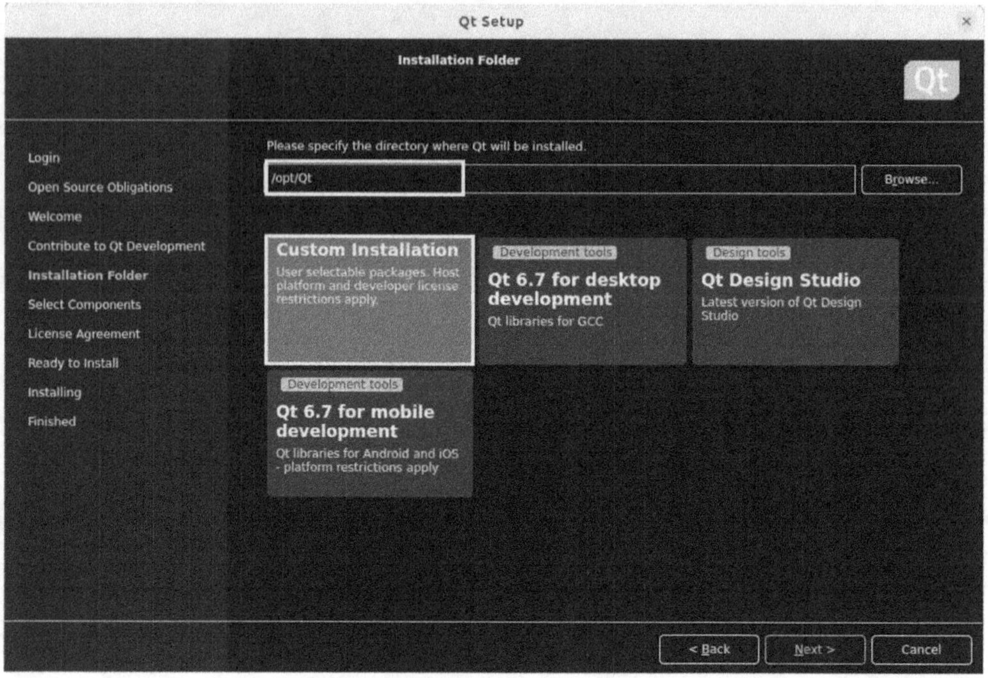

Figure 10.8 – Custom Qt installation

6. In the subsequent window, ensure that **Archive** is checked and click **Filter**. Then, scroll down and ensure that **Qt 5.15.2** and **Qt Creator 13.0.2** are checked, as shown in the following screenshot:

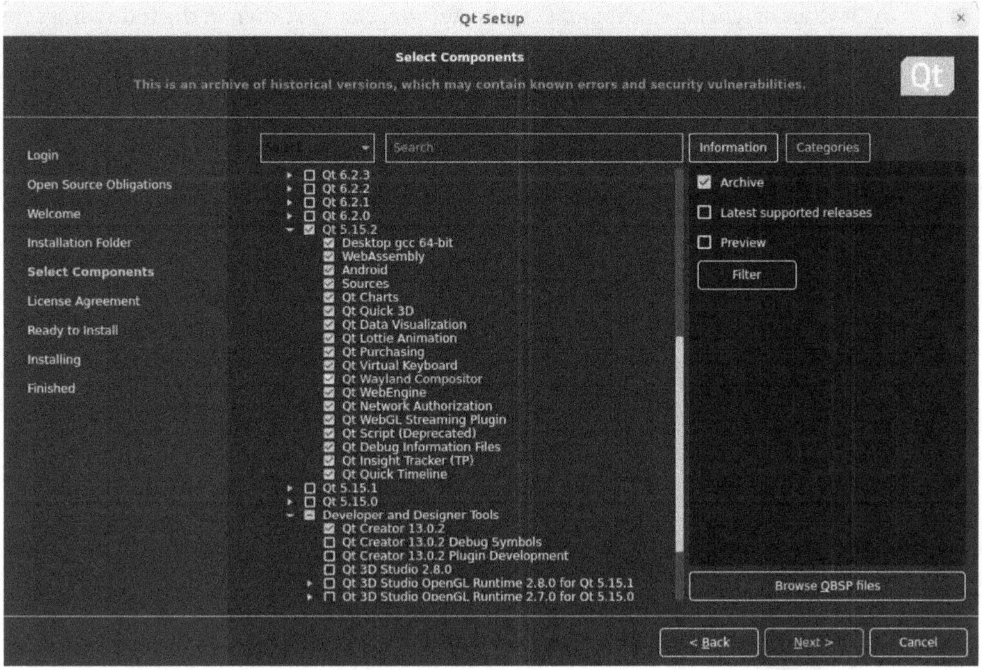

Figure 10.9 – Installing Qt 5.15.2

7. Click **Next** on the following windows, making sure to read and agree to any licenses, and complete the installation.

Now, we will create a *kit* by following these steps:

> Important note
>
> A "kit" consists of the compiler, debugger, and Qt libraries specifically for the Raspberry Pi 5. We will use the components part of the toolchain we created in the previous section.

1. Launch Qt Creator by executing this command:

```
$ /opt/Qt/Tools/QtCreator/bin/qtcreator
```

2. In Qt Creator, click on **Edit** and then **Preferences...**, as shown in the following screenshot:

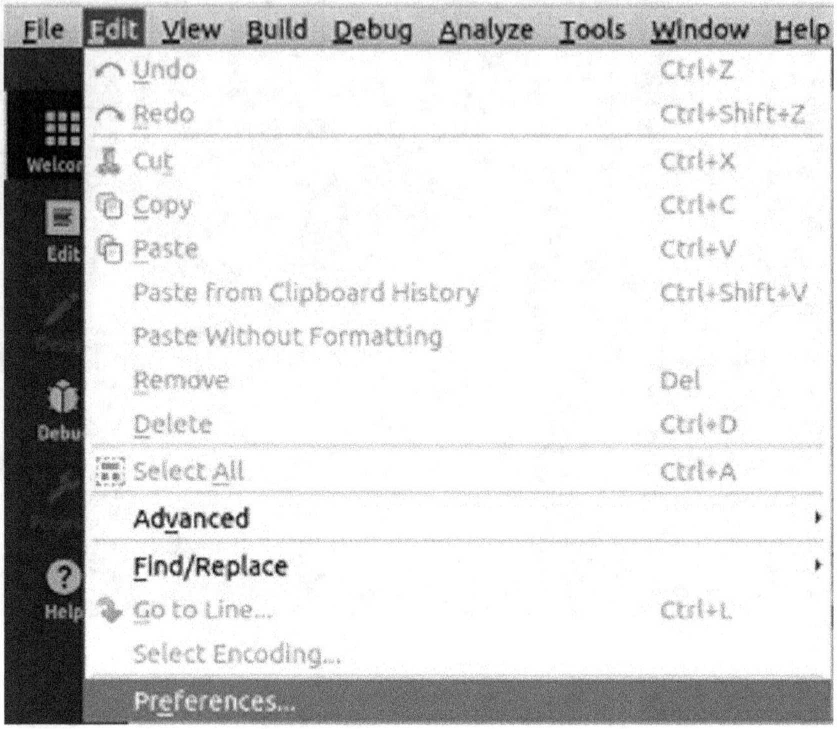

Figure 10.10 – Opening the Qt Creator preferences

3. In the resulting window, click on **Kits** in the left pane and then on the **Compilers** tab. Afterward, click on the **Add** button, and then select **GCC** and then **C**. These steps are shown in the following screenshot:

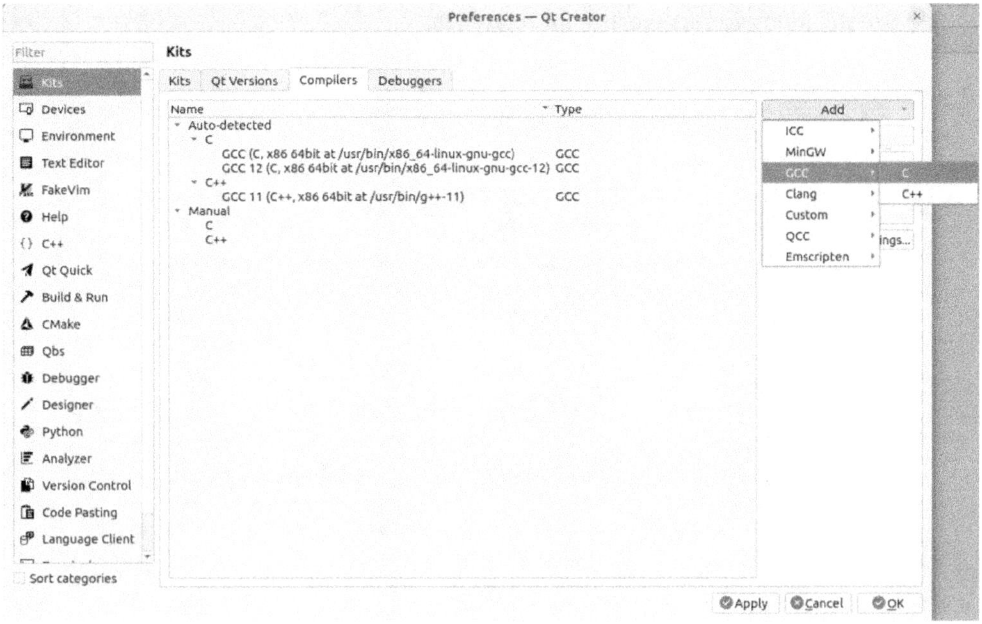

Figure 10.11 – Adding our compiler

4. In the pane that appears, enter the following information and click **Apply**:

    1. **Name**: `packt-gcc`

    2. **Compiler path**: <path to the Qt toolchain installed in the previous section>/sysroots/x86_64-pokysdk-linux/usr/bin/aarch64-poky-linux/aarch64-poky-linux-gcc

5. See the following screenshot for reference:

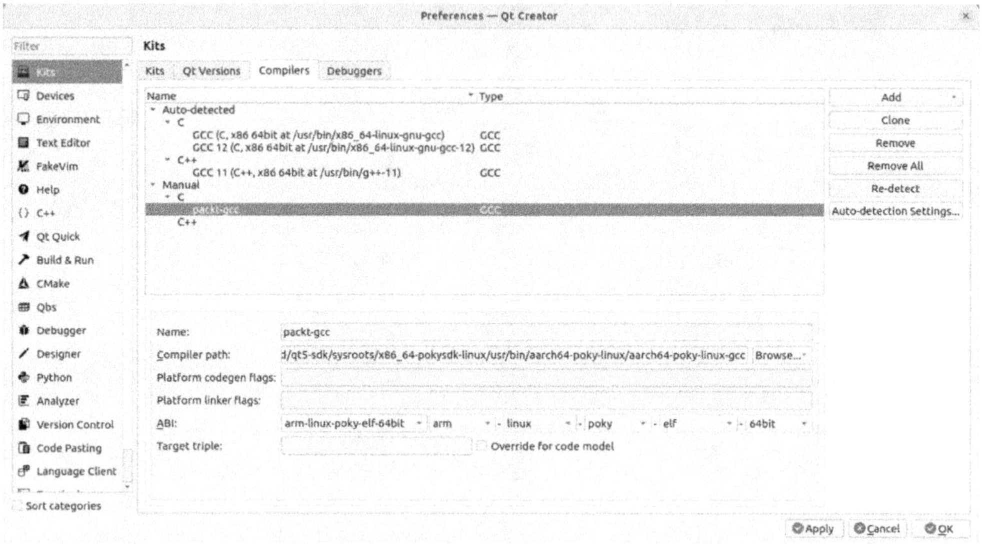

Figure 10.12 – Adding details of our compiler

6. Follow similar steps for the C++ compiler. Instead of specifying `aarch64-poky-linux-gcc` as the path to the compiler, specify `aarch64-poky-linux-g++`. Also, replace `packt-gcc` with `packt-g++`.
7. Navigate to the **Debugger** tab and click on **Add**. Enter the following information in the pane that appears:
    1. **Name:** `packt-gdb`
    2. **Path:** `<path to the Qt toolchain installed in the previous section>/sysroots/x86_64-pokysdk-linux/usr/bin/aarch64-poky-linux/aarch64-poky-linux-gdb`

8. Click on the **Qt Version** tab and click on **Add**, as shown in the following screenshot:

Figure 10.13 – Adding our custom Qt installation

9. In the resulting window, navigate to the location of the toolchain installation directory, navigate to `sysroots/x86_64-poky-sdklinux/usr/bin`, click on **qmake**, and click **Open**. See the following figure for reference:

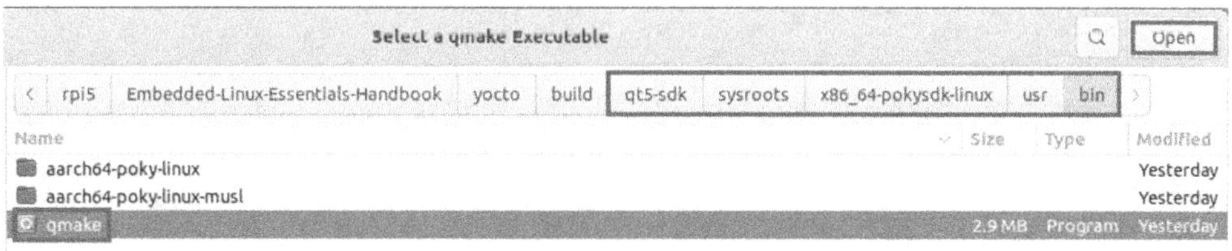

Figure 10.14 – Selecting our custom Qt installation

10. Click on the **Kit** tab, click on the **Add** button, and enter the following information in the pane that appears:

    1. **Name:** `packt`

2. **Compiler:**
   - C: `packt-gcc`
   - C++: `packt-g++`
3. **Debugger**: `packt-gdb`

11. Click on the **Browse** button next to the **Sysroot** option, select the path to the toolchain that we installed in the previous section, select **cortexa76-poky-linux**, and click **Open**. The following screenshot can be used for reference:

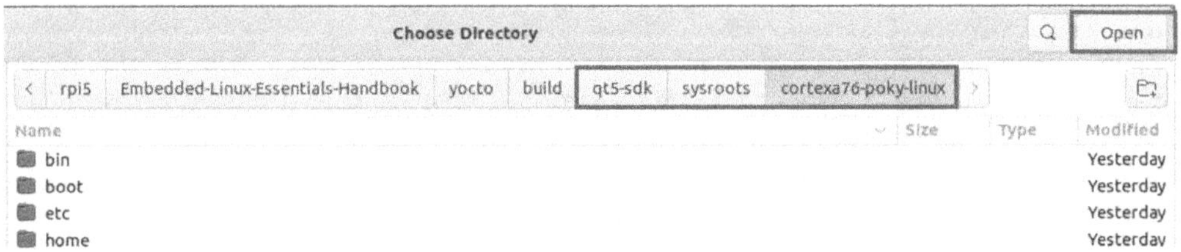

Figure 10.15 – Selecting our custom sysroot

12. For the **Qt version** option, select **Qt 5.15.7 (System)**, which represents our custom Qt installation.

The following screenshot shows an example of our custom kit in Qt Creator.

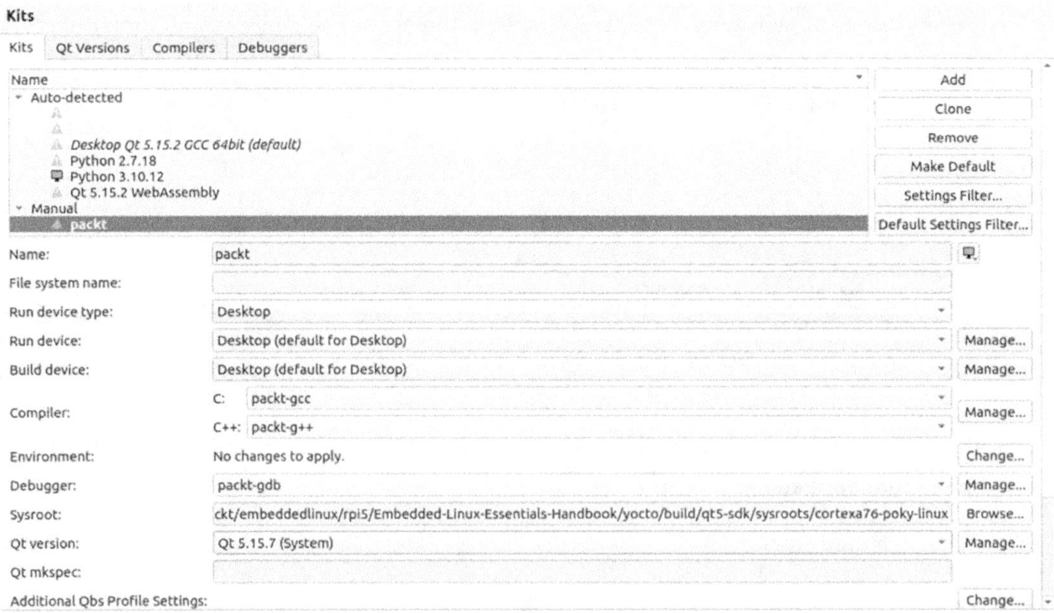

Figure 10.16 – Our custom Qt kit

In the next section, we will learn how to connect a display to our Raspberry Pi 5.

Attaching a display to the Raspberry Pi 5

In this section, we will learn how to connect the Raspberry Pi display (`https://www.raspberrypi.com/products/raspberry-pi-touch-display/`) to the Raspberry Pi 5.

In addition to purchasing the Raspberry Pi 5 display, we also need to purchase the Raspberry Pi 5 display cable (`https://www.raspberrypi.com/products/display-cable/`), which will allow us to connect the Raspberry Pi display to the Raspberry Pi 5.

The following figure shows the connections from the Raspberry Pi display to the Raspberry Pi 5:

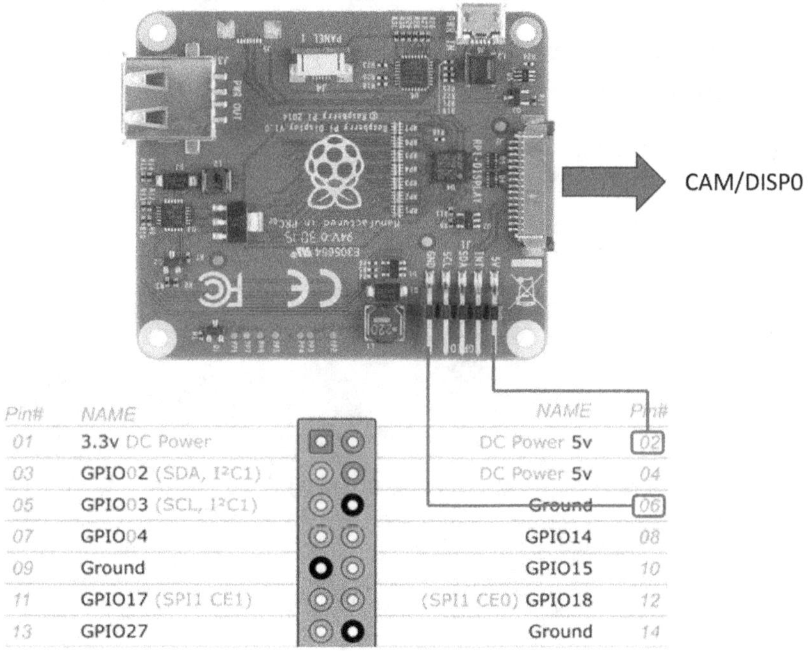

Figure 10.17 – Connections between Raspberry Pi display and Raspberry Pi 5

The following figure shows the physical connections between the two devices for the remainder of the chapter:

Figure 10.18 – Physical connections between the Raspberry Pi display and the Raspberry Pi 5

If we power on the Raspberry Pi 5, we should see the display showing the standard background, as shown in the following figure:

Figure 10.19 – Display output on Raspberry Pi 5

In the next section, we will learn how to add the necessary packages to our Raspberry Pi 5 to run our Qt application.

Installing Qt on the Raspberry Pi 5

In this section, we will learn how to install the necessary packages on our Raspberry Pi 5 to run applications.

We can execute the following commands to install the packages on our Raspberry Pi that are necessary to run a Qt application:

```
$ sudo apt-get install libqt5quickcontrols2-5 libqt5multimedia5
libqt5webengine5 libqt5quick5 libqt5qml5

$ sudo apt-get install qml-module-qtquick-controls

$ sudo apt-get install qtdeclarative5-private-dev

$ sudo apt-get install qml-module-qtquick-controls2
```

We will learn how to implement a simple "Hello Qt World!" application using the Qt framework in the next section.

Hello Qt World!

In this section, we will learn how to create, build, and deploy our first application. This application will be a single window that shows **Hello Qt World** in the title.

We can create this application by following these steps:

1. Launch Qt Creator by executing the following command (make sure to replace `/opt/Qt` in the following command with the location of the Qt installation directory if it's different):

   ```
   $ /opt/Qt/Tools/QtCreator/bin/qtcreator
   ```

2. In the window that opens, click on **Create Project...**, as shown in the following screenshot:

Figure 10.20 – Qt Creator

3. In the popup that appears, click on **Qt Quick Application (compat)** and then click **Choose...**, as shown in the following screenshot:

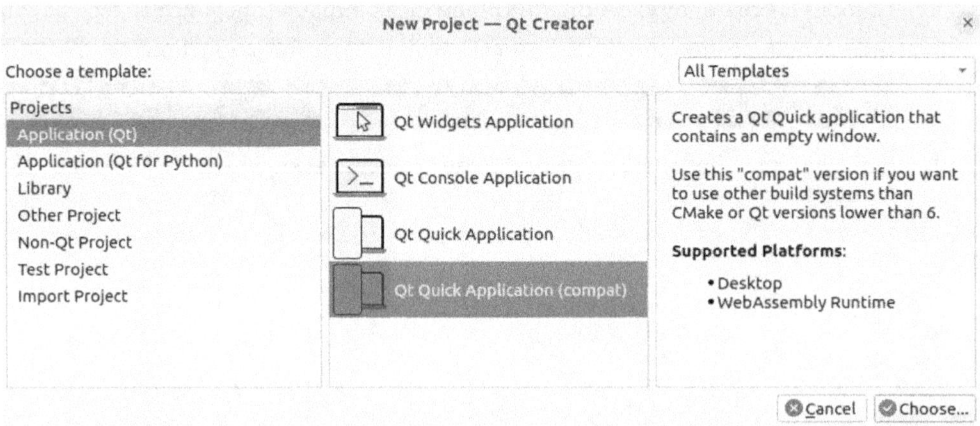

Figure 10.21 – Creating a new project

4. In the subsequent window, enter `hello-world` for **Name** and enter an appropriate location for **Create in**, and click **Next**, as shown in the following screenshot:

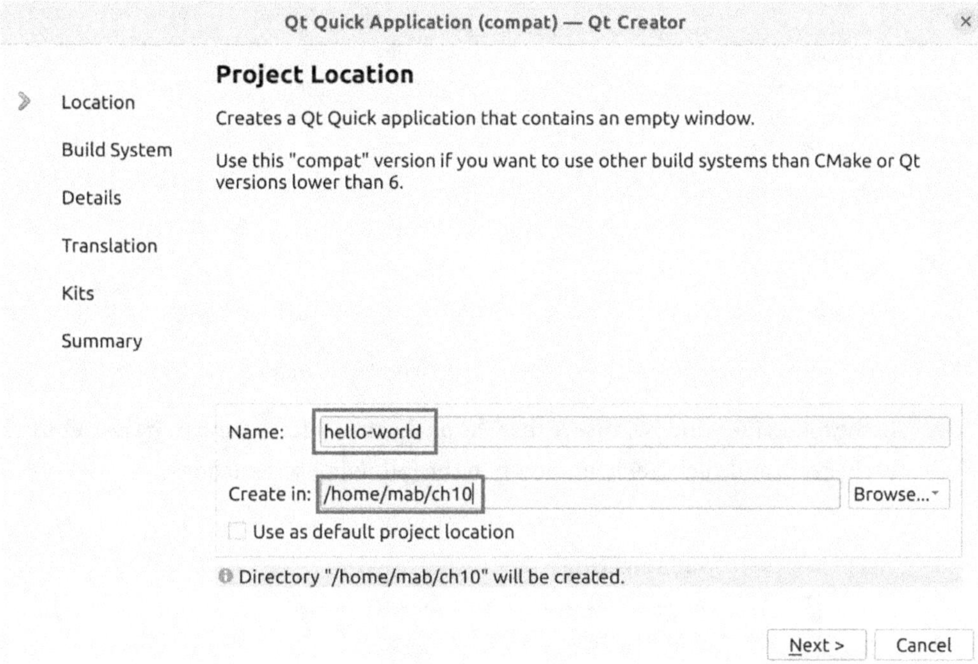

Figure 10.22 – Project options

5. In the following window, keep **qmake** for **Build system** and click **Next**.
6. In the subsequent window, select **Qt 5.15** for **Minimum required Qt version** and make sure that **Use Qt Virtual Keyboard** is unchecked.

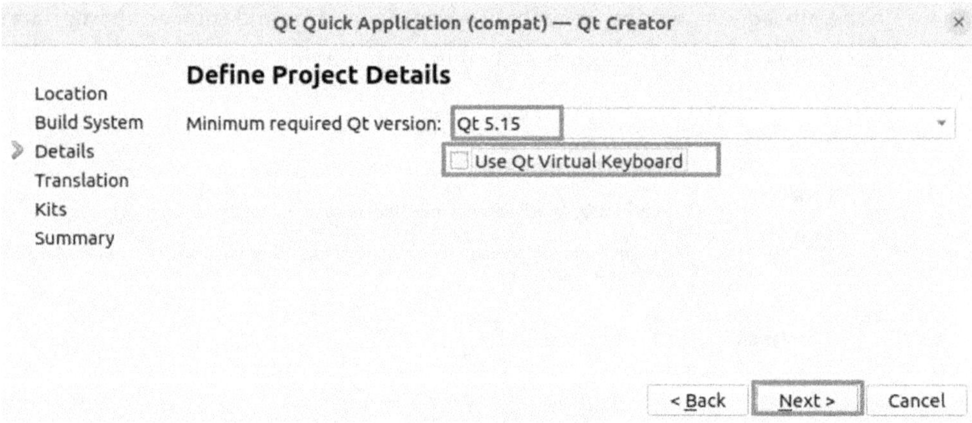

Figure 10.23 – Project details

7. In the following window, ensure that the **packt** kit is selected and that the **Debug** checkbox is checked, and click **Next**, as shown in the following screenshot:

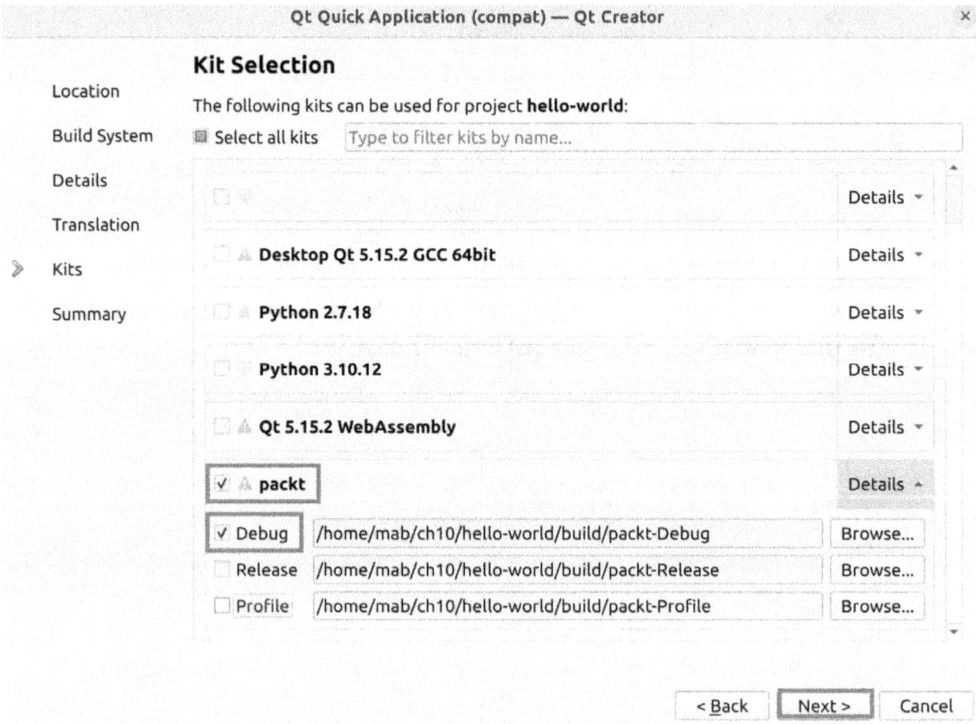

Figure 10.24 – Selecting the appropriate kit

8. Click on **Finish** in the next and final window.
9. In the main Qt Creator window, we see the source files (along with the QML file that represents our screen) on the left and the content of the selected file in the middle, as shown in the following figure:

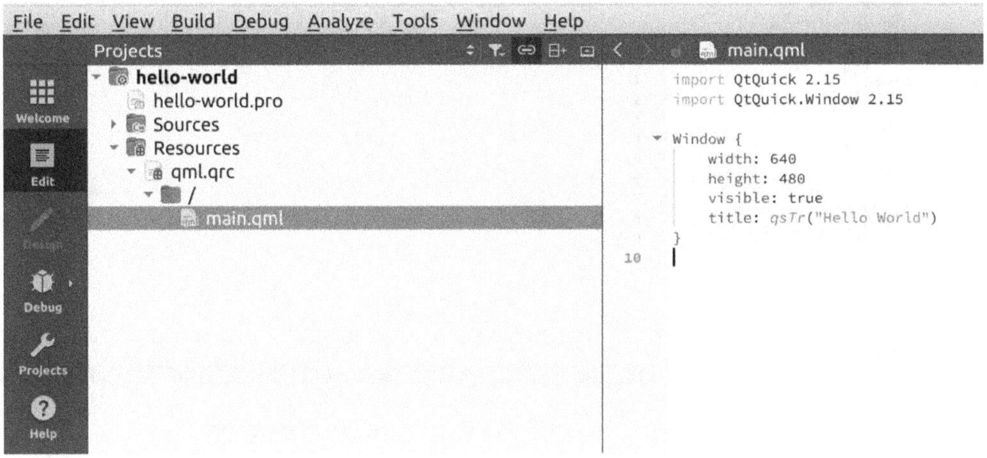

Figure 10.25 – Main Qt Creator window

10. Finally, we can right-click on **hello world** on the left and click on **Build**, as shown in the following screenshot:

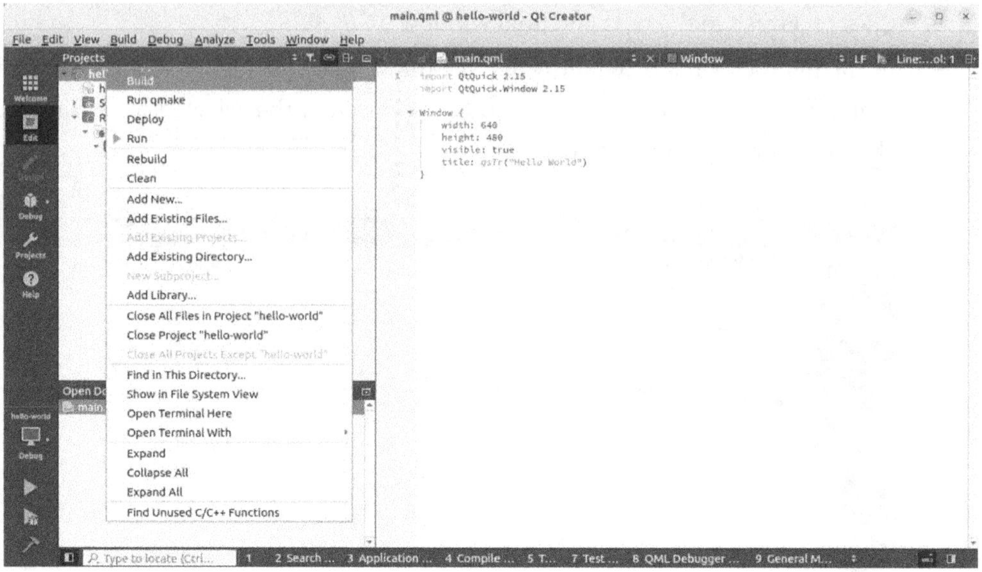

Figure 10.26 – Building our Qt application

After following the preceding steps, we have a binary file of our Qt application that we can execute on the Raspberry Pi 5. We can deploy the application to the Raspberry Pi and run it there by following these steps:

1. Navigate to the location of the Qt project by executing the following command (make sure to replace `/home/mab/` with the directory that matches the location where you created the project in the previous section):

```
$ cd /home/mab/ch13/hello-world
```

2. Execute the following command to transfer the file to the Raspberry Pi (make sure to replace the IP address with that of your Raspberry Pi):

```
$ scp build/packt-Debug/hello-world pi@10.10.2.247:~/
```

3. Connect a keyboard and mouse to the Raspberry Pi and physically log in to the Raspberry Pi (that is, *not over SSH*), and then execute the command shown here:

```
$ ./hello-world
```

After executing the preceding command, we should see the following window on our Raspberry Pi 5 display:

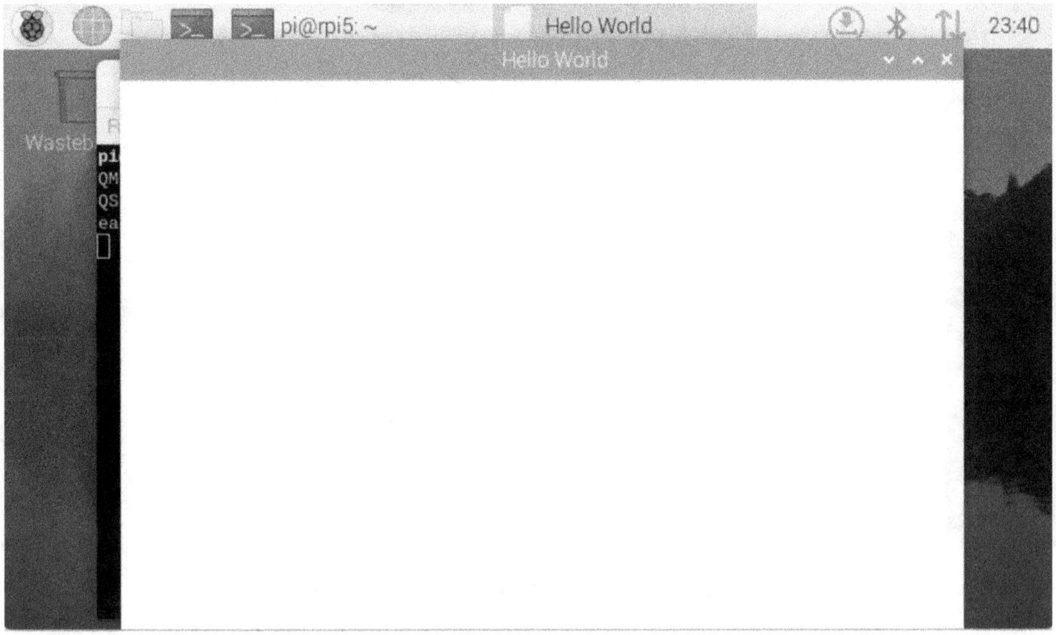

Figure 10.27 – Hello World Qt application

After following the preceding steps, we have created, deployed, and executed a Qt application on our Raspberry Pi 5. We can change `qsTr("Hello World")` to `qsTr("Hello Qt World")` in `main.qml`, as shown in the following figure:

```
import QtQuick 2.15
import QtQuick.Window 2.15

Window {
    width: 640
    height: 480
    visible: true
    title: qsTr("Hello Qt World")
}
```

Figure 10.28 – Modifying our Qt application

If we follow the preceding steps to deploy and execute our application again, we will see that the title of the window that is displayed is **Hello Qt World**, as shown in the following screenshot:

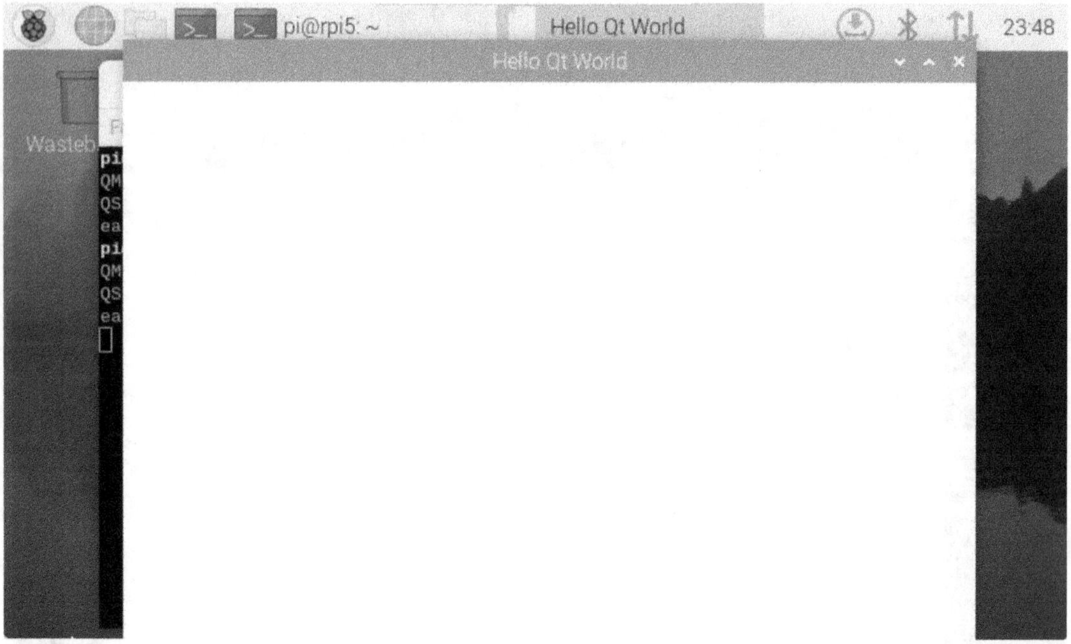

Figure 10.29 – Our "Hello Qt World" application

In the next section, we will learn how to add the remaining UI elements of our application.

Adding UI elements

In this section, we will learn how to add the remaining UI elements of our application. Recall that the screen of our application will have the following layout:

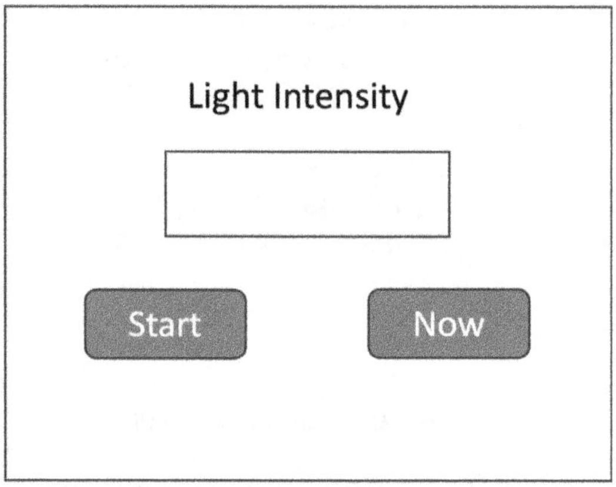

Figure 10.30 – Application screen layout

There are four main components of the screen:

- A label with the text **Light Intensity**.
- Another label that will be periodically updated with the numerical value of the light intensity.
- A button with the text **Start** that will perform the following tasks after it is pressed. Periodically update the label with the value reported by the TSL2591 sensor.
  - Change the text of the **Start** button to **Stop**.
  - Hide button with the text **Now**.
  - When the button is pressed again (after its text is changed to **Stop**), it will stop periodically updating the label with the value reported by the TSL2591 sensor and clear the label.
  - Unhide the button with the text **Now**.
- A button with the text **Now** that, when clicked, will update the label with the recently reported value from the TSL2591 sensor.

The following listing shows the implementation in QML:

```
import QtQuick 2.15
import QtQuick.Window 2.15
import QtQuick.Controls 2.15

Window {
    width: 640
    height: 480
    visible: true
    title: qsTr("TSL2591 Reading")

    property double lightIntensity: 0
    property bool isStarted: false

    Label {
        id: itmIntensityLbl
        anchors.horizontalCenter: parent.horizontalCenter
        anchors.top: parent.top
        anchors.topMargin: 100
        font.pixelSize: 24
```

```
        text: "Light Intensity"
    }

    Item {
        id: itmIntensityValue
        anchors.horizontalCenter: parent.horizontalCenter
        anchors.top: itmIntensityLbl.bottom
        anchors.topMargin: 10
        width: itmIntensityLbl.width
        height: (itmIntensityLbl.height * 2) + 20

        Rectangle {
            id: rectLabelVal
            color: "transparent"
            border.color: "black"
            border.width: 2
            width: itmIntensityValue.width
            height: itmIntensityValue.height
            anchors.horizontalCenter: parent.horizontalCenter

            Text {
                id: txtLightIntensity
                anchors.horizontalCenter: parent.horizontalCenter
                font.pointSize: 48
                text: lightIntensity
            }
        }
    }

     Button {
        id: btnPeriodic
        anchors.right: itmIntensityValue.horizontalCenter
        anchors.top: itmIntensityValue.bottom
        anchors.rightMargin: 50
        anchors.topMargin: 20
        font.pointSize: 24
        text: "Start"
```

```
50          onClicked: {
51              if (isStarted === false) {
52                  btnPeriodic.text = "Stop";
53                  isStarted = true;
54              } else {
55                  btnPeriodic.text = "Start";
56                  isStarted = false;
57              }
58          }
59      }

60      Button {
61          id: btnNow
62          anchors.left: itmIntensityValue.horizontalCenter
63          anchors.top: itmIntensityValue.bottom
64          anchors.leftMargin: 50
65          anchors.topMargin: 20
66          font.pointSize: 24
67          text: "Now"
68      }
69  }
```

The QML implementation is described in detail here:

- Lines 1–8 are from our "Hello Qt World" application. However, we modified the title to `TSL2591 Reading` to reflect the purpose of our application.
- Line 9 initializes a variable of type `double`, which is used to report the light intensity. Variables in QML can be declared using the `property` keyword and can be initialized using a colon.
- Similarly, line 10 initializes a variable of type `bool`, which keeps track of whether the background process to periodically report the light intensity has been started.
- Lines 11–18 define the label that contains the text **Light Intensity**:
    - Line 12 identifies the label, using the `id` identifier, which is later used to reference other GUI elements.
    - Line 13 defines the horizontal position of the label using the `anchors` property. In this instance, we have specified that the label should be horizontally centered in line with the overall window (the label's **parent**).

    - Line 14 defines the vertical position of the label. In this instance, we use the `anchors.top` property to specify that the top of the label should be in line with the top of the main window.
    - Line 15 specifies that there should be an offset of 100 pixels from the label's `anchors.top` property to the start of where the label should be drawn.
    - Line 16 indicates that the size of the label's text should be 24 points.
    - Line 17 defines the label's text.

- Lines 19–41 define the GUI element where the light intensity value will be displayed. It consists of three QML objects: an item, which contains a rectangle, which in turn contains a text box:

    - Line 20 identifies the item, using the `id` identifier, which is later used to reference other GUI elements.
    - Lines 21–23 specify the positioning of the item. In this case, we place the top of the item at the bottom of the **Light Intensity** label. Additionally, the offset from the top is 10 pixels.
    - Lines 24 and 25 specify the width and height of the entire item. The width is identical to the width of the **Light Intensity** label. However, the height is a little over double the height.
    - Lines 26–33 define a rectangle containing the light intensity value to be displayed. The specifics of the rectangle are defined here:

        - Line 27 identifies the rectangle.
        - Line 28 defines the rectangle as transparent, and line 29 specifies that the rectangle's border must be black. Line 30 specifies the width of the rectangle's border to be 2 pixels.
        - Line 31 defines the rectangle's width as identical to the width of the top-level item. Additionally, the rectangle's height is identical to the height of the top-level item.
        - Line 33 defines the horizontal position of the rectangle. Specifically, the rectangle should be horizontally centered to the center of the top-level item.

- Lines 34–39 define the text of the light value to be displayed, as specified here:
    - Line 35 identifies the text.
    - Line 36 defines the horizontal position of the text and specifies that it should be horizontally centered with the top-level item.
    - Line 37 specifies that the size of the text should be 48 pixels. Line 38 defines the text's value equal to the `lightIntensity` property defined previously.
- Lines 42–59 define the button that will trigger the process to periodically update the text box above with the light intensity reported by the TSL2591:
    - Line 43 identifies the button.
    - Lines 44–47 specify the position of the button. Like the preceding elements, we position it horizontally centered relative to the item above. However, this time, we offset it from the right by 50 pixels via the `anchors.rightMargin` property.
    - Line 48 defines the size of the text in the button, and line 49 specifies that the initial text should be `Start`.
    - Lines 50–57 define the behavior of the button when it is pressed via the `onClicked` callback function. Initially, the `isStarted` property is set to `false`. Thus, when the button is first pressed, the button text is updated to `Stop`, and the `isStarted` property is updated to `true`. The next time the button is pressed, since the `isStarted` property is now `true`, the text in the button is updated to `Start`, and the `isStarted` property is now set to `false`.
- Lines 60–68 define the button that displays the most recent value reported by the TSL2591 sensor. The properties of the button are identical to those we already covered earlier. The only difference is the use of `anchors.leftMargin`, which specifies that the button should be offset from the horizontal center to the right by 50 pixels.

After compiling, deploying, and running the preceding application on the Raspberry Pi, we see the following screen:

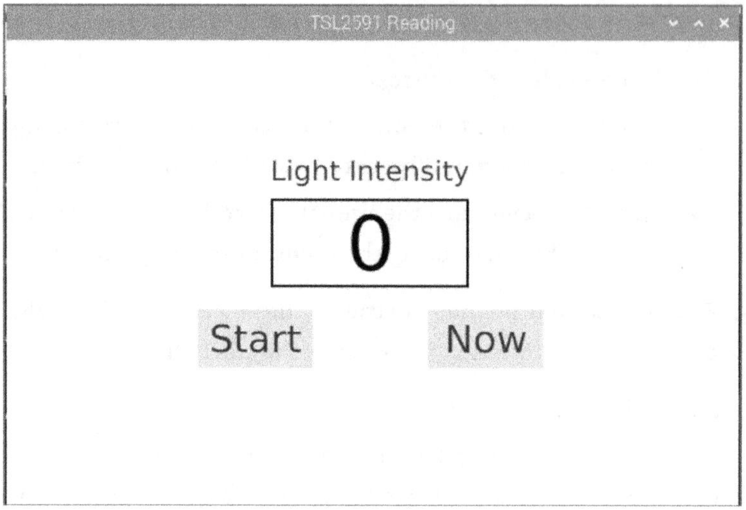

Figure 10.31 – Initial presentation of application

If we click on the **Start** button, we will see that the text of the button changes to **Stop**:

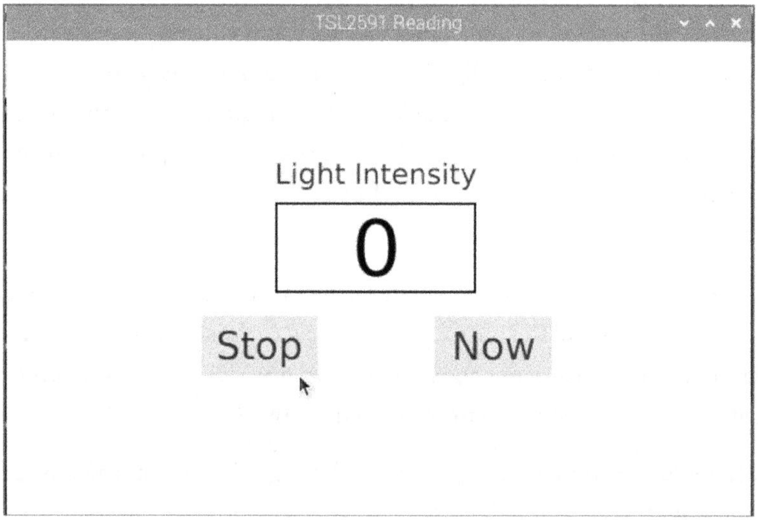

Figure 10.32 – Pressing the Start button and it changing to Stop

In the next section, we will implement the application's **backend** in C++.

Backend implementation using C++

In this section, we will learn how to implement the backend in C++. Initially, the backend will not report the value reported by the TSL2591 sensor. Instead, it will only report a contrived value, which the QML side will display. In later sections, we will add the logic to retrieve the value from the sensor.

We can create the initial backend implementation by following these steps:

1. Right-click on **hello-world** in the left pane and click on **Add New...**, as shown in the following screenshot:

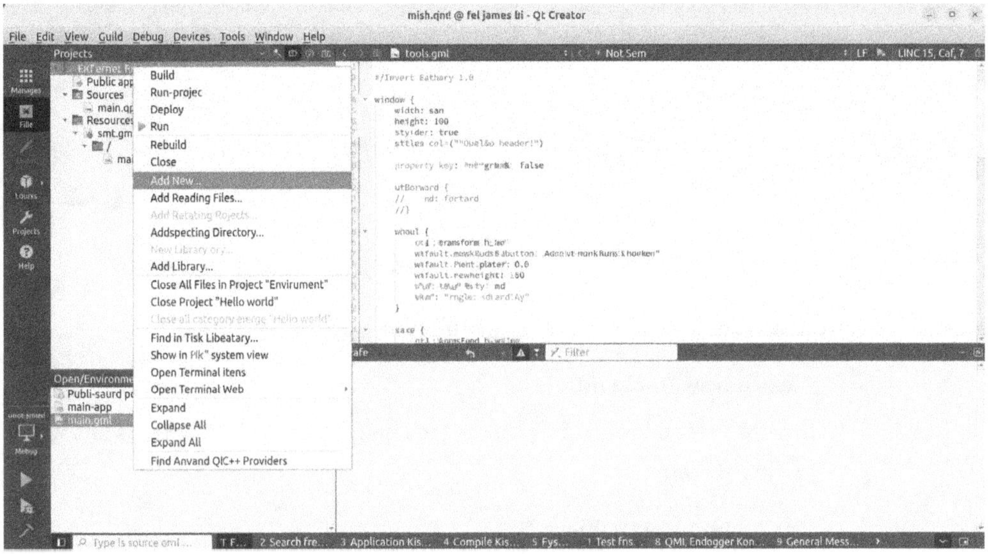

Figure 10.33 – Adding a new file

2. In the subsequent window, select **C/C++** under **Choose a template**, select **C++ Class**, and click **Choose...**, as shown in the following screenshot:

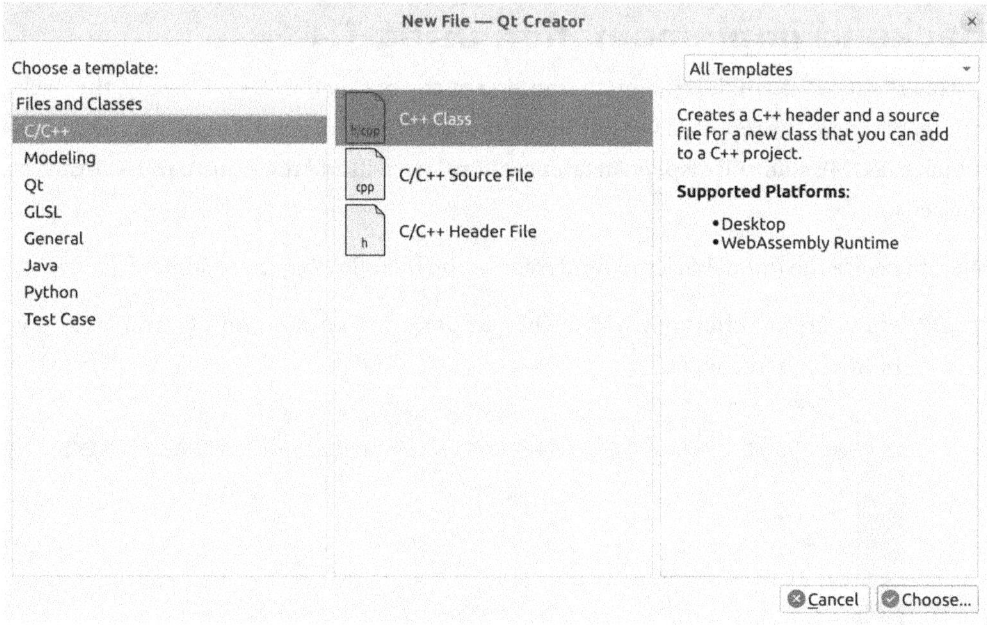

Figure 10.34 – Adding a C++ class

3. Finally, in the last window, specify the following options:
   - **Class name: Backend**
   - Ensure that the following boxes are checked and click **Next**, as shown in the following screenshot:
     - **Include QObject**
     - **Add Q_OBJECT**
     - **Add QML_ELEMENT**

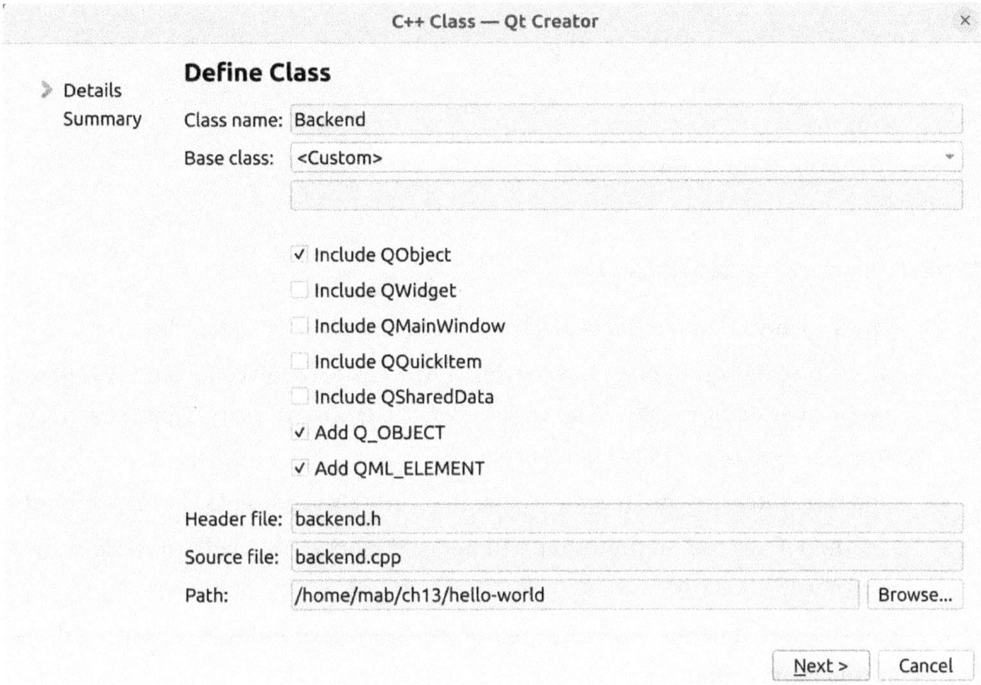

Figure 10.35 – Customizing a class

4. Click on **Finish** in the final window.

The next step is to modify the source code generated by Qt Creator. First, we need to modify the backend header file. The modifications are shown in bold in the following screenshot:

```
#ifndef BACKEND_H
#define BACKEND_H

#include <QObject>
#include <QQmlEngine>

class Backend : public QObject
{
    Q_OBJECT
    Q_PROPERTY(QString q_lightIntensity READ lightIntensity)
    QML_ELEMENT
public:
  explicit Backend(QObject *parent = nullptr);
```

```
12    QString lightIntensity();

13 private:
14    QString m_lightIntensity;
#endif // BACKEND_H
```

The modifications are described here:

- Line 5 ensures that our `Backend` class inherits from the `QObject` class.
- Line 8 specifies a property representing the intensity reported by the TSL2591 sensor that can be queried from QML. The variable on the QML side is `q_lightIntensity`, and the function used to query is `lightIntensity`.
- Line 11 updates the constructor so that it accurately represents the class inheritance.
- Line 12 defines the method that will be used by the QML side to retrieve the TSL2591 sensor value.
- Lines 13 and 14 define a private member variable containing a cached version of the reported sensor value.

Second, we need to modify the source file representing the backend, as shown:

```
1  #include "backend.h"

2  Backend::Backend(QObject *parent) :
3      QObject(parent)
4  {
5      m_lightIntensity = QString::number(12.3, 'f', 1);
6  }

7  QString Backend::lightIntensity()
8  {
9      return m_lightIntensity;
10 }
```

The relevant lines are described here:

- Line 5 initializes the cache variable representing the reported intensity as 12.3
- Lines 7–10 implement the method used by the QML side to retrieve the cached variable

Next, we need to modify `main.cpp` to register our backend with the QML side. This can be achieved by adding the following highlighted lines:

```
#include <QGuiApplication>
#include <QQmlApplicationEngine>

#include "backend.h"
.
.
.
    QGuiApplication app(argc, argv);

    qmlRegisterType<Backend>("Backend", 1,0, "Backend");
.
.
.
```

Then, we need to make the following changes, shown in bold, to our QML file to use the backend implementation:

```
import Backend 1.0

Window {
.
.
.
    Backend {
        id: backend
    }
.
.
.
            Text {
                id: txtLightIntensity
                anchors.horizontalCenter: parent.horizontalCenter
                font.pointSize: 48
                text: backend.q_lightIntensity
            }
```

In the preceding implementation, the text used to display the reading from the TSL2591 sensor is retrieved from the backend class.

Finally, we need to make the following changes to the `hello-world.pro` file:

```
.
.
.
# Additional import path used to resolve QML modules in Qt Creator's code
model
QML_IMPORT_PATH = $$PWD
.
.
.
HEADERS += \
    backend.h

QML_IMPORT_NAME = backend
QML_IMPORT_MAJOR_VERSION = 1
```

If we compile, deploy, and run the application with the preceding changes on the Raspberry Pi, we will see the following output:

Figure 10.36 – Updated implementation with backend

Important note

You may see a warning like the following reported when the application is run:

```
QQmlExpression: Expression qrc:/main.qml:49:17 depends on
non-NOTIFYable properties:
    Backend::q_lightIntensity
```

This warning informs us that we haven't implemented a mechanism where the backend can notify the QML of the change in the `q_lightIntensity` variable. Indeed, we should use notifications from the C++ side to the QML side as the appropriate mechanism. However, this will prevent us from understanding how to implement timing in a later section.

After making the preceding changes, we can see that the application reports the initialized value of the cache variable representing the TSL2591 sensor reading.

In the next section, we will learn how to interact with the TSL2591 sensor and display the value reported by the sensor.

Interacting with hardware asynchronously

In this section, we will learn how to interact with the TSL2591 sensor asynchronously. The backend C++ implementation will use the IIO infrastructure to query the TSL2591 sensor for the light intensity when requested by the UI from QML.

First, we will need to add the IIO library to our toolchain. We can achieve this by following these steps:

1. Navigate to the `meta-qt5` layer in our BSP based on The Yocto Project.
2. Make the following modification (in bold) to the `packagegroups/packagegroup-qt5-toolchain-target.bb` file:

```
    qtquickcontrols2 \
    qtquickcontrols2-dev \
    qtquickcontrols2-mkspecs \
    libiio \
```

3. Remove the existing Qt toolchain that was installed in the previous section.
4. Rebuild the Qt toolchain and install it using the steps outlined in the previous section.

5. We can confirm that the IIO library was added to our toolchain by executing the following commands:

```
$ find sysroots/ -name iio.h
sysroots/cortexa76-poky-linux/usr/include/iio.h
sysroots/cortexa76-poky-linux/usr/src/debug/libiio/0.23-r0/git/iio.h
```

Next, we have to use the IIO library in our Qt application to query the TSL2591 sensor from the C++ backend. We can achieve and confirm this by following these steps:

1. Apply the following change (in bold) to `backend.h`:

```
private:
    iio_channel *m_iioChannel;
    QString m_lightIntensity;
};
```

2. Make the following changes (in bold) to `backend.cpp`:

```
#include "backend.h"
#include <iio.h>

Backend::Backend(QObject *parent) :
    QObject(parent)
{
    iio_context* context = iio_create_local_context();
    iio_device* device = iio_context_find_device(context, "tsl2591");
    m_iioChannel = iio_device_find_channel(device, "illuminance", false);

    double intensity;
    iio_channel_attr_read_double(m_iioChannel, "input", &intensity);
    m_lightIntensity = QString::number(intensity, 'f', 1);
}

QString Backend::lightIntensity()
{
    return m_lightIntensity;
}
```

3. The changes are described here:
    - Line 2 includes the appropriate header file to allow us to use the IIO library
    - Lines 6–8 retrieve the channel associated with the light intensity from the TSL2591 sensor
    - Lines 9–11 retrieve the light intensity and set it to the `m_lightIntensity` member variable

If we compile the application and deploy and run it on the Raspberry Pi, we get the output shown in the following figure:

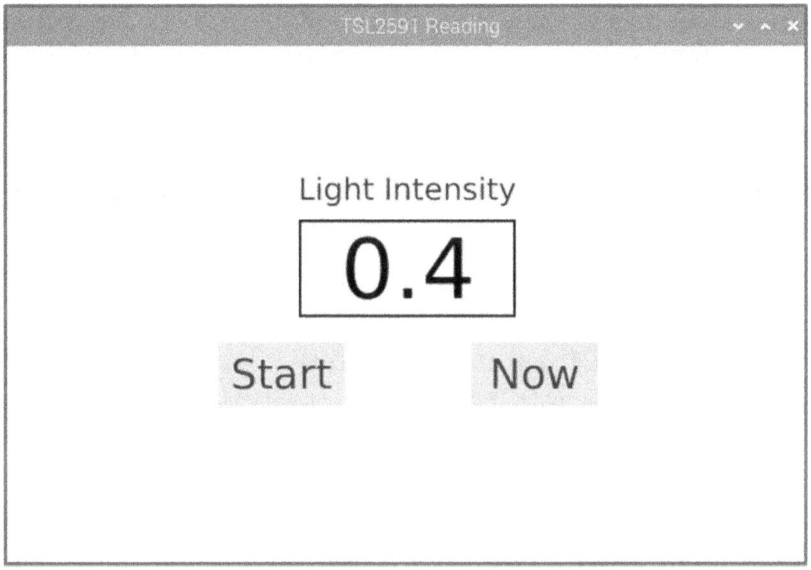

Figure 10.37 – IIO implementation of TSL2591

Finally, we can implement the necessary functionality where the UI can request the backend by following these steps:

1. Replace the existing implementation of the `lightIntensity` method in `backend.cpp` with the following lines, which is similar to the implementation in the preceding constructor:

```
QString Backend::lightIntensity()
{
    double intensity;
```

```
    iio_channel_attr_read_double(m_iioChannel, "input", &intensity);
    return QString::number(intensity, 'f', 1);
}
```

2. Remove the corresponding lines in the constructor so that it results in the following:

```
Backend::Backend(QObject *parent) :
    QObject(parent)
{
    iio_context* context = iio_create_local_context();
    iio_device* device = iio_context_find_device(context,
"tsl2591");
    m_iioChannel = iio_device_find_channel(device, "illuminance",
false);
}
```

3. Make the following modifications (in bold) to `main.qml`, which updates the text in the box to the most recent value sensed by the TSL2591 sensor:

```
    Button {
        id: btnNow
        anchors.left: itmIntensityValue.horizontalCenter
        anchors.top: itmIntensityValue.bottom
        anchors.leftMargin: 50
        anchors.topMargin: 20
        font.pointSize: 24
        text: "Now"
        onClicked: {
            txtLightIntensity.text = backend.q_lightIntensity
        }
    }
```

We can apply the preceding changes, compile the application, and deploy it to the Raspberry Pi. After running the application, we can click on the **Now** button and see the value in the text box being updated, as shown in the following screenshot:

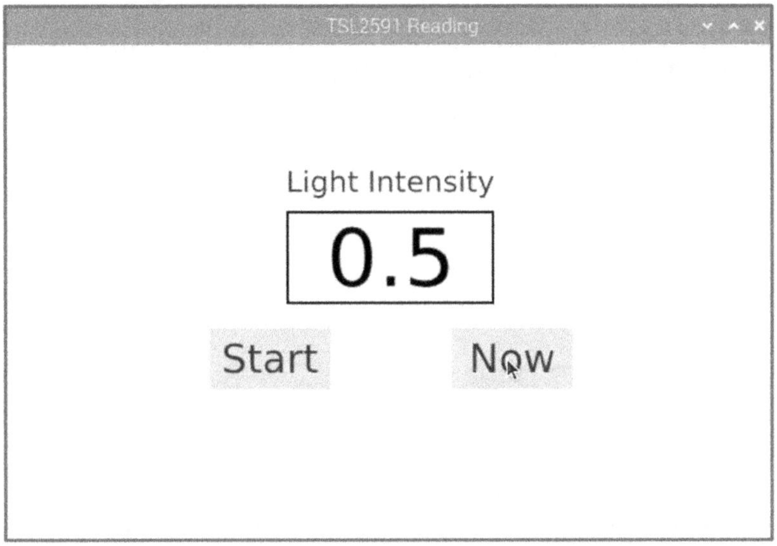

Figure 10.38 – Retrieving the light intensity from the GUI

In the next section, we will complete the application by implementing the functionality of the **Start** button.

Implementing timing

In this section, we will complete the application. Recall that when the **Start** button is pressed, the following actions should be taken:

- Change the text in the button to **Stop**
- Hide the **Now** button, and similarly, show the **Now** button when **Stop** is pressed
- Periodically query the TSL2591 and display the light intensity

We have already implemented the first action. We can implement the second one with the following modification (in bold) to `main.qml`:

```
Button {
    id: btnPeriodic
    anchors.right: itmIntensityValue.horizontalCenter
    anchors.top: itmIntensityValue.bottom
    anchors.rightMargin: 50
```

```
        anchors.topMargin: 20
        font.pointSize: 24
        text: "Start"
        onClicked: {
            if (isStarted === false) {
                btnPeriodic.text = "Stop";
                isStarted = true;
                btnNow.visible = false;
            } else {
                btnPeriodic.text = "Start";
                isStarted = false;
                btnNow.visible = true;
            }

        }
    }
```

After pressing the **Start** button with the preceding change in the application, we see the result shown in the following screenshot:

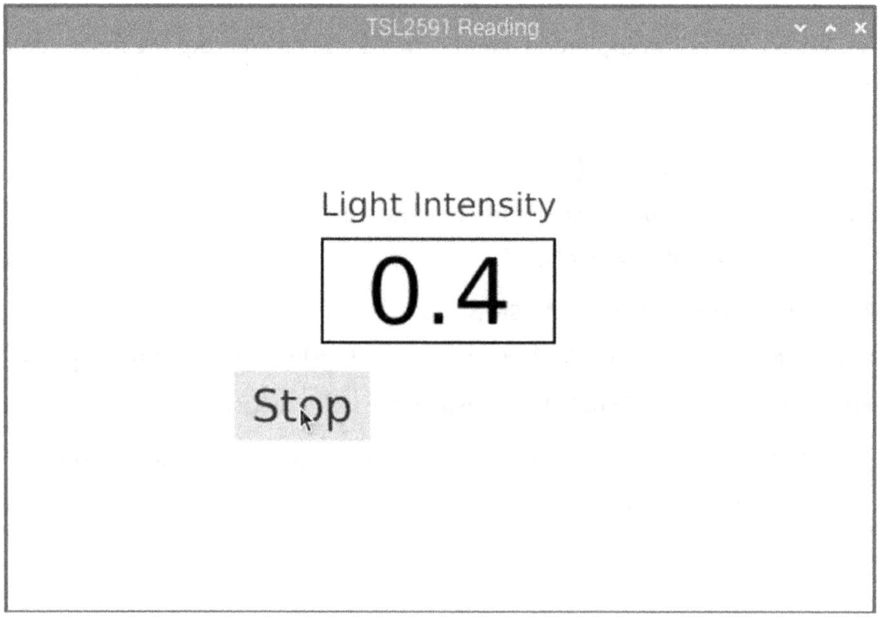

Figure 10.39 – Clicking on the Start button and it changing to Stop

Similarly, when we click on the **Stop** button, we can see that the **Now** button is visible.

Finally, we can make the following changes (in bold) to `main.qml` to periodically query the TSL2591 sensor:

```
    Timer {
      id: tmrSensor
      interval: 1000
      running: false
      repeat: true
      onTriggered: {
          txtLightIntensity.text = backend.q_lightIntensity
      }
    }

    Button {
        id: btnPeriodic
        anchors.right: itmIntensityValue.horizontalCenter
        anchors.top: itmIntensityValue.bottom
        anchors.rightMargin: 50
        anchors.topMargin: 20
        font.pointSize: 24
        text: "Start"
        onClicked: {
            if (isStarted === false) {
                btnPeriodic.text = "Stop";
                isStarted = true;
                btnNow.visible = false;
                tmrSensor.running = true;
            } else {
                btnPeriodic.text = "Start";
                isStarted = false;
                btnNow.visible = true;
                tmrSensor.running = false;
            }

        }
    }
```

We have added a QML **Timer**, which triggers a handler at a specific interval. The following describes the properties of the Timer defined in the preceding code block:

- `id`: Identifies the Timer and is used by the **Start/Stop** button to start the Timer.
- `interval`: Specifies how often the Timer should fire in milliseconds. In our implementation, the Timer fires every second.
- `running`: Defines whether the Timer is running or not. The Timer is not running on initialization. When the **Start** button is pressed, we start the Timer, and when the **Stop** button is pressed, we stop the Timer.
- `repeat`: Specifies whether the Timer should run periodically. Since we have defined this property as `true`, the Timer is periodic.
- `onTriggered`: This handler defines the logic to execute when the Timer expires. In our implementation, we retrieve the light intensity from the backend and update the text box.

With the preceding changes, when we click on the **Start** button, we should see the text box update with the value reported by the TSL2591 sensor. Try it for yourself under different lighting conditions!

Summary

In this chapter, we learned about the basics of Qt and how to install Qt Creator on our Linux development PC. We then used The Yocto Project BSP to create a toolchain that can be used to compile Qt applications that can be run on the Raspberry Pi 5. Finally, we implemented an application that can periodically query and display data retrieved from the TSL2591 sensor. We learned how to use Qt to build sophisticated applications with a polished GUI and deploy them to our Raspberry Pi. We will continue our exploration of using Qt in the next chapter by using Qt widgets, and develop a simple application similar for a medical device.

Get this book's PDF version and more

Scan the QR code (or go to `packtpub.com/unlock`). Search for this book by name, confirm the edition, and then follow the steps on the page.

UNLOCK NOW

Note: Keep your invoice handy. Purchases made directly from Packt don't require an invoice.

11

Project 3: Using Qt to Build a Medical Device

We will continue our journey of developing applications by exploring another mechanism to develop Qt applications, called **Qt Widgets**. Qt is a popular framework to develop medical devices because of its capability to develop sophisticated and polished UIs. It also has mature cross-development support to ensure that code bases can be leveraged across different platforms for a unified ecosystem. For example, a manufacturer can leverage the same code base for a bedside monitor running on an embedded Linux system and an app on a medical provider's tablet.

In this chapter, we will explore how to build a simple medical device using Qt Widgets. This application will use the same TSL2591 sensor from the previous two chapters. The application will collect and store data from the TSL2591 sensor every second in the background when it starts.

The GUI will also have a box that will be green if the light reading exceeds a threshold set by the user, and red otherwise. This box will be used to represent an "alarm" state. The GUI will also have a button that the user can press to inform the application that they have addressed the alarm and wish to clear it.

On that note, the GUI will also have a text box where the user can enter a threshold value and a button that will commit the value.

Medical devices usually have a requirement where a red alarm state cannot be cleared by the device on its own. Instead, the user must inform the device that they have taken action to clear the alarm. In our application, this is achieved by the user clicking on the **Clear** button.

We are going to cover the following topics in this chapter:

- Application overview
- Getting started with Qt Widgets
- Assembling the GUI elements
- Interacting with hardware synchronously
- Responding to user interaction
- Putting it all together

Technical requirements

You should be comfortable executing commands on a terminal. You should be comfortable reading, writing, and executing C++ applications. Finally, you should also ensure that you have downloaded the Git repository associated with this book, located at `https://github.com/PacktPublishing/Embedded-Linux-Essentials-Handbook`.

Application overview

In this section, we will review how the application will function. As mentioned earlier, our application will consist of the following GUI elements:

- A label will be green if the current light intensity is greater than or equal to the threshold and red if it is less than the threshold. The red color will signify that the system has entered an "alarm" state, which is a common feature in medical devices.
- A label that will display the current light intensity.
- A button to clear the device's alarm state. If the label is red, it will change to green.
- A text box where the user can enter the threshold.
- A button that the user can click that will set the threshold for the device to use to set the alarm state.

The following figure shows the GUI elements we just outlined:

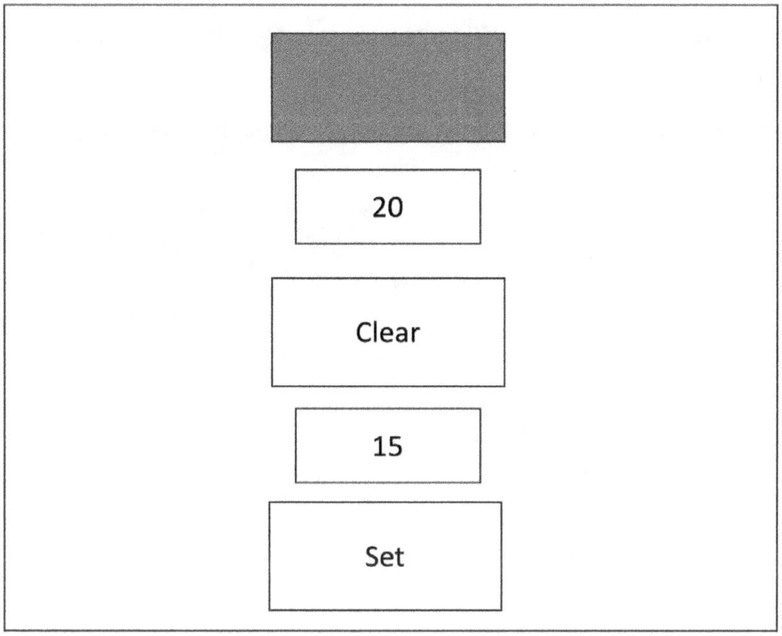

Figure 11.1 – Medical device application block diagram

In the next section, we will walk through the process of creating a Qt Widgets project using Qt Creator.

Getting started with Qt Widgets

We will now learn how to create a Qt Widgets project in Qt Creator. The following steps guide you in setting this up:

1. Open Qt Creator and click on **File** and then select **New Project...**, as shown in the following figure:

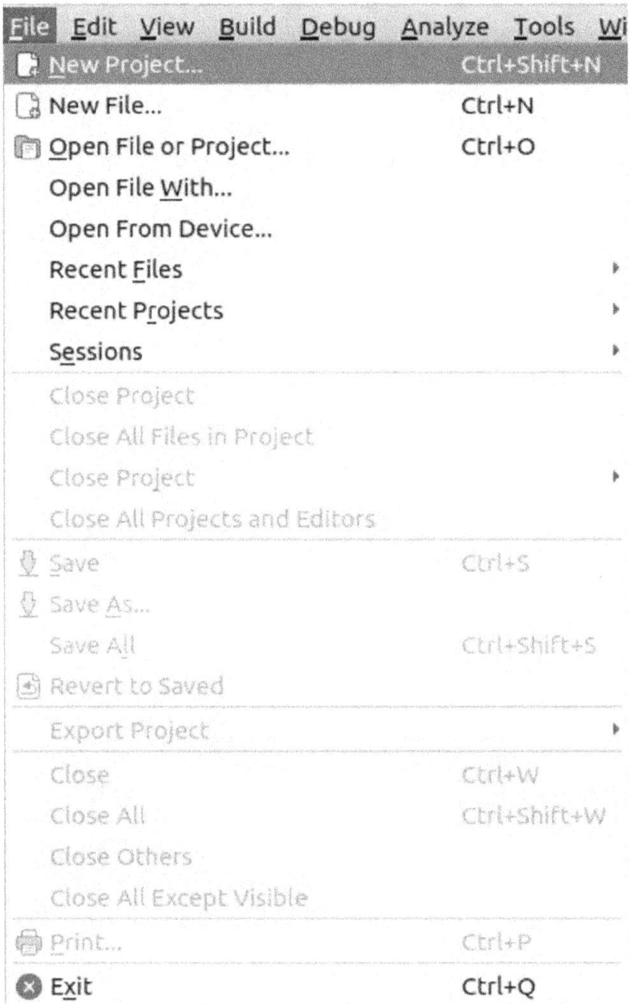

Figure 11.2 – Creating a Qt project

2. Highlight **Qt Widgets Application** and click on **Choose...** in the resulting window, as shown in the following figure:

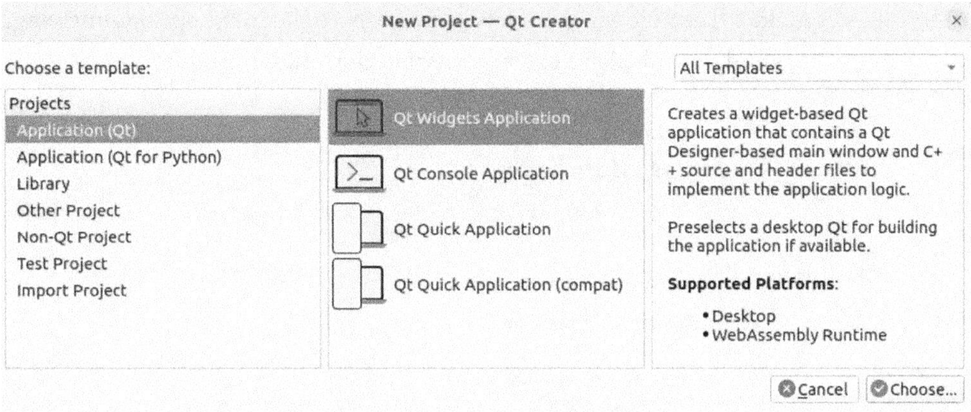

Figure 11.3 – Choosing a Qt Widgets application

3. In the following window, enter `medicalDevice` for the **Name** entry and choose an appropriate location for the **Create in** entry, as shown in the following figure:

Figure 11.4 – Specifying the details of our medical device

4. Select **qmake** in the following window and click **Next**. Keep the options unchanged in the following window and click **Next**, as shown in the following figure:

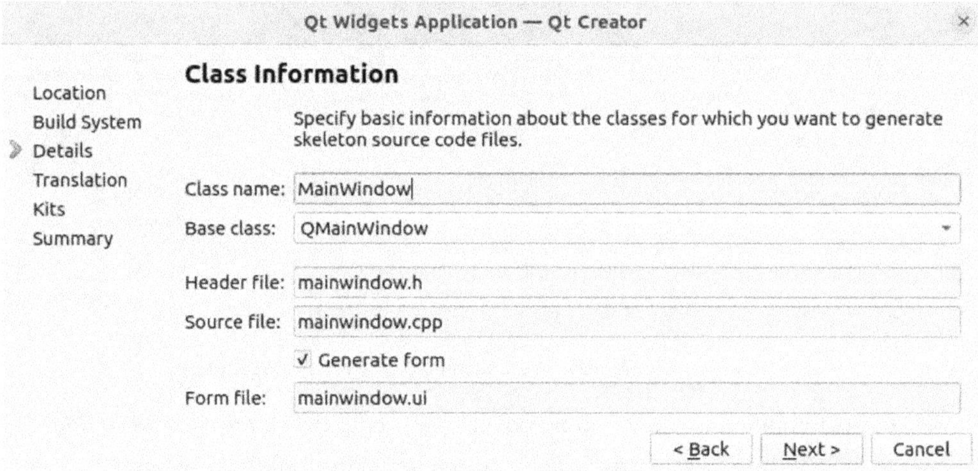

Figure 11.5 – Choosing default class options

5. Click **Next** on the **Translations File** window. In the following window, uncheck **Desktop Qt 5.15.2 GCC 64bit**, select **packt**, and ensure that only **Debug** is checked, as shown in the following figure:

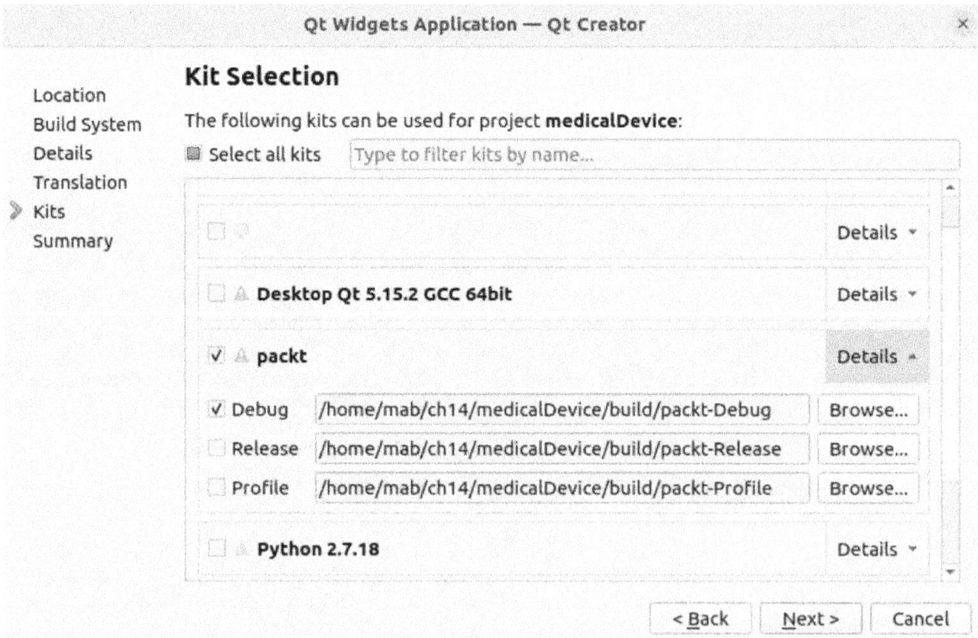

Figure 11.6 – Selecting our custom packt kit

6. Click **Finish** in the final window after clicking **Next** in the preceding figure.

In the next section, we will learn how to assemble our GUI elements in Qt Creator.

Assembling the GUI elements

In this section, we will learn how to assemble the GUI elements of our application in Qt Creator. After clicking **Finish** in the previous section, double-click on **mainwindow.ui** under **Forms** in the **Projects** pane, as shown in the following figure:

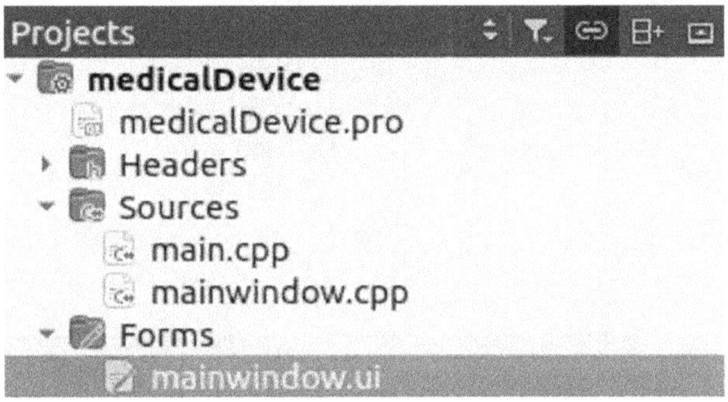

Figure 11.7 – Selecting our main GUI screen

Afterward, Qt Creator will present our main GUI screen in a view where we can drag and drop and customize the necessary elements, as shown in the following figure:

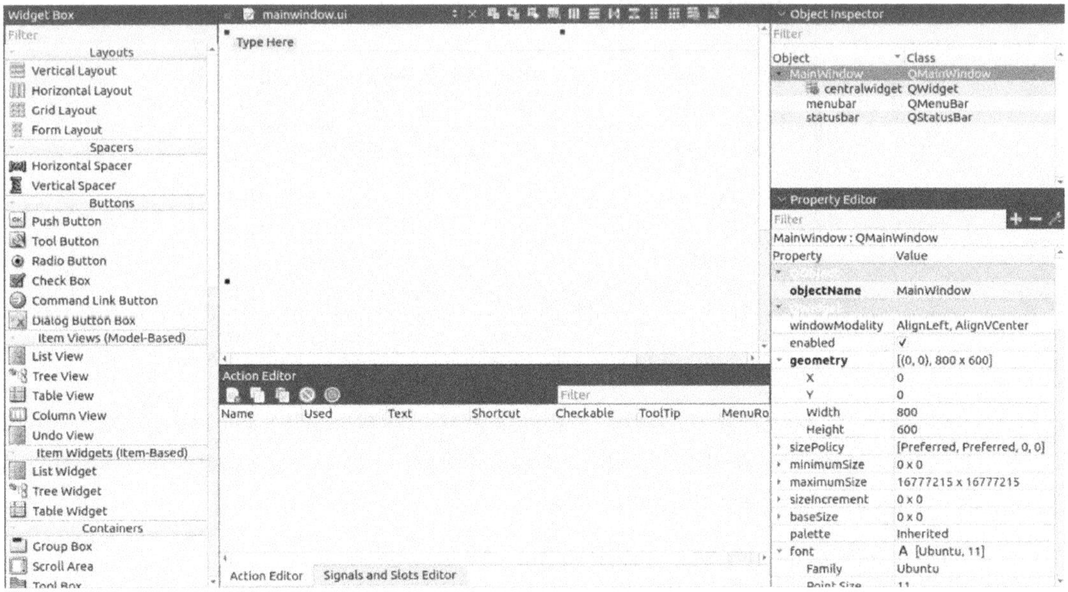

Figure 11.8 – Customizing our main GUI screen

We can assemble our GUI elements by following the steps outlined here:

1. Highlight **MainWindow** in the **Filter** pane at the top right, select **geometry** in the **Property Editor** pane at the bottom right, and modify **Width** to `640` and **Height** to `480`, as shown in the following figure (note that the default units of these properties are pixels):

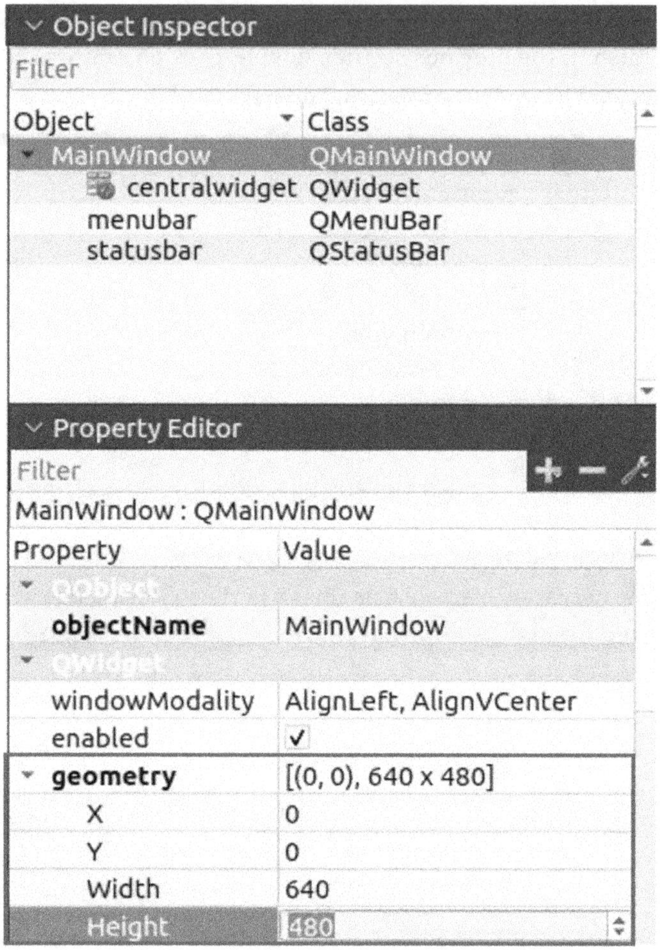

Figure 11.9 – Setting the dimensions of our GUI

2. Drag and drop **Label** from **Display Widgets** in the bottom-left pane to the main GUI in the center pane. Make the following modifications to the label's properties under the **Property Editor** pane at the bottom right:

   - Click on **label** next to **objectName** and enter `Status`.
   - Click the value next to **X** and enter `235`, and click the value next to **Y** and enter `50`.

- Click on the value next to **Width** and enter `130`, and click the value next to **Height** and enter `50`.
- Click on the value next to **styleSheet** and enter `background-color: green`. The label color should change to green.
- Click on the value next to **text** and delete it.

3. Drag and drop another **Label** widget from **Display Widgets** in the left pane to the main GUI in the center pane. Make the following modifications to the label's properties:

    - Click on **label** next to **objectName** and enter `lightIntensity`
    - Click on the value next to **X** and enter `235`, and click the value next to **Y** and enter `120`
    - Click on the value next to **Width** and enter `130`, and click the value next to **Height** and enter `50`
    - Click on the value next to **text** and delete it

4. Drag and drop **Push Button** from **Buttons** in the left pane to the main GUI in the center pane. Make the following modifications to the button's properties:

    - Click on **pushButton** next to **objectName** and enter `clearButton`
    - Click on the value next to **X** and enter `235`, and click the value next to **Y** and enter `200`
    - Click on the value next to **Width** and enter `130`, and click the value next to **Height** and enter `50`
    - Click on the value next to **text** and enter `Clear`

5. Drag and drop **Text Edit** from **Input Widgets** in the left pane to the main GUI in the center pane. Make the following modifications to the text box's properties:

    - Click on **textEdit** next to **objectName** and enter `Threshold`
    - Click on the value next to **X** and enter `235`, and click the value next to **Y** and enter `280`
    - Click on the value next to **Width** and enter `130`, and click the value next to **Height** and enter `50`
    - Expand **inputMethodHints** and check **ImhPreferNumbers** and uncheck **ImhMultiLine**

6. Drag and drop another **Push Button** from **Buttons** in the left pane to the main GUI in the center pane. Make the following modifications to the button's properties:

    - Click on **pushButton** next to **objectName** and enter `clearButton`
    - Click on the value next to **X** and enter `235`, and click the value next to **Y** and enter `360`
    - Click on the value next to **Width** and enter `130`, and click the value next to **Height** and enter `50`
    - Click on the value next to **text** and enter `Set`

The resulting GUI should match the following figure:

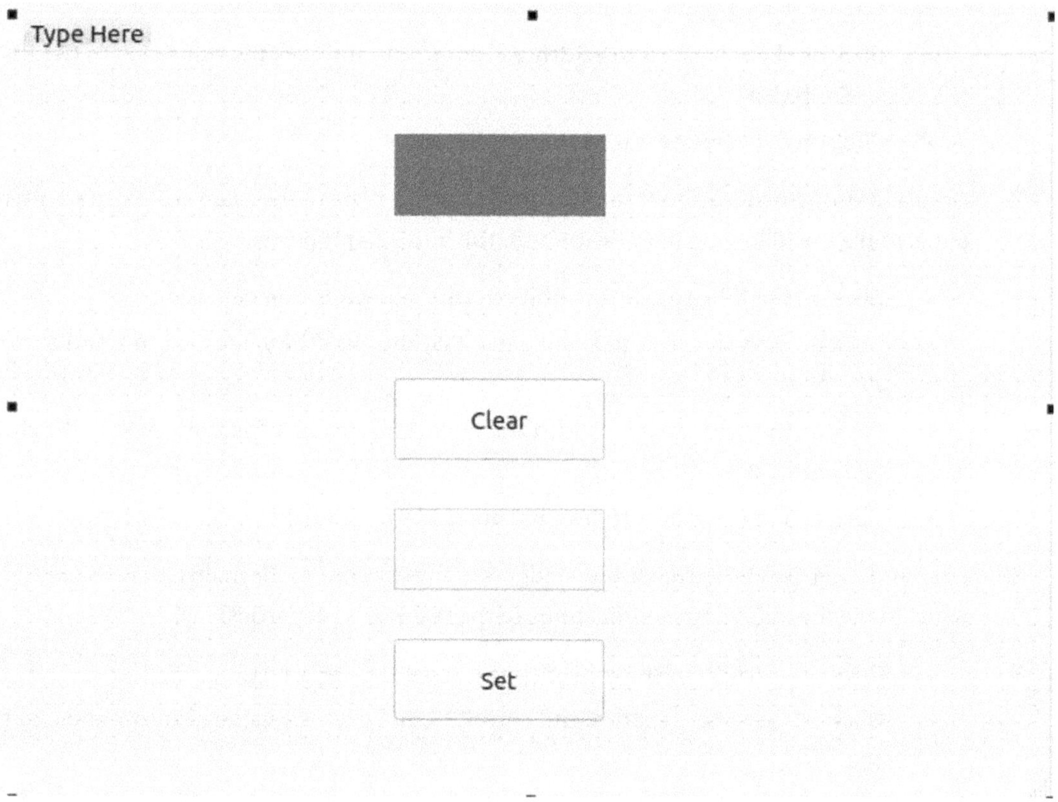

Figure 11.10 – Final GUI layout

In the next section, we will learn how to retrieve the light intensity sensor synchronously, which means on a regular interval.

Interacting with hardware synchronously

In this section, we will learn how to query the light intensity sensor regularly using the C++ implementation, or "synchronously." Specifically, we will query the sensor every second and update the `lightIntensity` label. We will use the **QTimer** construct in Qt to achieve this functionality. Also, we will be using `libIIO` to interact with the TSL2591 sensor, as we did in *Chapter 13, Securing Code Execution with eBPF.*

First, we need to edit `mainwindow.h` with the following modifications shown in bold:

```
#ifndef MAINWINDOW_H
#define MAINWINDOW_H

#include <QMainWindow>
#include <QTimer>
#include <iio.h>
.
.
.
private:
    Ui::MainWindow *ui;
    iio_channel *m_iioChannel;
    QTimer *lightTimer;
```

Second, we need to edit `mainwindow.cpp` with the modifications outlined here:

1. Add the `libIIO` functionality to the constructor, as shown here:

```
MainWindow::MainWindow(QWidget *parent)
    : QMainWindow(parent)
    , ui(new Ui::MainWindow)
{
    ui->setupUi(this);

    iio_context* context = iio_create_local_context();
    iio_device* device = iio_context_find_device(context,
"tsl2591");
    m_iioChannel = iio_device_find_channel(device, "illuminance",
false);
```

2. Create the `QTimer` in the constructor, set it to expire every second, and start it, as shown here:

```
    lightTimer = new QTimer(this);
    lightTimer->setInterval(1000);
    lightTimer->start();
```

3. Inform Qt to call the `getLightIntensity` function when the timer expires, by adding the following line to the constructor:

```
    connect(lightTimer, SIGNAL(timeout()), this,
SLOT(getLightIntensity()));
```

4. Create a section called `private slots` in `mainwindow.h` and add the `getLightIntensity` function under this section, as shown here:

```
private slots:
        void getLightIntensity();
```

5. Add the implementation of the `getLightIntensity` function to `mainwindow.cpp`. As shown here, this function will query the TSL2591 sensor using `libIIO`:

```
void MainWindow::getLightIntensity()
{
    double intensity;
    iio_channel_attr_read_double(m_iioChannel, "input", &intensity);

    ui->lightIntensity->setText(QString::number(intensity, 'f', 1));
}
```

6. Add the following entry to `medicalDevice.pro` to inform Qt to link our application against `libIIO`:

```
LIBS += -liio
```

Important note

Signals and slots are used for communication between objects in Qt. When a Qt timer expires, it fires a signal, which is received by the corresponding slot, and the appropriate function is executed. In the preceding implementation, we have instructed Qt that the `getLightIntensity` function is a slot that will receive signals fired by `lightTimer`.

After compiling, deploying, and running the application on our Raspberry Pi 5, we should see the label for the light intensity updated every second.

In the next section, we will learn how to respond to button clicks in our application.

Responding to user interaction

In this section, we will learn how to respond to user interaction in our application. Specifically, we will learn how to act appropriately when a user clicks on a button.

First, we need to add the methods that will be called when either of the two buttons is clicked under the `private slots` section of `mainwindow.h`, as shown here:

```
private slots:
        void getLightIntensity();
        void on_setButton_clicked();
        void on_clearButton_clicked();
```

Second, we can edit `mainwindow.cpp` with the following modifications:

1. Add a test implementation of the `on_setButton_clicked` method, as shown here:

   ```
   void MainWindow::on_setButton_clicked()
   {
       qDebug() << "on_setButton_clicked";
   }
   ```

2. Add a test implementation of the `on_clearButton_clicked` method, as shown here:

   ```
   void MainWindow::on_clearButton_clicked()
   {
       qDebug() << "on_clearButton_clicked";
   }
   ```

After applying the preceding changes, compiling, deploying, and running the application on our Raspberry Pi 5, if we click on the **Set** button, we should see the following in the terminal:

```
$ on_setButton_clicked
```

Similarly, if we click on the **Clear** button, we should see the following in the terminal:

```
$ on_clearButton_clicked
```

In the next section, we will combine the GUI elements with the business logic to implement and test the complete application.

Putting it all together

In this section, we will complete the application implementation.

Since our application will have two main states, we need to represent this state information using an enumeration. Additionally, we need a class variable to store the threshold that we will use to set the application state.

We can accomplish this by first making the following modifications in bold to `mainwindow.h`:

```
private:
.
.
.
    typedef enum {
            ALARM_STATE_GREEN,
            ALARM_STATE_RED,
    } AlarmState_e;

    AlarmState_e currentAlarmState;
    double threshold;
```

Second, we need to make the following modifications to `mainwindow.cpp`:

1. Initialize the threshold to `0` and set the initial state to `GREEN` by making the following modifications to the constructor:

```
MainWindow::MainWindow(QWidget *parent)
    : QMainWindow(parent)
    , ui(new Ui::MainWindow)
{
.
.
.
    threshold = 0;
    currentAlarmState = ALARM_STATE_GREEN;
}
```

2. If the most recent light intensity reading is less than the threshold, set the alarm state to `RED` and fill the `Status` label in red. This can be accomplished by modifying the `getLightIntensity` function in the following manner (note that we will not set the status to green because that can only be done if the user clicks on the **Clear** button):

```
void MainWindow::getLightIntensity()
{
    double intensity;
    iio_channel_attr_read_double(m_iioChannel, "input", &intensity);

    ui->lightIntensity->setText(QString::number(intensity, 'f', 1));

    if (intensity < threshold) {
            currentAlarmState = ALARM_STATE_RED;
            ui->Status->setStyleSheet("background-color: red");
    }
}
```

3. Update the `threshold` member variable when the **Set** button is clicked, by making the following modification to the `on_setButton_clicked` method:

```
void MainWindow::on_setButton_clicked()
{
    threshold = ui->Threshold->toPlainText().toDouble();
}
```

4. When the **Clear** button is clicked, the application state should be reset to `GREEN`, and the `Status` label should be colored green. This can be accomplished with the following modifications to `mainwindow.cpp`:

```
void MainWindow::on_setButton_clicked()
{
    threshold = ui->Threshold->toPlainText().toDouble();
}

void MainWindow::on_clearButton_clicked()
{
    ui->Status->setStyleSheet("background-color: green");
    currentAlarmState = ALARM_STATE_GREEN;
}
```

After applying the preceding changes, compiling, deploying, and running the application on our Raspberry Pi 5, we should see the application behave as expected. For example, if the threshold is set to `20`, and the light intensity is less than `20`, we should see the `Status` label turn red, as shown in the followimg figure:

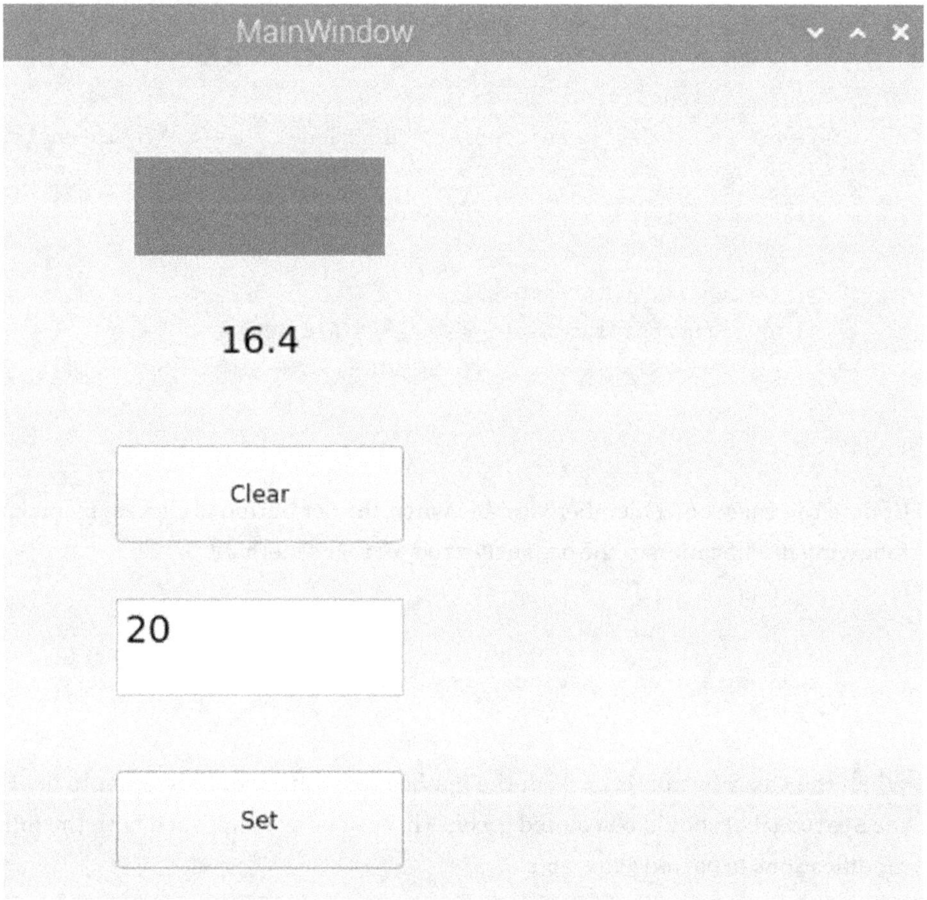

Figure 11.11 – Setting the threshold

If we click **Clear**, the `Status` label should momentarily turn green and return to red. If we reduce the threshold to 15 and click **Set**, the `Status` label should turn red. Finally, if we now click **Clear**, the `Status` label should turn and stay green, as shown in the following figure:

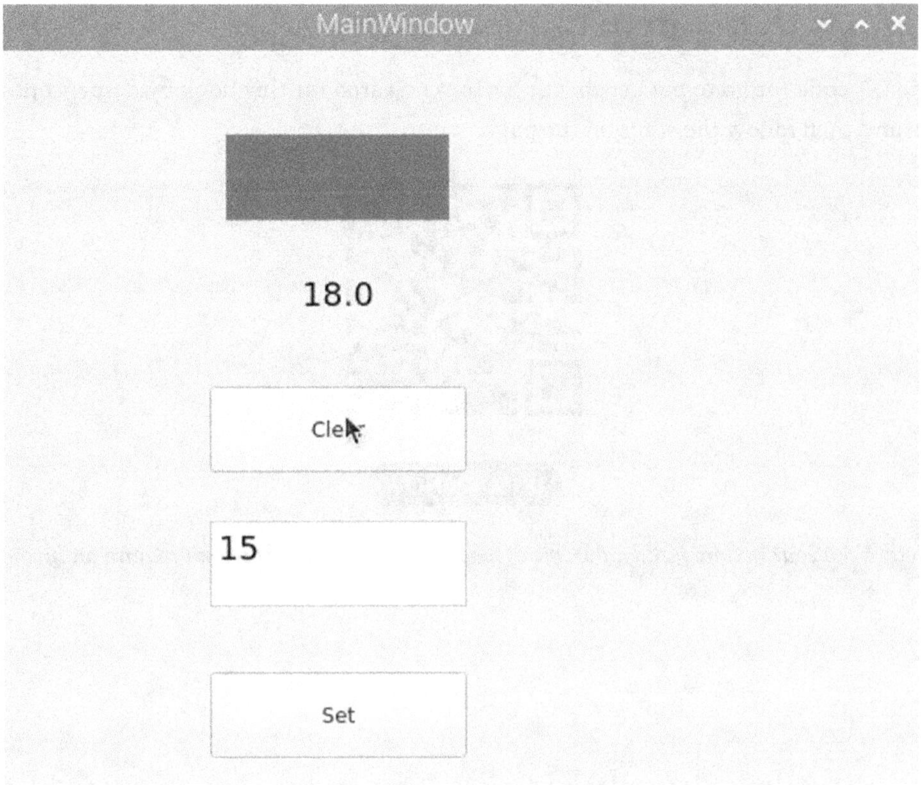

Figure 11.12 – Resetting and maintaining the application state

Thus, we have implemented the complete application as defined by our original requirements.

Summary

In this chapter, we used Qt Widgets to implement a simple medical device application. We defined a set of requirements where the application would enter certain states, depending on the light intensity reading and a threshold set by the user. We also defined a critical requirement that is typical of most medical devices. Specifically, if the application enters a red alarm state, it can only be cleared by the user clicking on a particular button.

We then learned how to add widgets to our application using Qt Creator, synchronously querying the TSL2591 using the LibIIO framework using the QTimer construct. Finally, we implemented the complete set of requirements.

This chapter concludes *Part 2*. In *Part 3*, we will cover advanced topics and hypothesize about the future of embedded Linux systems.

Get this book's PDF version and more

Scan the QR code (or go to `packtpub.com/unlock`). Search for this book by name, confirm the edition, and then follow the steps on the page.

UNLOCK NOW

Note: Keep your invoice handy. Purchases made directly from Packt don't require an invoice.

Part 4

Advanced Topics, Implementing CI/CD, Best Practices, and Looking Ahead

In this part, we will discuss advanced topics associated with the development of an Embedded Linux System. Then, we will see how Continuous Integration/Continuous Delivery (CI/CD) can mitigate these issues. Finally, we will review topics which are relevant for Embedded Linux enthusiasts in the future.

This part has the following chapters:

- *Chapter 12, Debugging the Linux Kernel*
- *Chapter 13, Securing Code Execution with eBPF*
- *Chapter 14, Rust in Embedded Linux: The Kernel and Applications*
- *Chapter 15, Implementing Continuous Integration/Continuous Delivery (CI/CD)*
- *Chapter 16, Looking to the Future*

12

Debugging the Linux Kernel

Debugging is an important skill for an embedded software developer to master. We learned how to debug Linux userspace applications in *Chapter 8*. However, due to the nature of embedded systems, debugging the Linux kernel is different.

Custom hardware in embedded systems may require custom drivers or modifications directly to the Linux kernel. Additionally, the nature of the final application may require that the embedded system operate optimally. Thus, it may not be sufficient for the embedded software, specifically the Linux kernel and corresponding drivers, to be functional. Instead, they must also be performant.

This chapter aims to teach the different mechanisms to debug the Linux kernel, for both functionality and optimal performance. First, we will learn about functional and performance issues encountered when using the Linux kernel in an embedded system.

Second, we will understand the hardware and software tools that can be used to perform step-through debugging in the Linux kernel. **Step-through debugging** is an important mechanism that embedded software engineers use to ensure that their implementation is functionally correct. However, step-through debugging in Linux-based embedded systems differs from traditional step-through debugging for bare-metal and Real Time Operating System (RTOS)-based embedded systems.

Third, we will learn about and understand how to debug an *oops*, a specific type of error encountered by the Linux kernel.

Fourth, we will learn about `ftrace`, a tool that efficiently traces function calls in the driver or kernel subsystem under test.

Finally, we will review `lockdep`, a tool that can help us ensure that our driver implementation or kernel modification does not introduce locking errors, such as a deadlock.

In this chapter, we are going to cover the following main topics:

- Issues encountered in the Linux kernel
- `kgdb`: step-through debugging the Linux kernel
- `ftrace`: efficiently tracing function calls
- `lockdep`: debugging deadlocks

Important note

Using `printk` statements is one technique to debug issues encountered in the Linux kernel. While `printk` statements (or their derivatives) are easy to include and can be useful to identify implementation bugs and functional issues, they shouldn't be used to identify and resolve performance issues. Logging using `printk` statements is surprisingly heavyweight.

Important note

Debugging the Linux kernel is an extensive topic that cannot be covered in earnest in one chapter. Thus, we will review a few useful techniques in this chapter. You are encouraged to explore the following to read about Linux kernel debugging in detail: `https://www.packtpub.com/en-us/product/linux-kernel-debugging-9781801075039`.

Technical requirements

You should be comfortable reading and writing C code and executing commands on a terminal. You can follow the examples in this chapter using the following Github link: `https://github.com/PacktPublishing/Embedded-Linux-Essentials-Handbook/tree/main/Chapter12`

Issues encountered in the Linux kernel

In this section, we will learn about the possible issues encountered when implementing device drivers or modifying the Linux kernel for custom hardware. The Linux kernel has been architected and designed to keep the overall system running even if a particular driver or subsystem crashes. The Linux kernel's architecture also aims to ensure that each device driver and subsystem is performant. Nonetheless, issues may still arise.

We will learn about the functional issues that may result in incorrect or incomplete behavior of our device driver. We will also understand how an inefficient implementation of our device driver may degrade the performance of our embedded system.

Functional issues

Bugs are always a concern in software development. In the case of embedded systems, they can be catastrophic since we are operating so close to the hardware. Defects introduced during the course of implementing a device driver or modifying the Linux kernel may result in certain functional issues, including the following:

- They may cause our hardware to behave differently than expected
- They may also cause the Linux kernel to limit the functionality of our driver to ensure that the overall system continues to function

In the following subsections, we will learn about the most common functional issues in the Linux kernel.

Kernel panic

A **kernel panic** is a catastrophic error that occurs in the Linux kernel. The entire system comes to a halt in the case of a kernel panic. Three general mechanisms can be used to recover from a kernel panic, which are outlined here:

- **Hard reboot**: The system can be power cycled to allow the Linux kernel to boot from a clean start. The advantage of this mechanism is that it is instantaneous. However, it usually requires direct and physical access to the system.
- **Watchdog timeout**: The processor usually contains a hardware watchdog timer, which is responsible for resetting the processor if it locks up. The Linux kernel contains a device driver that periodically exercises, or *feeds/pets*, the watchdog timer to ensure it doesn't reset the system. However, in the event of a kernel panic, the watchdog driver stops running and fails to pet the hardware watchdog timer, causing the watchdog timer to reset the processor.
- **Soft reboot**: The Linux kernel has a mechanism that can perform a soft reset after some time has elapsed after a kernel panic. The timeout value can be set using the `CONFIG_PANIC_TIMEOUT` Kconfig parameter.

Let's walk through an example of triggering a kernel panic on the Raspberry Pi 5:

1. Before demonstrating a kernel panic, connecting to the Raspberry Pi 5 using a serial interface is best. This way, we can observe interesting kernel output presented on the console.
2. Unlike previous iterations of the Raspberry Pi, the serial console interface of the Raspberry Pi 5 is not available on the GPIO pins of the header. Instead, there is a dedicated UART port, as shown in the following figure (courtesy of `https://www.raspberrypi.com/documentation/computers/raspberry-pi-5.html#uart-connector`):

Figure 12.1 – UART console from the Raspberry Pi 5

3. We need to connect this port to the port labeled **U** on the Raspberry Pi Debug Probe (`https://www.raspberrypi.com/products/debug-probe/`), and connect the Micro-USB cable on the Debug Probe to our PC, as shown in the following figure:

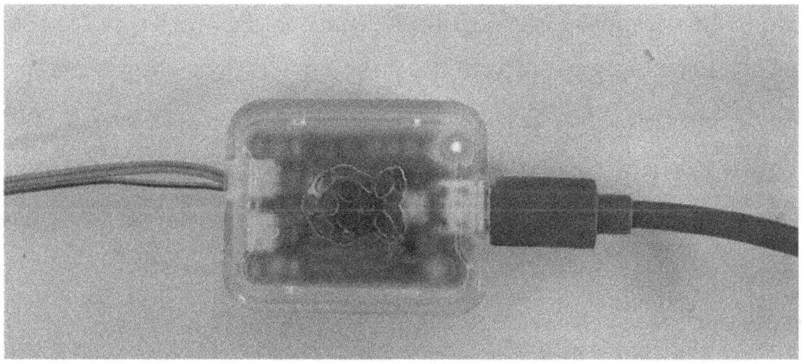

Figure 12.2 – Connecting the ribbon cable to the Debug Probe

The following figure shows the connection to the Raspberry Pi 5:

Figure 12.3 – Connecting the ribbon cable to the Raspberry Pi 5

4. The Debug Probe should appear as a **teletype** (`tty`) device on our PC, as shown in the following, in the case of a Linux host PC:

```
[~]$ ls --color=none /dev/ttyACM*
/dev/ttyACM0
```

5. We can open a terminal application on our host PC, such as `minicom`, and we will be presented with the login prompt to the Raspberry Pi 5, as shown here:

```
raspberrypi login: mab-rpi
Password:
Linux raspberrypi 6.1.69-v8-16k+ #4 SMP PREEMPT Fri Jan  5 19:28:14 EST 2024 aarch64

The programs included with the Debian GNU/Linux system are free software;
the exact distribution terms for each program are described in the
individual files in /usr/share/doc/*/copyright.

Debian GNU/Linux comes with ABSOLUTELY NO WARRANTY, to the extent
permitted by applicable law.
Last login: Tue Jan 23 19:06:31 EST 2024 on tty1
mab-rpi@raspberrypi:~$ [    21.380700] hwmon hwmon2: Undervoltage detected!
[    27.428693] hwmon hwmon2: Undervoltage detected!
```

Figure 12.4 – Raspberry Pi 5 login prompt over serial console

6. We can then trigger a kernel panic by executing the following commands in the terminal. The second command writes a `c` character to the `/proc/sysrq-trigger` file:

```
mab-rpi@raspberrypi:~$ sudo su
root@raspberrypi:/home/mab-rpi# echo c > /proc/sysrq-trigger
```

After executing the preceding command, we will see the following output, and the Raspberry Pi 5 will become unresponsive:

```
root@raspberrypi:/home/mab-rpi# echo c > /proc/sysrq-trigger
[  210.706414] sysrq: Trigger a crash
[  210.710719] Kernel panic - not syncing: sysrq triggered crash
[  210.716484] CPU: 2 PID: 1982 Comm: bash Tainted: G         C         6.1.69-v8-16k+ #4
[  210.724433] Hardware name: Raspberry Pi 5 Model B Rev 1.0 (DT)
[  210.730285] Call trace:
[  210.732733]  dump_backtrace.part.0+0xe8/0xf4
[  210.737019]  show_stack+0x20/0x30
[  210.740340]  dump_stack_lvl+0x68/0x84
[  210.744013]  dump_stack+0x18/0x34
[  210.747335]  panic+0x18c/0x358
[  210.750396]  sysrq_handle_crash+0x24/0x2c
[  210.754416]  __handle_sysrq+0x94/0x1a0
[  210.758174]  write_sysrq_trigger+0x7c/0xb0
[  210.762280]  proc_reg_write+0xac/0x100
[  210.766040]  vfs_write+0xcc/0x2b4
[  210.769361]  ksys_write+0x70/0x100
[  210.772770]  __arm64_sys_write+0x24/0x30
[  210.776701]  invoke_syscall+0x50/0x120
[  210.780461]  el0_svc_common.constprop.0+0x4c/0x100
[  210.785268]  do_el0_svc+0x38/0xe0
[  210.788591]  el0_svc+0x2c/0x84
[  210.791651]  el0t_64_sync_handler+0xbc/0x140
[  210.795933]  el0t_64_sync+0x18c/0x190
[  210.799604] SMP: stopping secondary CPUs
[  210.803537] Kernel Offset: 0x100004000000 from 0xffff800008000000
[  210.809650] PHYS_OFFSET: 0x0
[  210.812534] CPU features: 0x00000,001700a0,66600720b
[  210.817426] Memory Limit: none
[  210.820486] ---[ end Kernel panic - not syncing: sysrq triggered crash ]---
```

Figure 12.5 – Triggering a kernel panic

The `proc/sysrq-trigger` interface allows us to send keys to the Linux kernel, regardless of its state, to trigger certain behavior in the Linux kernel. According to the Linux kernel documentation for this interface (`https://www.kernel.org/doc/html/v6.9/admin-guide/sysrq.html`), we can send the `c` character to this interface to perform a system crash.

During a panic, before either the kernel performs a soft reset after the specified timeout, the user pulls power, or the watchdog timer resets the CPU, the kernel prints a **backtrace** of the functions that were called immediately before the panic occurred. The backtrace, or **stack trace**, can help diagnose the problem that led to the kernel panic. The interesting portion of the preceding backtrace is shown in the output here:

```
[ 210.737019] show_stack+0x20/0x30
[ 210.740340] dump_stack_lvl+0x68/0x84
[210.747335] panic+0x18/0x358
[210.750396] sysrq_handle_crash+0x24/0x2c
[210.754416] __handle_sysrq+0x94/0x1a0
[210.758174] write_sysrq_trgger+0x7c/0xb0
```

Each line of the backtrace has the following format:

```
[timestamp] function+offset/size
```

- `timestamp`: The time in seconds after boot when the function was called
- `function`: The name of the function that was invoked in the backtrace
- `offset`: The offset (which corresponds to the line) inside the function that was called
- `size`: The total size of the function in the backtrace

Although we know what triggered the kernel panic in this instance, in a typical scenario, we would need to debug further to identify the underlying cause. We can use the `faddr2line` utility, available in the Linux kernel repository, to convert each line in the backtrace into a source file and line in the Linux kernel.

We can determine which line in the Linux kernel source code led to the preceding kernel panic by following the steps outlined here:

1. Configure and compile the Linux kernel using the steps outlined in *Chapter 3, Navigating the Linux Kernel*. The `vmlinux` file, an uncompressed version of the Linux kernel that contains its debugging symbols, can be passed to the `f2addrline` utility to convert an entry from the backtrace to a source file and line.

2. Execute the following command to determine the line and source file where the `panic` function was called. Since the `sysrq_handle_crash` function in the backtrace is immediately before the `panic` function, we can use it to identify the source file and line that triggered the kernel panic:

```
$./scripts/faddr2line vmlinux sysrq_handle_crash+0x24/0x2c
sysrq_handle_crash+0x24/0x2c:
sysrq_handle_crash at drivers/tty/sysrq.c:155
```

3. If we open the `drivers/tty/sysrq.c` source file and navigate to line 155, we can see the call to the `panic` function, highlighted here:

```
static void sysrq_handle_crash(int key)
{
        /* release the RCU read lock before crashing */
        rcu_read_unlock();

        panic("sysrq triggered crash\n");
}
```

4. We can go up one level in the backtrace and see the source and line corresponding to `__handle_sysrq+0x94/0x1a0` by using the `faddr2line` utility:

```
$ ./scripts/faddr2line vmlinux __handle_sysrq+0x94/0x1a0
__handle_sysrq+0x94/0x1a0:
rcu_read_unlock at include/linux/rcupdate.h:823
(inlined by) __handle_sysrq at drivers/tty/sysrq.c:626
[linux]$ vim drivers/tty/sysrq.c
```

5. However, if we navigate to line 626 of the `drivers/tty/sysrq.c` source file, we notice that it points to the call to the `rcu_read_unlock` function. This isn't the actual line and function call that triggers the panic. This is because the locking mechanism used in the **Read-Copy-Update** (**RCU**) framework masks the exact location of certain function calls. Additional details of the RCU framework are outside of this book's scope.

6. We can go up another level in the backtrace and see the source and line corresponding to `write_sysrq_trgger+0x7c/0xb0`, by executing the following command:

```
$ ./scripts/faddr2line vmlinux write_sysrq_trigger+0x7c/0xa0
write_sysrq_trigger+0x7c/0xa0:
write_sysrq_trigger at drivers/tty/sysrq.c:1164
```

7. If we navigate to line 1,164 of `drivers/tty/sysrq.c`, it corresponds to the call to the `__handle_sysrq` function in the backtrace, in the `write_sysrq_trigger` function, as shown highlighted here:

```
static ssize_t write_sysrq_trigger(struct file *file, const char
__user *buf,
                                   size_t count, loff_t *ppos)
{
        if (count) {
                char c;

                if (get_user(c, buf))
                        return -EFAULT;
                __handle_sysrq(c, false);
        }

        return count;
}
```

8. The `__handle_sysrq` function takes a character as its argument, looks up the function that should be called based on the character, and calls that function. As shown next, in the case of the `c` character, which is what we wrote to the `/proc/sysrq-trigger` file, the `sysrq_handle_crash` function is called:

```
static const struct sysrq_key_op sysrq_crash_op = {
        .handler        = sysrq_handle_crash,
        .help_msg       = "crash(c)",
        .action_msg     = "Trigger a crash",
        .enable_mask    = SYSRQ_ENABLE_DUMP,
};
.
.
.
static const struct sysrq_key_op *sysrq_key_table[62] = {
        &sysrq_loglevel_op,             /* 0 */
        &sysrq_loglevel_op,             /* 1 */
.
.
.
```

```
        &sysrq_reboot_op,                  /* b */
        &sysrq_crash_op,                   /* c */
};
```

9. Finally, as shown in the following snippet, the `write_sysrq_trigger` function is invoked when we write to the `/proc/sysrq-trigger` file:

```
static const struct proc_ops sysrq_trigger_proc_ops = {
        .proc_write     = write_sysrq_trigger,
        .proc_lseek     = noop_llseek,
};

static void sysrq_init_procfs(void)
{
        if (!proc_create("sysrq-trigger", S_IWUSR, NULL,
                         &sysrq_trigger_proc_ops))
                pr_err("Failed to register proc interface\n");
}
```

Important note

The `proc` filesystem is an antiquated mechanism that the Linux kernel uses to allow users and other user-space applications to interact with different Linux kernel subsystems, drivers, and modules.

We have successfully traced the origin of the kernel panic!

Kernel oops

A **kernel oops** is a mechanism in the Linux kernel that identifies and notifies the user that the operation performed by a particular device driver or subsystem has resulted in an exception. On a kernel oops, a message is printed to the device console and stored in the kernel log. Similar to a kernel panic, this message contains a backtrace and the contents of the relevant processor registers. If a critical subsystem or device driver causes a kernel oops, it may result in a kernel panic.

If the device driver or subsystem is not critical, and the system can continue to operate, the Linux kernel simply terminates the user-space process that ultimately triggered the oops.

Let's see how we can create and trigger a kernel oops on the Raspberry Pi 5:

1. Navigate to the `Chapter3` directory of the GitHub repository associated with this book (`https://github.com/PacktPublishing/Embedded-Linux-Essentials-Handbook`). The lines that trigger the kernel oops are shown in bold in the following code:

```
#include <linux/init.h>
#include <linux/module.h>

static void test_generate_oops(void)
{
    *(int *) 0 = 0;
}

static int __init test_oops_init(void)
{
    printk("Hello World!\n");
    test_generate_oops();
    return 0;
}

static void __exit test_exit(void)
{
    printk(KERN INFO "Goodbye World!\n");
}

module_init(test_oops_init);
module_exit(test_exit);

MODULE_AUTHOR("Mohammed Billoo");
MODULE_DESCRIPTION("Hello World kernel module");
MODULE_LICENSE("GPL");
```

Note

We're dereferencing and writing a value to a `NULL` pointer, which is an invalid operation and is the root cause of the kernel oops.

2. Then, we need to configure and compile the Linux kernel by following the instructions in *Chapter 3, Navigating the Linux Kernel.*
3. We can navigate to the `kernel-oops` directory and compile the kernel module by executing the following command:

```
[kernel-oops]$ ARCH=arm64 make
```

4. Finally, we need to transfer the kernel module to our Raspberry Pi 5, load the module in our console window, and observe the kernel output, as shown here:

```
mab-rpi@raspberrypi:~$ sudo insmod kernel-oops.ko
[  235.413957] Unable to handle kernel NULL pointer dereference at
virtual address 0000000000000000
[  235.422799] Mem abort info:
[  235.425599]   ESR = 0x0000000096000045
[  235.429358]   EC = 0x25: DABT (current EL), IL = 32 bits
[  235.434689]   SET = 0, FnV = 0
[  235.437750]   EA = 0, S1PTW = 0
[  235.440898]   FSC = 0x05: level 1 translation fault
[  235.445791] Data abort info:
[  235.448676]   ISV = 0, ISS = 0x00000045
[  235.452523]   CM = 0, WnR = 1
[  235.455493] user pgtable: 16k pages, 47-bit VAs,
pgdp=000000003a950000
[  235.462046] [0000000000000000] pgd=0000000000000000,
p4d=0000000000000000, pud=0000000000000000
[  235.470785] Internal error: Oops: 0000000096000045 [#1] PREEMPT
SMP
.
.
.
[  235.470889] pc : test_oops_init+0x20/0x1000 [test_module]
[  235.471093] lr : test_oops_init+0x18/0x1000 [test_module]
.
.
.
Call trace:
[ 235.472402]  test_oops_init+0x20/0x1000 [test_module]
[ 235.473949]  do_one_initcall+0x60/0x1dc
```

```
.
.
.
[ 235.481075] ---[ end trace 0000000000000000 ]--
mab-rpi@raspberrypi:~$
```

As we can see in the preceding output, besides CPU registers that we could potentially use to debug the oops, the Linux kernel has also output the **program counter** (`pc`) and the **link register** (`lr`). The program counter contains information regarding the line that was being executed when the oops occurred. Similarly, the link register contains information about the calling function.

At the end of the oops, we can also see that a backtrace is provided. We can use the steps outlined previously to confirm that the line where we dereference and write to a `NULL` pointer is the cause of the oops.

Performance issues

Unlike functional issues, which may be obvious to identify but not easily reproduce, performance-related issues may be more nuanced. The following are examples of symptoms indicative of performance-related issues:

- "Normal" operations are taking longer than usual. For example, opening a terminal or browser window that was previously snappy takes a noticeably longer amount of time. Additionally, the sluggish behavior may be sporadic and under hard-to-reproduce conditions.
- With the system idle and only running performance monitoring tools, the user observes momentary spikes in increased CPU load or memory use. While this doesn't directly impact day-to-day system operation, it may result in observed sluggish behavior as the system takes on additional load due to a demanding operation.
- During brief intervals, there is substantial latency in writing a file to disk or sending data over the network.

Performance-related issues are usually more difficult to troubleshoot than functional issues. However, there are tools that can help us identify specific drivers or subsystems in the kernel that may be the cause of such issues. In a later section, we will learn about `ftrace`, which can be used to identify performance-related issues.

In the next section, we will see how we can debug the Linux kernel using step-through debugging.

kgdb: step-through debugging the Linux kernel

Step-through debugging is an especially important skill for an embedded software engineer to master. Step-through debugging of bare-metal or RTOS-based embedded systems is usually performed by an IDE provided by the silicon vendor. The hardware and software, for the most part, are proprietary and costly. On the other hand, the Linux kernel contains the necessary tools to support step-through debugging, and we can use the GDB utility and a UART connection. In this section, we will walk through the necessary steps to connect the GDB debugger to a running kernel. Afterward, we can use the available GDB commands to perform typical debugging operations.

Before we can start debugging the kernel, it needs to be configured appropriately. First, we need to configure the kernel to enable debugging and *not* to randomize the address of the kernel image, which is used as a security feature.

We can disable the feature to randomize the address of the kernel image by using the kernel's configuration interface. As we learned in *Chapter 3, Navigating the Linux Kernel*, we can bring up the configuration interface by executing the following command in the directory of the Linux kernel code base:

```
$ ARCH=arm64 make menuconfig
```

Then, we need to navigate to the `Kernel Features` menu and hit the spacebar after highlighting the `Randomize the address of the kernel image` option, which is shown here:

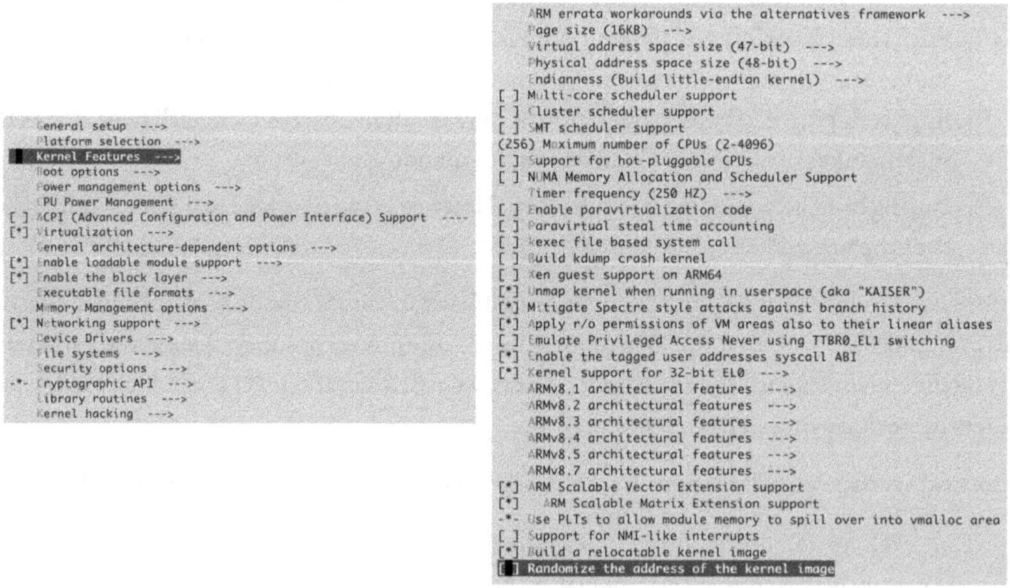

Figure 12.6 – Disabling kernel image address randomization

We also need to ensure that the following options are also enabled:

- `Magic SysRq key`, which is found under `Kernel hacking` | `Generic Kernel Debugging`
- `Enable magic SysRq key functions by default`, which is found under the same menu, and should be set to `0x1`
- `KGDB`, which is found under `Kernel hacking` | `Generic Kernel Debugging Instruments` | `KGDB: kernel debugger`
- `KGDB: use kgdb over serial console`, which is found in the same menu

After enabling the preceding options, we need to save the configuration, recompile the kernel and kernel modules, and install both onto the Raspberry Pi 5. We learned how to accomplish these tasks in *Chapter 3, Navigating the Linux Kernel.*

Then, we need to execute the following commands on the Raspberry Pi 5 to put the Linux kernel in debug mode:

```
$ sudo su
root@raspberrypi:# echo ttyAMA10 > /sys/module/kgdboc/parameters/kgdboc
root@raspberrypi:# echo g > /proc/sysrq-trigger
```

The Raspberry Pi 5 will no longer be responsive since it is waiting for a connection from the debugger on the host PC.

On the host PC, we will need to navigate to the directory containing the compiled kernel and execute the following command to start a `gdb` session with the Linux kernel with all of the debugging symbols:

```
$ gdb-multiarch vmlinux
.
.
.
Reading symbols from vmlinux...
(gdb)
```

Then, we will need to execute the following commands in the `gdb` terminal to begin interacting with the kernel using our UART connection:

```
(gdb) set serial baud 115200
(gdb) target remote /dev/ttyACM0
Remote debugging using /dev/ttyACM0
warning: multi-threaded target stopped without sending a thread-id, using
first non-exited thread
[Switching to Thread 4294967294]
arch_kgdb_breakpoint () at ./arch/arm64/include/asm/kgdb.h:21
21              asm ("brk %0" : : "I" (KGDB_COMPILED_DBG_BRK_IMM));
```

And we can see exactly where the Linux kernel has stopped as it awaited a connection from GDB! The exact details of why the Linux kernel has hit this particular breakpoint are outside of the scope. However, we can use the mechanisms available in GDB, such as stepping through code, adding more breakpoints, and running to a breakpoint to ensure that a kernel module we have written behaves as expected. Additionally, if we encounter issues when our kernel module or device driver is running on our embedded Linux system, we can use `kgdb` and `gdb` to step through the source code to resolve any issues.

In the next section, we will learn how to use `ftrace`, which is a tool that we can use to efficiently trace function calls.

ftrace: efficiently tracing function calls

The process of debugging functional issues in the Linux kernel is generally straightforward. First, we need to be able to reproduce the issue being reported. Then, we can trace the cause of the issue using the procedure previously outlined.

However, performance issues are trickier to debug. Stepping through the code base is usually insufficient to debug performance issues since the debugger significantly slows down the overall system. Additionally, `print` statements may add a non-trivial amount of overhead that may artificially add overhead to our system.

Ftrace is an efficient tracing utility built directly into the Linux kernel. `ftrace` uses special features in the `gcc` compiler to achieve this efficiency. Although the main interaction with the `ftrace` system occurs through the `tracefs` filesystem, we will be using the `debugfs` filesystem in our discussion on a Raspberry Pi 5. `ftrace` requires the following configuration options to be enabled in the Linux kernel:

- `CONFIG_FUNCTION_TRACER`
- `CONFIG_FUNCTION_GRAPH_TRACER`
- `CONFIG_STACK_TRACER`
- `CONFIG_DYNAMIC_FTRACE`

We will need to be the root user to interact with the tracing subsystem, which we can achieve by executing the following command:

```
$ sudo su
```

We can navigate to the main `ftrace` directory by executing the following command:

```
$ cd /sys/kernel/debug/tracing
```

We can execute the following command to determine the "tracers," or capabilities that we can trace, available on the system:

```
# cat available_tracers
blk function_graph wakeup_dl wakeup_rt wakeup function nop
```

As we see in the preceding output after executing the command on our Raspberry Pi 5, the following tracers are available:

- `blk`: This tracer is used to get detailed information about the I/O requests on the system
- `function_graph`: This tracer is used to trace function entry and exit, and is used to generate a call graph
- `wakeup_dl`: This tracer is used to gain insight into tasks that are scheduled using the `SCHED_DEADLINE` policy
- `wakeup_rt`: This tracer is used to gain insight into **real-time** (**RT**) tasks
- `wakeup`: This tracer provides insight into the maximum latency that it takes for the highest priority to get scheduled after it has been woken up
- `function`: This tracer traces all kernel functions
- `nop`: This disables all tracing

We can see the 10 most recently invoked functions in the Linux kernel at any given time by executing the following commands:

```
# echo function > current_tracer
# cat trace | head -10
```

After executing the preceding command on our Raspberry Pi 5, we may observe the output similar to the following, which shows the functions that may have been called at the time of invocation:

```
# tracer: function
#
# entries-in-buffer/entries-written: 155568/162575   #P:4
#
#                                _-----=> irqs-off/BH-disabled
#                               / _----=> need-resched
#                              | / _---=> hardirq/softirq
#                              || / _--=> preempt-depth
#                              ||| / _-=> migrate-disable
#                              |||| /     delay
```

We can get a graph of the 10 most recently invoked functions at any given time by executing the following commands:

```
# echo function_graph > current_tracer
# cat trace | head -10
```

If we execute the preceding commands on our Raspberry Pi 5, we may observe an output similar to the following:

```
# tracer: function_graph
#
# CPU  DURATION                  FUNCTION CALLS
# |     |   |                     |   |   |   |
 1)   0.315 us    |                          } /* check_cfs_rq_
runtime */
 1)   0.371 us    |                          pick_next_entity();
 1)               |                          put_prev_entity() {
 1)   0.315 us    |                            update_curr();
 1)   0.315 us    |                            check_cfs_rq_
runtime();
 1)   0.315 us    |                            __update_load_avg_
se();
```

It is sometimes helpful to understand when a particular function in the Linux kernel is called in relation to an action in user space. However, the times shown in the preceding trace are shown relative to when the trace was started. The `trace_marker` interface can help coordinate times in the Linux kernel trace and user space. For example, we can execute the following commands:

```
# echo nop > current_tracer
# echo helloworld > trace_marker
# cat trace
```

If we execute the preceding command, we may observe an output similar to the following:

```
# cat trace
# tracer: nop
#
# entries-in-buffer/entries-written: 1/1   #P:4
#
#                                _-----=> irqs-off/BH-disabled
#                               / _----=> need-resched
#                              | / _---=> hardirq/softirq
#                              || / _--=> preempt-depth
#                              ||| / _-=> migrate-disable
#                              |||| /     delay
#           TASK-PID     CPU#  |||||  TIMESTAMP  FUNCTION
#              | |         |   |||||     |         |
            bash-2844    [003] ..... 49320.851867: tracing_mark_write:
helloworld
```

The preceding output shows the `helloworld` string we injected into the trace buffer and subsequent functions in the Linux kernel that were called afterward.

In the next section, we will review a utility in the Linux kernel that can help us ensure that locks are properly used and avoid deadlocks.

lockdep: debugging deadlocks

Locking mechanisms are often used in embedded systems to ensure that hardware resources are not accessed simultaneously. As embedded software engineers, we know that incorrectly using locking mechanisms can result in a **deadlock**. A deadlock occurs when a system stalls because multiple software entities are vying for the same hardware resource. The following figure shows how a deadlock may occur (borrowed from `https://www.mathworks.com/products/polyspace/static-analysis-notes/what-deadlocks-how-prevent-during-software-development.html`):

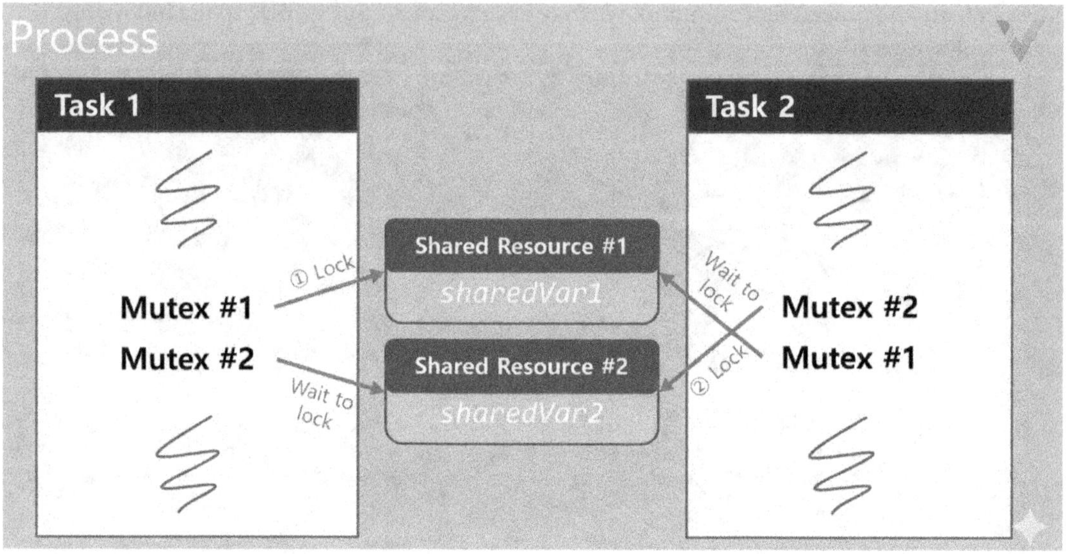

Figure 12.7 – Deadlock occurrence

The following sequence occurs in the preceding figure:

1. *Task 1* uses *Mutex #1* to lock *Shared Resource #1*. *Task 1* attempts to use *Mutex #2* to lock *Shared Resource #2*.
2. *Task 2* preempts *Task 1* and uses *Mutex #2* to lock *Shared Resource #2*.
3. Then, *Task 2* attempts to use *Mutex #1* to lock *Shared Resource #1*. However, since *Task 1* is already holding the lock to *Shared Resource #1*, *Task 2* blocks.
4. However, since *Task 1* is already attempting to lock access to *Shared Resource #2* before it is preempted, it can't unlock access to *Shared Resource #1*.

We have a deadlock!

While simple scenarios such as this may be obvious and easy to avoid when implementing device drivers, it becomes increasingly difficult to identify such scenarios in more complex drivers and systems. Deadlocks can occur randomly depending on the interaction of different hardware elements and drivers in the system. Since deadlock scenarios can halt the entire system, it is important to identify them before they occur.

lockdep is a utility built into the Linux kernel that can be used to identify *potential* deadlock scenarios. Although the implementation may not directly result in a deadlock, the utility can be used to identify incorrect or suboptimal implementations that may trigger a deadlock.

We can enable `lockdep` in the Linux kernel by running the `menuconfig` utility and searching for `LOCKDEP` (by entering the / character and typing `LOCKDEP`), as shown here:

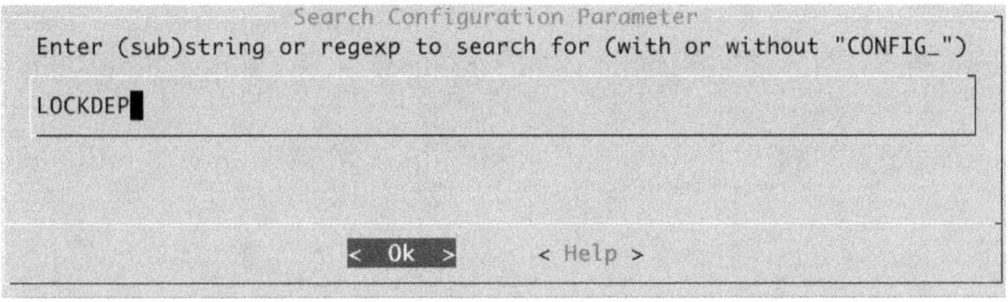

Figure 12.8 – Searching for LOCKDEP in the Linux kernel

The search results are shown here:

```
Symbol: LOCKDEP [=n]
Type  : bool
Defined at lib/Kconfig.debug:1389
  Depends on: DEBUG_KERNEL [=y] && LOCK_DEBUGGING_SUPPORT [=y]
Selects: STACKTRACE [=y] && KALLSYMS [=y] && KALLSYMS_ALL [=y]
Selected by [n]:
  - PROVE_LOCKING [=n] && DEBUG_KERNEL [=y] && LOCK_DEBUGGING_SUPPORT [=y]
  - LOCK_STAT [=n] && DEBUG_KERNEL [=y] && LOCK_DEBUGGING_SUPPORT [=y]
  - DEBUG_LOCK_ALLOC [=n] && DEBUG_KERNEL [=y] && LOCK_DEBUGGING_SUPPORT [=y]
```

Figure 12.9 – lockdep disabled by default

As we can see in the preceding figure, `lockdep` is disabled because we don't have the following features enabled:

- `PROVE_LOCKING`
- `LOCK_STAT`
- `DEBUG_LOCK_ALLOC`

We can enable the `LOCK_STAT` feature by searching for it using the `menuconfig` utility and noticing that it is located under `Kernel hacking` | `Lock Debugging`, as shown here:

```
Symbol: LOCK_STAT [=n]
Type  : bool
Defined at lib/Kconfig.debug:1303
  Prompt: Lock usage statistics
  Depends on: DEBUG_KERNEL [=y] && LOCK_DEBUGGING_SUPPORT [=y]
  Location:
    -> Kernel hacking
      -> Lock Debugging (spinlocks, mutexes, etc...)
(1)     -> Lock usage statistics (LOCK_STAT [=n])
Selects: LOCKDEP [=n] && DEBUG_SPINLOCK [=y] && DEBUG_MUTEXES [=y] && DEBUG_RT_MUTEXES [=y] && DEBUG_LOCK_ALLOC [=n]
```

Figure 12.10 – Searching for LOCK_STAT

If we type `1` on our keyboard (identified in the parentheses in the preceding figure), `menuconfig` takes us to the exact entry. We can enable it by hitting the spacebar on our keyboard, as shown here:

```
[ ] Lock debugging: prove locking correctness
[ ] Lock usage statistics
[*] RT Mutex debugging, deadlock detection
[*] Spinlock and rw-lock debugging: basic checks
[*] Mutex debugging: basic checks
[ ] Wait/wound mutex debugging: Slowpath testing
[ ] RW Semaphore debugging: basic checks
[ ] Lock debugging: detect incorrect freeing of live locks
[ ] Sleep inside atomic section checking
[ ] Locking API boot-time self-tests
< > torture tests for locking
< > Wait/wound mutex selftests
< > torture tests for smp_call_function*()
[ ] Debugging for csd_lock_wait(), called from smp_call_function*()
```

```
[ ] Lock debugging: prove locking correctness
[*] Lock usage statistics
-*- RT Mutex debugging, deadlock detection
-*- Spinlock and rw-lock debugging: basic checks
-*- Mutex debugging: basic checks
[ ] Wait/wound mutex debugging: Slowpath testing
[ ] RW Semaphore debugging: basic checks
-*- Lock debugging: detect incorrect freeing of live locks
(15) Bitsize for MAX_LOCKDEP_ENTRIES
(16) Bitsize for MAX_LOCKDEP_CHAINS
(19) Bitsize for MAX_STACK_TRACE_ENTRIES
(14) Bitsize for STACK_TRACE_HASH_SIZE
(12) Bitsize for elements in circular_queue struct
[ ] Lock dependency engine debugging
[ ] Sleep inside atomic section checking
[ ] Locking API boot-time self-tests
< > torture tests for locking
< > Wait/wound mutex selftests
< > torture tests for smp_call_function*()
[ ] Debugging for csd_lock_wait(), called from smp_call_function*()
```

Figure 12.11 – Enabling LOCK_STAT

Finally, as we've done in the past, we can save our kernel configuration, rebuild the kernel and kernel modules, and transfer them to our system. With `lockdep` enabled, we can identify possibilities for a deadlock by looking at the kernel log. Let's try with an example!

We can compile, transfer, and load the `lockdep-test.ko` kernel module on our Raspberry Pi 5. This kernel module creates a kernel thread that simply locks two spinlocks and unlocks them after one second:

```
int thread_function(void *params)
{
        while (1) {
                spin_lock(&l1);
                spin_lock(&l2);
                msleep(1000);
```

```
                spin_unlock(&l2);
                spin_unlock(&l1);
        }
        return 0;
}
```

While this doesn't look problematic, let's see what happens if we load the kernel module and see how the kernel responds in the log. We can load the kernel module by executing the following command:

```
$ sudo insmod lockdep-test.ko
[  179.782875] lockdep_test: loading out-of-tree module taints kernel.
[  179.783402] BUG: scheduling while atomic: locktest-fn/2000/0x00000003
[  179.783415] 2 locks held by locktest-fn/2000:
[  179.783418]  #0: ffffc00001744418 (&l1){....}-{2:2}, at: thread_
function+0x28/0x4c [lockdep_test]
[  179.783434]  #1: ffffc00001744460 (&l2){....}-{2:2}, at: thread_
function+0x30/0x4c [lockdep_test]
```

As we can see in the output, `lockdep` has identified a possible issue in our kernel module and has notified us in a kernel oops. Although there is no obvious issue since our contrived example is simple, `lockdep` can be invaluable as implementations become more complex and interactions between locks and threads may not be obvious.

Summary

In this chapter, we learned about techniques to debug issues in the Linux kernel. Debugging the Linux kernel is different from debugging applications because of its affinity to hardware and the sheer complexity of the code base. We can't use the lessons learned in *Chapter 8, Building, Debugging, and Launching Applications on Startup,* to debug the Linux kernel, and need to use other techniques that we covered in this chapter. However, before we can use any specific techniques, we need to understand the different types of issues that can be encountered in the Linux kernel, including both functional and performance issues. For example, we learned about a kernel oops, which is a specific type of issue in the Linux kernel. Afterward, we learned how to perform traditional step-through debugging of the Linux kernel using `kgdb`, which is significantly different from `gdb`. Finally, we learned about `ftrace` and `lockdep`, which are two tools included in the Linux kernel that we can use to identify performance issues.

In the next chapter, we will learn how to execute applications inside the Linux kernel using the **extended Berkeley Packet Filter (eBPF)**.

Get this book's PDF version and more

Scan the QR code (or go to `packtpub.com/unlock`). Search for this book by name, confirm the edition, and then follow the steps on the page.

UNLOCK NOW

Note: Keep your invoice handy. Purchases made directly from Packt don't require an invoice.

13

Securing Code Execution with eBPF

In *Chapter 3, Navigating the Linux Kernel*, we learned that the Linux kernel has many responsibilities, including managing the execution of different applications and providing an interface for the underlying hardware to these applications. We also learned that if we wish to change the behavior of the Linux kernel, we either need to modify a portion of the kernel itself or a kernel module that gets loaded by the Linux kernel. As we saw in that chapter, this process can be arduous. We need to recompile either the entire kernel or the individual kernel module, install the kernel or module onto our system, and reboot the system. If we are modifying the Linux kernel or module to resolve a bug or implement a feature, we may need to go through this process numerous times to ensure our modification. This process can also be destructive. If we make an incorrect change to the Linux kernel, our system may be unable to boot. However, **eBPF**, which is what we will cover in this chapter, is an alternative technique we can use that avoids recompiling the Linux kernel.

The **Berkeley Packet Filter** (**BPF**) was developed to allow operating systems to capture and filter network packets. In the Linux kernel, user-space programs can load a BPF into the kernel to allow or prevent certain types of data from passing through a network interface. The acceptance of the BPF in the Linux kernel introduced a new paradigm of packet filtration. With the BPF, packets are filtered immediately after being received on the network interface and require minimal intervention from the Linux kernel. Depending on how the BPF is created and used, packets may get intercepted before the kernel can act on them.

Extended BPF (**eBPF**) expands on the traditional BPF, more commonly known as **cBPF** (or **classical BPF**). eBPF provides a set of tools for writing generic applications that are executed strictly in kernel space. The eBPF infrastructure also includes complementary tools to ensure that eBPF applications are run securely.

This chapter aims to explain eBPF and how it can be used to execute code in the Linux kernel securely. First, we will learn about the basics of eBPF and its advantages over other mechanisms of executing code in kernel space. We will explore the components that comprise an eBPF program.

Second, we will learn about the process of creating an eBPF application. Then, we will walk through some examples of building eBPF applications. The first example will demonstrate how eBPF can be used to monitor packets, and the second example will demonstrate how to monitor files using eBPF.

We are going to cover the following main topics in this chapter:

- eBPF overview and advantages
- Creating and executing eBPF applications
- Example #1: Packet monitoring
- Example #2: File monitoring

Technical requirements

You should be comfortable reading and writing C code and executing commands on a terminal. You should also be familiar with running Python applications and reading Python code. You can follow along with the examples in the chapter using the following GitHub repository: `https://github.com/PacktPublishing/Embedded-Linux-Essentials-Handbook/tree/main/Chapter13`.

eBPF overview and advantages

In this section, we will learn about the eBPF. We will start by learning about the motivation behind using eBPF. As we learned in *Chapter 3, Navigating the Linux Kernel*, the Linux kernel provides a mechanism for user-space applications to access the underlying hardware safely. For example, if the application wishes to access a file on the filesystem, it doesn't directly interact with the underlying storage device. Instead, the application interacts with the Linux kernel to access a particular file. This interaction is performed using **system calls**.

As we also learned in *Chapter 3*, having clear interfaces between the Linux kernel and user-space applications to perform common operations is an extremely advantageous paradigm. The Linux kernel guarantees that a user-space application can access the underlying hardware using a well-defined series of functions. Device drivers can be implemented with a predefined infrastructure in place. However, this paradigm still has certain drawbacks, which are outlined here:

- **Performance limitations**: When a user-space application interacts with the Linux kernel, data from user space needs to be copied to kernel space (and vice versa if the kernel returns a response). These memory copies incur a massive penalty. These copies may not result in apparent performance degradation when performing low-duty-cycle operations, such as infrequent file operations or periodically accessing peripherals. However, reduced performance becomes more obvious when conducting frequent operations, which are typical for networking operations.
- **Restricted operation**: Since the Linux kernel acts as a strict barrier between user-space applications and the underlying hardware, user-space applications have to operate within the constraints presented to them by the kernel. If a driver doesn't exist to interface with a certain peripheral, the user space may not be able to use the peripheral.

> Important note
>
> Even though a specific driver may not exist, workarounds may be possible for user-space applications to access the peripheral. For example, if the peripheral is connected to the processor using the I2C bus, the `i2c-dev` interface (`https://www.kernel.org/doc/Documentation/i2c/dev-interface`) can be used to perform I2C transactions. Similarly, if the peripheral is connected using the SPI bus, `spidev` (`https://www.kernel.org/doc/Documentation/spi/spidev`) can be used by user-space applications to perform individual SPI transactions.

To mitigate the performance limitation incurred when crossing the user space and kernel boundary and to ease the restrictions that user-space applications must follow, kernel modules can be developed. As we learned in *Chapter 3*, kernel modules have much more latitude. They can access the hardware directly and have the entire kernel infrastructure available. However, since kernel modules operate in kernel space, a bug in the implementation can be disastrous. It can result in system-wide vulnerabilities or sporadic crashes.

eBPF is an excellent middle ground that offers the best of both worlds. It facilitates applications to be executed within kernel space, so that maximum performance may be achieved. Additionally, eBPF applications are thoroughly vetted before they are executed in the kernel to eliminate catastrophic behavior.

History

The predecessor of the eBPF is the cBPF. cBPF was originally designed with networking in mind. As its name implies, it was developed to filter network packets efficiently. cBPF was designed to intercept packets immediately when they are received by the hardware and before they are passed up to the rest of the kernel's networking stack. cBPF makes use of a virtual machine that runs inside the kernel itself.

> Important note
>
> The *virtual machine* referenced here is not a full-blown virtual machine you may be accustomed to running in an application such as VirtualBox or VMware. Instead, the virtual machine here refers to a **just-in-time** (JIT) compiler that resides in the Linux kernel and is capable of understanding instructions from a BPF program.

The virtual machine supports a limited set of operations designed specifically for networking operations. It allows utilities, such as **tcpdump**, to compile a primitive application to filter packets and run it entirely inside the kernel.

The advantage of using a packet filter with cBPF is that changing the Linux kernel or a separate kernel module is unnecessary. Instead, all operations can be done in user space! The downside is that the cBPF applications are restricted to operations that only operate on network packets.

Let's look at an example of a cBPF application and learn how we can view the instructions executed by the cBPF compiler inside the Linux kernel on our Raspberry Pi 5. As we mentioned earlier, `tcpdump` is an application that leverages the BPF virtual machine to filter packets. We can also use `tcpdump` to view the instructions executed by the cBPF virtual machine by following these steps (the steps assume that Raspbian is installed on our Raspberry Pi 5):

1. Install `tcpdump` by executing the following command:

   ```
   $ sudo apt-get install tcpdump
   ```

2. Execute the following `tcpdump` command to view the instructions used to filter packets that are received on port 22 of the specified interface:

```
$ sudo tcpdump -i eth0 -d 'port 22'
(000) ldh      [12]
(001) jeq      #0x86dd          jt 2    jf 10
(002) ldb      [20]
(003) jeq      #0x84            jt 6    jf 4
(004) jeq      #0x6             jt 6    jf 5
(005) jeq      #0x11            jt 6    jf 23
(006) ldh      [54]
(007) jeq      #0x16            jt 22   jf 8
(008) ldh      [56]
(009) jeq      #0x16            jt 22   jf 23
(010) jeq      #0x800           jt 11   jf 23
(011) ldb      [23]
(012) jeq      #0x84            jt 15   jf 13
(013) jeq      #0x6             jt 15   jf 14
(014) jeq      #0x11            jt 15   jf 23
(015) ldh      [20]
(016) jset     #0x1fff          jt 23   jf 17
(017) ldxb     4*([14]&0xf)
(018) ldh      [x + 14]
(019) jeq      #0x16            jt 22   jf 20
(020) ldh      [x + 16]
(021) jeq      #0x16            jt 22   jf 23
(022) ret      #262144
(023) ret      #0
```

The preceding snippet shows the assembly instructions executed by the cBPF virtual machine!

> Important note
>
> We won't cover the instructions themselves in further detail. Instead, if you're interested, the Linux kernel documentation is an excellent resource to help you understand the details of these instructions. You can find this documentation under `Documentation/bpf` inside the Linux kernel source code repository.

From cBPF to eBPF

cBPF is limited to filtering network packets. However, eBPF was the result of years of enhancements to cBPF. It extended the virtual machine to support performing operations inside the kernel beyond just filtering network packets. Although eBPF is still constrained to preserve the safeguards that the kernel provides, it supports operations including the following:

- High-performance networking
- System observability
- File monitoring
- Security
- Tracing and profiling

Generally, there are three distinct components of eBPF applications:

- **Toolchain**: Originally, eBPF applications were implemented by manually writing the assembly instructions. Eventually, tools were created that allowed developers to write eBPF applications in C, compile the application into bytecode, and load it into the kernel. Ultimately, these tools were expanded to support more languages, such as Rust.
- **Probes**: It can be useful to trigger eBPF applications based on certain conditions. eBPF probes are constructs that the eBPF infrastructure uses to execute applications inside the Linux kernel under certain conditions.
- **Maps**: Sometimes, data needs to be shared between the kernel and user space. eBPF applications can use maps specifically for this purpose.

In the next section, we will see how to build and execute eBPF applications.

Creating and executing eBPF applications

In this section, we will learn how to create and execute eBPF applications on our Raspberry Pi 5. Similar to how we get started with other software languages and paradigms, we will start with a *Hello World* example.

> Important note
>
> Creating and executing eBPF applications differs from developing "traditional" user-space applications in a compiled language, such as C. While traditional user-space applications require a compilation step before execution, there is no explicit compilation step. Instead, with eBPF, there are three options. First, the C source code can be compiled using the BCC toolchain to generate the bytecode. Then, the bytecode can be transferred to the Linux kernel for execution.
>
> The second option is to use an interpreted language, such as Python, to compile the C source code and transfer it to the Linux kernel for execution. In this section, we will use the latter process. The third option is most similar to traditional software development. This involves embedding the eBPF application inside a separate C or C++ application that is compiled and executed as a traditional application.

Kernel configuration

The kernel must be appropriately configured before eBPF applications can be loaded and executed. We can follow the steps outlined in *Chapter 3* and use the Linux kernel Kconfig GUI to enable the following options:

- `CONFIG_BPF`: Enables the BPF subsystem in the Linux kernel.
- `CONFIG_BPF_SYSCALL`: Adds support for the `bpf` system call.
- `CONFIG_BPF_JIT`: Enables the BPF JIT compiler (allowing the Linux kernel to compile passed-in source code during runtime).
- `CONFIG_HAVE_EBPF_JIT`: Enables instructions for eBPF (beyond just cBPF) in the kernel's JIT compiler.
- `CONFIG_BPF_EVENTS`: Allows us to attach our BPF applications to the Linux kernel tracing subsystem.
- `CONFIG_IKHEADERS`: Instructs the Linux kernel to expose the headers as a compressed file, located at `/sys/kernel/kheaders.tar.xz`. Since we're not using the stock Linux kernel on the Raspberry Pi 5, we need the header files corresponding to our kernel version.

After configuring the Linux kernel, we need to install it and the kernel modules on our Raspberry Pi 5.

Installing kernel headers

Since we are using a custom version of the Linux kernel, we need to install the corresponding header files for use by the eBPF subsystem. We can follow the steps outlined here to do so:

1. Navigate to the `/usr/src` directory on our Raspberry Pi 5 and observe the existing directories by executing the following commands:

```
$ cd /usr/src
$ ls
linux-headers-6.1.0-rpi7-common-rpi  linux-headers-6.1.0-rpi7-
rpi-2712  linux-headers-6.1.0-rpi7-rpi-v8  linux-kbuild-6.1
python3.11  sense-hat
```

   We can see that the headers corresponding to the stock Linux kernel on our Raspberry Pi 5 are already present. Since we're using a custom (and newer) kernel, we have to add the headers corresponding to our kernel version.

2. Execute the following commands to extract the headers corresponding to our kernel version:

```
$ sudo cp /sys/kernel/kheaders.tar.xz ./
$ sudo mkdir linux-headers-$(uname -r)
$ cd linux-headers-$(uname -r)
$ sudo tar ../kheaders.tar.xz ./
```

Installing additional packages

Before executing our eBPF application, we need to install a package allowing us to interact with the Linux kernel's eBPF subsystem from user space. We can do so by executing the following command:

```
$ sudo apt-get install bpfcc-tools
```

Hello eBPF World!

Now that we have all the necessary infrastructure in place, we can see our first eBPF application in action. We can run our *Hello eBPF World* application by following these steps:

1. After cloning the repository referenced in the *Technical requirements* section, change to the `Chapter13` directory.
2. Transfer `hello-world.c` and `hello-world.py` to the Raspberry Pi 5.

3. Run the Python script by executing the following command:

```
$ sudo python ./hello-world.py
```

You should see the following output:

```
b' systemd-journal-278     [001] d..31    38.731985: bpf_trace_printk:
Hello, World!\\n'
b' systemd-journal-278     [001] d..31    38.732022: bpf_trace_printk:
Hello, World!\\n'
b'            <...>-311     [002] d..31    38.744768: bpf_trace_printk:
Hello, World!\\n
```

Important note

The Python application will continue to run until it is terminated by hitting *Ctrl* + *C* on the keyboard.

The Python portion of the eBPF application, shown here, only contains two lines:

```
from bcc import BPF

BPF(src_file="hello-world.c").trace_print()
```

The first line imports the BPF object from the bcc Python module. The second line creates a class of the BPF object with the src_file variable set to hello-world.c. This instructs the BPF object to load, parse, and compile the application specified in the hello-world.c source file. Then, the trace_print() method of the BPF class is called, which attaches to the underlying Linux trace subsystem and passes any output to the console.

The C portion of the eBPF application is similarly simple, and is shown here:

```
int kprobe__sys_clone(void *ctx)
{
        bpf_trace_printk("Hello eBPF World!\\n");
        return 0;
}
```

The kprobe__sys_clone function is called whenever the clone system call is invoked. kprobe__ is a special prefix defined in the eBPF framework. If a function name is prepended with this prefix, a **kprobe** is created associated with the kernel function name in the remainder.

In the preceding example, kprobe__sys_clone will be called when the sys_clone kernel function is called. sys_clone is called whenever a new process is created, such as when we run our Python script. Inside kprobe__sys_clone, the bpf_trace_printk function is called with the Hello eBPF World!\\n string. This function outputs the string to the Linux kernel tracing subsystem, which gets routed to the console by our call to the trace_print() method in the Python portion.

In the next section, we will create a slightly more sophisticated application that monitors packets received on a particular network interface and takes action based on the packet contents.

Example #1: Packet monitoring

In this section, we will create a slightly more complex eBPF application. The application developed in this section will do the following:

- It will monitor packets being received by our Raspberry Pi 5 over the Ethernet interface
- If the packet is a TCP packet and is destined for the IP address associated with the Ethernet interface, the eBPF will print a message to the tracing subsystem

The example is contained in the only-for-me.c and only-for-me.py source files. Let's transfer these files to our Raspberry Pi 5 and execute the Python script, and observe the result, as shown here:

```
$ sudo python ./only-for-me.py
b''
b'          <idle>-0       [000] d.s31  4295.970616: bpf_trace_printk:
packet for us!'
b''
b'          <idle>-0       [000] d.s31  4295.970786: bpf_trace_printk:
packet for us!'
b''
b'          <idle>-0       [000] d.s31  4295.970955: bpf_trace_printk:
packet for us!'
b''
b'          <idle>-0       [000] d.s31  4295.971046: bpf_trace_printk:
packet for us!'
```

Important note

As with the previous example, the Python application will continue to run until it is terminated by hitting *Ctrl* + *C* on the keyboard.

Let's review the C implementation of the eBPF application first. Since we will be performing operations on network packets, the function in our eBPF application takes a `__sk_buff` data structure. This data structure is central to all network operations in a Linux system. The implementation is described as follows:

1. We declare two variables, as shown here:

   ```
   unsigned char ip_octets[4];
   u8* cursor = NULL;
   ```

   The first variable declares an array of four bytes containing the packet's destination IP address. The second variable is a pointer to the elements in the packet passed to us by the network interface.

2. We extract the information associated with the Ethernet header and move the pointer in the packet past this data structure, as shown in the following line:

   ```
   struct ethernet_t *ethernet = cursor_advance(cursor,
   sizeof(*ethernet));
   ```

3. We check whether the packet type is an IP packet, and if it is, we continue processing it, as shown in the following `if` statement (`0x800` indicates an IP packet):

   ```
   if (ethernet->type == 0x800) {
   ```

4. We extract the information in the IP header of the packet and advance the pointer again:

   ```
   struct ip_t *ip = cursor_advance(cursor, sizeof(*ip));
   ```

5. We check that the packet type is a TCP packet using the following `if` statement (`6` indicates a TCP packet):

   ```
   if (ip->nextp == 6) {
   ```

   If it is, we continue the filtration process. If it is not, we exit the function. Then, we store the IP address in the 4-byte array we allocated previously:

   ```
   ip_octets[0] = ip->dst & 0xff;
   ip_octets[1] = (ip->dst >> 8) & 0xff;
   ip_octets[2] = (ip->dst >> 16) & 0xff;
   ip_octets[3] = (ip->dst >> 24) & 0xff;
   ```

6. We check to see whether the IP address matches our own, and if it does, we print a statement to the trace buffer:

```
if (ip_octets[3] == FIRST_OCTET
    && ip_octets[2] == SECOND_OCTET
    && ip_octets[1] == THIRD_OCTET
    && ip_octets[0] == FOURTH_OCTET)
        bpf_trace_printk("packet for us!\n");
```

> **Important note**
>
> You will need to change the macros in bold in the preceding snippet, which are defined at the top of the C file, to match the IP address of your own board.

Now, let's review the Python portion of the application:

1. We import the `BPF` object from the `bcc` Python module, and we import the `socket` object, as shown here:

```
from bcc import BPF
import socket
```

2. As we did previously, we instantiate an object of the `BPF` type. But this time, we store the resulting object in a variable, as shown here:

```
bpf = BPF(src_file = "only-for-me.c")
```

3. We load the function that we implemented in the C portion and instruct the virtual machine that this is to filter network packets (by specifying `SOCKET_FILTER`):

```
fn_ofm = bpf.load_func("only_for_me", BPF.SOCKET_FILTER)
```

4. We attach our application to the `eth0` interface of our Raspberry Pi 5:

```
BPF.attach_raw_socket(fn_ofm, "eth0")
```

> **Important note**
>
> You can also use the `wlan0` interface and observe the resulting behavior. Is it any different?

5. Finally, as we did with the previous example, we capture any output to the Linux tracing subsystem and print it to the console:

   ```
   bpf.trace_print()
   ```

In the next section, we will see how eBPF can help us perform operations outside of networking and understand its value in other subsystems of an embedded Linux system.

Example #2: File monitoring

In this section, we will create an eBPF application that will monitor and notify us when content has been written to a specific file.

To get started, we will need to create an empty file in the home directory on our Raspberry Pi 5. We can do so by executing the following command:

```
$ touch test.txt
```

Next, we'll need to determine the **inode number** associated with the file we created.

> Important note
>
> An **inode** is a data structure that the Linux kernel uses to represent underlying files. The inode number is a unique number assigned to each file and is part of the inode data structure.

We can determine the inode number of the file that we just created by executing the following command:

```
$ ls -i test.txt
168567 test.txt
```

We need to place the inode number into the `FILE_NODE` macro definition of the `monitor-file-write.c` source file, as shown here (and marked by `TODO`):

```
// TODO: Change this based on your file
#define FILE_INODE 168567
```

Then, in a separate window, we can execute the following command to write the `test` string to our empty file:

```
$ while sleep 1; do echo test > test.txt; done
```

Important note

The > operator in Bash overwrites all content in the file. Thus, if we check the file's contents at the end of this experiment, it will only contain a single line with `test`. If we want to append to the file, we would need to use the >> operator.

Finally, if we execute our eBPF application, we can see the expected output, as shown here:

```
$ sudo python monitor-file-write.py
b'            bash-3422    [000] d..31 13278.955304: bpf_trace_printk:
Wrote to our file!'
```

Let's review the Python portion of the eBPF application. First, we perform the usual operations to import the `BPF` object from the `bcc` module and create an instance of the `BPF` class, as shown here:

```
from bcc import BPF

bpf = BPF(src_file="monitor-file-write.c")
```

Then, we call the `attach_kprobe` method, as shown here:

```
bpf.attach_kprobe(event="vfs_write", fn_name="trace_write")
```

This method instruments the Linux kernel filesystem subsystem so that the `trace_write` function gets called whenever `vfs_write` is called, which happens whenever data is written to a particular file.

Finally, we call the `trace_print()` method to capture any output to the Linux tracing subsystem and redirect it to the console, as shown here:

```
bpf.trace_print()
```

Now, let's review the C portion of the implementation. The `trace_write` function takes the following arguments:

- `struct pt_regs *ctx`: A pointer to the registers that are stored on the stack, which is commonly used as part of the tracing subsystem
- `struct file *file`: A pointer to a data structure that represents the file
- `char __user *buf`: An array of characters that will be written to the file
- `size_t count`: The size of the data that will be written to the file

Finally, we compare the inode number of the file that is being written to against the inode number defined by the macro in the C source file, as shown here:

```
if (file->f_path.dentry->d_inode->i_ino == FILE_INODE)
    bpf_trace_printk("Wrote to our file!");
```

If the inode number matches, then we print the string to the tracing subsystem.

Summary

In this chapter, we learned about the eBPF subsystem of the Linux kernel. eBPF is a valuable tool that can be used for monitoring network traffic, filtering packets, and gaining insight into other kernel subsystems. eBPF is a fascinating feature added to the Linux kernel that allows us to dynamically add functionality to the kernel without having to recompile it. It has mechanisms in place to ensure that the program we embed inside the kernel is safe for execution. In this chapter, we created a few examples and understood their behavior as a way to reinforce our learning.

In the next chapter, we will explore Rust in the context of Embedded Linux.

Get this book's PDF version and more

14

Rust in Embedded Linux: The Kernel and Applications

Rust is one of the fastest-growing languages. Its promise of reducing memory-related issues and its compatibility with C have made it an appealing programming language for use in embedded systems. As shown in the following figure, the number of commits on GitHub that are associated with projects written in Rust has exploded in the past few years:

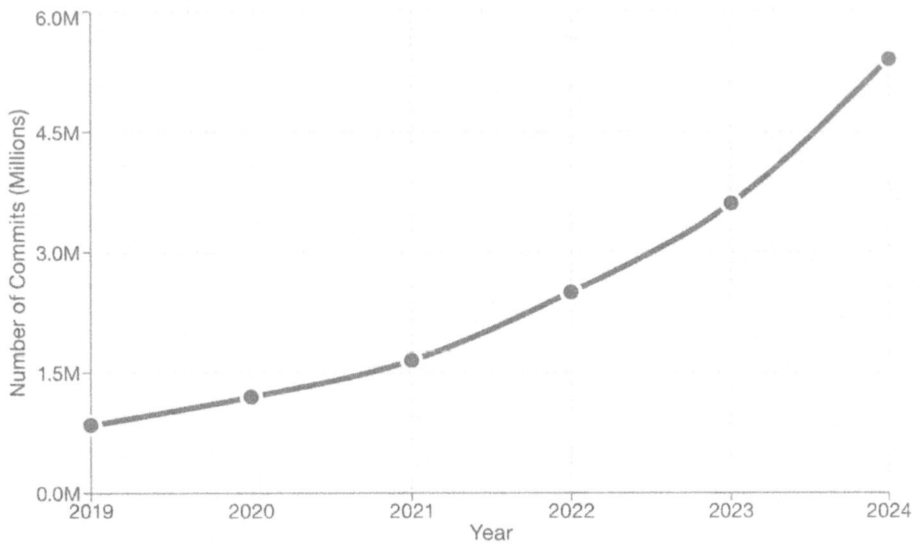

Figure 14.1 – Number of GitHub commits over time

We will explore Rust in detail in this chapter and examine how to use Rust in both user space and kernel space. First, we will learn the basics of Rust, including its syntax and data structures. While some of Rust's syntax will be familiar to us based on our experience with C, there are some nuanced differences and paradigms, such as traits and match, that we will need to understand.

Then, we will explore how Rust's promise of memory safety works in detail. We will learn about variable ownership, lifetime, and mutability. We will briefly examine the Rust borrow checker, a core component of the Rust compiler that enforces Rust's ownership and borrowing rules.

Next, we will explore how complex Rust programs are typically managed, using **crates** and **packages**. On that same topic, we will learn how the **Cargo** utility can be used to manage Rust dependencies and help us manage and build our Rust applications.

Then, we will transition from the theoretical to the practical, understanding how to utilize Rust in an embedded Linux system. First, we will learn how to cross-compile Rust applications. We will see how the cross-compilation process is much more streamlined when using Rust compared to what we are accustomed to in C. We will learn how to cross-compile a simple Rust application that prints `Hello Rust World!` to the Raspberry Pi's console.

Then, we will migrate from user space to kernel space. First, we will enable Rust support in the Linux kernel, deploy the Rust-enabled Linux kernel to our Raspberry Pi 5, and confirm the deployment. Then, we will learn how to develop a simple Linux kernel module in Rust that prints messages to the kernel log when it is loaded and unloaded.

We will cover the following topics in this chapter:

- An introduction to Rust
- Rust and memory safety
- Crates and Cargo
- Rust cross-compilation
- Hello Rust World!
- Rust in the Linux kernel
- A Linux kernel module in Rust

Important note

One chapter is not sufficient for a thorough review of the Rust programming language. *The Rust Programming Language*, available at `https://doc.rust-lang.org/book/title-page.html`, is an excellent reference that provides more detailed information. *The Rustonomicon*, available at `https://doc.rust-lang.org/nomicon/`, is also a great reference that provides more details on advanced Rust topics.

Technical requirements

You should be comfortable using an editor to write code and navigating a Linux system using the terminal. You can follow the code snippets for yourself using the GitHub link here: `https://github.com/PacktPublishing/Embedded-Linux-Essentials-Handbook/tree/main/Chapter14`.

An introduction to Rust

Rust is becoming one of the most widely adopted programming languages for systems development. In November 2025, Debian officially announced that it will integrate Rust code into the APT package manager by May 2026. Rust's most significant advantage over other systems programming languages, such as C/C++, is its guarantee of **compile-time** memory and thread safety. This section provides an introduction to Rust, describing the language's syntax, implementing patterns in familiar languages, and exploring new paradigms specific to Rust.

Rust source files end with a `.rs` extension and are compiled using the Rust compiler into an executable application. The Rust compiler, officially known as `rustc`, serves not only as an application to translate source code into an executable but also functions to verify that your implementation is safe before it is executed.

Variables are created in Rust using the `let` keyword. For example, the following line creates a new variable called `packt` and binds it to a value of `10`:

```
let packt = 10;
```

Rust variables are **immutable** by default. This means that once a variable has been assigned a value, the value of the variable can't be changed. For example, let's say we had the following lines in our Rust application:

```
let packt = 10;
packt = 20;
```

If we attempt to compile the application with the preceding two lines in sequence, the Rust compiler will throw an error, as shown here:

```
error[E0384]: cannot assign twice to immutable variable `packt`
 --> rust-test.rs:3:2
  |
2 |     let packt = 10;
  |         ----- first assignment to `packt`
3 |     packt = 20;
  |     ^^^^^^^^^^ cannot assign twice to immutable variable
```

However, we can allow the value of a variable to change by using the `mut` keyword. For example, the following line will allow us to change the value of the `packt` variable later in our program:

```
let mut packt = 10;
```

Like C, Rust also has functions. The entry point to any Rust application is the `main` function, and it has the following structure:

```
fn main() {
     .
     .
     .
}
```

There are two obvious differences between the `main` function in C and the `main` function in Rust:

- The `main` function in C can take the number of arguments passed to the application, usually via the `argc` parameter, and the arguments themselves, usually via the `argv` parameter. Rust doesn't take any parameters to the `main` function. Any arguments that are passed to the application are accessed through an iterator using the `std::env::args()` function.
- The `main` function in C must return an integer, whereas the `main` function in Rust doesn't have to return a value.

Rust functions can be defined to have parameters. For example, the following function accepts a parameter called `packt_arg`, which is of the `i32` type:

```
fn packt_function(packt_arg: i32) {
     .
     .
     .
}
```

Rust functions can also return values. The following function returns a constant of `10`:

```
fn packt_ret_func() -> i32 {
    10
}
```

You may notice that the preceding function definition is strange. Although the function signature specifies that it returns a variable of the `i32` type, we don't see a `return` statement in the function. This is because, unlike C, Rust has a clear syntactical difference between a **statement** and an **expression**. A statement in Rust is an instruction that performs an action and does not return a value, whereas an expression evaluates to a value that can be bound to a variable. For example, the following line is a statement:

```
let packt = 10;
```

Since statements don't return values, the following line in Rust is incorrect:

```
let packt_var = (let packt = 10);
```

Although the preceding line will result in an error during compilation, this pattern is common in C, since the assignment returns the value of the assignment.

Macros are another unique and extensive feature of Rust. While macros also exist and are commonly used in C, Rust's use of macros is significantly more expansive. Macros in Rust are a technique of writing code that writes other code. For example, `println!` is a commonly used macro for printing messages to the console. Macros differ from functions in that they can accept a variable number of parameters, whereas functions can only accept the number of parameters that is specified in the function signature. The disadvantage of implementing and using macros over functions is that they can be difficult to debug and maintain.

Traits are another unique feature of Rust. They are used to define shared behavior across different data types. While there is no obvious analogy to traits in C, the concept of **interfaces** in other languages, such as Java and Go, would be the closest comparison. Traits are a core feature of Rust, allowing developers to write highly flexible and reusable code. We can implement a trait using the `impl` keyword and then define the relevant functions that are required to implement the trait. As we will see later in the section titled *A Linux kernel module in Rust*, we will use a trait when implementing a Linux kernel module.

A **match** in Rust is a powerful feature that allows us to control the flow of an application. A match can be used to compare a variable against a series of patterns and execute code based on a particular pattern match. Although a Rust match is similar to a C **switch/case**, it is significantly more powerful because it's based on pattern matching rather than just a simple value comparison. The following snippet shows an example of how to use a Rust match to print the demographic of a person based on their age:

```
match age {
    0..=12 => "child",
    13..=19 => "teen",
    20..=64 => "adult",
    _ => "senior",
}
```

In the next section, we will explore how Rust enforces memory safety.

Rust and memory safety

One of Rust's biggest advantages is its guarantee of memory safety. It accomplishes this by implementing an **ownership** model. Rust has a specific set of rules that define how memory is owned and managed, which the compiler checks against. We saw an example of the ownership model earlier in the chapter when we attempted to change the value of an immutable variable.

The following are three ownership rules that the Rust compiler enforces:

- Every variable in Rust has an **owner**
- Each variable can only have one owner at a time
- When the variable owner goes out of **scope**, the variable is **dropped**

The concept of scope in Rust is similar to that of other programming languages. For example, in the following example, the `packt_var` variable of the `String` type is only in scope between the two curly braces and is not valid outside of the curly braces:

```
{
    let packt_var = String::from("packt");
    // Perform actions on packt_var
}
```

After the closing curly brace and `packt_var` goes out of scope, the memory allocated for the variable is returned. Rust accomplishes this by calling the `drop` function, which is implemented as part of the `Drop` trait. The `String` type in Rust implements the `Drop` trait.

The following example demonstrates how Rust can help mitigate a **dangling reference** error, a common memory safety issue only encountered during runtime when implementing software in traditional systems programming languages, such as C:

```
fn main() {
    let packt_ref;
    {
        let packt_var = 10;
        packt_ref = &packt_var;
    }

    println!("packt reference is: {}", packt_ref);
}
```

We will see the following error if we compile the preceding snippet:

```
error[E0597]: `packt_var` does not live long enough
 --> src/main.rs:5:15
  |
4 |         let packt_var = 10;
  |             --------- binding `packt_var` declared here
5 |         packt_ref = &packt_var;
  |                     ^^^^^^^^^^ borrowed value does not live long
enough
6 |     }
  |     - `packt_var` dropped here while still borrowed
7 |
8 |     println!("packt reference is: {}", packt_ref);
  |                                        --------- borrow later used
here

For more information about this error, try `rustc --explain E0597`
```

The following snippet is an analogous implementation in C of the preceding snippet in Rust:

```
#include <stdio.h>

int* create_dangling()
{
        int loc = 10;
        return &loc;
}

int main(void)
{
        int *packt_ref = create_dangling();

        printf("packt_ref = %d\n", *packt_ref);

        return 0;
}
```

The C compiler will successfully compile the preceding example, but there is an issue. Since the `create_dangling()` function returns the memory address to a local variable, we have no guarantee that the value will not be modified after we have used it.

In the next section, we will learn how to manage complex Rust applications using crates and the Cargo utility.

Crates and Cargo

Rust provides a framework to manage large and complex applications. Similar to writing large applications in C, it is good practice to organize a large application across different source files. Additionally, if we want to share the features of our application with other developers and organizations, it is best practice to compile our source code into a library.

Unlike C, Rust uses crates as the framework for developing libraries and applications. A binary crate compiles to an executable program and must have a `main()` function. The entry point to a binary crate is usually the `src/main.rs` source file. On the other hand, a library crate compiles to a library that other developers can use in their application. The entry point to a library crate is usually the `src/lib.rs` file, and the library crate can't be executed directly.

Crates are managed using the Cargo utility. Cargo is Rust's official build system and package manager. We can use Cargo to create and build Rust projects, which consist of crates. We can use the `cargo new` command to create a new crate. As shown here, this command creates a directory structure with bare `src/main.rs` and `Cargo.toml` files:

```
$ cargo new packt-rust
    Creating binary (application) `packt-rust` package
note: see more `Cargo.toml` keys and their definitions at https://doc.
rust-lang.org/cargo/reference/manifest.html
$ tree packt-rust/
packt-rust/
├── Cargo.toml
└── src
    └── main.r
```

`Cargo.toml` is Rust's project manifest file, and a bare one created from the `cargo new` command is shown here:

```
[package]
name = "packt-rust"
version = "0.1.0"
edition = "2024"

[dependencies]
```

Dependent crates can be added under the `[dependencies]` section of the `Cargo.toml` file. For example, if we need to generate random numbers in our application, we can include the `rand` crate in our application by adding the following line in bold in `Cargo.toml`:

```
[package]
name = "packt-rust"
version = "0.1.0"
edition = "2024"

[dependencies]
rand = "0.8"
```

In the next section, we will learn how to cross-compile a Rust application so that we can run it on the Raspberry Pi 5.

Rust cross-compilation

As we learned in *Chapter 1*, one of the key components of an embedded Linux system is the **toolchain**. Recall that the toolchain is a utility that converts the source code representing a particular component of an embedded Linux system into a binary that can be executed by the processor.

Rust is no different. We write source code in the Rust programming language and use the Rust compiler to convert the source code into a binary or application that can be executed on the target processor. However, the Rust cross-compilation process has a significant advantage over the traditional process when using C/C++.

When we are writing source code using C/C++, there are two tools we can use to convert the source code for execution:

- **Native compiler**: This tool is used to convert source code written in C/C++ into an application that can be executed on the processor of the machine that was used to write the source code. In this instance, the final application is usually *not* executed on the Raspberry Pi 5.
- **Cross compiler**: This tool is used to convert source code written in C/C++ into an application that can be executed on the processor of the target system. In this instance, the final application is executed on the Raspberry Pi 5.

The advantage of Rust is that there is no distinction between the native compiler and the cross compiler. The same tool can be used for native compilation and cross-compilation. We can choose whether we want to compile our application for execution on the processor of our development PC or the processor of the Raspberry Pi 5 by using command-line arguments.

The following outlines the necessary steps to cross-compile a Rust application for execution on the Raspberry Pi 5:

> Note
>
> The following steps assume that the development PC is running Ubuntu 24.04.

1. Ensure that you have the appropriate dependencies installed by executing the following command:

```
$> sudo apt-get install curl build-essential file
```

2. Execute the following command to install the Rust toolchain:

```
$> curl --proto '=https' --tlsv1.2 -sSf https://sh.rustup.rs | sh
```

3. Rust provides the `cross` tool, which leverages Docker containers, that can significantly ease the cross-compilation process. The following command can be executed to install `cross`:

```
$> cargo install cross
```

> Important note
>
> Even though we will be using the Rust tools to cross-compile an application for execution on the Raspberry Pi 5, they still require a cross-compilation toolchain. This is because, at a minimum, the compilation process still requires a linker to generate the final binary for execution on the Raspberry Pi 5. The `cross` tool, which is provided by Cargo, retrieves and sets up the appropriate toolchain inside a container.

In the next section, we will learn how to use these tools to cross-compile a sample application that prints `Hello Rust World!` to the console of the Raspberry Pi 5.

Hello Rust World!

In this section, we will cross-compile a simple Rust application that displays `Hello Rust World!` to the console of the Raspberry Pi 5. The steps to accomplish this are outlined next.

Execute the following command to create a new sample project, which will create a directory titled `packt-ch14-hello-world`:

```
$> cargo new packt-ch14-hello-world
    Creating binary (application) `packt-ch14-hello-world` package
note: see more `Cargo.toml` keys and their definitions at https://doc.
rust-lang.org/cargo/reference/manifest.html
```

The following shows the resulting directories and files that are generated:

```
[packt-ch14-hello-world]$ tree
.
├── Cargo.toml
└── src
    └── main.rs

1 directory, 2 files
```

Each file is described here:

- `Cargo.toml`: As mentioned before, this is the Rust manifest file that we can use to help Cargo understand specific details about our project. It has the following content:

  ```
  [packt-ch14-hello-world]$ cat Cargo.toml
  [package]
  name = "packt-ch14-hello-world"
  version = "0.1.0"
  edition = "2024"

  [dependencies]
  ```

  Since the application doesn't require any external libraries, the `dependencies` section of the manifest file is blank.

- `src`: This directory contains the source code for our Rust application. Since this is a simple application, we only have a single source file.
- `main.rs`: This is a simple Rust source file that is created by Cargo to help us get started. It only has the following `main` function, which is the entry point for our application:

  ```
  fn main() {
      println!("Hello, world!");
  }
  ```

We can modify the `println!` macro to the following, which prints `Hello Rust World!` to the console:

```
fn main() {
    println!("Hello Rust World!");
}
```

The Rust `cross` project can help us cross-compile our application so it can be executed on the Raspberry Pi 5. It fetches and installs the necessary libraries and tools to manage cross-compilation. We can execute the following command to configure `cross` to support the ARM64 architecture:

```
$ cargo install cross
```

Finally, we can use `cross` to cross-compile our application by executing the following command:

```
$ cross build --target aarch64-unknown-linux-gnu
```

The final binary is located at `target/aarch64-unknown-linux-gnu/debug` and is named `packt-ch14-hello-world`, as seen here:

```
[packt-ch14-hello-world]$ ls target/aarch64-unknown-linux-gnu/debug/
build  deps  examples  incremental  packt-ch14-hello-world  packt-ch14-
hello-world.d
```

We can use the `file` command to confirm that the application binary has indeed been compiled for ARM64, which is the architecture of the Raspberry Pi 5 CPU:

```
[packt-ch14-hello-world]$ file  target/aarch64-unknown-linux-gnu/debug/
packt-ch14-hello-world
target/aarch64-unknown-linux-gnu/debug/packt-ch14-hello-world: ELF 64-
bit LSB pie executable, ARM aarch64, version 1 (SYSV), dynamically
linked, interpreter /lib/ld-linux-aarch64.so.1, for GNU/Linux 3.7.0,
BuildID[sha1]=d31e32e8a235257e5a28726beb54888d3a1626af, with debug_info,
not stripped
```

Finally, we can use the `scp` command to transfer the binary to the Raspberry Pi 5 and execute it on the Raspberry Pi 5. As shown here, we should see `Hello Rust World!` on the Raspberry Pi 5 console:

```
mab@packt-rpi:~ $ ./packt-ch14-hello-world
Hello Rust World!
```

In the next section, we will see how we can use Rust in the Linux kernel.

Rust in the Linux kernel

The following steps illustrate how to enable Rust support in the Linux kernel that will be used on the Raspberry Pi:

1. Clone the Raspberry Pi's Linux kernel repository and check it out at the commit used in this book by executing the following commands:

   ```
   $ git clone https://github.com/raspberrypi/linux
   $ cd linux
   $ git checkout 987e4eb6edf9d7b9e3b26924d79ca351543649a3
   ```

2. Execute the following command to configure the Linux kernel for the BCM2712, which is the System on a Chip (SoC) on the Raspberry Pi 5:

```
$ ARCH=arm64 LLVM=1 make bcm2712_defconfig
```

The components of the preceding command are described here:

- `ARCH=arm64`: This informs the build system that we are targeting the ARM64 architecture, which is the architecture of the BCM2712.
- `LLVM=1`: This instructs the build system to use the LLVM/Clang toolchain instead of the default GCC toolchain for compilation. Clang is needed to enable Rust in the Linux kernel.
- `make`: This is the core command used to compile the Linux kernel.
- `bcm2712_defconfig`: This instructs the build system to configure the Linux kernel for the BCM2712 SoC.

3. Launch the kernel configuration interface by executing the following command:

```
$ ARCH=arm64 LLVM=1 make menuconfig
```

4. In the resulting interface, search for the `MODVERSIONS` configuration option and disable it, as shown in the following figure:

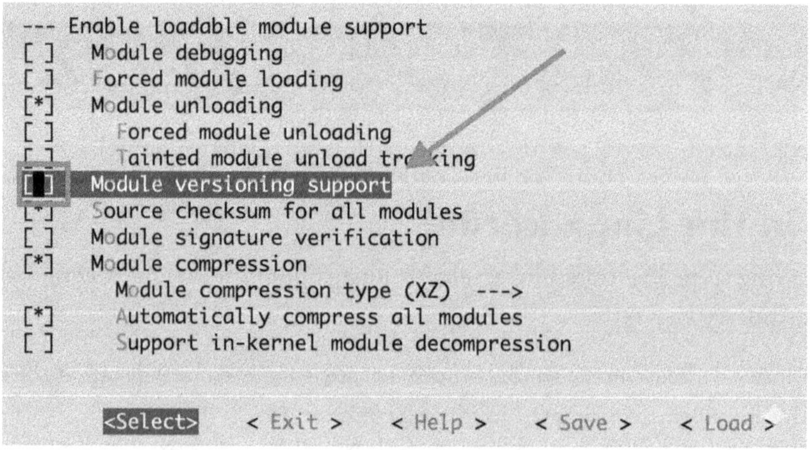

Figure 14.2 – Disabling module versioning

> Important note
>
> The `MODVERSIONS` configuration option enables support for module versioning. Module versioning is used to ensure binary compatibility between kernel modules and the kernel itself. Rust didn't support module versioning at the time of writing the book. Thus, module versioning needs to be disabled to enable Rust support in the Linux kernel.

5. Search for `RUST` in the Linux kernel's `menuconfig`, and you should see the following results:

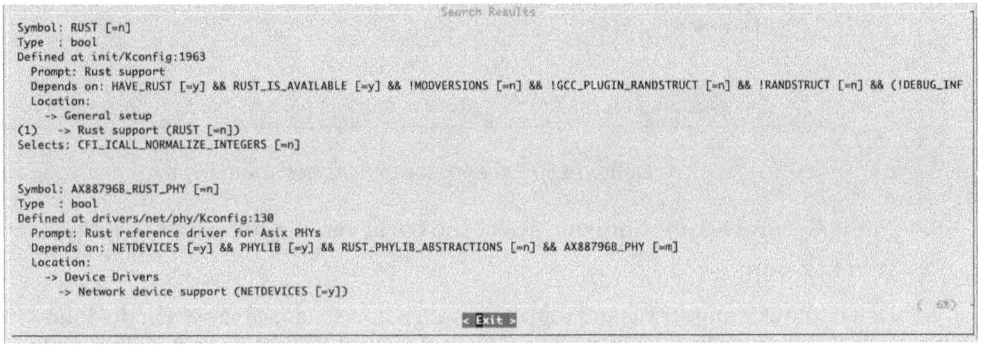

Figure 14.3 – Searching for RUST in the Linux kernel

6. Type `1` and then hit the spacebar on your keyboard to enable Rust support in the Linux kernel, as shown in the following figure:

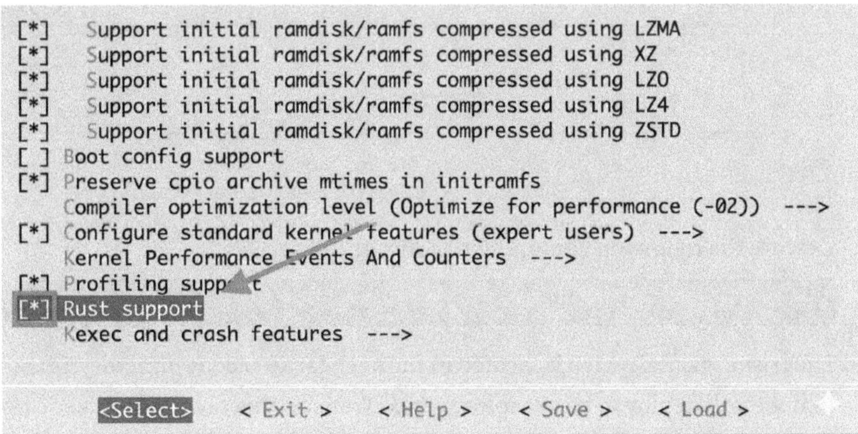

Figure 14.4 – Enabling Rust support in the Linux kernel

7. Go back to the main menu of the configuration interface, and enter the **General setup** submenu, as shown here:

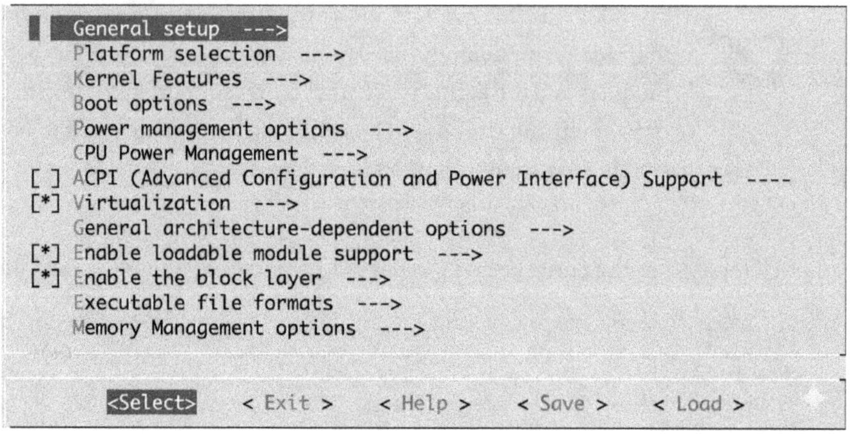

Figure 14.5 – Entering the General setup submenu

8. In the **General setup** submenu, select the **Local version** option and hit the *Enter* key on your keyboard.
9. Delete the existing string and replace it with `packt-rust`, as shown in the following figure, and hit the *Enter* key:

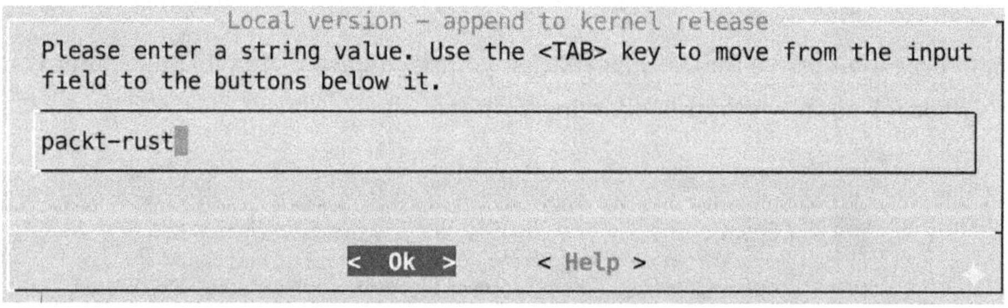

Figure 14.6 – Setting the Linux kernel version

10. Execute the following command to compile the kernel:

```
$ make ARCH=arm64 LLVM=1 -j$(nproc)
```

11. The `Image.gz` file, which is located in the `arch/arm64/boot` directory, is the kernel image that we will deploy to the Raspberry Pi 5. Transfer this file to your user's home directory on the Raspberry Pi 5.

12. Execute the following command to copy `Image.gz` from your home directory to the appropriate file in the boot directory of the Raspberry Pi:

```
$ sudo cp Image.gz /boot/firmware/kernel_2712.img
```

13. Reboot the Raspberry Pi by executing the following command:

```
$ sudo reboot
```

14. After the Raspberry Pi has successfully rebooted, execute the following command to confirm that the Raspberry Pi has booted using our customized kernel:

```
$ $ uname -a
Linux packt-rpi 6.12.53packt-rust+ #2 SMP PREEMPT Sun Nov  9
15:31:04 EST 2025 aarch64 GNU/Linux
```

In the next section, we will see how to implement a simple Linux kernel module using Rust.

A Linux kernel module in Rust

We will learn how to implement a simple Linux kernel module in Rust. Our kernel module will perform the following:

- Print the following messages to the kernel log when the module is loaded:
    - `Hello from Rust on Raspberry Pi 5!`
    - `Module loaded successfully`
- Print `Goodbye from Rust on Raspberry Pi 5!` when the module is unloaded

Follow the steps outlined here to implement the kernel module:

1. Navigate to the same directory where you cloned the Raspberry Pi Linux kernel and create a directory called ko, and enter this directory by executing the following commands:

```
$ mkdir ko
$ cd ko
```

2. Create a file named `packet_hw.rs` with the following content:

```
// SPDX-License-Identifier: GPL-2.0

//! Rust Hello World module for Raspberry Pi 5

use kernel::prelude::*;
```

```
6
7 module! {
8     type: RustHelloRpi5,
9     name: "rust_hello_rpi5",
10     author: "Your Name",
11     description: "A Hello World Rust module for Raspberry Pi 5",
12     license: "GPL",
13 }
14
15 struct RustHelloRpi5;
16
17 impl kernel::Module for RustHelloRpi5 {
18     fn init(module: &'static ThisModule) -> Result<Self> {
19         pr_info!("Hello from Rust on Raspberry Pi 5!\n");
20         pr_info!("Module loaded successfully\n");
21         Ok(RustHelloRpi5)
22     }
23 }
24
25 impl Drop for RustHelloRpi5 {
26     fn drop(&mut self) {
27         pr_info!("Goodbye from Rust on Raspberry Pi 5!\n");
28     }
29 }
```

The following outlines the lines of the kernel module source:

- Lines 1–3 are comments that delineate the kernel module license and provide a short description of the kernel module.
- Line 5 imports the **kernel prelude**, which is a curated set of commonly used types, traits, and macros that can be leveraged to develop kernel modules in Rust.
- Lines 7–13 describe the kernel module using the Rust `module!` macro. The following outlines each field in the macro:
    - `type`: Describes the Rust struct that implements the kernel module logic. As we see in later lines, this struct type implements the `kernel::Module` trait.
    - `name`: Defines the kernel module's name.
    - `author`: Specifies the kernel module's author.

   - `description`: Describes the purpose of the kernel module.
   - `license`: Defines the kernel module's license.
- The `module!` macro also generates the necessary code to perform the following operations:
   - Register the module with the kernel
   - Call the module's `init` method, which needs to be defined by the kernel module, since it implements the `kernel::Module` trait
   - Unloads the kernel module by using the `Drop` trait
- Line 15 defines a **unit struct**. A Rust unit struct doesn't contain any fields and is used to implement a specific trait. In this case, our kernel module is implementing the `kernel::Module` trait.
- Lines 17–20 implement the `kernel::Module` trait for our kernel module:
   - Line 18 defines the `init` method, which takes a reference to the kernel module as a parameter. The reference to the kernel module has a lifetime of the entire duration that the kernel module is loaded. The method returns the `Result` type.
   - Lines 19 and 20 use the `pr_info!` macro to print the specified strings to the kernel log.
   - Line 21 returns the `Ok` result with the `RustHelloRpi5` struct.
- Lines 25–29 implement the `Drop` trait, which is used to unload the kernel module:
   - Line 26 defines the `drop` method, which needs to be defined for any type that implements the `Drop` trait
   - Line 27 prints a message to the kernel log using the `pr_info!` macro

3. Create a file named `Makefile` alongside `packt_hw.rs` with the following content. This is similar to the `Makefile` file we wrote in *Chapter 3*, with the only difference being the `LLVM=1` flag in the `default` target. The `default` target is used to compile the kernel module:

```
# SPDX-License-Identifier: GPL-2.0

KDIR ?= $(shell pwd)/../linux/

default:
```

```
	$(MAKE) ARCH=arm64 LLVM=1 -C $(KDIR) M=$(PWD) modules

clean:
	$(MAKE) -C $(KDIR) M=$(PWD) clean

install:
	$(MAKE) -C $(KDIR) M=$(PWD) modules_install

help:
	$(MAKE) -C $(KDIR) M=$(PWD) help
```

4. Compile the kernel module by executing the following command:

```
[ko]$ make
```

5. Use SCP to transfer `packt_hw.ko` to your home directory on the Raspberry Pi.
6. Execute the following command to load the kernel module on the Raspberry Pi:

```
$ sudo insmod ./packt_hw.ko
```

7. Confirm that the appropriate lines were printed to the kernel log by executing the `dmesg` command shown here:

```
$ dmesg
[59842.368828] packt_hw: loading out-of-tree module taints kernel.
[59842.369174] rust_hello_rpi5: Hello from Rust on Raspberry Pi 5!
[59842.369178] rust_hello_rpi5: Module loaded successfully
```

8. Execute the following command to unload the kernel module:

```
$ sudo rmmod packt_hw
```

9. Finally, confirm that the message in the kernel module has been successfully printed using the `dmesg` command, as shown here:

```
$ dmesg
[59928.627073] rust_hello_rpi5: Goodbye from Rust on Raspberry Pi 5
```

Summary

Rust has rapidly emerged as a leading systems programming language, offering strong guarantees of memory safety and thread safety at compile time. Its compatibility with C and modern design features make it an ideal choice for embedded Linux development. In this chapter, we explored Rust's syntax, ownership model, and tools such as Cargo and crates, learned how to cross-compile Rust applications for Raspberry Pi, and even integrated Rust into the Linux kernel by building a kernel module. These capabilities highlight Rust's growing role in creating secure, efficient, and maintainable software for embedded systems. You should now have the tools necessary to continue developing more sophisticated applications and kernel modules using Rust.

The next chapter will focus on automating the Embedded Linux build process using CI/CD practices and tools such as GitHub Actions.

15

Implementing Continuous Integration/Continuous Delivery (CI/CD)

In *Part 2*, we learned how applications can be implemented and built for execution on an Embedded Linux system. We covered, in detail, how to compile, execute, and efficiently debug Embedded Linux applications. We learned how to use popular programming languages, such as C and C++, along with a popular UI framework – Qt – to implement applications across different verticals.

To wrap up the book, *Part 4* will cover topics that combine the lessons learned in the previous chapters. For example, we will learn how to automate builds to eliminate variations across developer machines. We will also learn about best practices we can leverage across all portions of the Embedded Linux development system. Finally, we will cover future trends in Embedded Linux that would be useful to pay attention to.

In this chapter, we will learn how to automate the build process for all elements of the Embedded Linux system, including the following:

- The custom Embedded Linux operating system, with the bootloader, kernel, and root filesystem, with any custom applications
- The toolchain, when any component of the Embedded Linux operating system changes
- Any custom userspace applications developed in a separate repository, using the previously mentioned toolchain

Although we will use GitHub Actions as our CI/CD platform, the lessons learned translate easily to any other platform. The difference will only be in the implementation details.

We are going to cover the following topics in this chapter:

- The importance of CI/CD
- Docker: eliminating build variations
- Strategies for automated builds
- CI/CD examples in GitHub Actions

Technical requirements

You should be comfortable executing commands on a terminal. You should also be comfortable reading, writing, and executing C++ applications. Finally, you should ensure that you have downloaded the Git repository associated with this book, located at `https://github.com/PacktPublishing/Embedded-Linux-Essentials-Handbook`. You should also have an account with GitHub to be able to follow along with the instructions in this chapter.

The importance of CI/CD

In this section, we will understand the importance of **CI/CD**, which stands for **Continuous Improvement** and **Continuous Delivery**. CI/CD is a crucial aspect of the software development process, regardless of the type of software being developed, especially when working on a team.

The goal of CI/CD is to improve the speed, quality, and reliability of the software being developed. As mentioned, there are two aspects of CI/CD: Continuous Integration and Continuous Delivery.

Continuous Integration (CI)

Continuous Integration (CI) involves developers frequently integrating code changes into the repository. The exact frequency of integration depends on the software that is being developed. For example, if the **board support package** (**BSP**) is being customized, code changes may only be frequent at the beginning and end of the project. Changes may be frequent at the beginning of the project as device drivers, software libraries, and third-party packages are added to the BSP. Once the BSP is finalized, it can be given to the application development team. Finally, once application development is complete, the application can be included in the BSP for final delivery. Thus, CI will be relevant at the beginning and end of the project for BSP development. However, for application development, code changes should be integrated into the shared repository daily, if not multiple times a day.

Continuous Delivery (CD)

Continuous Delivery (**CD**) complements CI. CD involves the process of automatically building, testing, and releasing code changes integrated into the mainline by developers. The testing process can be invaluable in identifying any regressions that may have been introduced. However, one of the challenges with automated testing of embedded software is the inclusion of actual or representative hardware. There are two general techniques to mitigate this challenge.

First, feedback can be incorporated into the embedded software application itself. Depending on the hardware interfaces available on the underlying board, the application can send messages out for validation. Then, when any **hardware-in-the-loop** (**HIL**) testing is performed, the CD platform can run a series of tests where a certain response is expected from the application for each test. If the response from the application doesn't match the expected response, the test is deemed to fail. Then, the team is responsible for identifying and rectifying the problem's root cause. Of course, the feedback mechanism must be tested before it can be used as part of the CD testing infrastructure. However, the in-band feedback mechanism can be invaluable for CD testing once it is verified.

The second technique is to use an external entity, such as a development PC, to monitor the outputs of the embedded system. Certain facets of embedded software applications cannot be tested with messages from the software itself. For example, let's say our embedded software application blinked an LED every second. It would not be a sufficient test if we relied on feedback from the application to tell us that it was illuminating the LED. The application would toggle a particular GPIO, but in-band feedback would not indicate whether the LED was illuminated. Instead, we would need an out-of-band mechanism where we independently verify a particular output. For example, when illuminating an LED at a particular rate, we can have a webcam connected to our development PC that analyzes the captured video and confirms that the LED is blinking at 1 Hz. Of course, using out-of-band feedback mechanisms incurs increased development time and cost. Additionally, the complexity of the validation mechanism may increase depending on the feature. For example, verifying the timing of a critical aspect of our embedded software design could require specialized equipment and corresponding software to interact with the equipment and analyze the data.

Thus, CI/CD testing can require some significant upfront development and setup costs for independent, out-of-band testing.

To summarize, CI/CD is an invaluable process to ensure that code changes made by developers to implement features or resolve bugs are thoroughly tested before embedded software is released.

In the next section, we will learn how Docker can eliminate build variations that can arise.

Docker: eliminating build variations

In this section, we will learn how Docker (`https://www.docker.com/`) can eliminate build variations and ensure that embedded software releases are not dependent on the nuances of individual build machines.

Docker is a tool that uses operating system-level virtualization to allow us to run a different operating system on our local machine. The operating system run by Docker is referred to as a **container**, and it operates in a sandbox from the local operating system.

Docker can run multiple containers with entirely different operating systems on the same development machine. Each container can have a completely different set of software packages from each other and the local development machine. Assuming that each container is running a variant of Linux, this includes the following:

- **Kernel version**: Each container can have different versions of the Linux kernel.
- **Linux distribution**: Each container can run completely different distributions. For example, the host development machine can run Fedora, while one container can run Ubuntu, and another can run Arch Linux.
- **Software packages**: Each container can have a complete set of application packages. For example, if one container is designed to emulate a wireless-enabled device, it may have a wpa_supplicant installed. However, another container may be designed to emulate a Bluetooth-enabled device, and it may have BlueZ installed.

If multiple containers are running on a system, they are also isolated from one another unless explicit provisions are made to enable networking among the containers.

> Important note
>
> Docker is best used for embedded software development on a Linux development machine. While substantial strides have been made to run Linux-based Docker containers on Windows, it is not seamless. Thus, you should use a Linux development machine if you will use Linux-based containers.

A **Docker container** is an instance of a Docker image, which is created using a **Dockerfile**. For Docker to successfully parse a Dockerfile and create the image, the Dockerfile must follow a strict set of rules. A Dockerfile is portable and can be used to reproduce an identical environment on a different host machine. The following list describes common instructions found in Dockerfiles:

- `FROM`: This instruction informs Docker which base operating system to use for the image. For example, the following instruction informs Docker to use Ubuntu 22.04 as the base Linux distribution for the image:

```
FROM: ubuntu:22.04
```

- `RUN`: This instruction informs Docker of a command to execute in the shell during the generation process. For example, the following instructs Docker to install Python 3.x in the image:

```
RUN apt-get install -y python3
```

Important note

You may wonder why we didn't have to add "sudo" to the preceding instruction. This is because Docker executes the instructions to create the image as an elevated user, unless instructed otherwise in the Dockerfile. It is also common practice to combine multiple commands in a single `RUN` instruction in a Dockerfile. For example, we will typically see the following `RUN` instruction in a Dockerfile, which updates the local Ubuntu packages from the repositories and installs several different packages:

```
RUN apt-get update && apt-get install -y \
    apt-utils \
    ca-certificates \
    git
```

- `COPY`: This instruction copies files or directories from the host machine to the image.
- `EXPOSE`: This instruction instructs Docker to open a particular port on the container during runtime. For example, the following instruction will inform Docker to open port 2222.

```
EXPOSE 2222
```

- `ENV`: This instruction sets an environment variable, which the container can later use during runtime. For example, the following instructions inform the container of the location and language settings during runtime:

```
ENV LC_ALL en_US.UTF-8
ENV LANG en_US.UTF-8
ENV LANGUAGE en_US.UTF-8
```

- `ARG`: This instruction can set temporary variables for Docker to use when building the image. The following example uses ARG and RUN instructions to create a `dev` user in the image, and sets its user and group ID to match the local user on the host machine:

```
ARG user_name=dev
ARG user_uid=1000
ARG user_gid=1000
RUN groupadd -g $user_gid $user_name && \
    useradd -g $user_gid -m -s /bin/bash -u $user_uid $user_name
```

- `USER`: This instruction sets the user used by Docker to execute subsequent instructions. For example, the following instruction sets the user in the container to `dev`, assuming that such a user was created using the preceding example:

```
USER dev
```

- `WORKDIR`: This instruction sets the working directory for subsequent instructions. For example, the following instruction sets the working directory to `/home/dev/`:

```
WORKDIR /home/dev
```

- `CMD`: This instruction specifies the default command to run when Docker starts a container. For example, the following instruction will echo `Hello World` when the container is run:

```
CMD ["echo", "Hello World"]
```

> **Important note**
>
> If no command is specified and the container is run by executing `docker run` on the command line, we will be presented with a shell.

- `ENTRYPOINT`: This instruction sets the default executable to be run when Docker starts the container. For example, the following instruction will execute the `app.py` Python script:

```
ENTRYPOINT ["python", "app.py"]
```

> Important note
>
> The difference between `CMD` and `ENTRYPOINT` is subtle. `ENTRYPOINT` is the application executed inside the container, while `CMD` is the default set of arguments passed to it.
>
> If `ENTRYPOINT` is specified in the Dockerfile, passing arguments to `docker run` when running the container will add arguments to the application. To override the application executed when the container is started, the `--entrypoint` must be specified.
>
> If `CMD` is specified in the Dockerfile, any arguments passed to the `docker run` command will override the `CMD` instruction.

In the next section, we will discuss some useful strategies for automating Embedded Linux releases.

Strategies for automated builds

In this section, we will learn useful strategies for automating builds associated with software running on an Embedded Linux system. Generally, we need to automate build creation when the following actions take place during the software development process:

- **Developer commits code to their own branch**: If a developer commits a change to the relevant repository in their own branch, a build should be created for their own testing. However, that build should not result in a release. Instead, the build should be placed in a central location only accessible to developers. Example locations include the following:
  - A server with sufficient disk space inside the organization's VPN. The location where the builds are placed should only be accessible to developers.
  - A cloud storage solution, such as Amazon AWS S3 (`https://aws.amazon.com/s3/`). Developer builds should be placed in a bucket that is only accessible to developers.

- **Developer branch merged to the mainline**: Once the developer has thoroughly tested their feature or bug fix, they will want to have their implementation reviewed and merged into the mainline branch. After the branch is merged, a build will need to be created for validation by the test team. These builds should be placed in a location that is accessible to both the test and development teams. Of course, the test team will need to access the build for validation. The development team should also have access to the build to confirm any regressions identified by the test team.
- **Build ready for release**: Once the test team has performed its due diligence to validate the build from the latest mainline branch, it will need to be **versioned** and **tagged**. Afterward, a proper release will need to be created for deployment. This release can be placed in a location that is widely available throughout the organization. However, a separate team should be responsible for deploying the release as an update to devices out in the field. The following list outlines general strategies for deployment to ensure that the release is further validated before it is widely distributed to all devices:
    - The release is deployed to several devices under the manufacturer's control. These devices are under nearly or exactly identical conditions as those widely deployed. The devices are observed for a certain amount of time to identify any regressions or anomalies.
    - Once the handful of devices under the organization's control have not demonstrated any regressions or anomalous behavior, the release can be deployed to a subset of devices under customer control, whether single or multiple customers. Of course, customers would be aware that these devices would be used to validate a particular release. These devices are observed for a certain time to identify regressions or anomalies.
    - Once the subset of customer devices has not exhibited any regressions, the release can be deployed further. The release can be deployed to either another subset of customer devices or all devices in the field. However, it is still vital to continue to monitor the devices that have been updated to the latest release to identify any regressions.

In the next section, we will learn how to use GitHub to employ CI/CD for Embedded Linux systems.

CI/CD examples in GitHub Actions

In this section, we will learn how to use GitHub's CI/CD platform, called **GitHub Actions**, to create releases for different components of an Embedded Linux system.

The different components that are relevant to GitHub Actions are described here:

- **Workflow**: Workflows are the top-level mechanism used by GitHub Actions to run a series of tasks under certain conditions.
- **Event**: An event is a particular action that triggers a workflow. Examples of events include the following:
  - Any push to a repository by a developer.
  - When the mainline branch is updated, such as when a developer merges their feature branch into the mainline branch.
  - When the mainline branch is tagged.
- **Job**: A job is a series of tasks, or steps, performed to achieve the objective in a workflow.
- **Step**: A step is a single task that is performed in a job.
- **Runner**: A runner is a server or virtual machine that executes a workflow. A runner can run a single job at a time. There are two types of runners when using GitHub Actions:
  - **GitHub-hosted runners**: These are virtual machines offered by GitHub that are specifically configured to run GitHub Actions. While the free offering provided by GitHub is sufficient for most use cases, GitHub also offers larger virtual machines for a nominal fee. The advantage of GitHub-hosted runners is that it eliminates the necessary setup that we would need to perform if we wanted a self-hosted runner. The disadvantage is that the free tier is limited in its computational resources. Additionally, customization is limited on GitHub-hosted runners.
  - **Self-hosted runners**: These are machines that we can deploy and manage ourselves that can serve as runners and execute GitHub Actions workflows. The advantage of a self-hosted runner is that we can customize it as much as we want, both in terms of hardware and software. The disadvantage is that it requires time and resources to manage another machine, especially if we are working on a team.

Now, we will learn how to use GitHub Actions to create an Embedded Linux BSP image using the Yocto Project. Specifically, we will use the customizations we developed in *Chapter 6, Building an Image Using the Yocto Project*.

The crux of our workflow will be a Docker container that we will use to generate our BSP. The Dockerfile is shown here:

```
FROM ubuntu:20.04
ARG DEBIAN_FRONTEND=noninteractive
RUN apt-get update && apt-get install -y \
    apt-utils \
    bison \
    ca-certificates \
    ccache \
    check \
    curl \
    flex \
    git \
    git-core \
    gperf \
    lcov \
    libncurses-dev \
    libusb-1.0-0-dev \
    make \
    ninja-build \
    python3 \
    unzip \
    wget \
    xz-utils \
    zip \
    python \
    python3-pip \
    python3-pexpect \
    python3-git \
    python3-jinja2 \
    libegl1-mesa \
    libsdl1.2-dev \
    locales \
    locales-all \
    chrpath \
```

```
    cpio \
    diffstat \
    gawk \
    texinfo \
    iputils-ping \
    python3-distutils \
    gcc-multilib \
    build-essential \
    socat \
    debianutils \
    pylint3 \
    xterm \
    vim \
    rsync \
    bc \
    tmux \
    git-lfs \
    liblz4-tool \
    zstd \
    ca-certificates \
    parted \
    && apt-get autoremove -y \
    && rm -rf /var/lib/apt/lists/*

ENV LC_ALL en_US.UTF-8
ENV LANG en_US.UTF-8
ENV LANGUAGE en_US.UTF-8

ARG host_user dev
ARG host_uid=1000
ARG host_gid=1000
RUN groupadd -g $host_gid $host_user && \
    useradd -g $host_gid -m -s /bin/bash -u $host_uid $host_user

USER dev
```

```
66 WORKDIR /home/dev

67 RUN mkdir /home/dev/bin
68 RUN curl https://storage.googleapis.com/git-repo-downloads/repo > /
home/dev/bin/repo

69 RUN chmod a+x /home/dev/bin/repo
```

The following bullet points describe the relevant lines from the preceding Dockerfile:

- Line 1 instructs Docker to use the 20.04 Ubuntu distribution as the baseline image for the image that we are creating.
- Line 2 informs Docker that we wish to use a non-interactive interface during the image creation process, since we don't have a display or mechanism to interface with Docker.
- Lines 3 – 56 install the packages we need to create a BSP using the Yocto Project.
- Lines 57 – 59 set the localization and language settings for our image.
- Lines 60 – 64 create a dev user for the image and add it to the appropriate group. The `host_uid` and `host_gid` parameters can be altered to match those of the host machine.
- Line 65 sets the current user of the image to the `dev` user that was just created.
- Line 66 sets the current working directory to `/home/dev`, which is the home directory of the `dev` user.
- Lines 67 – 68 create a `bin` directory to store the `repo` tool and download `repo` to that directory.
- Line 69 makes the `repo` tool executable.

The following shows an example GitHub Actions workflow, which leverages the Dockerfile just discussed:

```
name: yocto-bsp
on:
  push:
    tags:
      - 'v*'

jobs:
  make-release:
    runs-on: yocto
    steps:
```

```
      - name: Checkout Dockerfile for Yocto builds
        uses: actions/checkout@v3
        with:
          repository: mabembedded/dockerfiles
      - name: Create Docker container for Yocto builds
        run:  |
              docker build -t yocto-builder .
      - name: Create repo manifest in Docker container
        run:  |
              mkdir yocto
              docker run -v${GITHUB_WORKSPACE}/yocto:/home/dev/src:z --user $UID --workdir /home/dev/src yocto-builder bash -c '/home/dev/bin/repo init -u <repo-manifest_url> -m default.xml -b main; /home/dev/bin/repo sync; source setup.sh; bitbake rpi-test-image'
              cp ${GITHUB_WORKSPACE}/yocto/build*/tmp/deploy/images/raspberrypi5/raspberrypi5.wic.bz2 ./
              echo "FINAL_IMAGE=$(ls ./*.wic.bz2)" >> $GITHUB_ENV
      - name: Create release
        id: create_release
        uses: actions/create-release@v1
        env:
          GITHUB_TOKEN: ${{ secrets.GITHUB_TOKEN }}
        with:
          tag_name: ${{ github.ref }}
          release_name: tps_cicd_${{ github.ref_name }}
          body: Actual release notes
          draft: false
          prerelease: false
      - name: Upload Release
        id: upload_release_asset
        uses: actions/upload-release-asset@v1
        env:
          GITHUB_TOKEN: ${{ secrets.GITHUB_TOKEN }}
        with:
          upload_url: ${{ steps.create_release.outputs.upload_url }}
          asset_path: ${{ env.FINAL_IMAGE }}
          asset_name: ${{ env.FINAL_IMAGE }}
          asset_content_type: application/x-bzip2
```

The following bullet points describe the relevant lines from the preceding Dockerfile:

- Line 1 names this workflow `yocto-bsp`.
- Lines 2 – 5 specify that this workflow should be executed if a tag beginning with "v" is pushed up.
- Line 6 outlines the job that this workflow should execute.
- Line 7 defines a job called `make-release`.
- Line 8 dictates that this job should be executed on a custom runner called `yocto`. This runner contains a fair number of computational resources for the BSP generation.
- Line 9 defines the steps that will be executed with this job.
- Lines 10 – 13 retrieve a Dockerfile that can be used to create a Docker container to build a BSP based on the Yocto Project.
    - Line 10 specifies the name of the step.
    - Line 11 uses a pre-defined GitHub action that can be used to retrieve a particular repository.
    - Lines 12 and 13 define the repository.
- Lines 14 – 16 create the Docker container using the Dockerfile that was just retrieved in the previous step.
- Lines 17 – 22 use the Docker container to create the BSP.
    - Line 19 creates a directory inside the workspace where the outputs of the Docker container will be stored.
    - Line 20 mounts the created directory inside the Docker container and performs the following tasks inside the container:
        - Sets the working directory to the directory that was mounted during the Docker container invocation.
        - Sets up the repository using the `repo` tool.
        - Executes the `bitbake` command to generate the BSP.
    - Line 21 copies the final build output from inside the Docker container to the root directory of the workspace.
    - Line 22 stores the name of the final build output in an environment variable that can be accessed by subsequent steps.

- Lines 23 – 33 create a release in GitHub using the specified parameters and the GitHub token stored in an environment variable.
- Lines 34 – 43 upload the final build output to GitHub releases. It uses the environment variable that was set in the previous step with the location of the final build output.

After adding the preceding workflow, we should see a new BSP created whenever a tag is created and pushed up.

Summary

In this chapter, we learned about **Continuous Integration** and **Continuous Delivery** (**CI/CD**) and their importance in overall software development. We learned about some challenges that can be encountered when using CI/CD in the context of embedded systems. Then, we learned how Docker can be used to eliminate variations across development machines to ensure that build artifacts are the same. Finally, we learned about GitHub Actions to automatically trigger builds on certain events. We learned how to incorporate the created Docker container into our GitHub Actions workflow to create a BSP when a tag is pushed up.

The next chapter turns to the future, examining trends that may become important for Embedded Linux software engineers.

16

Looking to the Future

In this chapter, we will look to the future and explore trends that may be relevant to us as embedded Linux software engineers. It is essential to be aware of rising trends that are relevant for embedded Linux systems because it ensures that we remain relevant amid rapid technological changes. By keeping up to date with such trends, we can anticipate how the field may evolve and learn of new tools that can be leveraged to enhance the development process. It is important to continue learning and stay engaged with innovations that could shape our careers as embedded software engineers and the industry at large.

Future trends

In this section, we will review some future trends that are useful for embedded Linux software engineers to be aware of as they progress. These trends may become extremely important across the software stack.

Edge AI

Artificial Intelligence (**AI**) has undergone a massive explosion in the past few years. As shown in the following graph, the explosion began in 2022, coinciding with the launch of OpenAI's ChatGPT and the subsequent proliferation of chatbots developed by other organizations, as well as applications that leverage these chatbots:

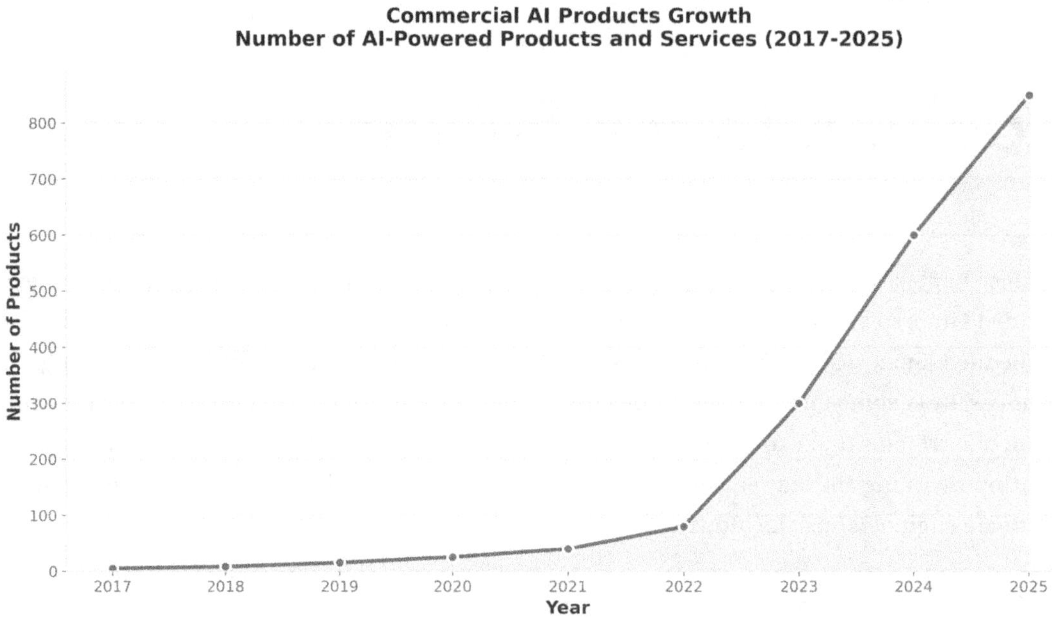

Figure 16.1 – Explosion of AI products

The traditional AI workflow championed by ChatGPT and other chatbots is outlined here:

1. First, the user begins interacting with the chatbot by sending a message, which serves as a **prompt**. This prompt gets transmitted to a backend that will process your prompt.
2. Then, the AI that is present in the backend analyzes the message to identify the **intent** and extracts the relevant **entities**.
3. Afterward, it performs state tracking to see whether your prompt has any relation to a previous prompt.
4. The AI system then uses the intent, entities, and context to query the **Large Language Model** (**LLM**) to gather an answer to your query.
5. Finally, the system packages the response and sends it back to you for presentation.

However, this flow has the following drawbacks:

- **Speed**: Since the prompt must be transmitted to the server and the response must be transmitted back to the device, there is an inherent latency in the process
- **Privacy**: Since potentially sensitive data is transmitted to a third-party server, there is an inherent concern that it may be exposed to unauthorized parties
- **Cost**: Depending on the amount of data transmitted and processed by the AI-based server, high costs can be incurred

Edge AI serves as an alternative to the traditional workflow and is ideal for embedded Linux systems. Edge AI moves the processing from a distant backend that requires data transmission and onto the device itself. The following are the advantages of edge AI when applied to embedded systems:

- **Speed**: Since data doesn't have to be transmitted by the embedded Linux system to a backend, and processing takes place on the device itself, edge AI is substantially faster when compared to the traditional AI workflow
- **Privacy**: Since the AI model processes data locally, there is less of a concern about sensitive data being exposed to unauthorized parties
- **Cost**: Since data is processed locally and no external entity is necessarily queried, significant cost savings can be achieved
- **Reliability**: Edge AI systems can be more reliable than traditional AI systems because they run the AI model locally and don't have a strict dependency on external systems

While the following list outlines some additional hardware and software requirements for an edge AI embedded Linux system, you can still leverage the lessons learned from this book:

- **Neural Processing Unit (NPU)**: This is the hardware component that enables edge AI on embedded Linux systems. The NPU in AI-ready SoCs is a specialized processor designed to perform matrix multiplication efficiently, a core operation required for edge AI. Examples of SoCs that contain an NPU include the NXP i.MX8M Plus, i.MX93, and i.MX95.
- **Linux device drivers**: You should apply what you have learned about Linux device drivers to NPU-specific drivers on the SoCs mentioned previously.
- **Userspace libraries**: Usually, edge AI applications don't interface directly with files exposed by NPU device drivers. Instead, they rely on intermediate libraries to interface with the underlying device driver. Examples include TensorFlow Lite, CUDA (for NVIDIA GPUs), and ONNX Runtime.

Real-time capabilities

There are times when real-time capabilities are needed in an embedded Linux system. As we learned in this book, the advantage of using an embedded Linux system is the capabilities and performance it offers. However, there may be instances where performance needs to be sacrificed for **predictability**.

For example, let's say our application is a machine vision-enabled robot that needs to perform the following tasks:

- Compress and stream video from a camera to a backend service for analysis
- If a sensor indicates that the robot is approaching an obstacle, the robot must immediately stop and take evasive actions

In a traditional embedded Linx environment, when the sensor triggers an interrupt, there is no guarantee that the interrupt will be handled in a timely manner. This can occur for a few reasons, including the following:

- **Spinlocks**: Certain operations in the Linux kernel require the use of a spinlock, which is used to protect a single resource from being accessed concurrently. If a spinlock is used to access a resource already in use, the task will sit in a busy loop, holding up the CPU. Thus, if our sensor fires an interrupt when it's in this busy loop, it may not address the interrupt in time.
- **Interrupt masking**: When a device driver interacts with certain hardware in a delicate manner, it may disable interrupts on the CPU to avoid any interruption. However, in this scenario, the CPU will never see the interrupt coming from our sensor.
- **SoftIRQs**: The Linux kernel handles interrupts in two parts:
    - **Top half**: This is usually where the interrupt handler routine is called in response to an interrupt, and it happens extremely quickly. Any CPU registers are cleared, and additional processing is then moved to the "bottom half."
    - **Bottom half**: This is where the crux of the interrupt handling occurs. However, there is no guarantee that the standard Linux kernel will execute a bottom-half function promptly. In our scenario, the bottom half of the function that handles the sensor interrupt may occur too late. In turn, our robot may not stop in time, resulting in destructive behavior.

In September 2024, support for **PREEMPT_RT** was introduced in version 6.12 of the Linux kernel. `PREEMPT_RT` can help address the issues outlined previously in the following manner:

- **Preemptible spinlocks**: The `PREEMPT_RT` feature converts the spinlock described previously into a mutex. Instead, if a task holds a spinlock, it is put to sleep until the spinlock is available. Thus, the CPU has an opportunity to address any interrupts that arise when a task is holding a spinlock.
- **Interrupt masking**: Interrupt masking is primarily a result of the use of spinlocks in traditional Linux. Since `PREEMPT_RT` converts spinlocks to mutexes, it enables the CPU to acknowledge interrupts. However, engineers must take care to ensure that they continue to mask interrupts as needed, especially when working with sensitive portions of the kernel and hardware. Additionally, they must take care to ensure that they only mask interrupts when absolutely necessary.

Asymmetric multiprocessing

An alternative to enabling `PREEMPT_RT` in the Linux kernel is to leverage the disparate cores present on certain SoCs. As shown in the following figure, it is becoming increasingly common for SoCs to have an ARM Cortex-A core and an ARM Cortex-M core on the same silicon.

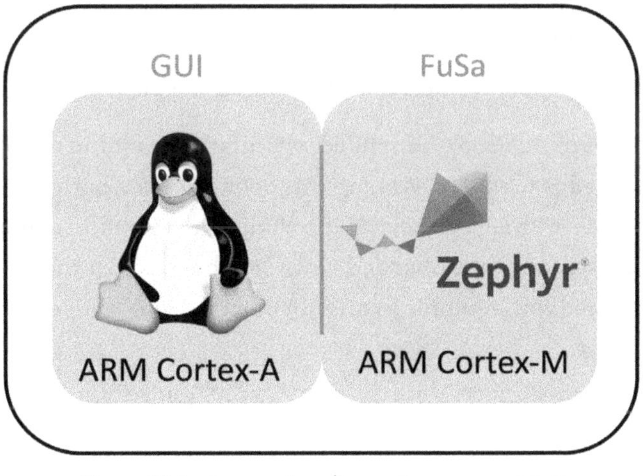

Figure 16.2 – Leveraging disparate cores on a SoC

For example, standard Linux can be run on the ARM Cortex-A core to run a GUI that doesn't have any time-critical needs. Similarly, the ARM Cortex-M core can run a **real-time operating system (RTOS)**, such as **Zephyr**, for **functional safety (FuSA)** applications.

Since the cores are on the same silicon, we can leverage **The OpenAMP Project** for communication rather than traditional communication buses, such as SPI, UART, or I2C. As outlined in the following list, two main mechanisms in OpenAMP can be leveraged for communication:

- **Remoteproc**: This mechanism is responsible for loading firmware onto the Cortex-M core from Linux on the Cortex-A core, and for starting and stopping the firmware on the Cortex-M core
- **RPMSG**: This mechanism is responsible for sending messages from the Cortex-A core to the Cortex-M core and receiving messages

Summary

In this chapter, we learned about future trends relevant to embedded Linux and that software engineers should become comfortable with.

The recent inclusion of `PREEMPT_RT` in the Linux kernel has allowed the kernel to behave similarly to traditional RTOSs, with enforced deadlines. Additionally, the increased density and complexity of modern system-on-chips has allowed real-time cores, such as ARM Cortex-M, to be present on the same silicon as more sophisticated cores, such as ARM Cortex-A. This has opened up a plethora of opportunities for simplifying hardware designs and resulted in the increased popularity of the OpenAMP embedded software framework.

Edge AI is an increasingly popular vertical that is ripe for deployment on embedded Linux systems.

As I close the final pages of this book, I am filled with gratitude for the opportunity to share my experiences and knowledge with you. Writing this book has been both a technical exploration and a personal journey—a chance to revisit the challenges, breakthroughs, and lessons that have shaped my understanding of embedded Linux. My hope is that these pages have not only informed but also inspired you, equipping you with practical tools and renewed curiosity for the possibilities ahead.

Get this book's PDF version and more

Scan the QR code (or go to `packtpub.com/unlock`). Search for this book by name, confirm the edition, and then follow the steps on the page.

UNLOCK NOW

Note: Keep your invoice handy. Purchases made directly from Packt don't require an invoice.

17

Unlock Your Exclusive Benefits

Your copy of this book includes the following exclusive benefits:

EPUB PDF

DRM-Free PDF Version

Download DRM-free PDF and ePub copies of this book.

7-Day Packt Library Access

Get 7-day unlimited access to 8,000+ books and videos. No credit card required.

Available for first-time Packt+ trial users only.

Next-Gen Reader Access

Read this book on Packt Reader with progress sync, dark mode and note-taking.

Follow the guide below to unlock them. The process takes only a few minutes and needs to be completed once.

Unlock this Book's Free Benefits in 3 Easy Steps

Step 1

Keep your purchase invoice ready for *Step 3*. If you have a physical copy, scan it using your phone and save it as a PDF, JPG, or PNG.

For more help on finding your invoice, visit `https://www.packtpub.com/en-us/unlock?step=1`.

> **Note:** If you bought this book directly from Packt, no invoice is required. After *Step 2*, you can access your exclusive content right away.

Step 2

Scan the QR code or go to `packtpub.com/unlock`.

On the page that opens (similar to *Figure 17.1* on desktop), search for this book by name and select the correct edition.

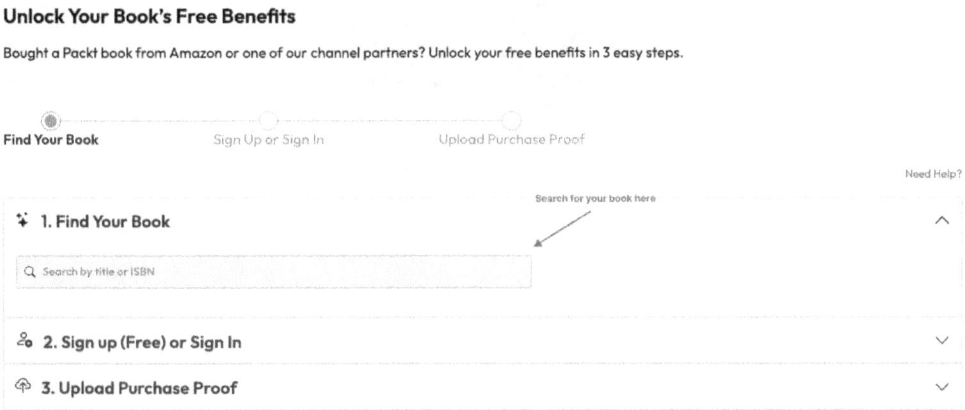

Figure 17.1: Packt unlock landing page on desktop

Step 3

After selecting your book, sign in to your Packt account or create one for free. Then upload your invoice (PDF, PNG, or JPG, up to 10 MB). Follow the on-screen instructions to finish the process.

Need Help

If you get stuck and need help, visit `https://www.packtpub.com/unlock-benefits/help` for a detailed FAQ on how to find your invoices and more. This QR code will take you to the help page.

Note: If you are still facing issues, reach out to `customercare@packt.com`.

Other Books You May Enjoy

If you enjoyed this book, you may be interested in these other books by Packt:

Mastering Embedded Linux Development

Frank Vasquez, Chris Simmonds

ISBN: 9781803232591

- Cross-compile embedded Linux images with Buildroot and Yocto
- Enable Wi-Fi and Bluetooth connectivity with a Yocto board support package
- Update IoT devices securely in the field with Mender or balena
- Prototype peripheral additions by connecting add-on boards, reading schematics, and coding test programs
- Deploy containerized software applications on edge devices with Docker
- Debug devices remotely using GDB and measure the performance of systems using tools like perf and ply

C++ in Embedded Systems

Amar Mahmutbegović

ISBN: 9781835881149

- Debunk myths and misconceptions about using C++ in embedded systems
- Set up build automation tailored for C++ in constrained environments
- Leverage strong typing to improve type safety
- Apply modern C++ techniques, such as Resource Acquisition Is Initialization (RAII)
- Use Domain Specific Language (DSL) with a practical example using Boost SML
- Implement software development best practices, including the SOLID principle, in embedded development

Packt is searching for authors like you

If you're interested in becoming an author for Packt, please visit `authors.packt.com` and apply today. We have worked with thousands of developers and tech professionals, just like you, to help them share their insight with the global tech community. You can make a general application, apply for a specific hot topic that we are recruiting an author for, or submit your own idea.

Share your thoughts

Now you've finished *Embedded Linux Essentials Handbook*, we'd love to hear your thoughts! Scan the QR code below to go straight to the Amazon review page for this book and share your feedback or leave a review on the site that you purchased it from.

`https://packt.link/r/1835469302`

Your review is important to us and the tech community and will help us make sure we're delivering excellent quality content.

Packt is searching for authors like you

[illegible]

Share your thoughts

[illegible]

Index

C

D

G

H

I

J

K

L

www.ingramcontent.com/pod-product-compliance
Lightning Source LLC
LaVergne TN
LVHW060018210926
848481LV00013B/3740
* 9 7 8 1 8 3 5 4 6 9 3 0 9 *